PSYCHOLOGY FROM
AN EMPIRICAL STANDPOINT

International Library of Philosophy

EDITED BY TIM CRANE AND JONATHAN WOLFF,
UNIVERSITY COLLEGE LONDON

The history of the International Library of Philosophy can be traced back to the 1920s, when C.K. Ogden launched the series with G.E. Moore's *Philosophical Papers* and soon after published Ludwig Wittgenstein's *Tractatus Logico-Philosophicus*. Since its auspicious start, it has published the finest work in philosophy under the successive editorships of A.J. Ayer, Bernard Williams and Ted Honderich. Now jointly edited by Tim Crane and Jonathan Wolff, the I.L.P. will continue to publish work at the forefront of philosophical research.

FRANZ BRENTANO

Psychology from an Empirical Standpoint

EDITED BY OSKAR KRAUS

ENGLISH EDITION EDITED BY
LINDA L. McALISTER

WITH A NEW INTRODUCTION BY
PETER SIMONS

Translated by
Antos C. Rancurello, D. B. Terrell
and Linda L. McAlister

LONDON AND NEW YORK

Originally published in 1874
by Duncker & Humblot, Leipzig, as
Psychologie vom empirischen Standpunkte
Second edition published in 1924
by Felix Meiner, Leipzig

First English edition published 1973
in the International Library of Philosophy and Scientific Method
under the editorship of Ted Honderich
by Routledge & Kegan Paul Ltd
Broadway House, 68–74 Carter Lane, London EC4V 5EL

Paperback edition published 1995
in the International Library of Philosophy
under the editorship of Tim Crane and Jonathan Wolff
by Routledge
11 New Fetter Lane, London EC4P 4EE

Simultaneously published in the USA and Canada
by Routledge
29 West 35th Street, New York, NY 10001

English translation © 1973, 1995 Routledge

Typeset in Times
Printed and bound in Great Britain by
Redwood Books, Trowbridge, Wiltshire

British Library Cataloguing in Publication Data
A catalogue record for this book is available from the British
Library.

Library of Congress Cataloging in Publication Data
A catalogue record for this book has been requested.

ISBN 0–415–10661–3

Contents

CONTENTS

ADDITIONAL ESSAYS FROM BRENTANO'S *NACHLASS*
CONCERNING INTUITIONS, CONCEPTS, AND OBJECTS
OF REASON

Introduction to the Second Edition

Psychologie vom empirischen Standpunkte[1] forged Franz Brentano's reputation and it remains his most important and influential
single work. Like Wilhelm Wundt's *Grundzüge der physiolo-
gischen Psychologie*, also published in 1874, it helped to establish
psychology as a scientific discipline in its own right. Through Brentano's illustrious circle of students it exerted a wide influence on
philosophy and psychology, especially in Austria, Germany,
Poland, and Italy. Knowledge of Brentano's views helps us to
understand such varied developments as Husserl's phenomenology, Meinong's theory of objects, gestalt psychology, and early
analytic philosophy in Poland and England. Brentano's emphasis
on the irreducible distinctness of psychology's subject matter and
his identification of intentional inexistence as the mark of the
mental have been revived within analytical philosophy of mind and
inform some approaches to cognitive science. The course of the
Psychology's influence has yet to be fully run.

Because we can view the *Psychology* with such hindsight it is
tempting to read back into the original text ideas which Brentano
and others developed later, but which cloud our appraisal of it. So
it pays to look more closely at its inception and the influences at
work in it.

It is not clear when Brentano first became interested in
psychology. His knowledge of the history of philosophy must have
led him to psychological topics. He had studied Aristotle under
Trendelenburg in Berlin and the Scholastics under Clemens in
Münster, while his interest in Aquinas went back to his youth.[2] He

---

[1] This was the title of the first edition: subsequently the final dative "e"
was dropped to give the more commonly cited *Standpunkt*. The 350-page
first edition was designated as Volume 1; this too was dropped.

[2] O. Kraus, "Biographical Sketch of Franz Brentano," in L. L. McAlister, ed., *The Philosophy of Franz Brentano*, London: Duckworth, 1976,
pp. 1–9: see p. 2.

also knew the work of the British empiricists, in whose hands psychological matters took on increased importance for philosophy. In 1866 Brentano achieved his habilitation in Würzburg with the book *Die Psychologie des Aristoteles, insbesondere seine Lehre vom "Nous Poietikos,"* published the following year. In Würzburg, where he embodied the hopes of the clerical faction, Brentano first lectured on psychology in 1871, dividing his course into two parts, the first dealing with mental phenomena and their laws, the second with the soul and the question of its immortality.[3] He also read and was impressed by the positivist philosophy of Comte. In his 1869 essay "Auguste Comte und die positive Philosophie" he indeed wrote, "Perhaps no other philosopher of recent times merits our respect to such a high degree as Comte."[4] In 1870 Brentano, prompted by inner doubts and the events surrounding the declaration of papal infallibility, became estranged from the Roman Catholic Church into which he had been ordained in 1864. During the period between 1870 and 1873, as his new views began to leak out, his position at Würzburg (where he was made *professor extraordinarius* in 1872) became increasingly untenable, and he determined to move elsewhere. In the spring of 1872 he took leave and went to England, visiting Herbert Spencer and corresponding with John Stuart Mill in France. In 1873 he resigned his position, left the Church, and travelled again in Europe. At this time he was writing the *Psychology,* a passport out of Würzburg, on the strength of which he might hope for a position elsewhere. His hopes were fulfilled: at the beginning of 1874 he was named *professor ordinarius* in Philosophy at the University of Vienna, where he had been in contention for some time, and in March of that year he completed work on the first two books of the *Psychology,* which appeared in May. Much of the writing was carried out at his family home in Aschaffenburg, from where the Foreword is signed.

Brentano's original plan, as explained in the Foreword, was for a large work consisting of six books. The first five would cover psychology as a science, mental phenomena in general, and their three basic classes; the final book was to deal with the mind–body problem, the soul, and immortality. But it turned out otherwise. After publishing the first two books, Brentano was ill with smallpox, and then he plunged into Viennese intellectual and

---

[3] C. Stumpf, "Reminiscences of Franz Brentano," in McAlister, ed., op. cit., pp. 10–46: see p. 37.

[4] See Brentano, *Die vier Phasen der Philosophie und ihr augenblicklicher Stand,* Hamburg: Meiner, 1968, p. 99.

cultural life. Brentano was a natural teacher, but not a natural producer of books. Papers and the occasional smaller monograph appeared, but the *Psychology* was his one attempt at a comprehensive treatise, and it did not get very far. Some work was done, but the project remained incomplete, overtaken by Brentano's changes of mind.[5] The plan of the *Psychology* ensured, however, that his position on the main questions was laid out in the two books we have, so that Brentano was happy to republish Book Two in 1911 under the new title *Von der Klassifikation der psychischen Phänomene*, appending supplementary remarks explaining his later views where they deviated significantly from those of 1874.

After Brentano had given up teaching and left Austria for Italy in 1895, he acquired a second generation of adherents among the Prague students of his old friend and Würzburg student Anton Marty. Most prominent among these were Alfred Kastil and Oskar Kraus, who corresponded frequently with Brentano, visited and generally assisted him, especially after he became blind. They became unswerving advocates of Brentano's views, intolerant of any criticism. After Brentano's death they set about publishing his *Nachlass*, aided by grants from the Czechoslovak government, for President Masaryk had also studied under Brentano in Vienna. Between 1922 and 1932, eleven volumes appeared, including a second edition of the whole *Psychology*, for which Kraus renumbered the chapters of Book Two to conform with the 1911 edition, added a number of further posthumous essays by Brentano, and copious explanatory notes of his own. This edition forms the basis of the present translation.

Aware that he was unable to bring his later views into publishable form, Brentano, impressed by what had been made of Bentham's disorderly manuscripts by their editors, gave Kastil and Kraus a free hand to make his views available as they thought best. This "creative editing" resulted in several compilations aimed at producing rounded, convincing works, but they made it difficult to gain a clear picture of the complex development of Brentano's ideas. Kraus's 1924 edition of the *Psychology* could not disturb Brentano's text, but his notes are frequently shrill and intrusive.[6] Passages in Chapter I, for instance, clearly accord mental phenomena an epistemological advantage over physical phenomena. Physical phenomena, says Brentano, like light, sound, heat, spatial

---

[5] Material corresponding to the third book, *Vom sinnlichen und noetischen Bewußtsein*, was published posthumously in 1928.

[6] In the German edition they are less intrusive, appearing as endnotes. In the present edition they are distinguished by being numbered.

location, and locomotion, "are not things which really and truly exist ... We have no experience of that which truly exists, in and of itself, and that which we do experience is not true" (p. 19). Kraus cannot forbear intervening several times to explain how Brentano expresses himself misleadingly, how this conflicts with other things he says elsewhere, and so on. This is all in the service of showing that, even if Brentano had been a little wrong in the past, his later views were unassailable and only prejudice or ignorance could stand in the way of their general adoption. Seventy years later, we can be more detached. Informative as Kraus's notes often are, they are best skipped on a reading aimed at attaining an untrammelled view of what Brentano meant in 1874.

Brentano wished to establish the independence of scientific psychology from both philosophy and physiology. The independence from philosophy is aimed at by seeking a subject matter common to all approaches to psychology, eschewing unnecessary and divisive metaphysical assumptions. One such assumption is the existence of a soul. Brentano, although he in fact believed in the soul as a substantial bearer of mental properties, put this view on one side for the purposes of psychology, embracing Lange's idea of psychology without a soul: "whether or not there are souls, the fact is that there are mental phenomena" (p. 18). This deliberate abstention from more speculative tenets presages Husserl's more radical (and unworkable) procedure of phenomenological reduction, the "bracketing" of anything not directly warranted in experience.

The common basis of subject matter Brentano believes, like Mill and Comte, to be mental phenomena. But Comte had thought inner observation of such phenomena impossible, requiring a division of oneself into observer and observed, so for him psychology could only be physiology, and hence part of biology. Brentano counters by distinguishing inner observation, which is impossible, from inner perception, which is the incidental awareness of all my mental phenomena concurrently with being aware of their objects. This inner perception, which Brentano, following Descartes, regards as infallible, is, assisted by memory, the experiential basis of all psychology. Only after the *Psychology* did Brentano distinguish between an a priori, philosophical, *descriptive* psychology, and an a posteriori, empirical *genetic* psychology. In the *Psychology* this distinction is at best latent, although Brentano's interests naturally lead him to emphasize the philosophical side.

The adjective "empirical" in the book's title aims to capture both these aspects: the lack of metaphysical speculation on the one hand and the provision of a firm experiential basis on the other.

But "empirical" does not mean quite the same as "experimental:" the deliverances of inner perception are indubitable yet synthetic, and while mental phenomena are amenable to testing with apparatus, their study can be embarked upon by pure introspection, or what perhaps in Brentano's case might better be termed *introception*. Had the short-sighted Austrian establishment not kept Brentano out of his professorial chair after 1880, it is likely he would have followed Wundt's lead in establishing a psychology laboratory in Vienna. As it was, the first Austrian psychology laboratory was founded by Meinong in Graz only in 1894, and in the meantime the cream of young European and American experimentalists learned their trade in Leipzig. It is unlikely that Brentano would have relished systematic experimentation, but he would certainly have found able assistants.

If psychology is to be a unified science, something must distinguish it from other sciences and yet bind it into a unity. It could not be method, since Brentano held (in his famous fourth habilitation thesis) that the true method of philosophy is none other than that of the natural sciences. Therefore it must be subject matter, and this Brentano sought in mental phenomena. The word "phenomena" is to be taken at face value. Natural science, according to Brentano, studies phenomena, too, namely physical phenomena, and all phenomena are appearances, not things in themselves. Appearances are mental entities, but not all mental entities are mental *phenomena*. Recall that for Brentano the subject matter of physics does not exist in itself and we can only indirectly infer anything about its causes. Thus Brentano's views are not dissimilar to those of Mach, whose subsequent appointment in Vienna in 1895 Brentano supported.[7] Despite his criticisms of Mach, Brentano saw him in 1894/95, with Mill, as representative of a thoroughgoing positivism, by contrast with the less well thought through versions of Comte and Kirchhoff.[8] Though his metaphysical views prevented him from being either a phenomenalist or a positivist, Brentano stood closer to these positions in 1874 than later; we could consider him a *methodological phenomenalist*.

Since, then, all (empirical) sciences study phenomena, how are mental phenomena to be distinguished from others? Brentano considers several distinguishing marks. Is it, as Descartes asserted, that they are nonspatial while physical phenomena are spatially

---

[7] See the correspondence between Brentano and Mach in Brentano's *Über Ernst Machs "Erkenntnis und Irrtum,"* Amsterdam: Rodopi, 1988, pp. 203 ff.

[8] Ibid., p. 204.

extended? While not denying this distinction, Brentano sets it aside, both because a negative characterization is undesirable and because it had been criticized, some seeing certain physical phenomena as unextended, others seeing certain mental phenomena as extended. While Brentano does not agree with these objections, he prefers to look for common ground. He also looks with favour on the views that mental phenomena are the distinctive objects of inner perception, and that they are all either ideas (*Vorstellungen*) or founded on ideas. But his preferred characteristic is that, unlike a physical phenomenon, "every mental phenomenon includes something as object within itself" (p. 88). Following Scholastic terminology, Brentano calls this the *intentional inexistence* of an object. Few passages in modern philosophy have been pored over so intensively as this, and few have given rise to such heated controversy. Yet Brentano's text gives historical antecedents for all to read: Aristotle's *De anima*, Philo of Alexandria, Augustine, and Aquinas. The most important is undoubtedly Aristotle, on whom Brentano had already published two books. The idea of intentional inexistence, though neither its use in demarcating psychology nor the Scholastic name, are already accepted by Brentano in *The Psychology of Aristotle*.[9] Even the plan of the *Psychology* parallels that of *De anima*.[10] The idea of intentional inexistence comes from Aristotle's theory of perception, in which the form but not the matter of the perceived object is literally within the soul. In Brentano's psychology without a soul, this emerges as the view that every mental phenomenon contains its object within itself. Again, this is to be understood literally: the sound I hear is part of my hearing it, the thought that I am hearing the sound has both my hearing and the sound as parts, and my delight in hearing the sound has the thought and the hearing and the sound as ever more mediate parts. The sound on the other hand is just a sound, it has nothing in it, and so is just a physical phenomenon. So inexistence does not mean nonexistence, but *inesse*, existence-in (the phenomenon).

[9] This is pointed out by R. George in "Brentano's Relation to Aristotle," in R. M. Chisholm and R. Haller, eds., *Die Philosophie Franz Brentanos*, Amsterdam: Rodopi, 1978, 249–66: see p. 253.

[10] Cf. D. Münch, *Intention und Zeichen: Untersuchungen zu Franz Brentano und zu Edmund Husserls Frühwerk*, Frankfurt am Main: Suhrkamp, 1993, p. 51. Münch holds more generally that the *Psychology* has an "Aristotelian origin." For an earlier statement of this view see B. Smith, "The Soul and its Parts: A Study in Aristotle and Brentano," *Brentano Studien* I (1988), 75–87.

Brentano himself and his students later found this view untenable, but it took a surprisingly long time for the criticisms to emerge, the first published evidence of demur being in an Austrian school logic textbook of 1890 published by Brentano's former students Alois Höfler and Alexius Meinong.[11] There two senses of "object" are distinguished: the immanent object in the sense of the *Psychology*, and the external object or referent, about which the *Psychology* has nothing to say. Brentano had contributed to the ambiguity by offering several paraphrases of the phrase "intentional inexistence:" mental inexistence, existence as an object (objectively) in something, reference to a content, direction to an object, immanent objectivity. In 1894 Twardowski proposed the terminology "content" (*Inhalt*) for the immanent object and simply "object" (*Gegenstand*) for the external object.[12] The controversy about the nature of intentionality rumbled (and rumbles) on, each view favoring some of Brentano's paraphrases while rejecting others. In 1874, however, he obviously thought the view was plain enough as he gave it.

Brentano did not use the term "intentionality" but it and its cognates have a complex and interesting history.[13] Clearly they do not here mean intention in the sense of purpose, design, intent to do something, though the two notions are related. The more general theoretical notion whose name Brentano probably took from Aquinas entered Scholasticism not directly from the Greeks but via Islamic philosophy, the Latin word being an attempt to render Al-farabi's and Avicenna's terms *ma'na, ma'qul*, whose concrete meaning had to do with drawing (stretching, hence *tension*) a bow whose metaphorical target is the object intended. Whatever the complex etymology and history of the term, it well served Brentano's purpose of 1874, and "intentionality" went on to become a powerful catchword, though the conscious archaism underscored Brentano's somewhat one-sided reputation as a modern Scholastic.

Much of the *Psychology* as we have it, however, is dedicated to a classificatory thesis. What are the basic, irreducibly distinct

[11] A. Höfler with A. Meinong, Logik, Vienna: Tempsky, 1890, pp. 6–7.

[12] K. Twardowski, *Zur Lehre vom Inhalt und Gegenstand der Vorstellungen*, Vienna: Hölder, 1894, reprinted Munich: Philosophia, 1982. Translated as *On the Content and Object of Presentations* by R. Grossmann, The Hague: Nijhoff, 1977.

[13] See P. Engelhardt, "Intentio," in *Historisches Wörterbuch der Philosophie*, vol. 4, Darmstadt: Wissenschaftliche Buchgesellschaft, 1976, pp. 466–74.

classes of mental phenomena? Brentano discerns just three: ideas, judgements, and a third class, comprising both emotions and volitions. They correspond to Descartes' *ideae, judicia* and *voluntates sive affectus*.[14] The last class is variously known: as emotions, phenomena of love and hate, phenomena of interest. There is no fully apt word, in German or English. Brentano expressly rejects the Aristotelian division into cognitions and desires, as well as the Kantian division into thoughts, feelings and will. Indeed if we look at the classifications used (less often argued for) by modern philosophers from Hobbes onwards we find a considerable diversity, and Brentano's concern with the basic division, pedantic though it may at times seem, is scientifically valid, whether or not his division is the best.

The central role of ideas (presentations, *Vorstellungen*) is also taken from Descartes, and from the British empiricists. Ideas furnish the raw material for all mental activity: no ideas, no content. Brentano assigns perceptions, however, to the class of judgements. Judgements have a yes/no polarity lacking among ideas: we either affirm or deny. But whereas the tradition had followed Aristotle in seeing judgement as requiring two ideas or terms, subject and predicate, so that in affirming I affirm the predicate *of* the subject, Brentano takes the basic form to be affirming or denying the existence of something, which needs only one idea. Judgements like "It is raining" and "Zeus does not exist" do not then need to be tortured into subject–predicate form to be regarded as meaningful. The one accepts rain, the other rejects Zeus. The verb "exist" does not stand for a property, not even a second-order property as in Kant (p. 211); it simply marks positive judgement or acceptance. On this basis, Brentano sketches in the *Psychology* how traditional syllogistic can be simplified, a project he had already presented in lectures in Würzburg in 1870/71.[15] The categorical propositions in Brentano, as in Boole, lack existential import in the subject position of universal propositions: "All A is B" becomes simply "There is no A non-B." The resulting economy is not inelegant, though Brentano later relented and admitted "double judgements" carrying import.

As Meinong and others (including Frege) later pointed out, it is possible to assume something, for example as the premiss of an

---

[14] See *The Origins of our Knowledge of Right and Wrong*, London: Routledge & Kegan Paul, 1969, pp. 15–16.

[15] In F. Mayer-Hillebrand's Brentano compilation *Die Lehre vom richtigen Urteil*, Berne: Franke, 1956, this reform is carried out in greater detail on pp. 202–26.

argument, or consider it within the context of a story, without judging it one way or the other. So Brentano's class of judgements appears not to cover all intellectual acts. Attempts by Brentano and his adherents to defend his view have not been convincing.

It is characteristic of interests that they show differences of degree or strength, whereas for Brentano judgement is an all or nothing affair. Theories of subjective degrees of belief or conviction seem to break down this difference, since they posit a continuum. Just as a sound may get subjectively louder as I approach its source, so my conviction that the girl I see is my friend Mary may get stronger as she comes closer. Brentano heard this objection, and was unimpressed (p. 286), but his counterargument fails to distinguish the subjective probability of a judgement, as *that this is Mary,* which concerns the degree of conviction with which it is held, from a judgement of probability, *that it is 70 percent likely that this is Mary.* The latter, as Brentano notes, is a more complex affair, and a different judgement, but it is for precisely that reason not the one whose degree of conviction is in question.

Not only did the name of the third class give Brentano trouble, but the justification for putting emotions and feelings in the same basic class as desires, intentions, and acts of will was unconvincing to most subsequent philosophers. Brentano's main argument (p. 236) is that there is a seamless continuum between feeling (e.g. sad at losing something) and willing (e.g. to act to replace it) and that all attempts to divide it are arbitrary. Meinong, Ehrenfels and others of Brentano's pupils concerned with the psychology of affects and interests found this argument unconvincing, and it becomes especially unconvincing when we drop Brentano's restriction to phenomena. A voluntary action, like picking up the telephone in order to call Mary, may or may not, depending on your theory, be immediately preceded by an "act of will" which can be frustrated by a physical impediment, but actions are generally not just mental, and the intents that go with them, even abortive ones, are intents by virtue of suitable connections of their kind with actions. But action raises questions of responsibility, right and wrong, precisely because its effects typically extend beyond the agent's mental life, and these are quite distinct from the issues surrounding emotions and feelings, no matter how like them the typical mental accompaniments of actions may otherwise be.[16] Brentano's ethics, which is based on the concepts of *correct* love

[16] See G. E. M. Anscombe, "Will and Emotion," in Chisholm and Haller, op. cit., pp. 139–48.

and hate, must have acts or agents as its objects if it is to graduate beyond the self-contemplative, and so it must go beyond the self-imposed restrictions of the 1874 *Psychology*.

The mental realm has then shown itself to be more complex than Brentano's classification would have us believe, but it proved fruitful to launch the classificatory project. Likewise Brentano's immanence theory of intentionality was soon overtaken, not least in his own mind, but the question of the nature of intentionality has proved not only astonishingly fecund in philosophy, but also extremely tough. So, while some of Brentano's concerns may now seem quaint, many others are still alive, and the quaint often has an uncanny way of reacquiring relevance.

When this translation first appeared, Brentano studies were the slightly exotic preserve of a small number of philosophers, foremost among them Roderick Chisholm. Under his guidance and influence, a new and larger generation of editors, translators and scholars has emerged in both America and Europe, many more works of Brentano have been edited and translated, new light has been cast on old issues and new avenues of research have opened up. There is a journal, *Brentano Studien*, and there are the beginnings of a textually accurate critical edition. The relevance of Brentano's work for the beginnings of analytic philosophy has become plain. Despite this, we are still some way from a full understanding of all the complexities of Brentano's views, the influences upon him, and his development. Yet all this activity leads back to the one major work that Brentano saw through the press, his 1874 *Psychology*. Its place in the history of philosophy and psychology is secure.

PETER SIMONS

University of Leeds

Preface to the English Edition

Franz Brentano's *Psychologie vom empirischen Standpunkt* was originally published in 1874 by Duncker & Humblot in Leipzig. It was divided into two books, and three additional books were supposed to follow, but never appeared. Another book entitled *Vom sinnlichen und noetischen Bewusstsein* is sometimes referred to as "*Psychologie* III"; it is not included here, although an English edition is planned. In 1911 Book Two of the *Psychologie* was reissued under the title *Von der Klassifikation der psychischen Phänomene* again by Duncker & Humblot. To this edition Brentano added some notes and appended several essays expanding upon and in some cases revising and correcting points made in the original text. In 1924 a second edition of *Psychologie vom empirischen Standpunkt*, edited by Oskar Kraus, was published in Felix Meiner's *Philosophische Biblothek* series in Leipzig. In addition to the supplementary essays which had been added in 1911, Kraus appended several more essays from Brentano's *Nachlass*, and provided an Introduction and explanatory notes.

The present edition is a translation of Kraus's 1924 edition although it differs in the following respects. It does not include the essay, "Miklosich on Subjectless Propositions." Kraus had included this essay in the 1924 edition of the *Psychologie* and omitted it from his 1934 edition of *Vom Ursprung sittlicher Erkenntnis*, the work to which Brentano had originally appended it. Since it has recently been restored to its place in that work in Roderick M. Chisholm's English edition, *The Origin of Our Knowledge of Right and Wrong* (London and New York, 1969), I omit it here. The notes from Kraus's edition, many of which are devoted to giving Kraus's own interpretation of Brentano's views, are included here. They can be distinguished from Brentano's notes by their numerical designations. I have, however, abbreviated some and omitted others. References have been brought up to date and English editions have been cited whenever possible. The few additional notes added by the translators and the editor are identified as such; most of these were contributed by D. B. Terrell.

The present translation has the following history. Working independently of each other, the late Professor Antos C. Rancurello of the University of Dayton and Professor D. B. Terrell of the University of Minnesota prepared translations of the *Psychologie.* Professor Rancurello and Professor Terrell both felt, however, that it would be better to publish one translation than two, and I was authorized to unify their two translations. The present work, therefore, is based upon what they have done, although the responsibility for any errors that may appear is mine.

The translators have, in general, followed Professor Chisholm's lead in translating certain difficult terms in Brentano's writings. As in his editions of *The True and the Evident* (London and New York, 1964), and *The Origin of Our Knowledge of Right and Wrong* (1969), "*Vorstellung*" is sometimes translated as "presentation," and sometimes as "idea," or "thought." The corresponding verb "*vorstellen*," is translated variously as "to think of," "to have before the mind," and as "to have a presentation of." "*Anschauung*" is rendered as "intuition," "*als richtig characterisiert*" is translated as "experienced as being correct," and, for reasons which Chisholm sets forth in his Preface to *The True and the Evident,* "*Realia*" is translated as "things."

I was privileged to have had the opportunity to consult with Franz Brentano's son, Dr. J. C. M. Brentano, before his death, and with Dr. George Katkov of St. Antony's College, Oxford, who was an associate of Oskar Kraus at the *Brentano Gesellschaft* in Prague before World War II. This book is one of a series of translations supported by the Franz Brentano Foundation under the general editorship of Professor Roderick M. Chisholm of Brown University. I am especially indebted to Professor Chisholm for his support and encouragement.

LINDA L. MCALISTER

Brooklyn College of the
City University of New York

Foreword to the 1911 Edition, The Classification of Mental Phenomena*

The greatest contributions to science are not made by treatises or manuals whose goal is to present a systematic view of a given scientific discipline, but by monographs which deal with a single problem. It is not surprising, therefore, that in spite of its incompleteness my *Psychology from an Empirical Standpoint* has aroused wide interest. In this work I offered entirely new solutions to certain elementary questions, and took pains to justify all my innovations in detail. In particular, my investigations concerning the classification of mental phenomena have attracted the general attention of scientists more and more. The fact that I was recently asked to authorize the Italian translation of the chapters dealing with these investigations testifies to the ever-increasing interest in the matter.

My book was published more than thirty years ago, and later investigations have not substantially altered the views expressed in it, although they have led to further developments or, as I myself at least believe, to improvements on some rather important points. It seemed impossible not to mention these innovations, yet at the same time it seemed advisable to retain the original format of my work, the form in which it had influenced its contemporaries. I was further prompted to follow this procedure by the realization that many eminent psychologists who had shown great interest in my doctrine, were more inclined to rally to it in its first form, than to follow me in my new lines of thinking. So I decided to reprint the old text with practically no changes, while at the same time supplementing it with certain observations which are to be found

*[Editor's note: Published in 1911 and containing only Chaps. 5–9 of Book Two, followed by an Appendix.]

partially in footnotes, but mainly in an Appendix. These observations contain a defense against certain attacks on my doctrine from various sources, and they develop those aspects of my doctrine which, in my own judgement, needed revision.

One of the most important innovations is that I am no longer of the opinion that mental relation can have something other than a thing [*Reales*] as its object. In order to justify this new point of view, I had to explore entirely new questions, for example I had to go into the investigation of the modes of presentation.

I am fully aware that the conciseness of my presentation does not facilitate the understanding of the subject matter. In view of this, I tried to express myself with greater precision.

Having come to know about the Italian translation and the additions included in it, some German psychologists have urged me to prepare a new German edition of my *Psychology from an Empirical Standpoint* as well, especially since the first edition has long been out of print. At their urging, then, everything included in the new Italian edition also appears here as the second edition of the original German text, augmented in the manner I have indicated.

FRANZ BRENTANO

Florence, 1911

Foreword to the 1874 Edition

The title which I have given this work characterizes both its object[1] and its method. My psychological standpoint is empirical; experience alone is my teacher. Yet I share with other thinkers the conviction that this is entirely compatible with a certain ideal point of view. The way in which I conceive of psychological method will be presented in more detail in the first of the six books into which this work is divided. The first book discusses psychology as a science, the second considers mental phenomena in general. A third book, to follow, will investigate the characteristics of, and the laws governing, presentations; the fourth will concern itself with the characteristics and laws of judgements; and the fifth with those of the emotions and, in particular, of acts of will. The final book will deal with the relationship between mind and body, and there we shall also pursue the question of whether it is conceivable that mental life continues after the disintegration of the body.[2]

Thus the plan of this work embraces all the different and essential fields of psychology. It is not our purpose, however, to write a compendium of this science, although we shall nevertheless strive to make our presentation clear and comprehensible enough for anyone interested in philosophical investigations. We often dwell at great length upon certain specific problems, and we are more concerned that the foundations be firmly established than we are with comprehensiveness. Perhaps people will find this careful method exaggerated and tedious, but I would rather be criticized for this than be accused of not having tried to justify my assertions

---

[1] Brentano deals with questions of descriptive and genetic psychology in this work, but it was not until later that he worked out the now commonly accepted distinction between them.

[2] Brentano dealt with the problems projected for Books Three through Six in various monographs as well as in his lecture courses, but he published only a little during his lifetime. Cp. for example, the *Untersuchungen zur Sinnespsychologie*, Leipzig, 1907.

sufficiently. Our most urgent need in psychology is not the variety and universality of the tenets, but rather the unity of the doctrine. Within this framework we must strive to attain what first mathematics and then physics, chemistry, and physiology have already attained, i.e. a core of generally accepted truths capable of attracting to it contributions from all other fields of scientific endeavor. We must seek to establish a single unified science of psychology in place of the many psychologies we now have.

In addition, just as there is no specifically German truth, there is no specifically national psychology, not even a German one. It is for this reason that I am taking into account the outstanding scientific contributions of modern English philosophers no less than those of German philosophers.

There is no doubt that science is badly served by indiscriminate compromises, since they sacrifice the unity and coherence of the doctrine to the unity and agreement of the teachers. Indeed, nothing has led to a splintering of philosophical outlooks more than eclecticism.

In science, just as in politics, it is difficult to reach agreement without conflict, but in scientific disputes we should not proceed in such a way as to seek the triumph of this or that investigator, but only the triumph of truth. The driving force behind these battles ought not to be ambition, but the longing for a common subordination to truth, which is one and indivisible. For this reason, just as I have proceeded without restraint to refute and discard the opinions of others whenever they seemed to be erroneous, so I will readily and gratefully welcome any correction of my views which might be suggested to me. In these investigations and in those which will follow I assail quite frequently and with great tenacity even the most outstanding investigators such as Mill, Bain, Fechner, Lotze, Helmholtz and others, but this should not be interpreted as an attempt either to lessen their merit or weaken the power of their influence. On the contrary, it is a sign that I, like many others, have felt their influence in a special way and have profited from their doctrines, not only when I have accepted them, but also when I have had to challenge them. I hope, therefore, that following my example, others can benefit from a thoroughgoing evaluation of their theories.

I am also very well aware of the fact that frequently my arguments will be directed against opinions which I do not consider to be of great intrinsic interest. I was prompted to undertake a rather detailed study of these opinions because at the present time they enjoy an undue popularity and exert a lamentable influence upon a public which, in matters of psychology even less than in other fields, has not yet learned to demand scientific cogency.

Quite frequently the reader will find that I advance opinions which have not been expressed before. It will, I believe, be readily apparent that in no instance have I been concerned with novelty for its own sake. On the contrary, I have departed from traditional conceptions only reluctantly and only when I was compelled to do so by the dominating force of reasons which seemed, to me at least, to be overpowering. Moreover, a closer analysis will reveal that even when I seem to be expressing the most original ideas, to some extent these views have already been anticipated. I have not failed to call attention to such earlier anticipations, and even when my viewpoint has developed independently of previous analogous views, I have not neglected to mention them, since it has not been my concern to appear to be the inventor of a new doctrine, but rather the advocate of a true and established one.

If earlier theories sometimes turn out to be viewed only as anticipations of more accurate doctrines, my own work can be no more than a mere preparation for future, more perfect accomplishments. In our own time a certain philosophy, which succeeded for a while in presenting itself as the final embodiment of all science, was soon seen to be unimprovable rather than unsurpassable.[3] A scientific doctrine which precludes further development toward a more perfect life is a stillborn child. Contemporary psychology, in particular, finds itself in a situation in which those who claim to be its experts betray a greater ignorance than those who confess with Socrates, "I know only one thing – that I know nothing."

The truth, however, lies in neither extreme. There exist at the present time the beginnings of a scientific psychology. Although inconspicuous in themselves, these beginnings are indisputable signs of the possibility of a fuller development which will some day bear abundant fruit, if only for future generations.

Aschaffenburg
March 7, 1874

---

[3] What is meant is speculative philosophy, especially Hegel's.

BOOK ONE

PSYCHOLOGY AS A SCIENCE

I

The Concept and Purpose of Psychology

There are certain phenomena which once seemed familiar and obvious and appeared to provide an explanation for things which had been obscure. Subsequently, however, these phenomena began to seem quite mysterious themselves and began to arouse astonishment and curiosity. These phenomena, above all others, were zealously investigated by the great thinkers of antiquity. Yet little agreement or clarity has been reached concerning them to this day. It is these phenomena which I have made my object of study. In this work I shall attempt to sketch in general terms an accurate picture of their characteristics and laws. There is no branch of science that has borne less fruit for our knowledge of nature and life, and yet there is none which holds greater promise of satisfying our most essential needs. There is no area of knowledge, with the single exception of metaphysics, which the great mass of people look upon with greater contempt. And yet there is none to which certain individuals attribute greater value and which they hold in higher esteem. Indeed, the entire realm of truth would appear poor and contemptible to many people if it were not so defined as to include this province of knowledge. For they believe that the other sciences are only to be esteemed insofar as they lead the way to this one. The other sciences are, in fact, only the foundation; psychology is, as it were, the crowning pinnacle. All the other sciences are a preparation for psychology; it is dependent on all of them. But it is said to exert a most powerful reciprocal influence upon them. It is supposed to renew man's entire life and hasten and assure progress. And if, on the one hand, it appears to be the pinnacle of the towering structure of science, on the other hand, it is destined to become the basis of society and of its noblest possessions, and, by this very fact, to become the basis of all scientific endeavor as well.

1. The word "psychology" means *science of the soul*. In fact,

3

Aristotle, who was the first to make a classification of science and to expound its separate branches in separate essays, entitled one of his works περί ψυχῆς. He meant by "soul" the nature, or, as he preferred to express it, the form, the first activity, the first actuality of a living being.* And he considers something a living being if it nourishes itself, grows and reproduces and is endowed with the faculties of sensation and thought, or if it possesses at least one of these faculties. Even though he is far from ascribing consciousness to plants, he nevertheless considered the vegetative realm as living and endowed with souls. And thus, after establishing the concept of the soul, the oldest work on psychology goes on to discuss the most general characteristics of beings endowed with vegetative as well as sensory or intellectual faculties.

This was the range of problems which psychology originally encompassed. Later on, however, its field was narrowed substantially. Psychologists no longer discussed vegetative activities. On the assumption that it lacked consciousness, the entire realm of vegetative life ceased to be considered within the scope of their investigations. In the same way, the animal kingdom, insofar as it, like plants and inorganic things is an object of external perception,[1] was excluded from their field of research. This exclusion was also extended to phenomena closely associated with sensory life, such as the nervous system and muscles, so that their investigation became the province of the physiologist rather than the psychologist.

This narrowing of the domain of psychology was not an arbitrary one. On the contrary, it appears to be an obvious correction necessitated by the nature of the subject matter itself. In fact, only when the unification of related fields and the separation of unrelated fields is achieved can the boundaries between the sciences be correctly drawn and their classification contribute to the progress of knowledge. And the phenomena of consciousness are related to one another to an extraordinary degree. The same mode of perception gives us all our knowledge of them, and numerous analogies relate higher and lower phenomena to one another.[2] The things which external perception has shown us about living beings are seen as if from a different angle or even in a completely different form, and the

---

* The Greek expressions are: ψύσις, μορφή, πρώτη ἐνέργεια, πρώτη ἐντελέχεια.

[1] "External perception" is to be understood in its extended, inexact sense here. Cp. Book Two, p. 91.

[2] According to Brentano the concept of consciousness is perfectly uniform; the individual species of consciousness are analogous to one another. For example, judgement is either affirmation or denial, emotive activity is either love or hate. Love is analogous to affirmation, hate to denial.

general truths which we find here are sometimes the same principles which we see governing inorganic nature, and sometimes analogous ones.

It could be said, and not without some justification, that Aristotle himself suggests this later and more correct delimitation of the boundaries of psychology. Those who are acquainted with him know how frequently, while expounding a less advanced doctrine, he sets forth the rudiments of a different and more correct viewpoint. His metaphysics as well as his logic and ethics provides examples of this. In the third book of his treatise *On the Soul*, where he deals with voluntary actions, he dismisses the thought of investigating the organs that serve as intermediaries between a desire and the part of the body toward whose movement the desire is directed. For, he says, sounding exactly like a modern psychologist, such an investigation is not the province of one who studies the soul, but of one who studies the body.* I say this only in passing so as perhaps to make it easier to convince some of the enthusiastic followers of Aristotle who still exist even in our own times.

We have seen how the field of psychology became circumscribed. At the same time, and in quite an analogous manner, the concept of life was also narrowed, or, if not this concept – for scientists still ordinarily use this term in its broad original sense – at least the concept of the soul.

In modern terminology the word "soul" refers to the substantial bearer of presentations (*Vorstellungen*) and other activities which are based upon presentations and which, like presentations, are only perceivable through inner perception. Thus we usually call soul the substance which has sensations such as fantasy images, acts of memory, acts of hope or fear, desire or aversion.[3]

We, too, use the word "soul" in this sense. In spite of the modification in the concept, then, there seems to be nothing to prevent us from defining psychology in the terms in which Aristotle once defined it, namely as the science of the soul. So it appears that just as the natural sciences study the properties and laws of physical bodies, which are the objects of our external perception,[4] psychology is the science which studies the properties and laws of the soul, which we discover within ourselves directly by means of inner perception, and which we infer, by analogy, to exist in others.

* *De Anima*, III, 10, 433 b 21.
[3] By "substance" we are to understand an entity in which other things subsist but which does not subsist in anything itself: the ultimate subject. The question as to whether the subject of consciousness is spiritual or material is not prejudged by assuming a "substantial substrate."
[4] Cp. above. note 1.

Thus delimited, psychology and the natural sciences appear to divide the entire field of the empirical sciences between them, and to be distinguished from one another by a clearly defined boundary.

But this first claim, at least, is not true. There are facts which can be demonstrated in the same way in the domain of inner perception or external perception. And precisely because they are wider in scope, these more comprehensive principles belong exclusively neither to the natural sciences nor to psychology. The fact that they can be ascribed just as well to the one science as to the other shows that it is better to ascribe them to neither. They are, however, numerous and important enough for there to be a special field of study devoted to them. It is this field of study which, under the name metaphysics, we must distinguish from both the natural sciences and psychology.

Moreover, even the distinction between the two less general of these three great branches of knowledge is not an absolute one. As always happens when two sciences touch upon one another, here too borderline cases between the natural and mental sciences are inevitable. For the facts which the physiologist investigates and those which the psychologist investigates are most intimately correlated, despite their great differences in character. We find physical and mental properties united in one and the same group. Not only may physical states be aroused by physical states and mental states by mental, but it is also the case that physical states have mental consequences and mental states have physical consequences.

Some thinkers have distinguished a separate science which is supposed to deal with these questions. One in particular is Fechner, who named this branch of science "psychophysics" and called the famous law which he established in this connection the "Psychophysical Law." Others have named it, less appropriately, "physiological psychology."*

Such a science is supposed to eliminate all boundary disputes between psychology and physiology. But would not new and even more numerous disputes arise in their place between psychology and psychophysics on the one hand and between psychophysics and physiology on the other? Or† is it not obviously the task of the

---

* Recently Wundt adopted this expression in his important work *Principles of Physiological Psychology* [trans. E. B. Titchener (London and New York, 1904)]. Even though it may not be the case in this context, such an expression could be misunderstood, and the term "physiological" taken to refer to the method used. As we shall soon see, some people have wanted to base all of psychology on physiological investigations. Cp. also F. W. Hagen, *Psychologische Studien* (Braunschweig, 1847), p. 7.

† [Translators' note: Reading "oder" with the 1874 edition.]

psychologist to ascertain the basic elements of mental phenomena?[5] Yet the psychophysicist must study them too, because sensations are aroused by physical stimuli. Is it not the task of the physiologist to trace voluntary as well as reflex actions back to the origins through an uninterrupted causal chain? Yet the psychophysicist, too, will have to investigate the first physical effects of mental causes.

Let us not, then, be unduly disturbed by the inevitable encroachment of physiology upon psychology and vice versa. These encroachments will be no greater than those which we observe, for example, between physics and chemistry. They do nothing to refute the correctness of the boundary line we have established; they only show that, justified as it is, this distinction, like every other distinction between sciences, is somewhat artificial. Nor will it be in any way necessary to treat the whole range of so-called psychophysical questions twice, i.e. once in physiology and once in psychology. In the case of each of these problems we can easily show which field contains the essential difficulty. Once this difficulty is solved, the problem itself is as good as solved. For example, it will definitely be the task of the psychologist to ascertain the first mental phenomena which are aroused by a physical stimulus, even if he cannot dispense with looking at physiological facts in so doing. By the same token, in the case of voluntary movements of the body, the psychologist will have to establish the ultimate and immediate mental antecedents of the whole series of physical changes which are connected with them, but it will be the task of the physiologist to investigate the ultimate and immediate physical causes of sensation, even though in so doing he must obviously also look at the mental phenomenon. Likewise, with reference to movements that have mental causes, the physiologist must establish within his own field their ultimate and proximate effects.

Concerning the demonstration that there is a proportional relationship between increases in physical and mental causes and effects, i.e. the investigation of the so-called "Psychophysical Law," it seems to me that the problem has two parts, one of which pertains to the physiologist, while the other is the task of the psychologist. The first is to determine which relative differences in the intensity of physical

---

[5] The task of "ascertaining the basic elements of mental phenomena" Brentano later assigned to "descriptive psychology," and the laws governing their coming into existence, duration, and passing away, to the investigations of "genetic psychology," which is then predominantly physiological in character. But before he had separated the two *disciplines*, he had already sharply discriminated between descriptive and genetic *questions*. Cp. Chap. 3, Sect. 2, p. 44.

stimuli correspond to the smallest noticeable differences in the intensity of mental phenomena. The second consists in trying to discover the relations which these smallest noticeable differences bear to one another. But is not the answer to the latter question immediately and completely evident? Is it not clear that all the smallest noticeable differences must be considered equal to one another? This is the view which has been generally accepted. Wundt himself, in his *Physiological Psychology* (p. 295), offers the following argument: "A difference in intensity which is just barely noticeable is . . . a psychic value of constant magnitude. In fact, if one just noticeable difference were greater or smaller than another, *then it would be greater or smaller than the just noticeable*, which is a contradiction." Wundt does not realize that this is a circular argument. If someone doubts that all differences which are just noticeable are equal, then as far as he is concerned, being "just noticeable" is no longer a characteristic property of a constant magnitude. The only thing that is correct and evident *a priori* is that all just noticeable differences are equally noticeable, but not that they are equal. If that were so, every increase which is equal would have to be equally noticeable and every increase which is equally noticeable would have to be equal. But this remains to be investigated, and the investigation of this question, which is the job of the psychologist because it deals with laws of comparative judgement, could yield a result quite different from what was expected. The moon does seem to change position more noticeably when it is nearer the horizon than when it is high in the sky, when in fact it changes the same amount in the same amount of time in either case. On the other hand, the first task mentioned above undoubtedly belongs to the physiologist. Physical observations have more extensive application here. And it is certainly no coincidence that we have to thank a physiologist of the first rank such as E. H. Weber for paving the way for this law, and a philosophically trained physicist such as Fechner for establishing it in a more extended sphere.*

So the definition of psychology which was given above appears to be justified, and its position among its neighboring sciences to have been clarified.

2. Nevertheless, not all psychologists would agree to defining psychology as the science of the soul, in the sense indicated above.

* In this connection Gustav Fechner says: "From physics outer psychophysics borrows aids and methodology; inner psychophysics leans more to physiology and anatomy, particularly of the nervous system . . ." *Elements of Psychophysics* [trans. Helmut E. Adler (New York, 1966)], p. 10. And again he says in the preface (p. xxix) "that this work would particularly interest physiologists, even though I would at the same time like to interest philosophers."

Some define it, rather, as the science of mental phenomena,[6] thereby placing it on the same level as its sister sciences. Similarly, in their opinion, natural science is to be defined as the science of physical phenomena, rather than as the science of bodies.

Let us clarify the basis of this objection. What is meant by "science of mental phenomena" or "science of physical phenomena"? The words "phenomenon" or "appearance" are often used in opposition to "things which really and truly exist." We say, for example, that the objects of our senses, as revealed in sensation, are merely phenomena; color and sound, warmth and taste do not really and truly exist outside of our sensations, even though they may point to objects which do so exist. John Locke once conducted an experiment in which, after having warmed one of his hands and cooled the other, he immersed both of them simultaneously in the same basin of water. He experienced warmth in one hand and cold in the other, and thus proved that neither warmth nor cold really existed in the water. Likewise, we know that pressure on the eye can arouse the same visual phenomena as would be caused by rays emanating from a so-called colored object. And with regard to determinations of spatial location, those who take appearances for true reality can easily be convinced of their error in a similar way. From the same distance away, things which are in different locations can appear to be in the same location, and from different distances away, things which are in the same location can appear to be in different locations. A related point is that movement may appear as rest and rest as movement. These facts prove beyond doubt that the objects of sensory experience are deceptive.[7] But even if this could not be established so clearly, we would still have to doubt their veracity because there would be no

---

[6] On this point, cp. Introduction, p. 402 ff.

[7] That is to say, it can be proved that the qualitatively extended thing which appears to us does not exist *as what it appears to us to be* (cp. Introduction, p. 392 ff.). Below (Book Two, Chap. 1, Sect. 9) it is maintained that the external world is not really "spatial" and "temporal" but "quasi-spatial" and "quasi-temporal." – Brentano expresses himself more clearly in his 1869 essay on Comte (reprinted) and in later essays. That the external world is "quasi-spatial" and "quasi-temporal" can only mean that it is *analogous* to what our perception of space and time shows us. "Analogous," means that the spatial and temporal world exhibits the *same relations* as those exhibited by the object of our perceptions of space and time. That this is how the terms "quasi-spatial" and "quasi-temporal' are to be understood can be seen in the lines that follow, which mention the fact that the real world displays "certain analogies" to the world of our perception, i.e. exhibits the same relationships. Cp. below Sect. 3, p. 19, end of the first paragraph and my note to it, and Chap. 3, Sect. 6, p. 60, Book Two, Chap. 2, p. 107.

guarantee for them as long as the assumption that there is a world that exists in reality which causes our sensations and to which their content bears certain analogies, would be sufficient to account for the phenomena.

We have no right, therefore, to believe that the objects of so-called external perception really exist as they appear to us. Indeed, they demonstrably do not exist outside of us. In contrast to that which really and truly exists, they are mere phenomena.

What has been said about the objects of external perception does not, however, apply in the same way to objects of inner perception. In their case, no one has ever shown that someone who considers these phenomena to be true would thereby become involved in contradictions. On the contrary, of their existence we have that clear knowledge and complete certainty which is provided by immediate insight. Consequently, no one can really doubt that a mental state which he perceives in himself exists, and that it exists just as he perceives it. Anyone who could push his doubt this far would reach a state of absolute doubt, a skepticism which would certainly destroy itself, because it would have destroyed any firm basis upon which it could endeavor to attack knowledge.

Defining psychology as the science of mental phenomena in order to make natural science and mental science resemble each other in this respect, then, has no reasonable justification.*

There is another, quite different reason which generally motivates those who advocate such a definition, however. These people do not deny that thinking and willing really exist. And they use the expression "mental phenomena" or "mental appearances" as completely synonymous with "mental states", "mental processes," and "mental events," as inner perception reveals them to us. Nevertheless, their objection to the old definition, too, is related to the fact that on such a definition the limits of knowledge are misunderstood. If someone says that natural science is the science of bodies, and he means by "body" a substance which acts on our sense organs and produces presentations of physical phenomena, he assumes that substances are the cause of external appearances. Likewise, if someone says that psychology is the science of the soul, and means by "soul" the substantial bearer of mental states, then he is expressing his conviction that mental events are to be considered properties of a substance. But what entitles us to assume that there are such substances? It has been said that such substances are not objects of experience; neither sense perception nor inner experience reveal substances to us.[8] Just

* Kant has certainly done this, and it is a mistake which has often been reproved, in particular by Überweg in his *System der Logik*.

[8] Brentano maintains the opposite view: according to his theory, which

as in sense perception we encounter phenomena such as warmth, color and sound, in inner perception we encounter manifestations of thinking, feeling and willing. But we never encounter that something of which these things are properties. It is a fiction to which no reality of any sort corresponds, or whose existence could not possibly be proved, even if it did exist. Obviously, then, it is not an object of science. Hence natural science may not be defined as the science of bodies nor may psychology be defined as the science of the soul. Rather, the former should be thought of simply as the science of physical phenomena, and the latter, analogously, as the science of mental phenomena. There is no such thing as the soul, at least not as far as we are concerned, but psychology can and should exist nonetheless, although, to use Albert Lange's paradoxical expression, it will be a psychology without a soul.*

We see that the idea is not as absurd as the expression makes it seem. Even viewed in this way psychology still retains a wide area for investigation.

A glance at natural science makes this clear. For all the facts and laws which this branch of inquiry investigates when it is conceived of as the science of bodies will continue to be investigated by it when it is viewed only as the science of physical phenomena. This is how it is actually viewed at present by many famous natural scientists who have formed opinions about philosophical questions, thanks to the noteworthy trend which is now bringing philosophy and the natural sciences closer together. In so doing, they in no way restrict the

---

* *The History of Materialism* [trans. Ernest Chester Thomas, 3rd ed. (London, 1892)], Book II, Sect. iii, Chap. 3, p. 168. "Calmly assume, then, a psychology without a soul! And yet the name will still be useful so long as we have something to study that is not completely covered by any other science."

---

follows Aristotle, both sensation and inner perception exhibit *substances* to us. In inner perception we apprehend ourselves as "thinking things" (thinking in the Cartesian sense = consciousness) or *"res cogitans."* In external perception we apprehend something as a subject which has accidents, for example, something extended which has a color. The assumption that there is a substance is not a fiction, but the assumption that there is an attribute without any subject supporting it is an immediately absurd fiction. (Cp. Condillac, cited in Vaihinger's *Philosophie des Als Ob*, p. 383.) But for quite a while – even in the study of "mental phenomena" – this fiction proves to be harmless, very much as one can study scientifically the transcendent "physical phenomena" of the external world and leave the question of their subject in doubt. – This comfortable fiction is not only harmless, but advantageous insofar as it eliminates a point of controversy in broad stretches of a large area of investigation.

11

domain of the natural sciences. All of the laws of coexistence and succession which these sciences encompass according to others, fall within their domain according to these thinkers, too.

The same thing is true of psychology. The phenomena revealed by inner perception are also subject to laws. Anyone who has engaged in scientific psychological research recognizes this and even the layman can easily and quickly find confirmation for it in his own inner experience. The laws of the coexistence and succession of mental phenomena remain the object of investigation even for those who deny to psychology any knowledge of the soul. And with them comes a vast range of important problems for the psychologist, most of which still await solution.

In order to make more intelligible the nature of psychology as he conceived it, John Stuart Mill, one of the most decisive and influential advocates of this point of view, has given in his *System of Logic** a synopsis of the problems with which psychology must be concerned.

In general, according to Mill, psychology investigates the laws which govern the succession of our mental states, i.e. the laws according to which one of these states produces another.†

In his opinion, some of these laws are general, others more special. A general law, for example, would be the law according to which, "whenever any state of consciousness has once been excited in us, no matter by what cause . . . a state of consciousness resembling the former but inferior in intensity, is capable of being reproduced in us, without the presence of any such cause as excited it at first." Every impression, he says, using the language of Hume, has its idea. Similarly, there would also be certain general laws which determine the actual appearance of such an idea. He mentions three such Laws of Association of Ideas. The first is the Law of Similarity: "Similar ideas tend to excite one another." The second is the Law of Contiguity: "When two impressions have been frequently experienced . . . either simultaneously or in immediate succession, then when one of these impressions, or the idea of it recurs, it tends to excite the idea of the other." The third is the Law of Intensity: "Greater intensity

---

* VI, Chap. 4, Sect. 3.
† Certainly sensations are also mental states. Their succession, however, is the same as the succession of the physical phenomena which they represent. Therefore, it is the task of the natural scientist to establish the laws of this succession insofar as it is dependent upon the physical stimulation of the sense organs.[9]
[9] The note means that the study of the *genetic* laws governing sensations is the business of the physiologist or the "psycho-physicist." Cp. p. 7. Just above Brentano proved that it is inevitable for both psychology and the natural sciences to mutually interact in the areas. Cp. also p. 98.

in either or both of the impressions, is equivalent, in rendering them excitable by one another, to a greater frequency of conjunction."

The further task of psychology, according to Mill, is to derive from these general and elementary laws of mental phenomena more specific and more complex laws of thought. He says that since several mental phenomena often work concurrently, the question arises whether or not every such case is a case of a combination of causes – in other words, whether or not effects and initial conditions are always related in the same way, as they are in the field of mechanics, where a motion is always the result of motion, homogeneous with its causes and in a certain sense the sum of its causes; or whether the mental realm also exhibits cases similar to the process of chemical combination, where you see in water none of the characteristics of hydrogen and oxygen, and in cinnabar none of the characteristics of mercury and sulphur. Mill himself believed it to be an established fact that both types of case exist in the domain of inner phenomena. Sometimes the processes are analogous to those in mechanics and sometimes to those in chemical reactions. For it may happen that several ideas coalesce in such a way that they no longer appear as several but seem to be a single idea of a completely different sort. Thus, for example, the idea of extension and three dimensional space develops from kinesthetic sensations.

A series of new investigations is linked with this point. In particular the question will be raised as to whether belief and desire are cases of mental chemistry, i.e. whether they are the product of a fusion of ideas. Mill thinks that perhaps we must answer this question negatively. In whatever way it should be decided, perhaps even affirmatively, it would nevertheless be certain that entirely different fields of investigation are opened here. And so there emerges the new task of ascertaining, by means of special observations, the laws of succession of these phenomena, i.e. of ascertaining whether or not they are the products of such psychological chemistry, so to speak. In respect to belief, we would inquire what we believe directly; according to what laws one belief produces another; and what are the laws in virtue of which one thing is taken, rightly or erroneously, as evidence for another thing. In regard to desire, the primary task would consist in determining what objects we desire naturally and originally, and then we must go on to determine by what causes we are made to desire things originally indifferent or even disagreeable to us.

In addition, there is yet another rich area for investigation, one in which psychological and physiological research become more closely involved with one another than elsewhere. The psychologist, according to Mill, has the task of investigating how far the production of one mental state by others is influenced by confirmable physical states. Individual differences in susceptibility to the same psychological causes can be conceived as having a threefold basis. They could be an original and ultimate fact, they could be consequences of the previous mental history of those individuals, and they could be the result of differences in physical organization. The attentive and critical observer will recognize, Mill thinks, that by far the greatest portion of a person's character can be adequately explained in terms of his education and outward circumstances. The remainder can, by and large, only be explained indirectly in terms of organic differences. And obviously this holds true not merely for the commonly recognized tendency of the deaf toward mistrustfulness, of the congenitally blind toward lustfulness, of the physically handicapped toward irritability, but also for many other, less easily intelligible phenomena. If there are still, as Mill grants, other phenomena, instincts in particular, which cannot be explained in any other way except directly in terms of one's particular physical organization, we see that a wide field of investigation is assured for psychology in the area of ethology, i.e. formulating the laws of the formation of character.

This is a survey of psychological problems from the point of view of one of the most important advocates of psychology as a purely phenomenalistic science. It is really true that in none of the above-mentioned respects is psychology harmed by this new conception of it or by the point of view which leads to such a conception. As a matter of fact, in addition to the questions raised by Mill and those implicit in them, there are still others which are equally significant. Thus there is no shortage of important tasks for psychologists of this school, among whom are, at the present time, men who have made themselves preeminently of service to the advancement of science.

Nevertheless, the above conception of psychology seems to exclude at least one question which is of such importance that its absence alone threatens to leave a serious gap in this science. The very investigation which the older conception of psychology considered its main task, the very problem which gave the first impetus to psychological research can, apparently, no longer be raised on this view of psychology. I mean the question of continued existence after death. Anyone familiar with Plato knows that above all else it was the desire to ascertain the truth about this problem which led him to the field of psychology. His *Phaedo* is devoted to it, and other dialogues such as the *Phaedrus*, *Timaeus* and the *Republic* come back to the question time and again. And the same thing is true of Aristotle. Admittedly he sets forth his proofs for the immortality of the soul in less detail than Plato, but it would be a mistake to conclude from this that the problem was any less important to him. In his logical works, where the doctrine of apodictic or scientific demonstration was necessarily the most important issue, he still discusses the problem, condensed into a few pages in the *Posterior Analytics*, in striking contrast to other long, extended discussions. In the *Metaphysics* he speaks of the deity only in a few short sentences in the last book,* yet this study was avowedly so essential to him that he actually applied the name "theology" to the entire science, as well as the names "wisdom" and "first philosophy." In the same way, in his treatise *On the Soul*, he discusses man's soul and its immortality only very briefly, even when he is doing more than merely mentioning it in passing. Yet the classification of psychological problems at the beginning of this work clearly indicates that this question seemed to him to be the most important object of psychology. We are told there that the psychologist has the task, first of all, of investigating what the soul is, and then of investigating its properties, some of which appear to inhere in it alone and not in the body, and, as such, are spiritual. Furthermore he must investigate whether the soul is composed of parts or whether it is simple, and whether all the parts are bodily states or whether there are some which are not, in which case its immortality would be assured. The various *aporiai* which are linked with these questions show that we have hit upon the point which aroused this great thinker's thirst for knowledge most of all. This is the task to which psychology first devoted itself, and which gave it its first impetus for development. And it is precisely this task which appears, at the present time, to have fallen into disrepute and to have become impossible, at least from the standpoint of those who reject psychology as the science of the soul. For if there is no soul, then, of course, the immortality of the soul is out of the question.

This conclusion appears to be so immediately obvious that we cannot be surprised if some partisans of the conception here developed, A. Lange, for one, consider it to be self-evident.† And so psychology offers us a drama similar to the one which occurred in the natural sciences. The alchemists' striving to produce gold from mixtures of elements first instigated chemical research, but the mature science of chemistry abandoned such ambitions as impossible. And somewhat in the manner of the well-known parable about the promise of the dying father, here too the heirs of earlier investigators have fulfilled the predictions of their predecessors. In the parable the sons industriously dug up the vineyard in which they believed a treasure was hidden, and if they did not find the buried gold, they

* I mean, of course, Book Lambda.
† *History of Materialism*, trans. Thomas, 3rd ed., Book II, Sect. i, Chap. 1, p. 162.

reaped the fruit of the well-tilled soil instead. Something similar has happened to chemists, and would be happening to psychologists too. The mature science would have to abandon the question of immortality, but we could say that, as consolation, the zealous efforts which stemmed from a desire for the impossible have led to the solution of other questions whose far-reaching significance cannot be called into question.

Nevertheless, these two cases are not wholly identical. In place of the alchemists' dreams, reality offered a higher substitute. But in comparison with Plato's and Aristotle's hopes of reaching certainty concerning the continued existence of our better part after the dissolution of the body, the laws of association of ideas, of the development of convictions and opinions, and of the origin and growth of desire and love, would hardly be real compensation. The loss of this hope would appear to be far more regrettable. Consequently, if the opposition between these two conceptions of psychology really implied the acceptance or rejection of the question of immortality, this issue would become of paramount importance and would compel us to undertake metaphysical research concerning the existence of substance as the bearer of mental states.

Yet, whatever appearance of necessity there is for restricting the range of inquiry in this connection, it may still be no more than an appearance. In his time David Hume strongly opposed the metaphysicians who claimed to have found within themselves a substance which was the bearer of mental states. "For my part," he says, "when I enter most intimately into what I call *myself*, I always stumble on some particular perception or other, of heat or cold, light or shade, love or hatred, pain or pleasure. I never can catch *myself* at any time without a perception, and never can observe anything but the perception. When my perceptions are removed for any time, as by sound sleep; so long am I insensible of myself, and may truly be said not to exist." If certain philosophers claim that they perceive *themselves* as something simple and permanent, Hume does not want to contradict them, but of himself and of everyone else (this sort of metaphysician alone excepted), he is convinced "that they are nothing but a bundle or collection of different perceptions, which succeed each other with an inconceivable rapidity, and are in a perpetual flux and movement."* We see, therefore, that Hume ranks unequivocally among the opponents of a substantial soul. Nevertheless, Hume himself remarks that in a conception such as his, all the proofs of immortality retain absolutely the same strength as in the traditional conception to which it is opposed. Of course, Albert Lange interprets this

---

* *Treatise on Human Nature*, Book I, IV, Sect. 6.

declaration as a mockery,* and he may very likely be right, for it is known that Hume did not elsewhere scorn the use of malicious irony as a weapon.† What Hume says, however, is not so obviously ridiculous as Lange and perhaps Hume himself might think. For even though it is self-evident that those who deny the existence of a substantial soul cannot speak of the immortality of the soul in the proper sense of the word, it still does not follow that the question of the immortality of the soul loses all meaning because we deny the existence of a substantial bearer of mental phenomena. This becomes evident as soon as you recognize that with or without a substantial soul you cannot deny that there is a certain continuity of our mental life here on earth. If someone rejects the existence of a substance, he must assume that such a continuity does not require a substantial bearer. And the question whether our mental life somehow continues even after the destruction of the body will be no more meaningless for him than for anyone else. It is wholly inconsistent for thinkers of this persuasion to reject, for the reasons mentioned, the question of immortality even in this, its essential sense, though it certainly would be more appropriate to call it immortality of life than immortality of the soul.

This was fully recognized by John Stuart Mill. In the passage from his *Logic* cited earlier, it is true that we do not find the question of immortality listed among those problems to be dealt with by psychology. In his work on Hamilton, however, he has developed with utmost clarity the very idea that we have just formulated.‡

Likewise, at the present time in Germany no important thinker has expressed his rejection of a substantial substrate for both mental and physical states as often and as categorically as Theodor Fechner. In his *Psychophysics*, in his *Atomenlehre* and in other writings, he criticizes this doctrine, sometimes in earnest, sometimes humorously. Nevertheless, he candidly acknowledges his belief in immortality. It is clear, therefore, that even if one accepts the metaphysical view which led modern thinkers to substitute the definition of psychology as the science of mental phenomena for the traditional definition as

* *History of Materialism*, trans. Thomas, 3rd ed., Book II, Sect. i, Chap. 1, p. 162.
† Alexander Bain says of him, "As he was a man fond of literary effects, as well as of speculation, we do not always know when he is in earnest." *Mental Science*, 3rd ed., p. 207.
‡ *An Examination of Sir William Hamilton's Philosophy*, Chap. XII: "As to immortality, it is precisely as easy to conceive that a succession of feelings, a thread of consciousness, may be prolonged to eternity, as that a spiritual substance forever continues to exist; and any evidence which proves the one, will prove the other."

17

the science of the soul, the field of psychology would not thereby be narrowed in any way, and, above all, it would not suffer any essential loss.

It would appear to be just as inadmissible, however, to accept this view without a thorough metaphysical investigation, as it is to reject it without a test. Just as there are eminent men who have questioned and denied that phenomena have a substantial bearer there also have been and still are other very famous scientists who firmly believe that they do. H. Lotze agrees with Aristotle and Leibniz on this point, as does Herbert Spencer, among contemporary English empiricists.* And, with his characteristic frankness, even John Stuart Mill has recognized, in his work on Hamilton, that the rejection of substance as the bearer of phenomena is not entirely free from difficulties and uncertainties, especially in the mental realm.† If, then, the new definition of psychology were connected with the new metaphysics just as inseparably as the old definition was with the old, we would be forced either to look for a third definition, or to descend into the fearful depths of metaphysics.

Happily, the opposite is true. There is nothing in the new definition of psychology which would not have to be accepted by adherents of the older school as well. For whether or not there are souls, the fact is that there are mental phenomena. And no one who accepts the theory of the substantiality of the soul will deny that whatever can be established with reference to the soul is also related to mental phenomena. Nothing, therefore, stands in our way if we adopt the modern definition instead of defining psychology as the science of the soul. Perhaps both are correct. The differences which still exist between them are that the old definition contains metaphysical presuppositions[10] from which the modern one is free; that the latter is accepted by opposing schools of thought, while the former already bears the distinctive mark of one particular school; and the one, therefore, frees us from general preliminary researches which the other would oblige us to undertake. Consequently, the adoption of the modern conception simplifies our work. Furthermore, it offers an additional advantage: any exclusion of an unrelated question not only simplifies, but also reinforces the work. It shows that the results of

* See his *First Principles.*

† *Exam. of Sir Wm. Hamilton's Philo.*, Chap. XII.

[10] The assumption that there is a substantial substrate of mental activities is not really a metaphysical, i.e., a transcendent assumption, according to Brentano's later doctrine, for a presentation without a subject is an absurd fiction. The subject of the presentation, or its subsistent substrate which does not subsist in anything further, is the only thing which deserves the name "substance." Cp. above Note 3 and the introduction.

our investigation are dependent on fewer presuppositions, and thus lends greater certainty to our convictions.

We, therefore, define psychology as the science of mental phenomena, in the sense indicated above. The preceding discussion should be sufficient to clarify the general meaning of this definition. Our subsequent investigation of the difference between mental and physical phenomena will provide whatever further clarification is needed.

3. If someone wanted to compare the relative value of the scientific field which we have just described with that of the natural sciences, using as a measuring stick only and exclusively the interest aroused at the present time by these two types of investigations, psychology would undoubtedly be overshadowed. It is a different matter if we compare the goals which each of the two sciences pursue. We have seen what kind of knowledge the natural scientist is able to attain. The phenomena of light, sound, heat, spatial location and locomotion which he studies are not things which really and truly exist.[11] They are signs of something real, which, through its causal activity, produces presentations of them. They are not, however, an adequate representation of this reality, and they give us knowledge of it only in a very incomplete sense. We can say that there exists something which, under certain conditions, causes this or that sensation. We can probably also prove that there must be relations among these realities similar to those which are manifested by spatial phenomena shapes and sizes. But this is as far as we can go. We have no experience of that which truly exists, in and of itself, and that which we do experience is not true. The truth of physical phenomena is, as they say, only a relative truth.[12]

The phenomena of inner perception are a different matter. They

[11] This passage is misleading; in order to understand it correctly, one must read and interpret it in connection with Chap. I, Sect. 2, p. 9, Chap. III, Sect. 4, pp. 47, 48, and Book Two, Chap. I, Sect. 9, p. 97 ff. In the sentence as it reads in the text "light" is to be understood as meaning the colored, "sound" as meaning the heard sound, just as in the beginning of Sect. 2 and repeatedly, for example pp. 69, 70, i.e. the *sense-quality* which we somehow perceive with relative spatial determination. Natural science, especially physics, has to do with these "mere phenomena" insofar as it (1) shows us that color and sound, etc., are merely appearances and so do not exist, and (2) investigates the transcendent causes of the perceptions (sensations) in which these qualities appear to us. This comes out unambiguously from pp. 10, 47, 48, 60, 98, 107. It also emerges from the immediately following sentences, moreover. In Chap. III, p. 44, and in other passages light and sound are spoken of in the physical sense, i.e. as the transcendent vibrations of the ether or air.

[12] Cp. Book Two, Chap. I, p. 98.

are true in themselves. As they appear to be, so they are in reality, a fact which is attested to by the evidence with which they are perceived. Who could deny, then, that this constitutes a great advantage of psychology over the natural sciences?

The high theoretical value of psychological knowledge is obvious in still another respect. The worthiness of a science increases not only according to the manner in which it is known, but also with the worthiness of its object. And the phenomena the laws of which psychology investigates are superior to physical phenomena not only in that they are true and real in themselves,[13] but also in that they are incomparably more beautiful and sublime. Color and sound, extension and motion are contrasted with sensation and imagination, judgement and will, with all the grandeur these phenomena exhibit in the ideas of the artist, the research of a great thinker, and the self-dedication of the virtuous man. So we have revealed in a new way how the task of the psychologist is higher than that of the natural scientist.

It is also true that things which directly concern us claim our attention more readily than things foreign to us. We are more eager to know the order and origin of our own solar system than that of some more remote group of heavenly bodies. The history of our own country and of our ancestors attracts our attention more than that of other people with whom we have no close ties. And this is another reason for conferring the higher value upon the science of mental phenomena. For our mental phenomena are the things which are most our own. Some philosophers have even identified the self with a collection of mental phenomena, others with the substantial bearer of such a collection of phenomena. And in ordinary language we say that physical changes are external to us while mental changes take place within us.

These very simple observations can easily convince anyone of the great theoretical significance of psychological knowledge. But even

[13] This passage is also misleading; in Brentano's opinion the physicist, too, is concerned with "things which are true and real in themselves," namely certain transcendent causes of sensations. Cp. Note 7 and pp. 95, 60. Of course, he also deals with the "color," the "sound," but this is primarily in order to study the causes of seeing the color, hearing the sound and, insofar as he is not a phenomenalist like Mach, to establish that colors and sounds are "mere phenomena," i.e. cannot be proved to exist. What exists is, on the one hand, the person who sees colors, hears sounds, and, on the other hand, the event which happens in the ether and is one of the causes of seeing and hearing. Psychology is distinguished by the fact that it has to do with phenomena which *are known immediately as true and real in themselves.* This, and nothing else, was and is Brentano's doctrine.

from the point of view of practical significance – and perhaps this is what is most surprising – psychological questions are in no way inferior to those which occupy the natural sciences. Even in this respect there is hardly another branch of science which can be placed on the same level with psychology unless perhaps it is one which merits the same consideration on the grounds that it is an indispensable preparatory step toward the attainment of psychological knowledge.

Let me point out merely in passing that psychology contains the roots of aesthetics, which, in a more advanced stage of development, will undoubtedly sharpen the eye of the artist and assure his progress. Likewise, suffice it to say that the important art of logic, a single improvement in which brings about a thousand advances in science, also has psychology as its source.[14] In addition, psychology has the task of becoming the scientific basis for a theory of education, both of the individual and of society. Along with aesthetics and logic, ethics and politics also stem from the field of psychology. And so psychology appears to be the fundamental condition of human progress in precisely those things which, above all, constitute human dignity. Without the use of psychology, the solicitude of the father as well as that of the political leader, remains an awkward groping. It is because there has been no systematic application of psychological principles in the political field until now, and even more because the guardians of the people have been, almost without exception, completely ignorant of these principles, that we can assert along with Plato and with many contemporary thinkers that, no matter how much fame individuals have attained, no truly great statesman has yet appeared in history. Even before physiology was systematically applied to medicine, there was no lack of famous physicians, as shown by the great confidence they won and by the astonishing cures attributed to them. But anyone who is acquainted with medicine today knows how impossible it would have been for there to have been a single truly great physician prior to the last few decades. The others were all merely blind empiricists, more or less skilful, and more or less lucky. They were not, and could not have been what a trained and discerning physician must be. Up to the present time the same thing holds true of statesmen. The extent to which they, too, are merely blind empiricists is demonstrated every time that an extraordinary event suddenly changes the political situation, and even more clearly every time one of them finds himself in a foreign country where conditions are different. Forsaken by their

[14] Concerning the charge of psychologism which was raised against Brentano because of this and other views, see the supplementary essays and the editor's introduction.

21

empirically derived maxims, they become completely incompetent and helpless.

How many evils could be remedied, both on the individual and social level, by the correct psychological diagnosis, or by knowledge of the laws according to which a mental state can be modified! What an increase in mental power mankind would achieve if the basic mental conditions which determine the different aptitudes for being a poet, a scientist, or a man of practical ability could be fully ascertained beyond any doubt by means of psychological analysis! If this were possible, we could recognize the tree, not from its fruit, but from its very first budding leaves, and could transplant it immediately to a place suited to its nature. For aptitudes are themselves very complex phenomena; they are the remote consequences of forces whose original activity suggests these consequences no more than the shape of the first buds suggests the fruit which the tree will bear. In both cases, however, we are dealing with relationships that are subject to similar laws. And just as botany can make accurate predictions, a sufficiently developed psychology must be able to do the same. In this and in a thousand other different ways, its influence would become most beneficial. Perhaps it alone will be in a position to provide us the means to counteract the decadence which sadly interrupts the otherwise steadily ascending cultural development from time to time.[15] It has long been noted, and correctly so, that the often-used metaphorical expressions, "old nation," and "old civilization," are not strictly appropriate, because, while organisms only partially regenerate themselves, society renews itself completely in each successive generation; we can speak of peoples and epochs becoming sick, but not old. There are, however, such sicknesses which have always appeared periodically up to now, and which, because of our lack of medical skill, have regularly led to death. Hence, even though the really essential analogy is missing, the similarity to old age in external appearance is undeniable.

It is apparent that the practical tasks I assign to psychology are far from insignificant. But is it conceivable that psychology will ever really approach this ideal? Doubt on this point seems to be well-founded. From the fact that up to now, for thousands of years, psychology has made practically no progress, many would like to believe that they are justified in concluding with certainty that it will also do little in the future to further the practical interests of mankind.

The answer to this objection is not far to seek. It is revealed by a

[15] See the title essay in Franz Brentano's *Die Vier Phasen der Philosophie und ihr augenblicklicher Stand*, ed. Oskar Kraus (Leipzig, 1926) and Kraus's book, *Franz Brentano*, p. 18.

simple consideration of the place which psychology occupies in the system of sciences.

The general theoretical sciences form a kind of hierarchy in which each higher step is erected on the basis of the one below it. The higher sciences investigate more complex phenomena, the lower ones phenomena that are simpler, but which contribute to the complexity. The progress of the sciences which stand higher in the scale naturally presupposes that of the lower ones. It is, therefore, evident that, apart from certain weak empirical antecedents, the higher sciences will attain their development later than the lower. In particular, they will not be able to reach that state of maturity in which they can meet the vital needs of life at the same time as the lower sciences. Thus we saw that mathematics had long been turned to practical applications, while physics still lay dozing in its cradle and did not give the slightest sign of its capacity, subsequently so brilliantly proved, to be of service to the needs and desires of life. Similarly, physics had long attained fame and multiple practical applications when, through Lavoisier, chemistry discovered the first firm basis upon which it could stand, in the next few decades, in order to revolutionize, if not the earth, at least the cultivation of the earth, and with it so many other spheres of practical activity. And once again, chemistry had already achieved many splendid results while physiology was yet to be born. And it is not necessary to go back too many years to find the beginnings of a more satisfactory development in physiology, and attempts at practical application followed immediately. They were incomplete perhaps, but nonetheless served to demonstrate that only from physiology is a re-birth of medicine to be expected. It is easy to explain why physiology developed so late. The phenomena it studies are much more complex than those studied by the earlier sciences and are dependent upon them, just as the phenomena of chemistry are dependent upon those of physics and the phenomena of physics are dependent upon those of mathematics. But it is just as easy to understand, then, why psychology has not borne more abundant fruit up until now.[16] Just as physical phenomena are under the influence of mathematical laws,

[16] On this point, see Brentano's inaugural lecture in Vienna, "Ueber die Gründe der Entmutigung auf philosophischem Gebiete," reprinted in *Ueber die Zukunft der Philosophie*, ed. Oskar Kraus (Leipzig, 1929). Brentano arranges the sciences in order somewhat as Comte does. Of course Comte leaves psychology out, while according to Brentano it is to be placed after physiology and prior to sociology. But it is only *genetic* and *physiological* psychology which presupposes the development of scientific knowledge of nature for its complete development. Descriptive-phenomenological psychology is independent of it to a great extent.

and chemical phenomena are under the influence of physical laws, and those of physiology under the influence of all these laws, so psychological phenomena are influenced by the laws governing the forces which shape and renew the bodily organs involved. Consequently, if someone knew from direct experience absolutely nothing about the state of psychology up to the present time, and were acquainted only with the history of the other theoretical sciences and with the recent birth of physiology and indeed even chemistry, he could affirm, without in any way being a skeptic about psychological matters, that psychology has achieved nothing as yet, or that it has achieved very little, and that at best it is only recently that it has shown a tendency toward a more substantial development. This implies that the most important fruits which psychology may bear for practical life, lie in the future. So, should this person turn his attention to the history of psychology, he would merely find in its barrenness confirmation of his expectations; and he would find himself in no way committed to an unfavorable judgement as to its future accomplishments.

We see that the backward condition in which psychology has remained appears to be a necessity, even if we do not doubt the possibility of a rich development in the future. That there is such a possibility is shown by the promising, though weak, beginning it has already in fact made. Once a certain level of its possible development has been reached, the practical consequences will not fail to materialize. For the individual and even more for the masses, where the imponderable circumstances which impede and promote progress balance each other out, psychological laws will afford a sure basis for action.

We may, therefore, confidently hope that psychology will not always lack both inner development and useful applications. Indeed the needs which it must satisfy have already become pressing. Social disorders cry out more urgently for redress than do the imperfections in navigation and railway commerce, agriculture and hygiene. Questions to which we might give less attention, if it were up to us to choose, force themselves upon everyone's attention. Many people have already seen this to be the most important task of our time. We could mention several great scientists who are devoting themselves, with this end in view, to the investigation of psychological laws and to methodological inquiries concerning the derivation and confirmation of conclusions to be applied in practice.

It cannot possibly be the task of political economy to put an end to the present confusion and to re-establish the peace in society which has been increasingly lost amid the clash of conflicting interests. Political economy has a role to play, but neither the whole task nor the major part depends upon it. And indeed even the growing interest which is being accorded to it can serve to corroborate these statements. In the introduction to his *Principles of Political Economy*, John Stuart Mill has touched upon the relation between this science and psychology. The differences in the production and distribution of goods by different peoples and at different times, in his opinion, would depend to a certain extent on differences in the states of their knowledge of physical matters, but would also have psychological causes. "Insofar as the economic condition of nations turns upon the state of physical knowledge," he continues, "it is a subject for the physical sciences, and the arts founded on them. But insofar as the causes are moral or psychological, dependent on institutions and social relations or on the principles of human nature, their investigation belongs not to physical, but to moral and social science, and is the object of what is called Political Economy."*

It seems beyond doubt, therefore, that in the future – and to a certain extent perhaps the not too distant future – psychology will exert a considerable influence upon the practical aspects of life. In this sense we could characterize psychology, as others have already done, as the science of the future, i.e. as the science to which, more than any other, the future belongs; the science which, more than any other, will mould the future; and the science to which, in the future, other sciences will be of service and to which they will be subordinate in their practical application. For this will be the position of psychology once it reaches maturity and is capable of effective action. Aristotle called politics the master art to which all others serve as subsidiaries. As we have seen, however, in order to be what it should be, it is necessary that politics pay heed to psychology, just as the lesser arts must heed the teachings of natural science. Its theory, I would like to suggest, will merely be a different arrangement and further development of psychological principles directed toward the attainment of a practical goal.

We have advanced four reasons which appear to be sufficient to show the outstanding importance of the science of psychology: the inner truth of the phenomena it studies, the sublimity of these phenomena, the special relationship they have to us, and finally, the practical importance of the laws which govern it. To these we must add the special and incomparable interest which psychology possesses insofar as it instructs us about immortality and thus becomes, in another sense, the science of the future. The question concerning the hope of a hereafter and our participation in a more perfect state of the world falls to psychology. As we have noted, psychology has

* P. 26.

already made attempts to solve this problem, and it does not seem that all its efforts in that direction have been without success. If this really is the case, we have here, without doubt, its highest theoretical achievement, which would be of the greatest practical importance as well,[17] besides lending new value to psychology's other theoretical achievements. When we depart from this life we separate ourselves from all that is subject to the laws of natural science. The laws of gravitation, of sound, of light and electricity disappear along with the phenomena[18] for which experience has established them. Mental laws, on the other hand, hold true for our life to come as they do in our present life, insofar as this life is immortal.[19]

So Aristotle had good reason for placing psychology above all the other sciences, as he did at the beginning of his treatise *On the Soul*, even though in so doing he took into consideration its theoretical advantages exclusively. He says,

> Holding as we do that, while knowledge of any kind is a thing to be honoured and prized, one kind of it may, either by reason of its greater exactness or of a higher dignity and greater wonderfulness in its objects, be more honourable and precious than another, on both counts we should naturally be led to place in the front rank the study of the soul.*

* [Editor's note: *De Anima*, 402 a 1–3, trans. J. A. Smith, in *The Works of Aristotle*, ed. W. D. Ross (Oxford, 1931), III.]

[17] Immortality, i.e. survival after death, is probable only if we assume an optimistic *Weltanschauung*, i.e. if we assume that the universe is subject to a rational necessity. Without such an assumption there would be no reason to suppose that, in some other mode of life, the subject would have an organ of consciousness such as the brain is in this life. In a world of blind necessity, as pessimists have realized, continued life is not worth desiring at all. Now psychology as such can very well initiate inquiries about the spirituality and indestructibility of the subject of consciousness and affirm both, but the question of immortality is really a metaphysical problem. The belief that the mental dispositions acquired in this world will be retained in the next can exert a powerful influence upon our behavior, and the "practical significance" of the problem of immortality lies in this fact. See Brentano's *The Origin of our Knowledge of Right and Wrong* (London and New York, 1969), pp. 40–41 n., 130. When we conjecture what the next world is going to be like, we need not limit ourselves to a three-dimensional world. See *Die vier Phasen*, p. 45.

[18] Here "phenomenon" is used for the transcendent event in nature, contrary to p. 95.

[19] In saying this, Brentano can only have been thinking of the laws of descriptive psychology, not the ultimate laws of genetic psychology. For the latter, insofar as they are physiological in nature, must be different in another sort of world (one of $3+n$ dimensions, for example).

What undoubtedly causes surprise is the fact that Aristotle here asserts that even with respect to its exactitude psychology is superior to the other sciences. For him the exactitude of knowledge is bound up with the imperishability of the object. According to him, that which changes continuously and in every respect evades scientific investigation, whereas that which is most permanent possesses the most abiding truth. Be that as it may, we, too, cannot deny that the laws of psychology at least possess a permanent important truth.

II

Psychological Method with Special Reference to its Experiential Basis

1. Scientists have begun to pay very special attention to the method of psychology. In fact you could say that no other general theoretical sciences are as noteworthy and instructive in this regard as psychology, on the one hand, and mathematics, on the other.

These two sciences are related to one another as polar opposites. Mathematics considers the most simple and independent phenomena, psychology those that are most dependent and complex. Consequently, mathematics reveals in a clear and understandable way the fundamental nature of all true scientific investigation. There is no better field of study for gaining one's first clear view of laws, deduction, hypothesis, and many other important logical concepts. Pascal had a real stroke of genius when he turned to mathematics to get a better understanding of certain basic logical concepts, and to clear up the confusion which had arisen about them, by distinguishing the essential from the non-essential. Psychology alone, on the other hand, demonstrates all the richness to which scientific method lends itself, by seeking to adapt itself to successively more and more complex phenomena. The two together shed light on the methods of investigation which are employed by the intermediary sciences. The difference exhibited by each successive science in comparison with its predecessor, and the basis of its own distinctive character, the increase in difficulty in proportion to the greater complexity of the phenomena, and the simultaneous refinement of techniques which to a certain extent at least compensate for the increase in difficulty – naturally all this becomes clear when we compare the first and the last link in the unbroken chain of sciences.[1]

[1] Compare what was said in the Introduction with the contrast between mathematics and psychology set up here. – That mathematics "considers

28

More light would undoubtedly be shed if psychological method itself were more clearly known and more fully developed. In this respect there remains much to be done, for only with the progress of the science does a true understanding of its method gradually develop.

2. Psychology, like the natural sciences, has its basis in perception and experience. Above all, however, its source is to be found in the *inner perception* of our own mental phenomena. We would never know what a thought is, or a judgement, pleasure or pain, desires or aversions, hopes or fears, courage or despair, decisions and voluntary intentions if we did not learn what they are through inner perception of our own phenomena. Note, however, that we said that inner *perception* [*Wahrnehmung*] and not introspection, i.e. inner *observation* [*Beobachtung*], constitutes this primary and essential source of psychology. These two concepts must be distinguished from one another. One of the characteristics of inner perception is that it can never become inner observation. We can observe objects which, as they say, are perceived externally.[2] In observation, we direct our full attention to a phenomenon in order to apprehend it accurately. But

[2] In 1906 Brentano said that objects of external perception could not be observed, in the strict sense of the word. On this point see the Introduction and the letter from Brentano to Stumpf reprinted there.

the simplest and most independent phenomena" is true only insofar as mathematics is independent of the investigation of "physical phenomena," while natural science does need mathematics. The relationship between mathematics and psychology is also ambiguous because a distinction must be made between descriptive and genetic psychology. Genetic psychology is for the most part psycho-physical; and it is true that it belongs at the other end of the hierarchy of sciences which Comte set up. Descriptive psychology, on the other hand, is independent of mathematics; as set forth in the Introduction and in *The Origin of our Knowledge of Right and Wrong*, descriptive psychology is a science which draws its concepts from inner experience. From these concepts we are then able to ascend to general laws without the help of induction. To that extent, then, it is as *a priori* as mathematics. But while psychology never leaves the domain of concepts based directly on perception, mathematics and geometry immediately turn to the most complicated conceptual constructions. For example, a concept of an ideal geometrical solid, which is never formed by simple abstraction but already involves a process of conceptual attribution not directly based on perception, belongs to such a class of concepts. This is, of course, even more true of a concept such as "3 + n dimensions." Mathematics, on the other hand, is dependent upon descriptive psychology insofar as a clarification of its *basic concepts* and *ultimate axioms* is impossible without analysis of consciousness; hence, of course, we also speak of "philosophy of mathematics."

29

with objects of inner perception this is absolutely impossible. This is especially clear with regard to certain mental phenomena such as anger. If someone is in a state in which he wants to observe his own anger raging within him, the anger must already be somewhat diminished, and so his original object of observation would have disappeared. The same impossibility is also present in all other cases. It is a universally valid psychological law that we can never focus our *attention* upon the object of inner perception. We will have to discuss this issue in more detail later on. For the moment it will suffice to call attention to the personal experience of any unbiased person. Even those psychologists who believe that inner observation is possible all acknowledge that it involves extraordinary difficulty. This is a clear admission that such observation eludes even their efforts in most cases. But, in those exceptional cases in which they think they have been successful, they are undoubtedly the victims of self-deception. It is only while our attention is turned toward a different object that we are able to perceive, incidentally, the mental processes which are directed toward that object. Thus the observation of physical phenomena in external perception, while offering us a basis for knowledge of nature, can at the same time become a means of attaining knowledge of the mind. Indeed, turning one's attention to physical phenomena in our imagination is, if not the only source of our knowledge of laws governing the mind, at least the immediate and principal source.

It is not without reason that we underline this difference between inner perception and introspection and emphasize the fact that the one but not the other can take place in connection with our mental phenomena. Until now, to my knowledge, no psychologist has drawn this distinction. And the indiscriminate interchange of these two terms has led to many harmful consequences. I know of examples of young people, desiring to devote themselves to the study of psychology, who, at the threshold of the science, began to doubt their own ability. They had been told that inner observation is the main source of psychological knowledge, and they repeatedly made strenuous attempts at it. But all these efforts were in vain; all they got for their trouble was a swarm of confused ideas and a headache. So they came to the conclusion that they had no capacity for self-observation, which is quite right. But on the basis of the notion which had been imparted to them, they took this to mean that they had no talent for psychological investigation.

Others who were not prevented from entering the field of psychology out of fear of this bogeyman fell victim to other errors. Many began to view physical phenomena, especially all those which appear to us in the imagination, as mental phenomena, thus confusing elements which are most disparate and heterogeneous. The preceding remarks concerning the advantage which psychology derives from the attentive study of imaginary things makes this misconception intelligible. But as long as such a misconception remained uncorrected, it was obviously impossible either to classify mental phenomena or to determine satisfactorily the characteristics and laws for each class. The confusion concerning these phenomena was necessarily accompanied by further confusion. This is how it happened that a would-be field of observation has often been turned into an arena for arbitrary notions. Fortlage gives us numerous illustrations of this in his *System der Psychologie als empirischer Wissenschaft aus der Beobachtung des innern Sinnes,** but he is by no means alone. Lange's comment about him in his *History of Materialism* is entirely correct: "First he fashions for himself an internal sense to which he attributes a series of functions which are *generally assigned to external senses*; then he defines this field of observation and begins to observe," (stating that the field of observation of psychology is man, insofar as he is perceived by the internal sense). The critique becomes caustic, but not without truth, when Lange goes on to state:

> It would be quite useless to offer a prize to anyone who should hunt out a single real observation in the two thick volumes. The whole book deals in general propositions, with a terminology of his own invention, without a single definite phenomenon being described of which Fortlage could tell us when and where he observed it, or how we must proceed in order to observe it too. We are very prettily told how, e.g., in considering a leaf, as soon as we are struck by its form, this form becomes the focus of attention, "of which the necessary consequence is that the *scale of forms fusing* with the form of the leaf on the law of similarity, becomes clear to consciousness." We are told that the leaf now "in the space of imagination disappears in the scale of forms," but when, how or where this has ever occurred, and upon what experience this "empirical" piece of knowledge is based, remains just as obscure as the mode and manner in which the observer applies the "inner sense," and the proofs that he makes use of such a sense and does not, it may be, crystallize his own crude guesses and inventions at haphazard into a system.†

Such errors, which are by no means isolated cases – indeed, introspection of the mental states which are present within us has been an

---

* [Editor's note: Leipzig, 1855.]
† *History of Materialism*, 3rd ed., Book II, Sect. iii, Chap. 3, pp. 171–172.

almost universally accepted dogma in psychology up to the present time – have led, on the other hand, to criticism of this conception. Psychologists came to realize that such inner observation does not really exist. But because the distinction between inner observation and inner perception was once again ignored, they came to deny the possibility of inner perception as well.

Comte has fallen victim to this error. He calls "illusory" that psychology which "pretends to accomplish the discovery of the laws of the human mind by contemplating it in itself."

> Lately, through peculiar subtlety, one has come to distinguish two types of observations of equal importance, i.e., external and inner observation, of which the latter is exclusively devoted to the study of intellectual phenomena. At this point I must restrict myself to mentioning only one line of reasoning which proves beyond doubt that this supposedly direct contemplation of the mind by itself is a pure illusion. Not long ago it was believed that seeing had been explained by saying that the influence of luminous objects projects on the retina images of their external form and color. To this the physiologists with good reason have objected that, if light impressions acted like images, another eye would be needed to see them. Does not this apply even more in our case? In fact, it is clear that on account of an ineluctable necessity the human mind can observe directly all phenomena except its own, since there is no one here who can perform the observation.*

With respect to moral phenomena, according to Comte, we can certainly assert that the organs of which these phenomena are a function are distinct from those of which thinking is a function, so that the only hindrance to reflective self-knowledge in connection with them is that being in a very decidedly emotional state is necessarily incompatible with the state of observation.

> As for observing in the same manner intellectual phenomena while they are taking place, this is clearly impossible. The thinking subject cannot divide himself into two parts, one of which would reason, while the other would observe its reasoning. In this instance, the observing and the observed organ being identical, how could observation take place? The very principle upon which this so-called psychological method is based, therefore, is invalid. Moreover, let us consider to what entirely contradictory procedures this method immediately leads. On the one hand we are told to isolate

* *Cours de Philosophie Positive*, 2nd ed. (Paris, 1864), I, 30 ff.

ourselves as much as possible from every external sensation, and especially to restrain ourselves from all intellectual work; even if we were only dealing with the most simple mathematical calculation, what would then happen to "inner" observation? On the other hand, after having finally attained through these measures this state of perfect intellectual sleep, we should devote ourselves to the contemplation of the operations which are occurring in our mind when nothing goes on in it any longer. To their amusement, our descendants will undoubtedly witness the disavowal of such an assumption.

Thus Comte rejects not only inner observation, whose impossibility he has rightly recognized, even though the explanation which he offers in this connection is of dubious value, but, without making any distinction between them, he rejects at the same time the inner perception of one's own intellectual phenomena. And what does he offer us in exchange? "We are almost ashamed to say," John Stuart Mill remarks in his critique of Comte, "that it is phrenology!"* In this critique he succeeds easily in showing that the ideas of judgement or inference could never have been derived from phenomena which are revealed to us by external perception. But Mill is not entirely fair to the element of truth contained in Comte's remarks. For this reason his authority was not strong enough to prevent the theory which he opposed from being well received by many of his countrymen. So, for example, Maudsley, too, rejects self-consciousness as a source of psychological knowledge in his *Physiology and Pathology of the Mind*.† His main reason is essentially Comte's argument to which he himself explicitly refers.‡ This argument, however, is of still greater importance to him, because, in opposition to the French thinker, he holds the same nerve centers to be the seat of both moral and intellectual phenomena. Yet Maudsley does not adhere strictly to the consequences which follow from this, and here and there he even ascribes a certain secondary importance to the testimony of self-consciousness which he really ought to deny entirely.

In Germany the confusion between inner observation and inner perception, and the above-mentioned muddle which resulted from it, led Albert Lange to pervert the notion of inner perception. According to him, Kant's own remarks on the consequences of attempts at inner observation show that we are not entitled to distinguish, as Kant himself does, between an external sense which observes

* [Editor's note: "August Comte and Positivism," *Westminster Review* (1865).]

† Henry Maudsley, *The Physiology and Pathology of the Mind*, 2nd ed. (London, 1868), pp. 17–18.   ‡ Pp. 37–38.

physical phenomena and an inner sense which observes mental phenomena. Indeed, he says that such attempts constitute "the very path that leads to mental derangement," and that here we "pretend to discover in us what we ourselves have introduced." But the confusion which Lange finds in Fortlage suggests to him the idea that "it is quite impossible to draw a fixed line between internal and external observation."* For example, concerning so-called subjective colors or tones, he asks himself into which of the two fields they should be placed. He would not ask such a question if he had not found the perceiving of colors which appear in the imagination to be included among the observations of the inner sense. Then, asserting correctly the analogy between the attentive perception of the phenomena which we represent in our imagination and observation through the sense of sight, he proceeds to declare "that the nature of any and every observation is the same, and that the difference chiefly depends merely on whether an observation is such that it may be also made by others at the same time or later, or whether it evades any such control and confirmation?"† Like Comte, therefore, he rejects inner perception, along with inner observation, accepting only external perception, of which he only complains that the term is inappropriate.

Thus the same omission of a single distinction has led various people on various opposing sides into error. That they really are in error should be evident from the preceding analysis. It will, however, become even more evident when we discuss inner consciousness and the difference between physical and mental phenomena.

Inner perception of our own mental phenomena, then, is the primary source of the experiences essential to psychological investigations. And this inner perception is not to be confused with inner observation of our mental states, since anything of that sort is impossible.

3. It is obvious that in this respect psychology appears to be at a great disadvantage compared with the other general sciences. Although many of these sciences are unable to perform experiments, astronomy in particular, none of them is incapable of making observations.

In truth, psychology would become impossible if there were no way to make up for this deficiency. We can make up for it, however, at least to a certain extent, through the observation of earlier mental states in *memory*. It has often been claimed that this is the best means of attaining knowledge of mental facts, and philosophers of entirely different orientations are in agreement on this point.

* *History of Materialism*, Book II, Sect. iii, Chap. 3, p. 172.
† *History of Materialism*, Book II, Sect. iii, Chap. 3, p. 174.

Herbart has made explicit reference to it; and John Stuart Mill points out in his essay on Comte that it is possible to study a mental phenomenon by means of memory immediately following its manifestation. "And this is," he adds, "really the mode in which our best knowledge of intellectual acts is generally acquired. We reflect on what we have been doing, when the act is past, but when its impression in the memory is still fresh."

If the attempt to observe the anger which stirs us becomes impossible because the phenomenon disappears, it is clear that an earlier state of excitement can no longer be interfered with in this way. And we really can focus our attention on a past mental phenomenon just as we can upon a present physical phenomenon, and in this way we can, so to speak, observe it. Furthermore, we could say that it is even possible to undertake experimentation on our own mental phenomena in this manner. For we can, by various means, arouse certain mental phenomena in ourselves intentionally, in order to find out whether this or that other phenomenon occurs as a result. We can then contemplate the result of the experiment calmly and attentively in our memory.

So at least one of the disadvantages can apparently be remedied. In all the experimental sciences memory makes possible the accumulation of observed facts for the purpose of establishing general truths; in psychology, it makes possible at the same time the observation of the facts themselves. I am certain that the psychologists who believed that they had observed their own mental phenomena in inner perception actually did what Mill described in the passage quoted above. They focused their attention on acts just past, whose impression was still fresh in their memory.

To be sure, this procedure, which we could call observation in memory, is obviously not fully equivalent to genuine observation of present events. As everyone knows, memory is, to a great extent, subject to illusion, while inner perception is infallible and does not admit of doubt. When the phenomena which are retained by the memory are substituted for those of inner perception, they introduce uncertainty and the possibility of many sorts of self-deception into this area at the same time. And once the possibility of deception exists, its actual occurrence is not far off, for that unbiased frame of mind which the observer must have is hardest to achieve in connection with one's own mental acts.

It is for this reason that while some authors extoll the infallibility of self-consciousness, others, for example Maudsley,* consider it entirely untrustworthy. The former appeal to the evidence of inner

* *Physiology and Pathology of the Mind,* pp. 9 ff.

perception, while the latter call attention to the frequent illusions about ourselves which befall not only the mentally ill, but all men, to a certain extent, one might say. This explains why psychologists have often been in disagreement on this point, even though the solution to the problem was available in inner perception, given with immediate evidence. What opened the door to doubt was the fact that the observation could take place only in memory. If even today there is disagreement on whether every mental phenomenon is accompanied by an emotion, be it pleasure or displeasure, this is the consequence of the confusion which we have just pointed out. Without such a confusion the fundamental question concerning the highest classes of mental phenomena would have been settled and finished long ago. The obstacle is so great that we shall often find ourselves in the position of having to refute by means of formal argumentation and *reductio ad absurdum* opinions which can actually be immediately recognized as false through the evidence of inner perception.

Nevertheless, no matter how great may be the disadvantage which is associated with the inadequate reliability of memory, it would obviously be a foolish exaggeration to deny on this basis that our own inner experience has any value at all. If the testimony of memory could not be used in scientific inquiry, not only psychology but all the other sciences as well would be impossible.

4. There remains another circumstance which threatens to place psychology at a disadvantage in comparison with the natural sciences. All that a person apprehends in inner perception and subsequently observes in memory are mental phenomena which appear within that person's own life. Every phenomenon which does not belong to the course of the life of this individual lies outside of his sphere of knowledge. However rich in remarkable phenomena even one life may be – and every life, even the poorest, exhibits a wonderful abundance – is it not obvious that it must be poor in comparison with what, contained in thousands upon thousands of other lives, is withheld from our inner perception? This limitation is all the more serious since the relation of one human being to another, as far as their inner life is concerned, is in no way comparable to that which exists between two inorganic individuals of the same species, e.g., between two drops of water. In the physiological realm two individuals of the same species always show certain variations; the same is true, but to a much greater degree, in the psychological realm. Even where there exists, as we say, the most intimate spiritual affinity between two people, the difference between them remains so pronounced that there are still occasions in which the one can neither agree with the other nor understand his behavior. And how very great are the differences

and contrasts in talents and character which appear in other instances, for example, when we compare the individual aptitudes of a
Pindar and an Archimedes, a Socrates and an Alcibiades, or even
when we make a general comparison between the masculine and
feminine character, not to mention the contrast between normal
people and cretins and insane people whom we consider abnormal or
sick. Consequently, if we are restricted in our observation to one
single individual, what else can we conclude but that our view of
mental phenomena is extremely incomplete. Will we not inevitably
fall into the error of mistaking individual peculiarities for general
characteristics? This is undeniably the case, and the disadvantage
appears even greater because we are never in a position to investigate
the entire development of our own mental life. No matter how far
back our memory may reach, the first beginnings of our mental life
are still shrouded in an impenetrable mist. Yet precisely these beginnings would best provide us with knowledge of the most universal
psychological laws, since the phenomena appear in their most simple
form at the beginning, while later on, because every mental impression is retained along with certain after-effects, we find ourselves in
the presence of an inextricable and infinitely complicated tangle of
innumerable causes.

The disadvantage of such a situation is also revealed in another
respect. Just as the object of observation is unique – a unique life of
which, as we have seen, we can only observe part – so the observer
himself is unique, and no one else is in a position to check his
observations. For someone else can no more apprehend my mental
phenomena through inner perception than I can those that belong to
him. In this respect too, the natural sciences appear to be in a much
more favorable position than psychology. The same solar eclipse and
the same comet can be perceived by thousands of individuals. The
observation made by a single individual which no one else can
confirm – for example, the observation of a new planet supposedly
seen by an astronomer, but which other astronomers are unable to
verify – would be received with less confidence.

The experimental foundation of psychology, therefore, would
always remain insufficient and unreliable, if this science were to
confine itself to the inner perception of our own mental phenomena
and to their observation in memory.

This is not the case, however. In addition to the direct perception
of our own mental phenomena we have an *indirect knowledge of the
mental phenomena of others*. The phenomena of inner life usually
express themselves, so to speak, i.e. they cause externally perceivable
changes.

They are expressed most fully when a person describes them

directly in words. Of course such a description would be incomprehensible or rather impossible if the difference between the mental lives of two individuals was such that they did not contain any common element. In that case their exchange of ideas would be like that between a person who was born blind and another who was born without the sense of smell trying to explain to one another the color and the scent of a violet. But this is not the case. On the contrary, it is obvious that our capacity for mutually intelligible communication encompasses all kinds of phenomena and that we ourselves are able to form ideas of mental states experienced by another person during a fever or under other abnormal conditions on the basis of his description.* Similarly, when an educated man wants to give an account of his inner states, he is not at a loss to find the necessary words with which to express himself. On the one hand, this fact demonstrates that individual differences among persons and their situations are not so pronounced as one might have supposed, and that, at least in terms of general kinds of phenomena, every individual experiences the complete range of mental phenomena in inner experience unless he is deprived of a sense organ, is abnormal, or is immature.[3] On the other hand, however, this makes it possible

* [Translators' note: We follow the 1874 edition here; the 1924 edition omits the words in brackets: "Es zeigt sich im Gegenteil, dass unsere Fähigkeit zu gegenseitiger verständlicher Mitteilung sich über [alle Gattungen der Erscheinungen erstreckt, und dass wir] uns selbst von psychischen Züstanden . . .".]

[3] Although it is perfectly true that my mental life can be perceived by no other creature, and is therefore simply transcendent for them, and although it is essential to check the results of psychological research against each other, it must nevertheless be pointed out that according to Brentano's later theory, inner perception does not reveal to me the specific difference by which the subject of my mental experiences is distinguished from another subject. It cannot even be decided directly on the basis of inner perception whether it is of a spiritual or corporeal nature, because *even inner perception exhibits a certain indefiniteness and generality* and conceals our individual differences from us. By virtue of this fact, however, our empirical psychological data are from the very beginning unbound by any individuating factor; rather, they are general ideas or general judgements. From this point, then, the ascent to apodictic truths, i.e. to insights which are obvious and self-evident from the general ideas obtained in this way, is accomplished directly without any inductive steps. As was already noted in the Introduction, the laws of descriptive or phenomenological psychology have an *a priori* axiomatic character. This is true, for example, of the law that judging or taking an interest in something is impossible without a presentation of that thing, and of many other laws. The indirect knowledge of someone else's mental phenomena based on the way they are externalized will tell me whether or not other beings also make judge-

for us to integrate our own inner experiences with the phenomena which others have observed within themselves, and, whenever the observations bear upon similar phenomena, to check one's own observations by means of someone else's, just as an experiment with light and heat made by an American scientist is confirmed or rejected by an experiment which another scientist performs in Europe on specifically similar phenomena. The language itself, which two people who speak with one another about their inner lives both have inherited from their people or from earlier science, can also further their knowledge of mental phenomena, just as it facilitates knowledge of external phenomena elsewhere, by displaying a sort of preliminary classification of the different main classes of phenomena clearly organized from the standpoint of their specific relationships.

Finally, the preceding statements show the value which the study of autobiographies has for the psychologist, provided that he takes due account of the fact that in this case the observer and reporter is more or less biased. Feuchtersleben says in this regard that in an autobiography we should pay attention not so much to what is reported, as to what it involuntarily reveals.

Less perfectly, perhaps, but often in a sufficiently clear way, mental states can be manifested even without verbal communication.

In this category belong, above all, human behavior and voluntary action. The conclusions that we can draw from them concerning the inner states from which they derive are often much more certain than those based on verbal statements. The old saying, *"verba docent, exempla trahunt,"* would not be a truth which can be verified daily if practical conduct were not generally considered as the more reliable expression of one's convictions.

Besides these voluntary ones, there are also involuntary physical changes which naturally accompany or follow certain mental states. Fright makes us turn pale, fear induces trembling, our cheeks blush red with shame. Even before the expression of emotions was an object of scientific study, as Darwin has recently made it once again, people had already learned a great deal about these relationships from simple custom and experience, so that the observed physical phenomena served as signs of the invisible mental phenomena. It is

---

ments, and whether or not they feel emotions, but if they do fall under the concept of someone who judges or someone who loves, it is certain *a priori* that they are also beings who have presentations. Differential psychology, referred to on p. 37, has to do with genetic distinctions; the differences between the endowments of Socrates and Alcibiades, between the masculine and feminine character and so on, are based upon the differences in their dispositions and tendencies.

obvious that these signs are not themselves the things that they signify. It is not possible, therefore, as many people have quite foolishly wanted to make us believe, that this external and, as it was pretentiously called, "objective" observation of mental states could become a source of psychological knowledge, quite independently of inner "subjective" observation. Together with subjective observation, however, it will do a great deal to enrich and supplement our own inner experiences by the addition of what others have experienced in themselves, and thus to correct the self-delusions into which we may have fallen.

5. It will be of especially great value if, by means of one or another of the above-mentioned methods, we can gain some insight into the states of *a conscious life simpler than our own*, whether it is simpler because it is less developed or because it is completely lacking in certain types of phenomena. The first is true of children in particular and the more so the younger they are. For this reason numerous observations and experiments have been made on the new-born. In addition, the study of adults in primitive societies is valuable in this respect. If, on the one hand such a study appears to be of lesser importance, it offers, on the other hand, the advantage of replacing signs which are more or less subject to misunderstanding with the more precise expression of verbal communication. It is for this reason that Locke made use of this method in his time and that recently, in the interests of psychology, scientists have been turning their attention more and more to the phenomena which are characteristic of primitive people.

An example of the second type of simpler mental life is that of the congenitally blind person in whom the idea of color is missing as well as all other ideas which can be acquired only by means of the sense of sight. Such cases are of two-fold interest: first, in determining to what extent a life of ideas can develop without the assistance of the sense of sight, particularly whether the congenitally blind have the same knowledge of spatial relations as we do; secondly, if a successful operation later on makes it possible for them to see, in investigating the nature of the first impressions they receive.

To this category also belong observations which are made on animals for psychological purposes. Not only the mental life of lower animals which are deprived of one or another sense, but also that of higher animals appears extremely simple and limited when compared with man's mental life. This may be due to the fact that they have the same faculties as we do but to an incomparably lesser degree, or it may be that they lack certain classes of mental phenomena altogether. The answer to this question is itself obviously of the utmost importance. If the latter view, which was maintained in earlier times by Aristotle and Locke and is still held today by the great majority of people, were found to be true, we would be in the presence of the most remarkable example of the isolated action of certain mental powers. Moreover, any theory which does not depart from sound common sense so far as to deny altogether that animals are endowed with mental life will maintain that the investigation and the comparison of the mental characteristics of animals with those of man is of the greatest value for the psychologist.

6. The attentive study of *diseased mental states* is important in another respect. Frequently theoretical interests, and even more often practical interests, have led scientists to observe idiots and insane people, and this has provided psychology with valuable data. Just as the phenomena involved here are themselves very different in kind, so are the services which they can perform for psychology. Sometimes mental illness manifests itself in the influence of a constant or, as they say, "fixed" idea, which affects a large portion of one's conscious life. Quite apart from the causes of this phenomenon, we find in it valuable illustrations of the laws of the association of complex ideas. Sometimes certain functions appear to be disproportionately strengthened or weakened and insofar as other functions connected with them are increased or decreased, the laws governing their connection are thereby clarified. The phenomena of imbecility and insanity and other diseased phenomena give us extremely valuable information concerning the connections between mental phenomena and our corporeal being when, as is almost always the case, such deteriorated mental phenomena are associated with observable organic abnormalities. It would be a mistake, however, to want to see greater or even equal attention paid to these diseased states than to those of normal mental life. First of all, we must establish the relations of coexistence and succession which are connected with normal physiological states. Only when these relations in themselves have been sufficiently observed and generalized, at least up to a certain point, will it prove useful to introduce anomalies. We shall then be in a position to appraise these anomalies more accurately since the same laws which govern normal life are operative in the abnormal, but, as it were, in different combinations and with new complications which are the result of radical upheavals in the vegetative functions. Then, but only then, will our understanding of these laws and of the usual sequence of phenomena be broadened and deepened by the introduction of anomalies, in that we can see how the law can explain even apparent exceptions. It is precisely those cases that we find most curious concerning which it will take the longest time to satisfy our desire for knowledge successfully. The explanation of these phenomena can be achieved

41

only little by little. Until psychology and physiology have reached a more advanced stage of development, preoccupation with these phenomena will be almost as idle and unfruitful as was zoologists' fondness for strange monstrosities in its time.

7. Therefore, since our first and foremost task is to learn about normal phenomena, it will be, on the whole, more instructive for us to observe first of all the extraordinary phenomena which are found in physically healthy persons. Valuable clues for psychological research can be found in biographies of men who have distinguished themselves as artists, scientists, or for outstanding character, as well as those of notorious criminals, and in studying* an eminent work of art, a remarkable discovery or a great deed or crime, at least to the extent that it is possible to gain insight into motives and antecedent circumstances. Thus, in its portrayal of great personalities and in its description of epoch-making events which generally revolve around some famous man who embodied the spirit of an age or a social movement, history provides many facts which are important to psychologists. The clear light in which these facts are presented is extremely useful to psychological observation.

In addition, the course of world history considered in and for itself, the succession of phenomena which are exhibited in the masses, progress and retrogression, the rise and fall of nations, can often render great service to those who want to investigate the general laws of man's mental nature. The most prominent characteristics of mental life can often be seen more clearly when you are dealing with large groups of people, while the secondary peculiarities cancel each other out and disappear. Even Plato hoped to find writ large in the state and in society the same characteristics which the soul of the individual contains on a smaller scale. He believed that his tripartite division of the soul corresponded to the three essential classes in the state: the workers, the guardians, and the rulers. Moreover, he found a further confirmation of this view in the comparison of the fundamental traits of different ethnic groups, such as Egyptians and Phoenicians, courageous Nordic barbarians and culture-loving Greeks. Perhaps someone else would expect to find a manifestation of the different fundamental structures of our higher mental life in the noble phenomena of art, science and religion. It has often been said, and certainly not without truth, that the history of the development of mankind exhibits on a large scale what takes place in an analogous manner but on a small scale in the history of the development of the individual. The observation of mental phenomena in human society undoubtedly sheds light upon the mental phenomena

* [Translators' note: Reading "Studium" with the 1874 edition.]

of the individual; the opposite, however, is even more true. Indeed, in general it is a more natural procedure to try to understand society and its development on the basis of what has been discovered about individuals than to proceed the other way around and to try to shed light on the problems of individual psychology by means of the observation of society.

What we have said is sufficient to show from which areas the psychologist gains the experiences upon which he bases his investigation of mental laws. We found *inner perception* to be his primary source, but it has the disadvantage that it can never become observation. To inner perception we added the contemplation of our previous mental experiences in *memory*, and in this case it is possible to focus attention on them and, so to speak, observe them. The field of experience which up to this point is limited to our own mental phenomena was then extended, in that *expressions* of the mental life of other persons allow us to gain some knowledge of mental phenomena which we do not experience directly. Certainly the facts which are important for psychology are thus increased a thousandfold. This last type of experience, however, presupposes observation through memory, just as the latter presupposes the inner perception of present mental phenomena. Inner perception, therefore, constitutes the ultimate and indispensable precondition of the other two sources of knowledge. Consequently, and on this point traditional psychology is correct as against Comte, inner perception constitutes the very foundation upon which the science of psychology is erected.

III

Further Investigations Concerning Psychological Method. Induction of the Fundamental Laws of Psychology

1. One task to which psychologists must first devote themselves is the determination of those characteristics which are common to all mental phenomena, assuming of course that there are such characteristics, for this is often denied. Bacon's assertion that it is always necessary to look for intermediate laws first and only then, ascending gradually, for the ultimate ones, has not stood the test of the history of the natural sciences, and therefore can have no value for the psychologist either. It is only correct insofar as in the induction of the most general laws we naturally find the common characteristic first in individuals, then in specific groups, until it is finally established throughout its entire range.

2. The principle of the subdivision of mental phenomena will emerge from a consideration of their general characteristics; and this will lead immediately to the determination of the fundamental classes of mental phenomena on the basis of their natural affinities. Until this is accomplished, it will be impossible to make further progress in the investigation of psychological laws, inasmuch as these laws apply for the most part only to one or another kind of phenomena. What would be the outcome of the researches of the physicist experimenting upon heat, light and sound[1] if these phenomena were not divided into natural groups for him by a patently obvious classification? By the same token, without having distinguished the different fundamental classes of mental phenomena, psychologists

---

[1] See Note 11 to Book One, Chap. I.

would endeavor in vain to establish the laws of their succession.[2] We have already observed that ordinary language prepared the way for psychological investigations by means of the general names it assigns to mental phenomena. Naturally ordinary language is not entirely reliable, and it would mislead those who depended upon it too much, just as it would facilitate the discovery of truth for those who utilize its definitions with caution. As we have already mentioned, there is conclusive proof that no fundamental class of mental phenomena which is found in other human beings is absent in our own individual life. This makes it possible to establish a complete list of mental phenomena. It is also easy to see that in spite of the great diversity of phenomena the number of fundamental classes is very limited.[3] This fact materially facilitates our investigation and excludes all fear that we may have completely overlooked some phenomenon belonging to a fundamental class distinct from all those previously considered. All the difficulty arises from the previously mentioned fact that inner perception can never become inner observation. The fact that even today psychologists have not reached an agreement concerning the problem of the fundamental classes of mental phenomena indicates how great this obstacle is in some circumstances. We shall have to establish the natural order as well as the number of fundamental classes of mental phenomena.

3. Among the investigations having primary and universal importance we must include the investigation of the ultimate[4] mental elements out of which more complex phenomena arise. This question would be solved immediately if we could remember more clearly the

---

[2] The notion of the distinction between descriptive and genetic psychology is clearly being expressed here. Cp. Chap. I, Note 5.

[3] In Book Two, Chap. V, Brentano shows that the number of ultimate classes does not exceed three (presentation, judgement, emotional attitude).

[4] This paragraph seems to be based on the presupposition that the phenomena which are temporally prior in mental life are also the simplest. But, as Brentano later came to believe, sensations and even affects (sensory pleasures and pains) are far from being the simplest mental occurrences, though they make their appearance very early. (See Brentano, *Untersuchungen zur Sinnespsychologie* and the Supplementary Essays.) So the earliest acts are not the least complex, but they *are*, however, the least bound up with other acts *by association* and association *which cannot be overcome*. The observations made on those who have been cured of congenital blindness by surgery are so valuable because they reveal to us someone who has come to see, someone whose visual perception is not yet tied by association to sensations of touch and interpretive judgements in such a way that one is tempted to speak of "fusion" and chemical combination. The general ideas, obtained by means of abstraction, are simpler than sensory perceptions; the most general are the simplest.

beginnings of our mental life. Unfortunately, we do not find ourselves in this happy situation. Moreover, observations of newborn infants provide somewhat of a substitute but they are by no means sufficient. The data gathered from these observations are ambiguous and even if our conclusions were more certain, there is still the objection that we may not be dealing even here with the first beginnings of mental life, since these beginnings extend back to the pre-natal period. We are forced, therefore, into an analytic procedure which has been compared with that of the chemist. The task is by no means an easy one. In fact, it is not enough merely to distinguish the various aspects presented by a phenomenon. Such a procedure would be equivalent to that of a chemist who chose to consider the color and taste of cinnabar as its constituent elements: a ridiculous mistake, even though many psychologists have actually fallen victim to it, a situation for which Locke is not entirely blameless. Just as the chemist separates the constituent elements of a compound, it seems that the psychologist, too, should try to separate out the elementary phenomena which make up the more complex phenomena. If only such an analysis could be done as perfectly and certainly here as in chemistry! Since, however, mental life never ever reverts from a later to an earlier stage, it seems absolutely impossible for us to relive an elementary phenomenon in the purity and simplicity in which we originally experienced it.* Under these circumstances, if the concrescence of ideas were a true fusion, if there were, as in the case of chemical compounds, a transformation into altogether different kinds of phenomena, and if this were universally the case, then the difficulty would obviously become insurmountable. Fortunately no psychologist goes so far in his assertions, and those who would like to do so could be easily refuted. In general, the theory of a mental chemistry of ideas has by no means met with consistent acceptance so far.

The investigation of the primary mental elements is mainly concerned with sensations, since sensations are undoubtedly a source of other mental phenomena, and more than a few scientists assert that sensations alone are the source of all phenomena. Sensations are effects of physical stimuli. Their origin is thus a psychophysical process. It is for this reason that physiology, especially the physiology of sense organs, provides appreciable help to psychology here. Nevertheless, the purely psychological means which are also available

---

* Even Kant complains that psychology "as a systematic science of analysis" can never approach chemistry because in it the manifold elements of inner observation are separated from one another only through a mere abstract operation, but cannot be kept isolated and recombined at will. *Metaphysische Anfangsgründe der Natürwissenschaft*, Preface [in *Kant's gesammelte Schriften*, Berlin Academy of Science edition, Vol. IV].

for the solution of the problem under discussion are often not sufficiently utilized. Otherwise no one would have come to ascribe separate origins to phenomena one of which includes the other. In this context, as we have already remarked, the observation of congenitally blind people who have undergone successful operations also becomes important, not only for the sense of sight, but also for the whole area of sense perception, because the investigation can be carried out more completely for sight, our highest sense, than it can for other senses.

4. The highest and most general laws of the succession of mental phenomena, whether these laws are valid for all phenomena or only for those of one fundamental class, are to be established directly by the general laws of induction. As Bain has rightly pointed out in his inductive logic* these laws are not the highest and ultimate laws in the sense in which we would characterize the Law of Gravity and the Law of Inertia as such. This is due to the fact that the mental phenomena to which these laws apply are entirely too dependent upon a variety of physiological conditions of which we have very incomplete knowledge. They are, strictly speaking, empirical laws which would require for their explanation an exact analysis of the physiological states with which they are connected.

What I say is not to be understood as though I believed that one should undertake to deduce the fundamental laws governing the succession of mental phenomena from physiological laws and then perhaps go still further and derive them from laws governing chemical phenomena and physical phenomena in the narrower sense. That would be foolishness. There are limits which cannot be exceeded in our attempt to explain nature; and, as John Stuart Mill quite rightly states, we run up against one of these limits when the transition from the mental realm to that of physical phenomena is involved.† Even if physicists had reduced all the causes which produce our sensations of color, sound, smell, etc. to molecular vibrations and impact and pressure, we would still have to assume special ultimate laws for the sensation of color, indeed for the sensation of each particular species of color, as well as for the sensations of sounds and smells. Any attempt to further reduce the number of such laws would be hopeless and unreasonable. Consequently, what I deem desirable and necessary for a further explanation of mental laws is not their deduction from physical laws. In simple cases the explanation which I have in mind would involve merely an enumeration of the immediate and proximate physiological preconditions or concomitant conditions with the utmost precision, excluding any element which is not

* *Logic*, II (Introduction), p. 284.
† *System of Logic*, III, Chap. 14, Sect. 2.

immediately connected with them. In those cases in which we must investigate the influence of previous mental phenomena on a subsequent phenomenon, perhaps after a rather long lapse of time has interrupted all mental activity, it would be necessary to take into account the purely physiological processes which have intervened in the meantime insofar as these processes influence the relationship between the earlier mental cause and its subsequent mental effect. If we could achieve this goal, we would be in possession of fundamental psychological laws which, while they would certainly be less transparently clear, would nonetheless possess the same rigorousness and exactitude as the axioms of mathematics – the highest psychological laws which could be considered ultimate laws in the full sense of the word. The laws which constitute our highest laws at present would, however, reappear in a somewhat altered form as derivative laws, and the major part, if not the whole, of psychology would take on a half-physiological, half-psychological character.

5. The undeniable dependence of mental processes upon physiological processes has repeatedly led psychologists to base psychology directly upon physiology. We have seen how Comte wanted to utilize phrenology as an instrument of psychological investigation, even though it was in a form which bore no close resemblance to that developed by Gall. In Germany, Horwicz has recently made a similar attempt to give psychology a new foundation.* The same author has already discussed the question of what he considers the only valid method in the realm of psychology at greater length in the *Zeitschrift für Philosophie und philosophische Kritik.*†

Horwicz does not fall into Comte's error of rejecting self-consciousness. On the contrary, my objection to him is that he over-emphasizes it to the point of considering it "scientific self-observation," and admits along with the other introspectionist psychologists only that "a good psychological observation is not within the reach of everyone and is certainly not always obtainable."‡ But despite this he does not really base his doctrine upon self-consciousness. He wishes to utilize it only in a preparatory way, believing that it will provide him with a rough preliminary survey of

---

* Adolf Horwicz, *Psychologische Analysen auf physiologischer Grundlage* (Halle, 1872).

† "Methodologie der Seelenlehre", *Zeitschrift für Philosophie und philosophische Kritik*, LX (1872), 164–205.

‡ "Methodologie," p. 170. It is difficult to understand how he reconciles this doctrine with the statement that "we are incapable of having more than one idea at the same time." (*Psych. Anal.*, I, 262.) Indeed, later on (I, 326), he himself seems to have strong doubts about the correctness of this statement.

the whole of mental activity.* He expects all further knowledge to be derived from physiology. From the fact that this science "furnishes the special conditions for the emergence of the mind in the organism, as well as of their mutual relationship," he forms "the methodological conviction that the organization of the mind – in its earliest and most general outlines – must . . . correspond to the organization of the body."† According to him we can find an answer to the question "of the most general organization and structure of mental life" only "if we first study the organization and structure of corporeal life." We must, therefore, begin with a general review of the physiology of the body, and then determine whether this provides us with a reliable survey of the total organization of the mind. His assurance that the enumeration of the different mental processes is complete is furnished by "the basic physiological principle, if it is in any way correct, that no mental process can take place without a material substrate."‡ Similarly he feels, as he expresses himself elsewhere, that in all subsequent investigations physiology is "not simply a useful accessory, but the methodological vehicle of research."§ In particular, by means of physiological comparison of all vital processes he hopes "to find the guide which will enable us to discover the simplest mental elements, from which mental life develops genetically."¶

These are enticing prospects, especially at a time when natural sciences enjoy a full measure of confidence and philosophy hardly any. Psychological perception, which is considered to be mainly a philosophical matter, and everything derived from it, is supposed to be merely a preliminary investigation. Then the natural scientist takes over. He determines by physiological means even how many classes of mental phenomena there are and their character relative to one another. He also determines the primitive mental element, discovers the laws of complexity and traces the origin of the highest mental phenomena.

We must not let ourselves be rashly deceived by what may appear to be a desirable goal. It does not seem difficult to show that Horwicz overestimates the services which physiology can render to psychology in much the same way that Comte does. He bases his conviction on the relationship of psychology to physiology. Since physiology deals with the immediately higher concept, namely the concept of life, its relationship to psychology must be similar to that of "mathematics to physics, and astronomy to geography."‖ But no

---

* "Methodologie," p. 187; cp. *Psych. Anal.*, I, 155 ff.
† "Methodologie," p. 189. ‡ "Methodologie," p. 190.
§ *Psych. Anal.*, I, 175. ¶ "Methodologie," p. 189.
‖ "Methodologie," p. 188.

matter how useful and even indispensable mathematics may be to the physicist, anyone can see that the physicist would not make any progress in his researches if he depended entirely upon mathematics and made it the vehicle of such researches, as Horwicz expects the psychologist to do with regard to physiology. To give just one example: what could mathematics tell us about the number of fundamental classes of phenomena with which the physicist deals?

Perhaps Horwicz will answer that the comparison of the relationship between physiology and psychology with the relationship between mathematics and physics, like any comparison, is not entirely satisfactory. Physiology, he might say, has a particularly intimate connection with the psychological sphere since, as he himself has pointed out, the phenomena it studies are the conditions for the occurrence of mental phenomena and there is very intimate interaction between them. But even if we grant that this is not so in the case of the relationship between mathematics and physics, we can still confidently point to the relationship between chemistry and physics of inorganic phenomena on the one hand and physiology on the other. The inorganic realm contains the conditions of organisms whose existence depends upon a constant and most intimate interaction with it. Nevertheless, no matter how much help inorganic chemistry and physics are to the physiologist, could he ever expect adequate information about the structure of organisms from them? Will he not, on the contrary, have to derive both the whole of this structure as well as the functions of the individual parts from the physiological phenomena themselves? There cannot be any doubt on this point.

Perhaps even this comparison will be criticized as inadequate. Inorganic phenomena, it will be said, are undoubtedly in a constant and mutual relationship with those of the organism, but they do not constitute their "material substrate" as physiological phenomena do for mental phenomena. But even Horwicz himself has admitted that it is not exactly easy to explain the special nature of this relationship and it would be even more difficult to prove it to hold universally for all mental phenomena in the same way. The only thing that is immediately obvious is that the relationship between mental phenomena and concomitant physiological phenomena is actually very different from that which exists between the inorganic phenomena with which the chemist deals and the organisms with which the physiologist deals. But the result of a more careful comparison and an analysis of all pertinent facts certainly seems to us to prove that much more information about physiological phenomena is to be expected from chemical phenomena than from physiological phenomena about mental phenomena. The difference between physiological processes and chemical and physical processes really seems to be only that physiological processes are more complex. More and more, since Lotze, scientists have abandoned the concept of a vital force which is of a nobler nature. The more comprehensive concept of chemical phenomena has been shown to apply uniformly to inorganic changes and to life in the physiological sense. We can hardly say the same thing of the concept of life when we apply it to the physiological and psychological realms. On the contrary, if we turn our attention from the external world to the inner, we find ourselves, as it were, in a new realm. The phenomena are absolutely heterogeneous, and even analogies either forsake us completely or take on a very vague and artificial character.* It was for this very reason that we separated the psychological and physical sciences as the main branches of empirical science in our earlier discussion of the fundamental divisions of that realm.

The unfortunate outcome of Horwicz's efforts, which could have been predicted in advance on the basis of these considerations, has proved to be a fact. Horwicz had hoped to provide a deeper and more firmly established psychology, but instead he relies upon superficial analogies and builds one hypothesis upon another. Just one example among many is provided by the two "important analogies between mental and corporeal life" which, in his psychological analyses, he finds in the "Ariadne's thread of the nervous system."† The first analogy is that between digestion in the ordinary sense of the word – which, through a progressive transformation and a gradual refinement, changes the raw materials ingested from the outside first into arterial blood, and then into muscles, tendons, bones, nerves, etc., – and digestion in the figurative sense of the word in the sphere of consciousness. According to him, the process of assimilation is very similar in the two cases. "The influences of things from outside act as stimuli on the perceptual organs of the sensory nerves. From them as the raw materials the mind, as we say in this case, derives its nourishment in the form of sensations. When we encounter a mass of completely unfamiliar impressions all of a sudden, we are correct in saying that first we have to digest them. But the mind digests by transforming the raw materials provided by the nerves into sensations and mental products of an increasingly higher order such as ideas, concepts, judgements, inferences, emotional tendencies, decisions, plans, maxims, etc." The second analogy, according to Horwicz, is that between the opposition of sensory and motor nerve activity, which dominates the whole nervous system (while the so-called

* Cp. Hermann Lotze, *Microcosmus* [English translation by Elizabeth Hamilton and E. E. Constance Jones (Edinburgh, 1885), I, 144 ff.].
† *Psych. Anal.*, I, 148 ff.

central organ consists of nothing but interpolated parts linking these polarically opposed currents) and the opposition of mental processes which in different forms manifests itself "in a polarity which is just as antagonistic, just as deep, and just as universal." It is the opposition between the theoretical and the practical orientation which, Horwicz believes, pervades the entire realms of consciousness. Relying on these two analogies, he arrives by way of physiological method at his fundamental classification of mental phenomena which, according to him, coincides essentially with "the really quite accurate skeleton of consciousness set up by Wolff." Mental phenomena are divided, on the one hand, into higher and lower phenomena, and into cognitive and appetitive phenomena, on the other, and both divisions overlap each other. There are transitional stages between cognitive and appetitive phenomena, just as between higher and lower phenomena. And this is the place for the class of feelings, which modern psychologists usually distinguish as a separate class. It is this class that is suggested by those interpolated parts of the central organ. Thus, on the basis of physiological considerations, we closely approximate the usual basic divisions of mental phenomena; we do so, however, only by means of a more exact procedure which also confirms and explains what it teaches.

It is really difficult to understand how, in spite of all his bias in favor of investigation based upon physical observation, a man endowed with as good judgement as Horwicz could delude himself into thinking that these crude analogies (of which the one has no more relation to the "nervous substrate of consciousness" than it has to other parts of the organism) could in any way confirm, let alone replace, things which we discover by means of mental observation. If these mental classifications were not certain, the hypothesis that the sensory nerves constitute the substrate of cognition and the motor nerves the substrate of appetition would be even less certain. Other physiologists have localized not only these phenomena but also thinking and willing in the same nerve-centers. As a matter of fact, why should we not assume that, just as many different kinds of physical properties are ascribable to one and the same substance, many different kinds of mental properties are too? Such a method, therefore, can tell us absolutely nothing about the number of mental faculties there are.*

* Horwicz himself says: We must "definitely assume that all mental action is connected with the central organs of the nervous system. We could not... find it likely that the different properties, powers, faculties (however you wish to express it) of the mind are separated, as the phrenologists claim, into distinct parts of the nervous mass. Instead, we are forced to assume that the different organs and groups and systems of organs fulfill essentially

We have seen that so far, while striving to establish and secure his theory, Horwicz has given us nothing but a whole series of bold hypotheses. And we shall find something similar at practically every subsequent step in his investigations. And, since probability diminishes in geometrical progression with every new hypothesis, we may long since have acquired the moral conviction that we have abandoned the way of truth when, under the undaunted leadership of the author, we reach the statement "that the intimate and necessary connection between sensation and movement constitutes the simple element from which all mental processes are constructed by means of mere repetition and complication."

Horwicz is entirely aware that Newton's motto "*hypotheses non fingo*" could not be applied to him as a physiological analyst of mental phenomena, and at times he even seems to be fully aware of the impossibility of his undertaking. Thus, in one place (I, 156) he states that physiology "is not capable of penetrating into the finer detail of mental processes." (We have already seen what a bright light it sheds upon their fundamental classification.) Furthermore he recognizes (I, 175) that "we still lack very essential connecting links" for the explanatory reduction of a mental phenomenon to its physiological foundation. Indeed, he assigns (I, 183) to physiology the "great task" of deriving the whole range of sensations and movements from one single state of excitation of the nerves, but at the same time he admits that we are "still a long way" from this goal. In addition, he asserts (I, 224) that it is "extremely dangerous to infer from physiological experiences the existence or nonexistence of consciousness." He acknowledges (I, 235) that "the physiological conditions of sleep are unknown," which implies that on the basis of physiology we would not have the least idea of the existence of such a remarkable phenomenon. Even in his opinion (I, 250) all that physiology can offer in this connection is "as yet only pious wishes and fantasies." Finally, the admission he makes (I, 288 n.) with respect to the phenomena of memory is very frank and comprehensive: "We call to mind once more that in the present state of science we can only deal with hypotheses and conceivable possibilities. In a subject matter in which measurement and precision are so completely absent there is obviously no question of saying how things really must be; that is just not known." So in his opinion we can show, on the basis of physiology, that something is wrong, but we can in no way determine what the truth is. There is plenty of room for diverse

___

the same functions, that different mental powers do not correspond to the different central organs or to their parts." (*Psych. Anal.*, I, 223.) But then, what value shall we attribute to the analogy which he has proposed?

hypotheses. If this is the case, we may indeed be thankful to physiology in many cases for forewarning us, but we certainly cannot take it as a guide in the proper sense of the word, as Horwicz wishes to do. Physiology cannot even give us an explanation of mental facts which are already well established, or such an explanation will resemble, for example, that which Horwicz gives (I, 325 ff.) of the unity of consciousness (which he accepts). Here too Horwicz asserts again and in all modesty that the matter is "still too much in the dark." The only thing that we can do for the time being is "to indicate the physiologically conceivable ways in which things *could* stand, ways which would at least be physiologically *possible* in this regard." "What sensible person who devotes himself to psychological research expects to see the last riddle of the psycho-physical connection solved by his analyses either?" He wants, he says, only to point out "how, in approximate terms, the theory must be constructed, in order to make the phenomenon of recollection to some extent physiologically conceivable and intelligible." He attempts only "to imagine, to get an idea of how things could be, physiologically." Some people may doubt, however, that he has achieved even this much.

6. The necessity of basing psychology upon physiology was emphasized just as much, if not more, by Maudsley than it had been by Horwicz. Sometimes, as we have already mentioned, he seems to agree with Comte in denying self-consciousness altogether; when he does recognize it, he emphatically stresses its total inadequacy.

In his critique of John Stuart Mill's work on Hamilton, which he published in the *Journal of Mental Science* in 1866, Maudsley reproaches Mill strongly for taking no account of physiological method, which had already proved so fruitful for psychology, and for believing that he could do by means of the old method based on inner perception what Plato, Descartes, Locke, Berkeley and a host of others had not been able to do. "Now we have not the slightest faith," he says "that ten thousand Mills will, following the same method, do what these great men have not done; but there can be no question that, had Mr. Mill chosen to avail himself of the new material and the new method which his great predecessors had not in their day, he would have done what no other living man could have done."

In his *The Physiology and Pathology of the Mind* he attempts to show very painstakingly the impossibility of achieving any appreciable result by means of the old method. To be sure, his conception of such a method is in no way adequate, since he believes that earlier psychologists paid attention only to their own individual phenomena and took no others into account. Because of this, he raises against them the drastic charge that they had tried to illuminate the universe with a rushlight.*[5] The simple fact that each of them utilized the investigations of the others should have made him aware of his error. Upon closer scrutiny, he would have found that James Mill and before him Locke and, two thousand years earlier, Aristotle, had already taken into consideration psychologically noteworthy phenomena observed in other men as well as in animals. But this remains a side issue; "Physiology or psychology?" that is the question which Maudsley himself clearly formulates, and he decides it wholly in favor of physiology.† Any attempt to develop a psychology without basing it upon physiology appears to him doomed to failure from the very beginning.

Since Maudsley, in his attacks against Mill, speaks of the fruitful results which physiological method has already yielded for psychology, and since he declares that it is only because Mill did not utilize them that he failed to attain successes unknown to any other mortal, I seemed entitled, upon opening this book, to expect a wealth of instruction on psychological questions. But I soon became aware that while he indeed made repeated attacks upon the old method, he said nothing concerning the achievements of the new one. Indeed, when he considers the problem to which he proposes to apply the physiological method, Maudsley's courage fails him and he declares that he himself and even our whole era is incapable of solving it. He recognizes openly (p. 7) "that, in the present state of physiological science, it is quite impossible to ascertain, by observation and experiment, the nature of those organic processes which are the bodily conditions of mental phenomena." And he adds (p. 28): "all that [physiology] can at present do is to overthrow the data of a false psychology." He admits that our ignorance of the pertinent areas of physiology is so great that it quite naturally raises doubt as to whether physiology will ever be in a position to lay a firm foundation for psychology. To console us, he recalls that in other fields of science, too, things have been achieved at a later date which centuries earlier would naturally have seemed impossible. But he adds: "there are really no grounds for expecting a positive science of mind at present."

From the point of view of physiological method this appears to be an indisputable truth which even Horwicz is not far from recognizing openly at times. If we compare his bolder and more abundant comments with the more circumspect and sparse psychological formula-

* *Physiology and Pathology*, p. 24.
† P. 24.
[5] See Note 3 to Chap. II, Sect. 4. In a certain sense we *are* able to light up the universe of the mental world with the rushlight of our own consciousness, as a consequence of the indefiniteness and generality of inner perception. See also Kraus, *Franz Brentano*, p. 34.

tions which we come across in the course of Maudsley's work, the contradiction between the two on essential points hardly serves to revive our faded hopes. Thus we see that, at least for the time being, it is not so much "Psychological method or physiological method?" as "Science – to be or not to be?" that is the question at hand. Consequently, it will be unavoidably necessary to clarify such a question completely so as not to waste our energies on a task that is impossible from the start.

We have heard how Maudsley settled the question. Now let us hear the motives behind his conclusion, for in his *Physiology of the Mind* Maudsley has set forth the arguments for the necessity of basing psychology methodologically on physiology in much more detail than Horwicz did.

These arguments are essentially as follows. First of all, according to Maudsley, *material conditions are the basis of consciousness*, conditions which vary in different individuals and undergo changes in the same individual, and whose properties determine the properties of mental life. Physiology alone can give us an account of them; inner consciousness obviously does not reveal anything about them.*

Furthermore, the brain, of which all consciousness is a function, according to Maudsley, also has *a vegetative life*. It is subject to an organic metabolism which, of course, ordinarily goes on, in a healthy state, without our being conscious of it. Yet, pressing its way into consciousness, it is often the cause of abnormal phenomena. Involuntary emotions appear followed by a disorderly confusion of ideas. Thus, for example, the presence of alcohol or some other such harmful agent in the blood leads to ideas which lie far outside the ordinary course of the association of ideas. How can we obtain information about these phenomena except by means of physiological method? How else, except through such a method, can we explain normal mental activity which certainly is no less dependent upon the organic life of the brain? This organic life consists of the assimilation of available material from the blood by the nerve cells. This process restores the static equilibrium after each expenditure of energy, including the consumption of neural energy produced by the activity of thought. "Statical functional potentiality thus following through the agency of nutritive attraction upon the waste of active idea through functional repulsion, and thereby the elements of the nerve cell or circuit grow to the form in which it energizes." Inner consciousness is completely silent as to all this.†

A further argument, according to Maudsley, is that *mental life does not necessarily involve mental activity*. Descartes, of course, main-

* *Physiology and Pathology*, p. 13.
† Pp. 22 ff.

tained that the mind always thinks and that non-thinking would mean non-existence. But the opposite is true. Anything which has once been present, with a certain amount of completeness, in consciousness, leaves behind it a trace, a potential or latent idea, when it disappears from consciousness. Thus, far from being constantly active, the fact is rather that at each moment the greatest part of the mind's life is inactive.

> Mental power exists in statical equilibrium as well as in manifested energy; . . . no man can call to mind at any moment the thousandth part of his knowledge. How utterly helpless is consciousness to give any account of the statical condition of mind! But as statical mind is in reality the statical condition of the organic elements which minister to its manifestations, it is plain that, if we ever are to know anything of inactive mind, it is to the progress of physiology that we must look for information.*

Still more! Not only does mental life not necessarily involve mental activity, but *mental activity does not necessarily involve consciousness.* Here Maudsley appeals to Leibniz and to his own countryman Sir William Hamilton who, following Leibniz's example, also defends the doctrine of unconscious thoughts. It would also be possible to show, Maudsley believes, that often, in fact usually, the organ of the mind appropriates influences from its environment unconsciously, i.e. in a state of complete inattention, through the senses. Although the impressions do not then produce definite ideas, nevertheless they are retained and permanently affect the mind's nature.† In the same way, the brain, as the central organ, responds to different internal stimuli which it received unconsciously from other organs, and in its turn reacts upon them. The influence of the sexual organs upon the mind is a clear example of this.‡ In addition, the brain unconsciously assimilates material and without consciousness reawakens the latent residua. "In composition," he states, "the writer's consciousness is engaged chiefly with his pen and with the sentences which he is forming, while the results of the mind's unconscious working, matured by an insensible gestation, rise from unknown depths into consciousness, and are by its help embodied in appropriate words."§ He quotes Goethe's statement: "I have never thought of thinking" which leads him to suspect that the human being in his highest development reaches an unconsciousness of the ego similar to that of a child and continues his organic evolution with a childlike un-

* *Physiology and Pathology*, p. 17.
† P. 15.
‡ P. 21.   § P. 18.

consciousness.* Thus he arrives at the assertion that not only is it the case that mental life does not necessarily involve mental activity and mental activity does not necessarily involve consciousness, but "that *the most important part of mental action*, the essential process on which thinking depends, is *unconscious mental . . . activity*." He then repeats the questions, "How can self-consciousness suffice to furnish the facts of a true mental science?"† In addition to all this, Maudsley, if I understand him correctly, finally introduces the *principle of heredity* from generation to generation.‡ Just as the residua of previous mental life persist in the individual, they are also preserved in the species. The genius differs from the common run of mortals as the butterfly which flies and feeds on honey differs from the caterpillar which crawls and gorges on leaves. But the crawling of the caterpillar is nevertheless a precondition for the flight of the butterfly; similarly, the toilsome conscious activity of ordinary labor is the precondition for the unconscious creations of the richly endowed mind. It is clear once again that this influence of heredity is far removed from the realm of consciousness.

These are, in essence, the grounds on which Maudsley considers it proved that no psychological efforts are adequate to the task unless they consider mental phenomena from a physiological standpoint.

That this is true, in a certain sense, I, at least, would have granted even before hearing his arguments. But whether it is true in the sense and to the extent to which he believes it to be is something that must be investigated. With this end in mind we will subject his arguments to a somewhat closer examination.

In the first place, it is worth noting that a good portion of the facts upon which Maudsley relies to demonstrate the inadequacy of the psychological and the necessity of the physiological method were themselves arrived at on the basis of psychological considerations; and the rest were obtained without any very thoroughgoing physiological analysis in any case, since they were already known before scientists had any idea of the physiology of the brain. It was psychological method which led people to assume the existence of innate knowledge and of genius which easily grasps by immediate intuition what others can approach only with difficulty after long discussions. Likewise, it was mental phenomena which first led Leibniz to believe in the existence of unconscious ideas, and subsequently induced Hamilton and others to assent to his theory. Moreover, it was on the basis of inner inexperience that even in antiquity Aristotle spoke of these unconscious habits and dispositions which Maudsley characterizes as the statical condition of mental life. The influence of

* *Physiology and Pathology*, p. 34.
† P. 20.   ‡ Pp. 32 ff. Cp. pp. 19 ff.

vegetative processes and the mental disturbances which follow the consumption of intoxicating beverages, as well as the connection between physical and mental properties generally, are facts the knowledge of which goes back to the dim past. Thus even for the knowledge that psychological method is inadequate Maudsley is indebted not to physiological method but, in the main, to psychological method itself.

Secondly, it should be noted that certain points upon which Maudsley bases his attacks are in no way as fully established as he seems to believe. This is true, for example, of heredity, if Maudsley really means *the inheritance of knowledge*. We will return to this question when we discuss innate ideas. If, on the other hand, Maudsley only meant to assert the inheritance of special aptitudes which are the basis for great psychological differences between different individuals, there would be no difficulty that would arise for psychological investigation from this conception which is not already included among those which we have pointed out above, and which would not be resolved along with them.

The existence of unconscious ideas is also far from being a proven fact. Most psychologists deny it. As far as I am concerned, not only do the reasons which are advanced in its favor seem to me to be inconclusive, but I even hope to prove later on, beyond a shadow of a doubt, that the opposite is true.* Maudsley appeals to facts such as the well-known story "which Coleridge quotes of the servant girl who, in the ravings of fever, repeated long passages in the Hebrew language, which she did not understand, and could not repeat when well, but which, when living with a clergyman, she had heard him read aloud." He also appeals to the prodigious memory found in certain idiots and to other similar facts. These phenomena, he believes, offer a clear proof of the existence of unconscious mental activity.

I do not see on what grounds. Just as she was conscious of hearing when she heard the clergyman, the servant girl was also conscious of the phenomena which recurred in a similar manner when she went back in her imagination to what she had previously heard. If, however, Goethe says he has never thought of thinking, while in his case thinking is certainly not absent, all he is saying is that he has never observed himself while he is thinking. But this, according to our previous discussion, in no way means that his thinking was unconscious. Otherwise we could ask him how he arrived at the very concept of thinking of which he speaks.

All this, therefore, appears neither certain nor even true. On the

* See Book Two, Chap. 2, where I return to Maudsley's arguments in Sects. 4, 5.

other hand, there are undoubtedly *habitual dispositions* resulting from previous actions. The fact that their existence cannot be denied is a sign that the psychological method is not as completely useless as Maudsley believes. In fact, as we said, these dispositions became known only by means of the psychological method. Of course it does indicate, on the other hand, that there definitely is a boundary which cannot be crossed by psychological means. For if we want to admit generally that it is certain that these acquired aptitudes and dispositions are tied up with real things (and I, at least, do not hesitate to do so, although there are other metaphysicians, John Stuart Mill for example, who would have reservations), we must also grant that they are not mental phenomena, because otherwise, as we shall show, they would be conscious. Psychological reflection informs us only that they are causes, unknown in themselves, which influence the rise of subsequent mental phenomena, as well as that they are in themselves unknown effects of previous mental phenomena. In either case psychological reflection can prove in isolated instances *that* they exist; but it can never in any way give us knowledge of *what* they are.

Will our knowledge of the "statical psychic states," which we attain in such a limited manner by means of psychological method be regarded as worthless for this reason? – If this were the case, then what value could we attribute to the natural sciences which are confronted by such boundaries much earlier? For, as we have already said, the physical phenomena of color, sound and temperature, as well as the phenomena of spatial location give us no idea of the realities which influence the phenomena we experience. We can say that such realities exist and can attribute to them certain relative properties. But what and how they are in and for themselves remains completely inconceivable to us.[6] Consequently, even if the physiology of the brain had reached its full development, it could give us no more information concerning the true nature of the realities with which these acquired dispositions are connected than pure psychological reflection could. It would tell us only about certain physical phenomena which are caused by the same unknown X.

Yet, in another respect at least, physiology would offer us more. If a mental phenomenon leaves behind a disposition from which another phenomenon similar to its cause will subsequently originate, inner experience reveals to us the previous and subsequent mental states and gives us knowledge of a law-like connection between them, but it gives us no indication of the intermediary links between them. It would be entirely different if we knew the sequence of physical phenomena which occurs in the brain, under given conditions,

[6] See above, Notes 11 and 7 to Chap. I, Sect. 3.

during the intermediate stages. We would then have a series of signs which would correspond in order of succession to the succession of the unknown reality, and as a result, by utilizing these signs, we could interpolate different intermediate steps between the two inwardly known phenomena. Thus we could explain a law discovered through psychological means much as we explain a natural law elsewhere when we discover the intermediary links in an indirect cause and effect relationship. And since it appears that these intermediary physical phenomena do always take place in the same way, and that differences in the way in which they unfold are connected with differences in subsequent mental phenomena, the increase in our knowledge would thus be of even greater importance. If in each case the empirical law connecting the two mental phenomena had been explained and more fully confirmed by physiological discoveries, it would at the same time attain greater precision. For the deviations from a rigid regularity are also obvious to an observer whose analysis is purely psychological, but he cannot take them into account except by weakening his law by such terms as "ordinarily" and "approximately." A psychology supported by physiology, on the other hand, will not only be able to explain the law, but will also be able to give a more accurate specification of its exceptions and modifications.

In this regard, therefore, Maudsley was undoubtedly right in pointing out the weakness of any non-physiological psychology. But he was wrong in ascribing no value rather than a limited value to its undertakings. – We grant that the law of succession, discovered by psychological means, is empirical and requires further explanation. – But do not the natural sciences also include many laws which are empirical and require further explanation, to which a high value is ascribed nevertheless? Or were the laws discovered by Kepler worthless before Newton explained them? – We admit further that the law of succession discovered by psychological method is not entirely accurate and precise. But is the same not true of laws in the natural sciences? To use the same prominent example, were not Kepler's laws themselves lacking in precision? And were not the laws which Copernicus thought to govern the course of the planets even more inaccurate? Nevertheless, his theory of the circular movement of the earth around the sun was a valuable and epoch-making approximation. As we said, it thus follows from the preceding considerations that investigations based upon psychological method certainly have limitations, but are not entirely without value.

Something quite similar is true of the preceding argument. Maudsley is not incorrect in saying that *mental activity depends on the organic life of the brain*. Whichever of the possible views we adhere to, no one can deny that the processes of the brain which manifest themselves in a succession of physical phenomena exert an essential influence upon mental phenomena and constitute their conditions. It is thereby clear that, even if the vegetative sequence of brain processes, apart from the differences due to the influence of mental phenomena themselves, always took place in the same way, pure psychological analysis would give us nothing but empirical laws requiring further elucidation, because it would not take account of such important joint causes. In other respects, at least the universal validity of its laws would suffer no limitation in this case. But this would not be so if the vegetative life of the brain can vary as a result of different physical influences, and if it is subject to strong abnormal disturbances which produce anomalous mental phenomena. Since this is actually the case, it is clear that the empirical laws discovered by psychological means are valid only within certain limits. It will be necessary, therefore, to determine, on the basis of reliable signs, if we are confronted with one of these limits. However, this has already been done with considerable success. Drunkenness, for example, betrays itself even to the non-psychologist in manifestations which cannot easily be misunderstood. Only within these limits may we trust the laws under discussion, but within these limits we are right in so trusting them.

Let it be further noted that if psychology thus discovers a limitation to the applicability of certain empirical laws, this limitation is not necessarily at the same time a limitation on its research. Psychology can give a characterization of anomalous states, and can determine for them, just as for normal states, the special laws of their succession. At first sight, it is not unlikely, and experience clearly confirms this, that these special laws are very complicated, and that ordinary laws are involved in their complexity. Perhaps the most essential part of the medical treatment of mentally disturbed persons, namely the so-called moral treatment of the insane, is based on the fact that to a certain extent we also know the laws governing the succession of mental events in abnormal states.

The result of examining this objection concerning the inaccessibility of the concomitant conditions of mental phenomena is thus very like the result of the analysis of the preceding objection which underlined the unavailability of the antecedent conditions of mental phenomena for psychological investigation.

Now anyone can see what answer is to be given to the first argument, the only one which still calls for a reply. When Maudsley asserts that mental life depends upon *material conditions*, all this proves is that the laws of succession discovered by means of psychological method alone are not really the ultimate basic laws. They demand a further explanation, which can only be attained by means of physiological investigations. Nothing else is proved. And if variations in physical conditions produce differences in the mental life of different people, this proves only that to the extent to which the laws established are indiscriminately general, they will be proportionately imprecise. To remedy this shortcoming, it is desirable to add to general psychology a special psychology (for example a psychology of women, on the one hand, and a psychology of men, on the other) not to mention an individual psychology, such as Bacon wanted, and which many of us are practicing to a certain degree with respect to some of our acquaintances. Besides, the general descriptions of zoologists and botanists, which also deal with species in which no individual completely resembles the other, show that even in such cases the general and average norms are not without a high value. Such a value, therefore, cannot be denied to the laws which are found by purely psychological means.

7. We have examined the views of those who say that psychology can accomplish its task only if it is based on physiology, and that consequently any attempt which depends exclusively on the analysis of mental phenomena must be unsuccessful. By reducing their assertion to its correct proportions we came to a conclusion which is in harmony with our previous conclusions. It proved to be false to say that nothing can be attained by psychological means, yet true to say that not everything can be attained by such means. We disproved the claim that no laws could be established on the basis of mental experience, but we agreed with the assertion that the discovery of the really ultimate laws of the succession of mental phenomena is possible only on the basis of physiological facts. The highest generalizations based upon the exclusive analysis of the succession of mental phenomena can only be empirical laws subject to inadequacies and imperfections, which is ordinarily the case with underived secondary laws.

If we ask whether psychology should strive toward that ultimate reduction of its highest laws to true fundamental laws on the basis of physiological data, it is clear that the answer must be similar to that given by Alexander Bain* in more general terms with respect to the advantages of physiological and psychological investigations. At *one* level of knowledge such an attempt may be useful, whereas at another level it is detrimental. Although we now hope and earnestly wish that brain physiology will one day be developed to the point where it is applicable to an explanation of the highest laws governing the succession of mental events, we believe nevertheless that the acknowledgements of the very people who most ardently advocate the

* *Logic*, II, 276.

utilization of physiology show with indubitable clarity that this day has not yet arrived. Thus John Stuart Mill is fully justified in asserting:

> To reject the resource of psychological analysis, and construct the theory of mind solely on such data as physiology affords, seems to me [a great] error in principle and an even more serious one in practice. Imperfect as is the science of mind, I do not scruple to affirm that it is in a considerably more advanced state than the portion of physiology which corresponds to it; and to discard the former for the latter appears to me an infringement of the true canons of inductive philosophy, which must produce, and which does produce, erroneous conclusions in some very important departments of the science of human nature.*

We can go even further. Not only the surrender of psychological investigation to physiological research, but also the mixing of the latter with the former seems by and large ill-advised in important areas. At the moment there are only a very few established physiological facts of the sort which could shed light upon mental phenomena. To explain the laws of their succession we would have to appeal to the flimsiest hypotheses. And, if many intelligent minds were to follow this path, we would soon see such a profusion of oddly combined systems and such a contrast of diverging opinions, as can be seen nowadays in the field of metaphysics. Far from having increased thereby the certainty of psychological laws in any way, we would subject them to the suspicion that they are equally hypothetical. For the same reasons which prompted us to eschew as much as possible all metaphysical theories, it also seems expedient to turn away from hypotheses that are advanced for the sake of physiological explanation. As John Stuart Mill points out in his Preface to the *Analysis of the Phenomena of the Human Mind*,† it is essentially because Hartley failed to do this that for a long time his ingenious attempt did not receive the consideration which it deserved.

---

* *System of Logic*, Book VI, Chap. 4, Sect. 2. [Translators' note: In quoting from Mill's *System of Logic*, Brentano used Schiel's translation, published in 1849 on the basis of the 1st edition (1843). The sentences quoted here are omitted from some editions, notably the American editions (New York, Harper & Bros.) of 1846 and 1970.]

† [Editor's note: By James Mill; John Stuart Mill, editor (London, 1869).]

IV

Further Investigations Concerning Psychological Method. The Inexact Character of its Highest Laws. Deduction and Verification

1. As we have seen, the fundamental laws from which we can derive the phenomena of mental succession, now and probably for a long time to come, are merely empirical laws. What is more, these laws have a somewhat indefinite and inexact character. The reason for this, as we have already shown, lies partly in what was just said; but it is partly the result of another factor.

Kant, in his time, denied that psychology was capable of ever becoming an explanatory science and a science in the proper sense of the word. The basic reason which prompted this judgement was the fact that mathematics is not applicable to mental phenomena since, although they have a temporal dimension, they have no spatial extension.*

Wundt tries to invalidate this objection in his *Physiological Psychology*. "It is not true," he asserts, "that inner experience has only one dimension, time. If this were the case, mathematical description would be impossible because such a description requires at least two dimensions, i.e. two variables, which can be subsumed under the concept of magnitude. But our sensations, thoughts and feelings are *intensive* magnitudes which form temporal series. Our inner life, therefore, has at least two dimensions which implies the general possibility of expressing them in mathematical form."† Thus Wundt seems to agree with Kant on the following point: if mental

---

* *Metaphysische Anfangsgründe der Naturwissenschaft*, Preface.
† *Principles of Physiological Psychology* [trans. Titchener, p. 6].

phenomena had no other constant magnitude except extension in time, the scientific character of psychology would be considerably impaired. It appears that, in Wundt's opinion, psychology is possible as an exact science only because of the fact that we find in the intensity of mental phenomena a second kind of constant magnitude, which he calls, rather inappropriately, a second dimension.

Unfortunately, I am afraid that the opposite is the case. Kant's objection would give me little pause. *In the first place*, it seems to me that it will always be possible to apply mathematics as long as there is something which can be counted. If there were absolutely no differences of intensity and degree, mathematics would still have to decide whether or not an idea is evoked through association when three conditions operate in favor and two against it. Secondly, mathematics appears to me necessary for the exact treatment of all sciences only because we now in fact find magnitudes in every scientific field. If there were a field in which we encountered nothing of the sort, exact description would be possible even without mathematics. If there were no intensities in the area of mental phenomena, it would be as if all phenomena had an equal and invariable intensity which we could quite properly ignore completely.[1] It is obvious that then the descriptions of psychology would be no less exact than they are now, only its task would be substantially simplified and facilitated. But differences of intensity do in fact exist in presentations and affects. This implies the necessity of mathematical measurement, if the laws of psychology are ever supposed to attain that precision and exactness which would belong to them if its phenomena had no intensity or at least no differences in intensity.

2. It was Herbart who first emphasized the necessity of such measurements. The merit which he earned thereby is just as generally recognized as is the complete failure of his attempt to discover actual determinations of quantity. The arbitrariness of the ultimate principle upon which he bases his mathematical psychology cannot be compensated for by his consistent adherence to the rigorous laws of mathematics in deducing consequences. So it becomes clear that by this method no progress is made toward the explanation of mental phenomena as revealed by experience. No predictions whatever can be made on the basis of Herbart's principles; indeed, the things which they would lead us to expect with the greatest certainty contradict what we actually observe to occur.

Later, following the example of E. H. Weber, Fechner made a new

[1] Brentano assumes such an invariable intensity in connection with visual sensation; Hering had denied that it had any intensity, just because of its constancy. See *Untersuchungen zur Sinnespsychologie.*

attempt to measure the intensity of mental phenomena in his *Psycho-physics*. Fechner avoided Herbart's mistake. His goal was simply to find a fundamental law of measurement within reach of experience. And just as scientists had long measured the duration of mental phenomena in terms of physical phenomena, i.e. regular spatial changes, he also sought a *physical* measurement of their intensity. The strength of the external impression which causes a sensation seemed to him to be such a physical measurement of the strength of a sensation. And what he called "Weber's Law" or "the Fundamental Psychophysical Law," asserted, for all senses, that one of the two is a function of the other, at least within certain limits.

I have already (Chap. I, Sect. 1) alluded to a rather serious oversight which may have crept into this assertion. It has been found that the increase of the physical stimulus which produces a just barely noticeable increase in the strength of the sensation always bears a constant relation to the magnitude of the stimulus to which it is added. And since it was assumed to be self-evident that each barely noticeable increase of sensation is to be regarded as equal, the law was formulated that the intensity of sensation increases by equal amounts when the relative increase of the physical stimulus is the same. In reality, it is by no means self-evident that each barely noticeable increase in sensation is *equal*, but only that it is *equally noticeable*. In addition, the quantitative relationship between equally noticeable increases in sensation remains to be examined. This investigation leads to the conclusion that all increases in sensation which have the same relationship to the intensity of the sensations to which they are added, are equally noticeable. This law also holds for other changes in the phenomena. So, for example, the noticeability is unequal, it is more noticeable, when you increase an inch by a certain amount than when you increase a foot by the same amount, provided we do not superimpose the two lengths upon one another for comparison. For if we do that, the length of the line which is increased makes no difference, since only the two increases are noticed. In other cases, though, the comparison takes place by way of memory which confuses phenomena with one another more easily the more they resemble one another. "More easily confused," however, simply means "hard to distinguish," i.e. that it is less easy to tell the difference between one thing and another. Now a foot which has been lengthened by a given line is obviously more similar to the original foot than an inch which has been lengthened by the same line is to the original inch. Therefore, only with an addition to the foot which is *proportionate* to what was added to the inch would the later appearance be dissimilar from the earlier in the same degree, and only then would the difference between them be equally noticeable.[2] But the very same thing must happen whenever we compare two successive phenomena which, alike in other respects, differ from one another in intensity. Memory certainly intervenes here too. Only if two phenomena differ from each other to the same degree will their difference strike us in the same way. In other words, their differences will only be equally noticeable if the relation of the increase to the previously given intensity is the same.

We have, therefore, the following two laws:

1. If the relative increases of the physical stimuli are equal, the sensations increase by equally noticeable amounts.

2. If sensations increase by equally noticeable amounts, the relative increases in the sensations are equal. From which it follows:

3. If the relative increase of the physical stimuli are equal, the relative increases in the sensations are equal. In other words, *if the strengths of the physical stimuli increase by the same number of times, the intensities of the sensations also increase by the same number of times.*

These results no longer contradict what common sense, and Herbart too, would have assumed in the first place: "in the region where the foundations of psychology lie . . . people quite simply say that two lights shine twice as brightly as one; that three strings sound three times as loud when struck as one," etc. (cp. p. 358). But this assertion has not yet been proved, either. Our law does not require that, whenever the stimulus increases by a certain number of times, the sensation increases by *the same* number of times. It would be satisfied if, whenever the stimulus increases by one half, the sensation increases by one third. In the case of our law, as in the case of Weber's Law, it can only be a question of validity within certain limits. It will always be incontestably to the great merit of Weber and Fechner to have rejected common sense judgement in this matter as a pre-

---

[2] The following comment, dated February 17, 1917, occurs among Brentano's manuscripts: "Elias Müller once accused me of a *circulus vitiosus*. I had said that the addition of an inch to a foot is more noticeable than the addition of an inch to a hundred feet, inasmuch as a length of 100 feet would be more similar to a length of 100 feet plus 1 inch than a length of 1 foot would be to a length of 1 foot plus 1 inch. Müller said 'more similar' means the same as 'less noticeably different.' But no such *idem per idem* is present. On the contrary, the similarity I spoke of is based on a geometrical relationship between the two quantities under consideration. The more closely the proportion approaches 1 : 1, the more similar (more nearly equal) the two things are. $\frac{1200}{1201}$ is much less different from 1 than $\frac{12}{13}$."

judice, and to have shown us the way to a sure demonstration. Although, if I am not mistaken, they assumed too soon that they had reached the goal, and thus, in correcting the original assumption, they only substituted an incorrect definition for one which could possibly have been correct. The contribution which I have made to their investigation, even if it should find unanimous assent, does not alter at all the fact that the credit for the work belongs exclusively to these two great researchers. Likewise, I hardly need to mention that the establishment of the relationship between the increase of the stimuli and a constant equally noticeable increase in the sensations is in itself of great significance.

However, whether you correct Weber's and Fechner's attempt in the manner I have indicated, or simply consider it accurate and definitive as it is, in no case can this attempt lead us to the desired goal.

In the first place, the possibility of measuring intensities according to their method is restricted entirely to those phenomena which are produced by external stimulation of the sense organs. We still lack, therefore, a measure of intensity for all mental phenomena which have their foundation in physical processes within the organism or which are caused by other mental phenomena. But the majority of mental phenomena including the most important ones belong in this category: the whole class of desires and actions of the will, as well as convictions and opinions of all kinds, and a wide range of presentations which have their origin in the imagination. Of all mental phenomena, sensations alone, and not even all of them, remain measurable.

Furthermore, even sensations depend not only on the strength of the external stimulus, but also on psychological conditions, e.g. on the level of attention. It will be necessary, therefore, to eliminate this influence, let us say, by assuming complete attention. Even if this procedure causes no other inconvenience, it nevertheless imposes at the very least a new and very important restriction upon our investigations.

Finally, it could be said that a clear understanding of what is actually measured by Fechner's method would show us that the object of measurement is not so much a mental as a physical phenomenon. What are physical phenomena if not the colors, sounds, heat and cold, etc., which manifest themselves in our sensations?[3] – So when we measure the intensities of colors, sounds, etc., as Fechner did, we are measuring the intensities of physical phenomena. Color is not seeing, sound is not hearing, warmth is not feeling warmth. – The reply may be made that even if seeing is not color, nevertheless its intensity corresponds to the intensity of the color seen by the

[3] See above, note 12 to Chap. I, and *Untersuchungen zur Sinnespsychologie.*

subject. In a similar way, the other sensations must correspond in their intensity to the physical phenomena which are presented in them. The strength of the mental phenomenon, therefore, would be determined along with the strength of the physical phenomenon. I do not want to deny that this is the case, although, as we shall see later, there are psychologists who distinguish between the intensity of the object which is presented and the intensity of the presentation. For my part, I admit that if, on the basis of Fechner's method, a measurement could be found for the physical phenomenon, it could also be found for the mental phenomenon in which the physical phenomenon is presented. Yet, it seems to me necessary to add the new restriction that only *one* aspect of the mental phenomenon should be measured according to its intensity, namely its reference to its primary object, for we shall see that the mental phenomenon has still other aspects and is not exhausted by this one reference.

For all of these reasons, then, it seems clear to me that Fechner's admirable attempt to measure psychological intensities cannot remedy, or can only remedy to an infinitesimally small degree, the deficiency which we are discussing.

We can now see how right I was in saying that unfortunately I, in opposition to Wundt, cannot in any way regard the existence of his so-called second dimension of mental phenomena as the condition which makes possible the scientific exactness of psychology. On the contrary, I think that it will be a great handicap to psychology and will make it completely impossible for the time being. For where Fechner's method fails us, it is absolutely impossible for us, at least as of now, to determine the comparative intensity of mental phenomena except through a vague "more" or "less."

These, then, are the two factors which prevent us from acquiring an accurate conception of the highest laws of mental succession: first, they are only empirical laws dependent upon the variable influences of unexplored physiological processes; secondly, the intensity of mental phenomena, which is really one of the decisive factors, cannot as yet be subjected to exact measurement. There will always be room for the application of mathematics; statistics also furnishes us numerical data, and statistical method will expand in proportion to the degree to which the laws become less exact, and to the degree to which the constant action of a cause can only be determined from statistical norms.[4] Thus mathematics proves to be the indispensable adjunct of all sciences, at every level of exactitude and in all kinds of different circumstances.

3. Although our psychological induction cannot discover the

[4] This comment is confirmed by the statistical procedure of modern physics.

genuinely basic laws, nevertheless, it does arrive at laws of a very comprehensive universality. It will be possible, therefore, to derive more specific laws from them. Accordingly, we can best establish laws for complex mental phenomena by taking as our model the method used by natural scientists, in particular by physiologists, to investigate more complex phenomena in their field of research. The physiologist is not satisfied with having derived the laws for more complex phenomena from higher laws; he takes pains to verify these laws by direct induction from experience. In the same way, the psychologist must seek an inductive verification of the laws which he has discovered deductively. Indeed, such a verification seems especially advisable in his case because, as we have seen, the higher laws which constitute the premises of his deduction often leave much to be desired in the way of precision. In such circumstances, even being able to point to individual outstanding cases is welcome corroboration, especially in the absence of other cases which appear contradictory. If the latter is the case, then a statistical confirmation will give the desired proof. Thus, psychology will be rich in examples which furnish an excellent illustration of deductive method in the empirical field, and of the three stages which the logicians have distinguished in it: induction of general laws, deduction of special laws, and verification of these laws by means of empirical facts.

It is clear from this analysis that, if on the one hand psychology cannot overlook demonstration by means of direct experience in its effort to establish the laws which govern more complex phenomena, on the other hand, it cannot regard such a demonstration as sufficient. It is not merely for the sake of the scientific interest of reducing, as far as possible, the multiplicity of facts to a unity which explains them that we strive to ascend to the highest attainable principles; not only does it give us more complete insight, derivation also provides us with greater certainty. For, as in any other field, here too general laws are more reliable. If general laws lack absolute precision and exactness, it is all the more true of special laws. If we can formulate general laws only by indicating what usually occurs and leaving room for exceptions, there will be even more exceptions to the special laws. And naturally so, because the chief factor responsible for the lack of precision in the general laws is present to an even greater extent in the case of the special laws. Thus these laws have even less right to be regarded as basic laws. Just as the discovery of the highest fundamental laws would account for both our present highest psychological laws and their exceptions and limitations, so the derivation of more special laws from them will often explain the laws themselves and their exceptions and will determine more exactly the instances falling under these exceptions, all at the same time.

Yet at least one thing can readily be admitted: we can reverse the relationship between derivation and its confirmatory induction. For it obviously makes no difference, either in terms of the insight or the certainty we obtain, whether we verify a law by induction after having deduced it, or whether we discover it by induction and then explain it by reference to more general laws. In that event we exchange the so-called deductive method of the natural scientist for what has been called the inverse deductive method. This method has also been called the historical method* because it is ideally suited for the discovery of the laws of history. It was in this way that Comte discovered the laws which he made the basis of his remarkable attempt at a philosophy of history.

This so-called historical method is also applicable, outside of history, to the psychological field, often to greater advantage than the usual deductive method. Preparatory direct induction shows the way to derivation and gives direction to it. Everyday experience has frequently been elevated to the status of low-level empirical laws which are expressed in the form of proverbs. "As the twig is bent the tree's inclined," "All beginnings are difficult," "New brooms sweep clean," "Variety is the spice of life," and the like, are expressions of such empirical generalizations. And the only thing that remains for the psychologist to do with them is to seek their explanation, verification and more exact delimitation by subordinating them to simpler and more general laws of which the common people know nothing. Pascal, as is well known, made a somewhat related attempt in one of his *Pensées*.

4. In the case of the investigation concerning immortality the procedure will also be deductive, and the deduction will rest upon factual generalizations which have been inductively established in earlier discussions. This investigation, which touches upon a problem that has always aroused the most vivid interest, will obviously have to assume a new character in many respects. On the one hand, it will be impossible to avoid taking greater account of some metaphysical laws than a phenomenalistic psychology[5] would ordinarily do. On the other hand, it will have to make much more use of the results of physiology than we do in the earlier investigations. In fact, the question of the possibility of a continuance of mental life after the disintegration of the organism is really a psychophysical question. It is but one of these questions which, according to our previous explanation, belongs to psychology rather than physiology because of the preponderance of psychological considerations. But will it be possible for us to find, by means of induction, factual generalizations

* Cp. John Stuart Mill, *System of Logic*, Book VI, Chap. 10.
[5] Re "Phenomenal psychology," see p. 14 above.

in the mental realm which will furnish the premises for a deduction which will solve the problem of immortality? Will we not be forced to go so deeply into metaphysics that we will lose the path of certainty and fall into vague, baseless dreaming? Will the facts which we have to borrow from physiology be of such a nature as to inspire too little confidence in us, given the present state of the science? It is not unjust to raise such questions. This, however, is not the place to answer them. Moreover, we do not even wish, at this time, to elaborate upon the method by which this question should be investigated. Just as the development of each earlier science furnishes hints concerning the method of the science which will follow it, so within one and the same science, the development of an earlier part of the science can also give us information concerning the method of treatment of a subsequent part. In addition, by its very nature this investigation is such that it will be best to assign to it the last place in the sequence of psychological discussions.

Let us just add, since it is obvious from the outset, that there can be no verification via direct experience concerning the problem of immortality. Thus there seems to be a dangerous gap here. Perhaps, however, we can substitute indirect for direct experience, inasmuch as numerous phenomena of experience become more intelligible if we accept the hypothesis of immortality than if we deny it. Similarly, the phenomena of falling bodies gives us only indirect evidence of the rotation of the earth on its axis.

In concluding our discussion of psychological method, let us add a final and more general remark concerning a methodological procedure which often prepares and facilitates investigations in other fields, but which does so especially in the psychological field. I have in mind the procedure which Aristotle used to be so fond of, namely, compiling "*aporiai.*" This method exhibits all the various conceivable assumptions, indicates for each of them the characteristic difficulties, and in particular gives a dialectical and critical survey of all the opposing views, whether formulated by eminent men or held by the people. John Stuart Mill also gave an insightful and positive evaluation of this method in his last essay on Grote's *Aristotle*, which he published a few months before his death in the *Fortnightly Review*. I believe that it is evident why psychologists in particular can derive even greater profit from the conflicting opinions of others than investigators in any other field. There is some truth, some experiential basis, underlying each of these opinions even though it may be viewed one-sidedly or interpreted erroneously. Moreover, when we are dealing with mental phenomena, each individual has his own special perceptions which are not accessible in the same way to anyone else.

BOOK TWO

MENTAL PHENOMENA IN GENERAL

I

The Distinction between Mental and Physical Phenomena

---

1. All the data of our consciousness are divided into two great classes – the class of physical and the class of mental phenomena. We spoke of this distinction earlier when we established the concept of psychology, and we returned to it again in our discussion of psychological method. But what we have said is still not sufficient. We must now establish more firmly and more exactly what was only mentioned in passing before.

This seems all the more necessary since neither agreement nor complete clarity has been achieved regarding the delimitation of the two classes. We have already seen how physical phenomena which appear in the imagination are sometimes taken for mental phenomena. There are many other such instances of confusion. And even important psychologists may be hard pressed to defend themselves against the charge of self-contradiction.* For instance, we encounter

---

* In this respect, I, at least, cannot reconcile the different definitions given by Bain in one of his latest psychological works, *Mental Science*, 3rd ed. (London, 1872). On p. 120, No. 59, he says that mental science (Science of Mind, which he also calls Subject science) is grounded on self-consciousness or introspective attention; the eye, the ear, the organs or touch being only the media for the observation of the physical world, or the "object world," as he expresses it. On the other hand, on p. 198, No. 4, he says that, "The perception of matter or the Object consciousness is connected with the putting forth of Muscular Energy, as opposed to Passive Feeling." And by way of explanation, he adds, "In purely *passive* feeling as in those of our sensations that do not call forth our muscular energies, we are not perceiving matter, we are in a state of subject consciousness." He illustrates this with the example of the sensation of warmth

statements like the following: sensation and imagination are distinguished by the fact that one occurs as the result of a physical phenomenon, while the other is evoked by a mental phenomenon according to the laws of association. But then the same psychologists admit that what appears in sensation does not correspond to its efficient cause. Thus it turns out that the so-called physical phenomenon does not actually appear to us, and, indeed, that we have no presentation of it whatsoever – certainly a curious misuse of the term "phenomenon"! Given such a state of affairs, we cannot avoid going into the question in somewhat greater detail.

2. The explanation we are seeking is not a definition according to the traditional rules of logic. These rules have recently been the object of impartial criticism, and much could be added to what has already been said. Our aim is to clarify the meaning of the two terms *"physical phenomenon"* and *"mental phenomenon,"* removing all misunderstanding and confusion concerning them. And it does not matter to us what means we use, as long as they really serve to clarify these terms.

To this end, it is not sufficient merely to specify more general, more inclusive definitions. Just as deduction is opposed to induction when we speak of kinds of proof, in this case explanation by means of subsumption under a general term is opposed to explanation by means of particulars, through examples. And the latter kind of explanation is appropriate whenever the particular terms are clearer than the general ones. Thus it is probably a more effective procedure to explain the term "color" by saying that it designates the class which contains red, blue, green and yellow, than to do the opposite and attempt to explain "red" by saying it is a particular kind of color. Moreover, explanation through particular definitions will be of even greater use when we are dealing, as in our case, with terms which are not common in ordinary life, while those for the individual phenomena included under them are frequently used. So let us first of all try to clarify the concepts by means of examples.

Every idea or presentation which we acquire either through sense

---

that one has when taking a warm bath, and with those cases of gentle contact in which there is no muscular activity, and declares that, under the same conditions, sounds and possibly even light and color could be "a purely subject experience." Thus he takes as illustrations to substantiate subject consciousness the very sensations from the eye, ear and organs of touch, which he had characterized as indicators of "object consciousness" in opposition to "subject consciousness."

perception or imagination is an example of a mental phenomenon.[1] By presentation I do not mean that which is presented, but rather the act of presentation. Thus, hearing a sound, seeing a colored object, feeling warmth or cold, as well as similar states of imagination are examples of what I mean by this term. I also mean by it the thinking of a general concept, provided such a thing actually does occur. Furthermore, every judgement, every recollection, every expectation, every inference, every conviction or opinion, every doubt, is a mental phenomenon. Also to be included under this term is every emotion: joy, sorrow, fear, hope, courage, despair, anger, love, hate, desire, act of will, intention, astonishment, admiration, contempt, etc.

Examples of physical phenomena,[2] on the other hand, are a color,

[1] "*Examples of mental phenomena.*" Brentano consequently understands "mental phenomenon" to mean the same as "mental activity," and what is characteristic of it, in his opinion, is the "reference to something as object," i.e. being concerned with something. With this the word φαινόμενον has become mere "internal linguistic form." The same thing holds true of the word "activity," since in Brentano's opinion every such activity, at least in men and animals, is a *passio*, an affection in the Aristotelian sense. So what we are concerned with is the sheer "having something as object" as the distinguishing feature of any act of consciousness, which Brentano also calls "state of consciousness," in Book One, Chap. 1, Sect. 2. Supplementary essay II is more precise on this point and on the further distinction between mental activity and mental reference. It would be better to avoid the expression "phenomenon," even though according to Brentano every consciousness not only has something appearing to it but appears to itself (see Book Two, Chap. 2).

[2] In citing examples of physical phenomena, Brentano intends to bring in first of all examples of "physical phenomena" which are given directly in perception. Thus he enumerates: colors, shapes, musical chords, warmth, cold, odors. In each of these cases we are concerned with objects of our sensations, what is sensed. Now "a landscape, which I see" has slipped in among these examples. But it was obvious for Brentano that I cannot see a landscape, only something colored, extended, bounded in some way. In his books and articles on the history of philosophy, Brentano repeatedly emphasized as one of the most fundamental rules of interpretation, that philosophical writers are to be interpreted in the context of all their work. Now anyone who takes notice of Brentano's *Psychologie des Aristotles* (Mainz, 1876), will find that on p. 84 he deals with that which is sensible *per accidens*. Aristotle uses an example to explain the sensible *per accidens*: someone sees the son of Diares. Now, to be sure, we can say that he sees the son of Diares, but he does not see him as such. He sees something white and it is a fact concerning the white thing he sees that it is the son of Diares. This should at least have called attention to the fact that Brentano does not believe one can see a landscape in the same way that one can see something variously colored. In other words, landscape is no sense-quality

a figure, a landscape which I see, a chord which I hear, warmth, cold, odor which I sense; as well as similar images which appear in the imagination.

These examples may suffice to illustrate the differences between the two classes of phenomena.

3. Yet we still want to try to find a different and a more unified way of explaining mental phenomena. For this purpose we make use of a definition we used earlier when we said that the term "mental phenomena" applies to presentations as well as to all the phenomena which are based upon presentations. It is hardly necessary to mention again that by "presentation" we do not mean that which is presented, but rather the presenting of it. This act of presentation forms the foundation not merely of the act of judging, but also of desiring and of every other mental act. Nothing can be judged, desired, hoped or feared, unless one has a presentation of that thing.[3] Thus the definition given includes all the examples of mental phenomena which we listed above, and in general all the phenomena belonging to this domain.

It is a sign of the immature state of psychology that we can scarcely utter a single sentence about mental phenomena which will not be disputed by many people. Nevertheless, most psychologists agree with what we have just said, namely, that presentations are the foundation for the other mental phenomena. Thus Herbart asserts quite rightly, "Every time we have a feeling, there will be something or other presented in consciousness, even though it may be something very diversified, confused and varied, so that this particular presentation is included in this particular feeling. Likewise, whenever

---

[3] The descriptive psychological law that Brentano here expresses is not obtained inductively but is self-evident in view of the concepts of presentation, judgement, and appetition. See Introduction, p. 370, and *The Origin of our Knowledge of Right and Wrong*.

---

and cannot be an object of direct sense-perception. What one sees, when one "sees" a landscape are extended colored shapes at some distance from us. Everything else is a matter of interpretation in terms of judgements and concepts. One can find fault with the example, then, in that it includes "landscape" among the "physical phenomena" belonging to our *direct perception*. Thus Husserl accuses Brentano of having confused "sense contents" with "external objects" that appear to us and of holding that physical phenomena "exist only phenomenally or intentionally." But this accusation is shown to be wrong in the Introduction to the present book. According to Brentano, we have perceptions of the mental and perceptions of the physical; the former exhibit nothing that is extended and the latter are restricted to what is qualitative and extended.

we desire something . . . we have before our minds that which we desire."*

Herbart then goes further, however. He sees all other phenomena as nothing but certain states of presentations which are derivable from the presentations themselves. This view has already been attacked repeatedly with decisive arguments, in particular by Lotze. Most recently, J. B. Meyer, among others, has set forth a long criticism of it in his account of Kant's psychology. But Meyer was not satisfied to deny that feelings and desires could be derived from presentations. He claims that phenomena of this kind can exist in the absence of presentations.† Indeed, Meyer believes that the lowest forms of animal life have feelings and desires, but no presentations and also that the lives of higher animals and men begin with mere feelings and desires, while presentations emerge only upon further development.‡ Thus Meyer, too, seems to come into conflict with our claim.

But, if I am not mistaken, the conflict is more apparent than real. Several of his expressions suggest that Meyer has a narrower concept of presentation than we have, while he correspondingly broadens the concept of feeling. "Presentation," he says, "begins when the modification which we experience in our own state can be understood as the result of an external stimulus, even if this at first expresses itself only in the unconscious looking around or feeling around for an external object which results from it." If Meyer means by "presentation" the same thing that we do, he could not possibly speak in this way. He would see that a condition such as the one he describes as the origin of presentation, already involves an abundance of presentations, for example, the idea of temporal succession, ideas of spatial proximity and ideas of cause and effect. If all of these ideas must already be present in the mind in order for there to be a presentation in Meyer's sense, it is absolutely clear that such a thing cannot be the basis of every other mental phenomenon. Even the "being present" of any single one of the things mentioned is "being presented" in our sense. And such things occur whenever something appears in consciousness, whether it is hated, loved, or regarded indifferently, whether it is affirmed or denied or there is a complete withholding of judgement and – I cannot express myself in any other way than to say – it is presented. As we use the verb "to present," "to be presented" means the same as "to appear."

---

* *Psychologie als Wissenschaft*, Part II, Sect. 1, Chap. 1, No. 103. Cp. also Drobisch, *Empirische Psychologie*, p. 38, and others of Herbart's school.
† *Kant's Psychologie* (Berlin, 1870), pp. 92 ff.
‡ *Kant's Psychologie*, p. 94.

Meyer himself admits that a presentation in this sense is presupposed by every feeling of pleasure and pain, even the lowliest, although, since his terminology differs from ours, he calls this a feeling and not a presentation. At least that is what seems to me to emerge from the following passage: "There is no intermediate state between sensation and non-sensation. . . . Now the simplest form of sensation need be nothing more than a mere *sensation of change* in one's own body or a part thereof, caused by some stimulus. Beings endowed with such sensations would only have a *feeling of their own states*. A sensibility of the soul for the changes which are favorable or harmful to it could very well be directly connected with this *vital feeling* for the events beneath one's own skin, even if this *new sensitivity* could not simply be derived from that feeling: such a soul could have *feelings* of pleasure and pain *along with the sensation* . . . . A soul so endowed still has no Presentations."* It is easy to see that what is, in our view, the only thing which deserves the name "feeling," also emerges according to J. B. Meyer as the second element. It is preceded by another element which falls under the concept of a presentation as we understand it, and which constitutes the indispensable precondition for this second phenomenon. So it would seem that if Meyer's view were translated into our terminology, the opposition would disappear automatically.

Perhaps a similar situation obtains, too, in the case of others who express themselves in a manner similar to Meyer's. Yet it may still be the case that with respect to some kinds of sensory pleasure and pain feelings, someone may really be of the opinion that there are no presentations involved, even in our sense. At least we cannot deny that there is a certain temptation to do this. This is true, for example, with regard to the feelings present when one is cut or burned. When someone is cut he has no perception of touch, and someone who is burned has no feeling of warmth, but in both cases there is only the feeling of pain.

Nevertheless there is no doubt that even here the feeling is based upon a presentation. In cases such as this we always have a presentation of a definite spatial location which we usually characterize in

* *Kant's Psychologie*, p. 92. J. B. Meyer seems to conceive of sensation in the same way as Überweg in his *Logik I*, 2nd ed., p. 64. "Perception differs from mere sensation in that in sensation we are conscious only of the subjective state, while in perception there is another element which is perceived and which therefore stands apart from the act of perception as something different and objective." Even if Überweg's view of the difference between sensation and perception were correct, sensation would still involve a presentation in our sense. Why we consider it to be incorrect will be apparent later.

relation to some visible and touchable part of our body. We say that our foot or our hand hurts, that this or that part of the body is in pain. Those who consider such a spatial presentation something originally given by the neural stimulation itself cannot deny that a presentation is the basis of this feeling. But others cannot avoid this assumption either. For there is in us not only the idea of a definite spatial location but also that of a particular sensory quality analogous to color, sound and other so-called sensory qualities, which is a physical phenomenon and which must be clearly distinguished from the accompanying feeling. If we hear a pleasing and mild sound or a shrill one, harmonious chord or a dissonance, it would not occur to anyone to identify the sound with the accompanying feeling of pleasure or pain. But then in cases where a feeling of pain or pleasure is aroused in us by a cut, a burn or a tickle, we must distinguish in the same way between a physical phenomenon, which appears as the object of external perception, and the mental phenomenon of feeling, which accompanies its appearance, even though in this case the superficial observer is rather inclined to confuse them.

The principal basis for this misconception is probably the following. It is well known that our perceptions are mediated by the so-called afferent nerves. In the past people thought that certain nerves served as conductors of each kind of sensory qualities, such as color, sound, etc. Recently, however, physiologists have been more and more inclined to take the opposite point of view.* And they teach almost universally that the nerves for tactile sensations, if stimulated in a certain way, produce sensations of warmth and cold in us, and if stimulated in another way produce in us so-called pleasure and pain sensations. In reality, however, something similar is true for all the nerves, insofar as a sensory phenomenon of the kind just mentioned can be produced in us by every nerve. In the presence of very strong stimuli, all nerves produce painful phenomena, which cannot be distinguished from one another.† When a nerve transmits different kinds of sensations, it often happens that it transmits several at the same time. Looking into an electric light, for example, produces simultaneously a "beautiful," i.e. pleasant, color phenomenon and a phenomenon of another sort which is painful. The nerves of the tactile sense often simultaneously transmit a so-called sensation of touch, a sensation of warmth or cold, and a so-called sensation of pleasure or pain. Now we notice that when several sensory phenomena appear at the same time, they are not infrequently regarded as *one*. This has been demonstrated in a striking manner in regard to the sensations of smell and taste. It is well established that almost

* Cp. especially Wundt, *Principles of Physiological Psychology* (trans. Titchener), pp. 322 ff.   † Cp. below, Book Two, Chap. III, Sect. 6.

all the differences usually considered differences in taste are really only differences in the concomitant olfactory phenomena. Something similar occurs when we eat food cold or warm; we often think that it tastes different while in reality only the temperature sensations differ. It is not surprising, then, if we do not always distinguish precisely between a phenomenon which is a temperature sensation and another which is a tactile sensation. Perhaps we would not even distinguish between them at all if they did not ordinarily appear independently of one another. If we now look at the sensations of feeling,[4] we find, on the contrary, that their phenomena are usually linked with another sort of sensation, and when the excitation is very strong these other sensations sink into insignificance beside them. Thus the fact that a given individual has been mistaken about the appearance of a particular class of sensory qualities and has believed that he has had one single sensation instead of two is very easily explained. Since the intervening idea was accompanied by a relatively very strong feeling, incomparably stronger than that which followed upon the first kind of quality, the person considers this mental phenomenon as the only new thing he has experienced. In addition, if the first kind of quality disappeared completely, then he would believe that he possessed only a feeling without any underlying presentation of a physical phenomenon.

A further basis for this illusion is the fact that the quality which precedes the feeling and the feeling itself do not have two distinct names. The physical phenomenon which appears along with the feeling of pain is also called pain. Indeed, we do not say that we sense this or that phenomenon in the foot with pain; we say that we feel pain in the foot. This is an equivocation, such as, indeed, we often find when different things are closely related to one another. We call the body healthy, and in reference to it we say that the air, the food, the color of the face, etc., are healthy, but obviously in another sense. In our case, the physical phenomenon itself is called pleasure or pain after the feeling of pleasure or pain which accompanies the appearance of the physical phenomenon, and there, too, in a modified sense of the words. It is as if we would say of a harmonious chord that it is a pleasure because we experience pleasure when we hear it, or, too, that the loss of a friend is a great sorrow for us. Experience shows that equivocation is one of the main obstacles to recognizing distinctions. And it must necessarily be the largest obstacle here where there is an inherent danger of confusion and perhaps the extension of the term was itself the result of this confusion. Thus many psychologists were deceived by this equivocation and this error fostered further errors.

[4] On "sensations of feeling," compare Brentano's controversy with Stumpf in *Untersuchungen zur Sinnespsychologie*.

Some came to the false conclusion that the sensing subject must be present at the spot in the injured limb in which a painful phenomenon is located in perception.[5] Then, since they identified the phenomenon with the accompanying pain sensation, they regarded this phenomenon as a mental rather than a physical phenomenon. It is precisely for this reason that they thought that its perception in the limb was an inner, and consequently evident and infallible perception.* Their view is contradicted by the fact that the same phenomena often appear in the same way after the amputation of the limb. For this reason others argued, in a rather skeptical manner, against the self-evidence of inner perception. The difficulty disappears if we distinguish between pain in the sense in which the term describes the apparent condition of a part of our body, and the feeling of pain which is connected with the concomitant sensation. Keeping this in mind, we shall no longer be inclined to assert that there is no presentation at the basis of the feeling of sensory pain experienced when one is injured.

Accordingly, we may consider the following definition of mental phenomena as indubitably correct: they are either presentations or they are based upon presentations in the sense described above. Such a definition offers a second, more simple explanation of this concept. This explanation, of course, is not completely unified because it separates mental phenomena into two groups.

4. People have tried to formulate a completely unified definition which distinguishes all mental phenomena from physical phenomena by means of negation. All physical phenomena, it is said, have extension and spatial location, whether they are phenomena of vision or of some other sense, or products of the imagination, which presents similar objects to us. The opposite, however, is true of mental phenomena; thinking, willing and the like appear without extension and without spatial location.

According to this view, it would be possible for us to characterize physical phenomena easily and exactly in contrast to mental phenomena by saying that they are those phenomena which appear extended and localized in space. Mental phenomena would then be definable with equal exactness as those phenomena which do not have extension or spatial location. Descartes and Spinoza could be cited in support of such a distinction. The chief advocate of this view, however, is Kant, who explains space as the form of the intuition of the external sense.

* This is the opinion of the Jesuit, Tongiorgi, in his widely circulated philosophy textbook.
[5] Here "perception" is taken in the loose and extended sense, for localization in the foot goes beyond sensation.

Recently Bain has given the same definition:

The department of the Object, or Object–World, is exactly
circumscribed by one property, Extension. The world of
Subject-experience is devoid of this property. A tree or a river is
said to possess extended magnitude. A pleasure has no length,
breadth, or thickness; it is in no respect an extended thing. A
thought or idea may refer to extended magnitudes, but it cannot
be said to have extension in itself. Neither can we say that an
act of the will, a desire or a belief occupy dimensions in space.
Hence all that comes within the sphere of the Subject is
spoken of as the Unextended.

    Thus, if Mind, as commonly happens, is put for the sum-total
of Subject-experiences, we may define it negatively by a single
fact – the absence of Extension.*

Thus it seems that we have found, at least negatively, a unified
definition for the totality of mental phenomena.

But even on this point there is no unanimity among psychologists,
and we hear it denied for contradictory reasons that extension and
lack of extension are characteristics which distinguish physical and
mental phenomena.

Many declare that this definition is false because not only mental
phenomena, but also many physical phenomena appear to be without
extension. A large number of not unimportant psychologists, for
example, teach that the phenomena of some, or even of all of our
senses originally appear apart from all extension and spatial location.
In particular, this view is quite generally held with respect to sounds
and olfactory phenomena.[6] It is true of colors according to Berkeley,
of the phenomena of touch according to Platner, and of the phenomena of all the external senses according to Herbart and Lotze, as
well as according to Hartley, Brown, the two Mills, H. Spencer and
others. Indeed it seems that the phenomena revealed by the external
senses, especially sight and the sense of touch, are all spatially
extended. The reason for this, it is said, is that we connect them with
spatial presentations that are gradually developed on the basis of
earlier experiences. They are originally without spatial location, and
we subsequently localize them. If this were really the only way in
which physical phenomena attain spatial location we could obviously
no longer separate the two areas by reference to this property. In
fact, mental phenomena are also localized by us in this way, as, for

* *Mental Science*, Introduction, Chap. 1.
[6] In the *Untersuchungen zur Sinnespsychologie*, Brentano attempts to show
that we experience all sense-qualities as being localized.

example, when we locate a phenomenon of anger in the irritated lion, and our own thoughts in the space which we occupy.

This is one way in which the above definition has been criticized by a great number of eminent psychologists, including Bain. At first sight he seems to defend such a definition, but in reality he follows Hartley's lead on this issue. He has only been able to express himself as he does because he does not actually consider the phenomena of the external senses, in and for themselves, to be physical phenomena (although he is not always consistent in this).*

Others, as we said, will reject this definition for the opposite reason. It is not so much the assertion that all physical phenomena appear extended that provokes them, but rather the assertion that all mental phenomena lack extension. According to them, certain mental phenomena also appear to be extended. Aristotle seems to have been of this opinion when, in the first chapter of this treatise on sense and sense objects he considers it immediately evident, without any prior proof, that sense perception is the act of a bodily organ.†
Modern psychologists and physiologists sometimes express themselves in the same way regarding certain affects. They speak of feelings of pleasure or pain which appear in the external organs, sometimes even after the amputation of the limb and yet, feeling, like perception, is a mental phenomenon. Some authors even maintain that sensory appetites appear localized. This view is shared by the poet when he speaks, not, to be sure, of thought, but of rapture and longing which suffuse the heart and all parts of the body.[7]

Thus we see that the distinction under discussion is disputed from the point of view of both physical and mental phenomena. Perhaps both of these objections are equally unjustified.‡ At any rate, another definition common to all mental phenomena is still desirable. Whether certain mental and physical phenomena appear extended or not, the controversy proves that the criterion given for a clear separation is

* Cp. above, p. 77, note.
† *De Sensu et Sensibili*, 1, 436, b. 7. Cp. also what he says in *De Anima*, I, 1, 403 16, about affective states, in particular about fear.
‡ The assertion that even mental phenomena appear to be extended rests obviously on a confusion of mental and physical phenomena similar to the confusion which we became convinced of above when we pointed out that a presentation is also the necessary foundation of sensory feelings.
[7] Brentano was entirely familiar, then, with such false localizations and interpretations. They did not lead him to doubt the evident nature of inner perception. In the Supplementary Essays he emphasizes that this evidence is not affected by the confused character of inner perception. Husserl takes "perception" to refer to complex interpretations and is thus led to dispute the evidence of inner perception.

not adequate. Furthermore, this criterion gives us only a negative definition of mental phenomena.[8]

5. What positive criterion shall we now be able to provide? Or is there perhaps no positive definition which holds true of all mental phenomena generally? Bain thinks that in fact there is none.* Nevertheless, psychologists in earlier times have already pointed out that there is a special affinity and analogy which exists among all mental phenomena, and which physical phenomena do not share.

Every mental phenomenon is characterized by what the Scholastics of the Middle Ages called the intentional (or mental)† inexistence of an object, and what we might call, though not wholly unambiguously, reference to a content, direction toward an object[9] (which is not to be understood here as meaning a thing),[10] or immanent objectivity. Every mental phenomenon includes something as object within itself, although they do not all do so in the same way. In presentation something is presented, in judgement something is affirmed or denied, in love loved, in hate hated, in desire desired and so on.‡

* *The Senses and the Intellect*, Introduction.

† They also use the expression "to exist as an object (objectively) in something," which, if we wanted to use it at the present time, would be considered, on the contrary, as a designation of a real existence outside the mind. At least this is what is suggested by the expression "to exist immanently as an object," which is occasionally used in a similar sense, and in which the term "immanent" should obviously rule out the misunderstanding which is to be feared.

‡ Aristotle himself spoke of this mental in-existence. In his books on the soul he says that the sensed object, as such, is in the sensing subject; that the sense contains the sensed object without its matter; that the object which is thought is in the thinking intellect. In Philo, likewise, we find the doctrine of mental existence and in-existence. However, since he confuses them with existence in the proper sense of the word, he reaches his contradictory doctrine of the *logos* and Ideas. The same is true of the Neoplatonists. St. Augustine in his doctrine of the *Verbum mentis* and of its inner origin touches upon the same fact. St. Anselm does the same in his famous ontological argument; many people have observed that his consideration of mental existence as a true existence is at the basis of his paralogism (cp. Überweg, *Geschichte der Philosophie*, II). St. Thomas Aquinas teaches that the object which is thought is intentionally in the thinking subject, the object which is loved in the person who loves, the object which is desired in the person desiring, and he uses this for theological purposes.

[8] Compare Book Two, Chap. 4, Sect. 3. [*note* ‡ *cont. on p. 89*]

[9] Brentano here uses "content" synonymously with "object." He later came to prefer the term "object."

[10] As we have noted, Brentano subsequently denies that we can have anything "irreal" as object; we can have as object only that which would be a substance or *thing* if it existed.

This intentional in-existence is characteristic exclusively of mental phenomena. No physical phenomenon exhibits anything like it. We can, therefore, define mental phenomena by saying that they are those phenomena which contain an object intentionally within themselves.[11]

But here, too, we come upon controversies and contradiction. Hamilton, in particular, denies this characteristic to a whole broad class of mental phenomena, namely, to all those which he characterizes as feelings, to pleasure and pain in all their most diverse shades and varieties.[12] With respect to the phenomena of thought and desire he is in agreement with us. Obviously there is no act of thinking without an object that is thought, nor a desire without an object that is desired. "In the phenomena of Feelings – the phenomena of Pleasure and Pain – on the contrary, consciousness does not place the mental modification or state before itself; it does not contemplate it apart – as separate from itself – but is, as it were, fused into one. The peculiarity of Feeling, therefore, is that there is nothing but what is subjectively subjective; there is no object different from the self – no objectification of any mode of self."* In the first instance

---

* *Lecture on Metaphysics*, I, 432.

[11] Brentano later acknowledged that the way he attempted to describe consciousness here, adhering to the Aristotelian tradition which asserts "the mental inexistence of the object," was imperfect. The so-called "inexistence of the object," the immanent objectivity, is not to be interpreted as a mode of being the thing has in consciousness, but as an imprecise description of the fact that I have something (a thing, real entity, substance) as an object, am mentally concerned with it, refer to it. There are more details on this point in the Supplementary Essays and the Introduction. The Table of Contents speaks more appropriately of "reference to an object." See note 20.

[12] Here, too, we are concerned with the question already mentioned in Note 1, whether it belongs to the essence of every act of consciousness to be a consciousness of something. Opinions are still divided on this most elementary question in psychology. There is still a distinction drawn today, as there was before Brentano, between objective acts of consciousness and mere states of consciousness. Brentano assails this doctrine with arguments which have remained unrefuted and indeed have gone largely unnoticed. His *Untersuchungen zur Sinnespsychologie* has, in particular, been largely ignored.

[*note* ‡ *cont.*]
When the Scriptures speak of an indwelling of the Holy Ghost, St. Thomas explains it as an intentional indwelling through love. In addition, he attempted to find, through the intentional in-existence in the acts of thinking and loving, a certain analogy for the mystery of the Trinity and the procession *ad intra* of the Word and the Spirit.

there would be something which, according to Hamilton's terminology, is "objective," in the second instance something which is "objectively subjective," as in self-awareness, the object of which Hamilton consequently calls the "subject-object." By denying both concerning feelings, Hamilton rejects unequivocally all intentional in-existence of these phenomena.

In reality, what Hamilton says is not entirely correct, since certain feelings undeniably refer to objects. Our language itself indicates this through the expressions it employs. We say that we are pleased with or about something, that we feel sorrow or grieve about something. Likewise, we say: that pleases me, that hurts me, that makes me feel sorry, etc. Joy and sorrow, like affirmation and negation, love and hate, desire and aversion, clearly follow upon a presentation and are related to that which is presented.

One is most inclined to agree with Hamilton in those cases in which, as we saw earlier, it is most easy to fall into the error that feeling is not based upon any presentation: the case of pain caused by a cut or a burn, for example. But the reason is simply the same temptation toward this, as we have seen, erroneous assumption. Even Hamilton recognizes with us the fact that presentations occur without exception and thus even here they form the basis of the feeling. Thus his denial that feelings have an object seems all the more striking.

One thing certainly has to be admitted; the object to which a feeling refers is not always an external object. Even in cases where I hear a harmonious sound, the pleasure which I feel is not actually pleasure in the sound but pleasure in the hearing.[13] In fact you could say, not incorrectly, that in a certain sense it even refers to itself, and this introduces, more or less, what Hamilton was talking about, namely that the feeling and the object are "fused into one." But this is nothing that is not true in the same way of many phenomena of thought and knowledge, as we will see when we come to the investigation of inner consciousness. Still they retain a mental inexistence, a Subject-Object, to use Hamilton's mode of speech, and the same thing is true of these feelings. Hamilton is wrong when he says that with

[13] The Supplementary Essays and the *Untersuchungen zur Sinnespsychologie* exclude sensual affects of pleasure from sensations of *hearing and seeing*, limit them, that is, to what Brentano called the "*Spürsinn.*" On this view, pleasure in hearing something is an affect of the "Spürsinn" which accompanies and is elicited by the hearing of it. [Translators' note: Brentano classified the sense-modalities in such a way that sensations other than visual and aural ones were grouped under one heading, to which he attached this term. Any attempt at a literal translation would merely be misleading.]

regard to feelings everything is "subjectively subjective" – an expression which is actually self-contradictory, for where you cannot speak of an object, you cannot speak of a subject either. Also, Hamilton spoke of a fusing into one of the feeling with the mental impression, but when carefully considered it can be seen that he is bearing witness against himself here. Every fusion is a unification of several things; and thus the pictorial expression which is intended to make us concretely aware of the distinctive character of feeling still points to a certain duality in the unity.

We may, therefore, consider the intentional in-existence of an object to be a general characteristic of mental phenomena which distinguishes this class of phenomena from the class of physical phenomena.

6. Another characteristic which all mental phenomena have in common is the fact that they are only perceived in inner consciousness, while in the case of physical phenomena only external perception is possible. This distinguishing characteristic is emphasized by Hamilton.*

It could be argued that such a definition is not very meaningful. In fact, it seems much more natural to define the act according to the object, and therefore to state that inner perception, in contrast to every other kind, is the perception of mental phenomena. However, besides the fact that it has a special object, inner perception possesses another distinguishing characteristic: its immediate, infallible self-evidence. Of all the types of knowledge of the objects of experience, inner perception alone possesses this characteristic. Consequently, when we say that mental phenomena are those which are apprehended by means of inner perception, we say that their perception is immediately evident.

Moreover, inner perception is not merely the only kind of perception which is immediately evident; it is really the only perception in the strict sense of the word.† As we have seen, the phenomena of the so-called external perception cannot be proved true and real even by means of indirect demonstration. For this reason, anyone who in good faith has taken them for what they seem to be is being misled by the manner in which the phenomena are connected. Therefore, strictly speaking, so-called external perception is not perception. Mental phenomena, therefore, may be described as the only phenomena of which perception in the strict sense of the word is possible.

* *Lecture on Metaphysics*, I, 432.

† [Translators' note: The German word which we translate as "perception" is "*Wahrnehmung*" which literally means taking something to be true. The English word does not reflect this literal meaning so this paragraph only makes sense if we bear in mind the German word.]

This definition, too, is an adequate characterization of mental phenomena. That is not to say that all mental phenomena are internally perceivable by all men, and so all those which someone cannot perceive are to be included by him among physical phenomena. On the contrary, as we have already expressly noted above, it is obvious that no mental phenomenon is perceived by more than one individual. At the same time, however, we also saw that every type of mental phenomenon is present in every fully developed human mental life. For this reason, the reference to the phenomena which constitute the realm of inner perception serves our purpose satisfactorily.

7. We said that mental phenomena are those phenomena which alone can be perceived in the strict sense of the word. We could just as well say that they are those phenomena which alone possess real existence as well as intentional existence. Knowledge, joy and desire really exist. Color, sound and warmth have only a phenomenal and intentional existence.[14]

There are philosophers who go so far as to say that it is self-evident that phenomena such as those which we call physical phenomena *could not* correspond to any reality. According to them, the assertion that these phenomena have an existence different from mental existence is self-contradictory. Thus, for example, Bain says that attempts have been made to explain the phenomena of external perception by supposing a material world, "in the first instance, detached from perception, and, afterwards, coming into perception, by operating upon the mind." "This view," he says, "involves a contradiction. The prevailing doctrine is that a tree is something in itself apart from all perception; that, by its luminous emanations, it impresses our mind and is then perceived, the perception being an effect, and the unperceived tree [i.e. the one which exists outside of perception] the cause. But the tree is known only through perception; what it may be anterior to, or independent of, perception, we cannot tell; we can think of it as perceived but not as unperceived. There is a manifest contradiction in the supposition; we are required at the same moment to perceive the thing and not to perceive it. We know the touch of iron, but we cannot know the touch apart from the touch."*

I must confess that I am unable to convince myself of the soundness of this argument. It is undoubtedly true that a color appears to us

---

* *Mental Science*, 3rd ed., p. 198.
[14] This passage also makes clear what Brentano intended as the object of outer perception; "color, sound, heat," in brief, sense-qualities, that someone having a sensation senses – what is sensed – but not "landscapes" or "boxes."

only when we have a presentation of it. We cannot conclude from this, however, that a color cannot exist without being presented. Only if the state of being presented were contained in the color as one of its elements, as a certain quality and intensity is contained in it, would a color which is not presented imply a contradiction, since a whole without one of its parts is indeed a contradiction. But this is obviously not the case. Otherwise, it would also be absolutely inconceivable how the belief in the real existence of physical phenomena outside our presentation could have, not to say originated, but achieved the most general dissemination, been maintained with the utmost tenacity, and, indeed, even been shared for a long time by the most outstanding thinkers. Bain said: "We can think of a tree as perceived, but not as unperceived. There is a manifest contradiction in the supposition." If what he said were correct, his further conclusions could not be objected to. But it is precisely this which cannot be granted. Bain explains this statement by remarking, "We are required at the same moment to perceive the thing and not to perceive it." It is not correct, however, to say that such a demand is placed upon us, for, in the first place, not every act of thinking is a perception. Secondly, even if this were the case, it would only follow that we can think only of trees that have been perceived by us, but not that we can think only of trees *as perceived by us*. To taste a piece of white sugar does not mean to taste a piece of sugar *as white*. The fallacy reveals itself quite clearly in the case of mental phenomena. If someone said, "I cannot think about a mental phenomenon without thinking about it; therefore I can only think about mental phenomena as thought by me; therefore no mental phenomenon exists outside my thinking," his method of reasoning would be identical to that of Bain. Nevertheless, even Bain will not deny that his individual mental life is not the only one which has actual existence. When Bain adds: "we know the touch of iron, but it is not possible that we should know the touch apart from the touch," he obviously uses the word "touch" first to mean the object that is sensed and secondly to mean the act of sensing. These are different concepts, even though the word is the same. Consequently, only those who would let themselves be deceived by this equivocation could grant the existence of immediate evidence as postulated by Bain.

It is not correct, therefore, to say that the assumption that there exists a physical phenomenon outside the mind which is just as real as those which we find intentionally in us, implies a contradiction.[15]

[15] We see from this that the account in the Table of Contents, Book Two, Chap. I, Sect. 7, is mistaken. Colors and sounds and so on *could* exist, i.e. their existence involves no direct contradiction. But critical inquiry and comparison convinces us of the blindness of our compulsive belief

It is only that, when we compare one with the other we discover conflicts which clearly show that no real existence corresponds to the intentional existence in this case. And even if this applies only to the realm of our own experience, we will nevertheless make no mistake if in general we deny to physical phenomena any existence other than intentional existence.[16]

8. There is still another circumstance which people have said distinguishes between physical and mental phenomena. They say that mental phenomena always manifest themselves serially, while many physical phenomena manifest themselves simultaneously. But people do not always mean the same thing by this assertion, and not all of the meanings which it has been given are in accord with the truth.

Recently Herbert Spencer expressed himself on this subject in the following vein: "The two great classes of vital actions called Physiology and Psychology are broadly distinguished in this, that while the one includes both simultaneous and successive changes the other includes successive changes only. The phenomena forming the subject matter of Physiology present themselves as an immense number of different series bound up together. Those forming the subject

---

[16] The attempt has been made to stamp Brentano as a phenomenalist on the basis of this sentence. That is completely mistaken. Brentano was always phenomenalism's most determined opponent. All he intends to say is that colored things, sounding extended things are intentionally given, i.e. we have them as objects, and that *such* qualitative extended things cannot be proved to exist, indeed that to affirm is in all probability a mistake. In this connection it is to be noted that the affirmation of colored extended things is false even when there *are* physical bodies. These bodies do not have qualities of color or sound, or the like; but every affirmation is an assertion of the entire content and our sensations are affirmative beliefs in what we sense. It is unconditionally certain that this belief, this impulse to grant their reality, is blind; i.e. it is not intrinsically logically justifiable, not experienced as being correct. This emerges from comparison with acts which are evident. At the same time it is extremely probable, according to all the rules of induction and the calculation of probability, that the belief in the existence of qualitatively extended things is false. The demonstrative force of Locke's experiments and Aristotle's experiment with the round ball already reach that far. There are certain equivocations which may still work in favor of naive realism today (as when the physicist speaks of "pressure," but without thinking of the quality of pressure which we sense).

---

in the objects of outer perception and natural science convinces us of its incorrectness. In this paragraph Brentano uses "perception" in a broader sense, following Bain's usage. One can no more perceive trees in the sense of sensing them than one can perceive landscapes.

matter of psychology present themselves as but a single series. A glance at the many continuous actions constituting the life of the body at large shows that they are synchronous – that digestion, circulation, respiration, excretion, secretions, etc., in all their many subdivisions are going on at one time in mutual dependence. And the briefest introspection makes it clear that the actions constituting thought occur, not together, but one after another."* Spencer restricts his comparison to physiological and physical phenomena found in one and the same organism endowed with mental life. If he had not done this, he would have been forced to admit that many series of mental phenomena occur simultaneously too, because there is more than one living being endowed with mental life in the world. However, even within the limits which he has assigned to it, the assertion he advances is not entirely true. Spencer himself is so far from failing to recognize this fact that he immediately calls attention to those species of lower animals, for example the *radiata*, in which a multiple mental life goes on simultaneously in *one* body. For this reason he thinks – but others will not readily admit it – that there is little difference between mental and physical life.† In addition he makes further concessions which reduce the difference between physiological and mental phenomena to a mere matter of degree. Furthermore, if we ask ourselves what it is that Spencer conceives as those physiological phenomena whose changes, in contrast to the changes of mental phenomena, are supposed to occur simultaneously, it appears that he uses this term not to describe specifically physical phenomena, but rather the causes, which are in themselves unknown, of these phenomena.[17] In fact, with respect to the physical phenomena which manifest themselves in sensation, it seems undeniable that they cannot modify themselves simultaneously, if the sensations themselves do not undergo simultaneous changes. Hence, we can hardly attain a distinguishing characteristic for the two classes of phenomena in this way.

Others have wanted to find a characteristic of mental life in the fact that consciousness can grasp simultaneously only *one object*, never more than one, at a time. They point to the remarkable case of the error that occurs in the determination of time. This error regularly appears in astronomical observations in which the simultaneous swing of the pendulum does not enter into consciousness simultaneously with, but earlier or later than, the moment when the

* *Principles of Psychology*, 2nd ed. I, Sect. 177, 395.
† *Principles of Psychology*, p. 397.
[17] See the preceding [Kraus] note. The word "phenomenon" is understood in the narrower sense here, not in the sense of "fact" or "event," as for example on p. 26.

observed star touches the hairline in the telescope.* Thus, mental phenomena always merely follow each other, one at a time, in a simple series. However, it would certainly be a mistake to generalize without further reflection from a case which implies such an extreme concentration of attention. Spencer, at least, says: "I find that there may sometimes be detected as many as five simultaneous series of nervous changes, which in various degrees rise into consciousness so far that we cannot call any of them absolutely unconscious. When walking, there is the locomotive series; there may be, under certain circumstances, a tactual series; there is very often (in myself at least), an auditory series, constituting some melody or fragment of a melody which haunts me; and there is the visual series: all of which, subordinate to the dominant consciousness formed by some train of reflection, are continually crossing it and weaving themselves into it."† The same facts are reported by Hamilton, Cardaillac, and other psychologists on the basis of their experiences. Assuming, however, that it were true that all cases of perception are similar to that of the astronomer, should we not always at least have to acknowledge the fact that frequently we think of something and at the same time make a judgement about it or desire it? So there would still be several simultaneous mental phenomena. Indeed, we could, with more reason, make the opposite assertion, namely, that very often many mental phenomena are present in consciousness simultaneously, while there can never be more than one physical phenomenon at a time.

What is the only sense, then, in which we might say that a mental phenomenon always appears by itself, while many physical phenomena can appear at the same time? We can say this insofar as the whole multiplicity of mental phenomena which appear to us in our inner perception always appear as a unity, while the same is not true of the physical phenomena which we grasp simultaneously through the so-called external perception. As happens frequently in other cases, so here, too, unity is confused by many psychologists with simplicity; as a result they have maintained that they perceive themselves in inner consciousness as something simple. Others, in contesting with good reason the simplicity of this phenomenon, at the same time denied its unity. The former could not maintain a consistent position because, as soon as they described their inner life, they found that they were mentioning a large variety of different ele-

* Cp. Bessel, *Astronomische Beobachtungen*, Sect. VIII Intro. (Königsberg, 1823), Intro. Struve, *Expedition Chronometrique*, etc. (Petersburg, 1844), p. 29.
† *Principles of Psychology*, p. 398. Drobisch likewise says that it is a "fact that many series of ideas can pass simultaneously through consciousness, but, as it were, at different levels."

ments; and the latter could not avoid involuntarily testifying to the unity of mental phenomena. They speak, as do others, of an "I" and not of a "we" and sometimes describe this as a "bundle" of phenomena, and at the other times by other names which characterize a fusion into an inner unity. When we perceive color, sound, warmth, odor simultaneously[18] nothing prevents us from assigning each one to a particular thing. On the other hand, we are forced to take the multiplicity of the various acts of sensing, such as seeing, hearing, experiencing warmth and smelling, and the simultaneous acts of willing and feeling and reflecting, as well as the inner perception which provides us with the knowledge of all those, as parts of one single phenomenon in which they are contained, as one single and unified thing. We shall discuss in detail later on what constitutes the basis for this necessity. At that time we shall also present several other points pertaining to the same subject. The topic under discussion, in fact, is nothing other than the so-called unity of consciousness, one of the most important, but still contested, facts of psychology.

9. Let us, in conclusion, summarize the results of the discussion about the difference between mental and physical phenomena. First of all, we illustrated the specific nature of the two classes by means of *examples*. We then defined mental phenomena as *presentations* or as phenomena which are based *upon presentation;* all the other phenomena being physical phenomena. Next we spoke of *extension,* which psychologists have asserted to be the specific characteristic of all physical phenomena, while all mental phenomena are supposed to be unextended. This assertion, however, ran into contradictions which can only be clarified by later investigations. All that can be determined now is that all mental phenomena really appear to be unextended.[19] Further we found that the *intentional in-existence*, the reference to something as an object,[20] is a distinguishing characteristic of all mental phenomena. No physical phenomenon exhibits anything similar. We went on to define mental phenomena as the exclusive *object of inner perception*; they alone, therefore, are perceived with immediate evidence. Indeed, in the strict sense of the

[18] This is another example of what Brentano means by "external perception" in the strict sense.

[19] The definition is negative: we do not perceive mental phenomena to be extended.

[20] This form of expression: "reference to something as an object" is the one which characterizes the situation more clearly. Brentano continues to use it after he had recognized that "mental inexistence of the object" was a defective description. He is also accustomed to saying: I make (have) something (as) my object. See the Introduction and Note 11.

word, they alone are perceived. On this basis we proceeded to define them as the only phenomena which possess *actual existence* in addition to intentional existence.[21] Finally, we emphasized as a distinguishing characteristic the fact that the mental phenomena which we perceive, in spite of all their multiplicity, *always* appear to us *as a unity*, while physical phenomena, which we perceive at the same time, do not all appear in the same way as parts of one single phenomenon.

That feature which best characterizes mental phenomena is undoubtedly their intentional in-existence. By means of this and the other characteristics listed above, we may now consider mental phenomena to have been clearly differentiated from physical phenomena.[22]

Our explanations of mental and physical phenomena cannot fail to place our earlier definitions of psychology and natural science in a clearer light. In fact, we have stated that the one is the science of mental phenomena, and the other the science of physical phenomena. It is now easy to see that both definitions tacitly include certain limitations.

This is especially true of the definition of the natural sciences. These sciences do not deal with all physical phenomena, but only with those which appear in sensation, and as such do not take into account the phenomena of imagination. And even in regard to the former they only determine their laws insofar as they depend on the physical stimulation of the sense organs. We could express the scientific task of the natural sciences by saying something to the effect that they are those sciences which seek to explain the succession of physical phenomena connected with normal and pure sensations (that is, sensations which are not influenced by special mental conditions and processes) on the basis of the assumption of a world which resembles one which has three dimensional extension in space and flows in *one* direction in time, and which influences our sense

[21] That is to say, I bring the "mental phenomena" before my mind in presentation and believe in them in the secondary consciousness with a correct, indeed evident belief. It is a blind compulsion which makes me believe in the "physical phenomena" (colors, sounds, etc.), on the other hand. They exist only intentionally, i.e. as present to my mind, i.e. I exist as someone perceiving or having a presentation of them, but they do *not* exist. See notes 13 and 15 to I, 1 and note 2 to II, 1. (See the Introduction on Brentano's appreciation of Comte, and p. 99.)

[22] So in Brentano's opinion the really characteristic property is *intentional* reference. The additional ones only "clarify" the definition of mental phenomena. That is to be noted as against Husserl's *Logical Investigations*, II, 856.

organs.* Without explaining the absolute nature of this world, these sciences would limit themselves to ascribing to its forces capable of producing sensations and of exerting a reciprocal influence upon one another, and determining for these forces the laws of co-existence and succession. Through these laws they would then establish indirectly the laws of succession of the physical phenomena of sensations, if, through scientific abstraction from the concomitant mental conditions, we admit that they manifest themselves in a pure state and as occurring in relation to a constant sensory capacity. We must interpret the expression "science of physical phenomena" in this somewhat complicated way if we want to identify it with natural science.†

We have nevertheless seen how the expression "physical phenomenon" is sometimes erroneously applied to the above mentioned forces themselves. And, since normally the object of a science is characterized as that object whose laws such a science determines directly and explicitly, I believe I will not be mistaken if I assume that the definition of natural science as the science of physical phenomena is frequently connected with the concept of forces belonging to a world which is similar to one extended in space and flowing in time; forces which, through their influence on the sense organs, arouse sensation and mutually influence each other in their action, and of

---

* Cp. Überweg (*System der Logik*) in whose analysis not everything can be accepted. In particular, he is wrong when he asserts that the world of external causes is extended in space and time, instead of saying that it resembles one which is spatially and temporally extended.[23]

† This explanation does not coincide entirely with Kant's premises, but it approaches as far as possible his explanation. In a certain sense it comes nearer to J. S. Mill's views in his book against Hamilton (Chap. 11), without, however, agreeing with it in all the essential aspects. What Mill calls "the permanent possibilities of sensation," is closely related to what we have called forces. The relationship of our view with, as well as its essential departure from, Überweg's conception was already touched upon in the previous note.

[23] See above, note 7 to I, 1. We directly and concretely perceive things that are spatially and temporally relative. The actual spatial and temporal properties of the "world" are similar since they exhibit like relations (of distance and direction), but there must also be absolute properties which are concealed from us in their specific forms. Since anything that is spatially and temporally relative still falls under the general concept of the spatial and temporal, Überweg's form of expression is unobjectionable. Later on Brentano himself used the same expression as Überweg, as he had earlier done in his article on Comte. See the Introduction, and Brentano's articles, "*August Comte und die positive Philosophie*" and "*Zur Lehre von Raum und Zeit.*"

which natural science investigates the laws of co-existence and succession. If those forces are considered as the object of natural sciences, there is also the advantage that this science appears to have as its object something that really and truly exists. This could, of course, also be attained if natural science were defined as the science of sensation, tacitly adding the same restriction which we have just mentioned. Indeed, the reason why the expression "physical phenomenon" is preferred probably stems from the fact that certain psychologists have thought that the external causes of sensations correspond to the physical phenomena which occur in them, either in all respects, which was the original point of view, or at least in respect to three-dimensional extension, which is the opinion of certain people at the present time. It is clear that the otherwise improper expression "external perception" stems from this conception. It must be added, however, that the act of sensing manifests, in addition to the intentional in-existence of the physical phenomenon, other characteristics with which the natural scientist is not at all concerned, since through them sensation does not give us information in the same way about the distinctive relationships which govern the external world.

With respect to the definition of psychology, it might first seem as if the concept of mental phenomena would have to be broadened rather than narrowed, both because the physical phenomena of imagination fall within its scope at least as much as mental phenomena as previously defined, and because the phenomena which occur in sensation cannot be disregarded in the theory of sensation. It is obvious, however, that they are taken into account only as the content[24] of mental phenomena when we describe the specific characteristics of the latter. The same is true of all mental phenomena which have a purely phenomenal existence.[25] We must consider only mental phenomena in the sense of real states as the proper object of psychology. And it is in reference only to these phenomena that we say that psychology is the science of mental phenomena.

[24] Content = object.

[25] *Imagined* mental phenomena have mere phenomenal existence, i.e. I make a primary object of something which is a secondary object of consciousness. (See further below and the Supplementary Essays.)

II

*Inner Consciousness**

---

1. Disputes about what concept a term applies to are not always useless quarrels over words. Sometimes it is a question of establishing the conventional meaning of a word, from which it is always dangerous to deviate. Frequently, however, the problem is to discover the natural boundaries of a homogeneous class.

We must have a case of the latter sort before us in the dispute about the meaning of the term "consciousness," if it is not to be viewed as mere idle quibbling over words. For there is no question of there being a commonly accepted, exclusive sense of the term. The surveys of the different uses of this term made by Bain,† in England, and by Horwicz‡ in Germany, show this beyond any doubt. Sometimes we understand it to mean the memory of our own previous actions, especially if they were of a moral nature, as when we say, "I am not conscious of any guilt." At other times we designate by it all kinds of immediate knowledge of our own mental acts, especially the perception which accompanies present mental acts. In addition, we use this term with regard to external perception, as for example when we say of a man who is awakening from sleep or from a faint that he has regained consciousness. And, we call not only perception and cognition, but also all presentations, states of consciousness. If something appears in our imagination, we say that it appears in consciousness. Some people have characterized every mental act as consciousness, be it an idea, a cognition, an erroneous opinion, a feeling, an act of will or any other kind of mental phenomenon. And psychologists (of course not all of them) seem to attach this meaning

* Just as we call the perception of a mental activity which is actually present in us "inner perception," we here call the consciousness which is directed upon it "inner consciousness."
† *Mental and Moral Science*, Appendix, p. 93.
‡ *Psychologische Analysen*, I, 211 ff.

101

in particular to the word when they speak of the unity of consciousness, i.e. of a unity of simultaneously existing mental phenomena.

For any given use of the word, we shall have to decide whether it
may not be more harmful than helpful. If we want to emphasize the
origin of the term, doubtless we would have to restrict it to cognitive
phenomena, either to all or to some of them. But it is obvious that
there is rarely any point in doing so, since words often change from
their original meaning and no harm is done. It is obviously much
more expedient to use this term in such a way as to designate an
important class of phenomena, especially when a suitable name for it
is lacking and a discernible gap is thereby filled.* For this reason,
therefore, I prefer to use it as synonymous with "mental phenomenon," or "mental act." For, in the first place, the constant use of
these compound designations would be cumbersome, and furthermore, the term "consciousness," since it refers to an object which
consciousness is conscious of,† seems to be appropriate to characterize mental phenomena precisely in terms of its distinguishing
characteristic, i.e., the property of the intentional in-existence of an
object, for which we lack a word in common usage.

2. We have seen that no mental phenomenon exists which is not,
in the sense indicated above, consciousness of an object. However,
another question arises, namely, whether there are any mental
phenomena which are not objects of consciousness. All mental
phenomena are states of consciousness; but are all mental phenomena conscious, or might there also be unconscious mental acts?

Some people would just shake their heads at this question. To
postulate an unconscious consciousness seems to them absurd. Even
eminent psychologists such as Locke and John Stuart Mill consider
it a direct contradiction. But anyone who has paid attention to the
foregoing definitions will hardly think so. He will recognize that a
person who raises the question of whether there is an unconscious
consciousness is not being ridiculous in the same way he would be
had he asked whether there is a non-red redness. An unconscious
consciousness is no more a contradiction in terms than an unseen
case of seeing.‡

---

* Cp. the remark of Herbart, *Lehrbuch zur Psychologie*, I, Chap. 2, 17,
and *Psychologie als Wissenschaft*, I, Sect. II, Chap. 2, 48.

† [Translators' note: "*von welchem das Bewusstsein Bewusstsein ist.*" This
linguistic support for the recommended usage of "*Bewusstsein*", depending
as it does on the structure of the German word, does not apply to the
English word "consciousness."]

‡ We use the term "unconscious" in two ways. First, in an active sense,
speaking of a person who is not conscious of a thing; secondly, in a passive
sense, speaking of a thing of which we are not conscious. In the first sense,

Most laymen in psychology, however, will immediately reject the assumption of an unconscious consciousness, even without being influenced by false analogies associated with this expression. Indeed, two thousand years had to go by before a philosopher appeared who taught such a thesis. Naturally philosophers were well familiar with the fact that we can possess a store of acquired knowledge without thinking about it. But they rightly conceived of this knowledge as a disposition toward certain acts of thinking, just as they conceived of acquired character as a disposition toward certain emotions and volitions, but not as cognition and consciousness. One of the first men who taught that there is an unconscious consciousness was Thomas Aquinas.* Later on, Leibniz spoke of *"perceptiones sine apperceptione seu conscientia,"* and *"perceptiones insensibiles,"*† and Kant followed his example. Recently, the theory of unconscious mental phenomena has found numerous proponents even among men who in other respects may adhere to doctrines which are not exactly congenial. The elder Mill, for example, states that there are sensations of which we are not conscious, because of habitual inattention. Hamilton teaches that the train of our ideas is often connected only by intermediate steps of which we are not conscious. Lewes, likewise, believes that many mental acts take place without consciousness. Maudsley considers the existence of unconscious mental activity a proven fact, and makes it one of the principal considerations in favor of his physiological method. Herbart speaks of ideas of which we are not conscious, and Beneke believes that only those ideas which possess a relatively high degree of intensity are accompanied by consciousness. Fechner, too, says that psychology cannot ignore unconscious sensations and presentations. Wundt,‡ Helmholtz, Zöllner and others maintain that there are unconscious inferences. Ulrici advances a whole series of arguments in support of his claim that not only sensations, but also other mental acts such as love and desire often go on unconsciously. And von Hartmann has worked out a complete "Philosophy of the Unconscious."

* See below, Sect. 7.

† *Nouveaux Essais*, II, 1. *Monadology*, 14. *Principles de la nature et de la grace*, 4.

‡ At least in his early work, *Vorlesungen über Menschen- und Tierseele.* Some passages of his *Physiologische Psychologie*, as it stands now, seem to indicate that he has retreated from the acceptance of unconscious mental activities.

---

the expression "unconscious consciousness" would be a contradiction, but not in the second. It is in the latter sense that the term "unconscious" is used here.

Nevertheless, however numerous the ranks of those who speak in favor of unconscious mental phenomena have become, the theory is still far from having attained general recognition. Neither has Lotze adopted it, nor have the famous English psychologists Bain and Spencer rallied to it. Even John Stuart Mill, who generally expresses the highest respect for the opinions of his father, has not refrained from opposing his doctrine on this issue. Moreover, even among those who assert that there are unconscious ideas, there are many who do this only because they attach a different meaning to these terms. This is true of Fechner, for example, who, when he speaks of unconscious *sensations* and *ideas*, clearly gives the terms "sensation" and "idea" different meanings from the ones we ascribe to them – so much so that he does not understand them to mean a mental phenomenon at all.[1] According to him, all mental phenomena are conscious, and, therefore, with regard to this matter, he is an opponent of the new conception.* By using the term "consciousness" in a different sense, Ulrici, likewise, denies any unconscious mental act in our sense.† We may well say that Hartmann, too, uses the term "consciousness" to refer to something different from what we do. He defines consciousness as "the emancipation of the idea from the will . . . and the opposition of the will to this emancipation," and as "the bewilderment of the will over the *existence* of the idea, which existence the will does not want but which, nevertheless, is sensibly present." This definition, if it does not just refer to something purely imaginary, at least seems to bear upon something different from what we called consciousness.‡ The reasons which he advances, however,

* This is clearly shown in a passage of his *Psychophysics*, II, 438: "Psychology cannot abstract from unconscious sensations and ideas, nor can it even abstract from the effects of unconscious sensations and ideas. In what way, then, can a thing which does not exist produce an effect? Or in what manner does an unconscious sensation or idea differ from a sensation or idea which we do not have at all?" In answer to the first question, Fechner states that there is really no sensation but something with which sensation stands in a functional relationship. "Sensations, ideas, have, of course, *ceased actually to exist* in the state of unconsciousness, insofar as we consider them apart from their substructure. Nevertheless, something persists within us, i.e. the psychophysical activity of which they are a function, and which makes possible the re-appearance of sensation, etc."

† In *Gott und Mensch*, I, 283, he says that "in general we have an immediate feeling of our inner states, processes, impulses and activities," and that there is no doubt "that this feeling accompanies all sensory impressions (perceptions), even those which are most commonplace," that in this way "we also feel *that* we see, hear, taste, etc."

‡ *Philosophie der Unbewusstsein*, 2nd ed., p. 366.

[1] Contemporaries also use the word in this sense.

at least show that he is an advocate of unconscious mental activities in the sense in which we speak of them.

The lack of unanimity among psychologists on this point cannot come as a surprise, since we have encountered disagreements at every step of our investigations. But in this case it provides no reasonable ground for concluding that the truth cannot be known with certainty. On the other hand, the peculiar nature of the question is such that some people may believe that the impossibility of answering it is obvious on the face of it and, therefore, while it can be the object of ingenious intellectual games, it cannot be the object of serious scientific investigation. For it is self-evident and necessarily the case that there can be no unconscious ideas in the domain of our experience, even if many such ideas should exist within us; otherwise, they would not be unconscious. It would seem, therefore, that one cannot appeal to experience as proof against them. For the same reason, however, one cannot testify to their existence, either. Forsaken by experience, how are we supposed to decide the question?

In answer to this charge the defenders of unconscious consciousness have rightly pointed out, nevertheless, that what cannot be directly experienced can perhaps be deduced indirectly from empirical facts.* They have not hesitated to gather such facts, and to offer a great variety of arguments as proof of their contention.[2]

3. There are four different ways in which one might proceed here with some hope of success.

First, we could try to prove that certain facts given in experience demand the hypothesis of an unconscious mental phenomenon as their *cause*.

Secondly, we could attempt to prove that a fact given in experience must bring about an unconscious mental phenomenon as its *effect*, even though none appears in consciousness.

Thirdly, we could try to show that in the case of conscious mental phenomena *the strength of the concomitant consciousness is a function of their own strength*, and that, because of this relationship, in certain cases in which the latter is a positive magnitude, the former must lack a positive value.

Finally, we could attempt to prove that the hypothesis that each mental phenomenon is an object of a mental phenomenon leads to an *infinite complexity* of mental states, which is both intrinsically impossible and contrary to experience.

4. The way which was, and still is, most frequently tried is the first.

* Cp. Kant, *Anthropologie*, 5.
[2] The question is, whether there can be a state of consciousness not accompanied by a secondary consciousness. *Unconscious determining factors* (Freud) are quite compatible with this.

Usually, however, not enough attention has been paid to the particular conditions under which this path can lead to its goal. In order to be able to draw any conclusion concerning an unconscious mental phenomenon as a cause, from a fact which is supposed to be its effect, it is necessary, first of all, that the fact itself be sufficiently established. This is the first condition. For this reason the attempted proofs which are based on the phenomena of so-called clairvoyance, presentiment, premonition, etc., can *only* be of dubious value. Hartmann himself, who cites them,* is fully aware of the fact that the starting point of the proof cannot inspire great confidence. Therefore, we shall be able to by-pass these arguments entirely.[3] But in addition, the things that Maudsley tells us about the accomplishments of geniuses,† which are not the product of conscious thinking, are not facts that are sufficiently certain to be used as the basis for a conclusive argument. Geniuses are even rarer than somnambulists. Moreover, the manner in which some of them, Newton, for example, reported their most brilliant discoveries clearly shows that these discoveries were not the product of unconscious thought. We follow them in their investigations and understand their success, without thereby being any less in awe of it. If other geniuses have not been able to give a like account of their accomplishments, is it more presumptuous to assume that they have forgotten the conscious steps of their discoveries, than to assume that unconscious thought processes bridged the gap? Goethe, who undoubtedly can claim a place among men of genius, says in his *Wilhelm Meister* that extraordinary talent is "only a slight deviation from the ordinary." If there are unconscious mental processes, therefore, it will be possible to discover them in less unusual cases too.[4]

There is a further condition, namely, that, on the hypothesis of a mental phenomenon of which we are not conscious, the fact of experience can really be explained as an effect brought about by a corresponding cause. To this end, it is necessary, first of all, to show through experience that conscious mental phenomena have always

---

* *Philosophie der Unbewusstsein*, 2nd ed., pp. 81 ff.

† *Physiology and Pathology of the Mind*, pp. 32 f. Cp. above Book One, Chap. III, Sect. 6.

[3] Many of the phenomena mentioned here have since been proved to be facts. So-called para-psychology is concerned with them, as is psychiatry. But it can be said very definitely that so far no counter instance has been found which would favor primary consciousness without any accompanying secondary consciousness.

[4] Brentano's essay, "Das Genie," deals with this question thoroughly in the same sense [reprinted in Franz Brentano, *Grundzüge der Aesthetik*, ed. Franziska Mayer-Hillebrand, Bern, 1959].

involved similar consequences. Furthermore, it is necessary to assume that they do not involve at the same time other consequences which are absent in the cases at hand, even though there is no reason to suspect that they are connected with the concomitant consciousness which is missing in these cases. Finally, it is necessary that the unconscious mental phenomena, to which the hypothesis appeals, do not contradict, in their succession or in their other characteristics, the recognized laws of conscious mental phenomena, so that any possible peculiarities can be understood on the basis of the lack of the concomitant consciousness. Their succession and other characteristics which they possess, naturally cannot be perceived directly, but they will reveal themselves in their effects, just as the laws of the external world, the law of inertia, the law of gravitation, etc., manifest themselves in the sensations which are their effects. So it is particularly necessary that the origin of the mental phenomena assumed to exist despite the absence of consciousness should not be considered to be something utterly and entirely inconceivable itself.

These conditions become particularly urgent if, as happens almost invariably, the assumed unconscious mental activities are considered homogeneous with conscious ones. We can also say that by and large those who, on the basis of facts of experience, have inferred unconscious mental acts as their cause, usually do not openly violate such conditions. The opposite is true only of individual thinkers, particularly Hartmann. He, however, differs from the majority of the proponents of unconscious mental acts in that he considers these acts to be heterogeneous as compared with conscious acts, indeed, as deviating from them in the most essential respects. It is obvious that anyone who adheres to such a view weakens the hypothesis of unconscious mental acts from the start. Many scientists whose views on logic agree with those of John Stuart Mill,* will reject the hypothesis in this form without further ado as unscientific because it does not make use of a *vera causa* as a principle of explanation. Reasoning by analogy undoubtedly loses force to the extent to which the similarity between the assumed cause and the observed ones diminishes. In this respect, therefore, the first divergent definition already represents a disadvantage and every new divergence, which does not stem from the one which precedes it as a necessary conclusion, cannot but affect considerably, by reason of the increasing complexity, the probability of the hypothesis. However, I believe that we cannot reject the hypothesis under discussion as a gratuitous and arbitrary fiction, if it fulfills, to the degree to which they remain valid, the conditions mentioned above, or other equivalent conditions. Even when arguing

* *System of Logic*, Book III.

107

from the phenomena of our sensations, to the conclusion that there is something like a spatially extended world which causes them, we assume something that was never discovered as an immediate fact of experience, and yet the inference may not be unjustified. But why not? Only because, by connecting the hypothesis of such a world with the hypothesis of certain general laws which govern it, we are able to understand and even to predict the otherwise unintelligible succession of our sensory phenomena in their relation to one another. Thus it will also be necessary here to set forth the laws of these alleged unconscious phenomena and to verify them through a unified explanation of a whole mass of empirical facts which otherwise would remain unexplained, and through prediction of other facts which nobody would otherwise anticipate. Furthermore, since the alleged unconscious phenomena are considered, if not homogeneous with conscious phenomena, at least analogous with them to a certain extent (otherwise it would be wrong to classify them as mental activities), it will be necessary to prove that the characteristics which they have in common with conscious facts are not violated, and, in general, that their assumption involves no contradictory assertions.

Hartmann has no more satisfied these requirements than he did the previous ones. On the contrary, at the very moment that we would expect to find the laws for unconscious mental phenomena,* it becomes evident that these phenomena are not mental phenomena at all. They merge into an eternal Unconscious, into a unique,† omnipresent, omniscient,‡ and all-wise being. A God appears who, in order fully to deserve this name, would need only a consciousness (pp. 486 ff.) even though he is also affected in other respects by some serious contradictions. He is being-in-itself,§ he knows being-in-itself (p. 337), but he doesn't know himself. He is above all time (p. 338) even though he not only acts, but also is acted upon in time.¶ He never grows weary (p. 336) and yet he goes to great length to spare himself whatever effort he possibly can (p. 554). The devices he contrives for the purpose are, of course, always imperfect, so that he has no alternative but to resort to direct intervention everywhere and continuously (p. 555). But he does not even do this all of the time. In fact, contrary to his usual behavior, he even allows it to happen that goals which would undoubtedly be attained by his direct "all-wise"

* *Philosophie der Unbewusstsein*, 2nd ed., pp. 334 ff.
† Pp. 473 ff.
‡ Pp. 552 ff.
§ P. 480. Nothing exists outside the Unconscious (p. 720).
¶ P. 472, where, for example, Hartmann speaks of a "reciprocal action of certain material parts of the organic individual with the Unconscious."

intervention (pp. 339 ff.) miscarry, and the mechanisms he created for preservation lead to destruction (p. 129). In a word he is playing utterly the role of a *deus ex machina*, which Plato and Aristotle in times past found reprehensible in Anaxagoras's *Nous* which was always at hand as a stopgap whenever the mechanistic explanation fails.* Anyone who is any kind of a rigorous thinker will reject as inadmissible such a hypothetical nonentity, even if he does not accept the limits assigned by Mill to scientific hypotheses. There can be no doubt, therefore, that all the arguments which Hartmann advances in support of the hypothesis of unconscious mental phenomena fail to satisfy the second condition, in the form in which he offers them. He has not proved that the facts of experience, from which the unconscious mental activity is to be inferred, would really be explained by such a hypothesis.

Finally, a third condition for the validity of the conclusion concerning unconscious mental phenomena as the cause of certain empirical facts would consist in the proof that the phenomena under discussion cannot be understood, at least not without the greatest improbability, on the basis of other hypotheses. Even if it is certain that in some cases conscious mental phenomena involve similar phenomena as effects, this fact alone does not prove that these effects never stem from other causes. It is not true that similar effects always have similar causes. Very often physical objects of very different kinds cannot be distinguished from one another on the basis of color. In this instance the effect is the same, but the causes are nonetheless different from one another. It was mainly because Bacon disregarded this possibility that his inductive experiments attained so few successful results. What is possible in the physical realm, however, is also possible in the psychological realm. In fact, starting from different premises, we often arrive at the same conclusion. Aristotle himself recognized and emphasized this point. This great thinker also pointed out that judgements, which are at first inferred in the proper sense of the term, are later made directly on the basis of experience alone, or (to use another expression in order to avoid any misunderstanding), on the strength of habit. It is due to the force of habit that certain principles, which are frequently applied but which are far from being self-evident, seem to us to be immediately evident, since they thrust themselves upon us with an almost irresistible strength. Likewise, it may be because of habit alone that, when placed in similar situations, animals anticipate similar effects. What is here an acquired disposition, however, could in other cases be an inborn disposition to

* Cp. for example, in order to find striking illustration in this connection, the chapter which deals with the increasing evolution of the organic life on earth.

make immediate judgements.* In that event, we would be wrong in speaking of unconscious inferences, i.e., of inferences the premises of which remained unconscious.

To what extent have these different attempts to prove the existence of unconscious mental phenomena complied with this third condition? I do not hesitate to say that not a single one has taken proper account of it, and I will prove this in detail with respect to the most important ones.

Like Hamilton,† many philosophers have deduced the hypothesis of unconscious ideas from the fact that, when an earlier train of ideas is recalled, sometimes a whole series of intermediate steps appears to be skipped over. This fact would undoubtedly be reconciled with the laws of association if we were to assume that the intermediate steps in question had intervened on this occasion but without appearing in consciousness. Neither Hamilton nor others, however, have shown, or have even tried to show, that this is the only possible method of explanation. Actually, this is by no means the case. In his critique of Hamilton,‡ John Stuart Mill was able to offer two other explanations without any difficulty. In addition, in our discussion of the association of ideas[5] we shall see that the number of these possible hypotheses, of which sometimes one and sometimes another appears to be the most probable, can be increased considerably.

With regard to the phenomenon of the blind spot, of which we shall have to speak again later, Lange remarks§ that the eye infers the color which seemingly fills this spot, and that through further and properly performed experiments it discovers its deception. In this case, therefore, we would have an unconscious act of thinking, for

---

* A so-called "instinctive" judgement.
† *Lecture on Metaphysics*, I, 244 f.
‡ *Examination of Sir William Hamilton's Philosophy*, Chap. 15; and James Mill, *Analysis of the Phenomena of the Human Mind*, 2nd ed., note 34 (I, 352 ff.) (I, 106 ff.).
§ *Geschichte der Materialimus*, 1st ed., pp. 494 ff. Cp. also E. Weber, *Ueber den Raumsinn und die Empfindungskreise in der Haut und im Auge* (Report of the Royal Saxon Society of Sciences, 1852, p. 158).
[5] See Brentano, "Das Genie." Brentano derives the so-called laws of the association of ideas, as James did after him, from the law of habituation. He formulates it as follows: "One experience of a mental phenomenon facilitates the recurrence of the same or a similar phenomenon under the same or similar circumstances."
In the special case of presentations: "A presentation experienced on one occasion will enter into consciousness again if all or some of the phenomena connected with it before, or similar ones are given."

we are in no way conscious of the intermediate inferential processes.*
I leave it undecided whether the explanation given by Lange even
satisfies the first condition that it should itself seem to be possible in
every respect, even though there is much to make us doubt it. In any
case, Lange has failed to exclude the possibility of any other hypothesis. If he had paid attention to the laws of association, he would
have found, as we shall find later on, that these laws readily explain
both the occurrence of this phenomenon without unconscious false
inference, as well as its disappearance without an unconscious
correction.

Helmholtz† and Zollner‡ have been guilty of the same omission.
Without exception, the same is true of all the other investigators, no
matter how competent, who traced back to unconscious inferences
the spatial ideas which we connect with perceived colors on the basis
of previous experience, as well as a whole series of other optical
phenomena. They never took into account the means which psychology already offers for doing justice to the facts without such unconscious intermediate terms. It would be inappropriate to deal in
detail with these means at this time. Subsequent discussions will
familiarize us with them. For the present, it is sufficient to have
pointed out that the alleged consequences from unconscious inference cannot furnish any proof for the existence of unconscious
mental activity, as long as the impossibility or extreme improbability of any other conception has not been established, and that so
far no one has fulfilled this condition. This is true in the case of the
above mentioned optical phenomena. It is also true of the argument
that the belief in the existence of the external world, already present
at a tender age, is due to unconscious induction.§ Likewise, it is true
of the attempts that are made to conceive of every recurrence of a
thought as a consequence of unconscious processes which are just
as protracted and complicated as those we sometimes come across
when we try to recall and, progressing from one thought to another,
trace back a previous experience. Hartmann¶ has done this and

* It is not quite clear whether Lange really wants to admit an intermediate
process similar to conscious reasoning. In iii, p. 220, he says, "The eye
makes, as it were a probable inference; an inference from experience, an
imperfect induction." And on p. 222, "The eye obtains, as it were, the
consciousness that there is nothing seen at this spot, and corrects its
original wrong inference." But in the same passage he speaks of it as a
process in the purely sensory realm, which is "essentially related with
rational inferences."
† *Physiologische Optik*, pp. 430, 449 and other passages.
‡ *Ueber die Natur der Kometen*, pp. 378 ff.
§ Cp. Hartmann, pp. 286 ff.
¶ P. 25.

Maudsley,* too, seems to be of this opinion. The latter conceives of every thought which emerges in us without being the result of purposive and strenuous searching, as a product of unconscious mental activity. It is on the basis of this conception alone that he arrives at the above mentioned conclusion that "the most important part of mental action, the essential process on which thinking depends, is unconscious mental . . . activity."†

In addition, Lewes, Maudsley, and Ulrici appeal to another set of facts in support of unconscious mental phenomena. Ulrici, as we have said, simply gives another meaning to the term "unconscious," while Lewes and Maudsley understand it in the same sense as we do. Indeed, on the basis of these facts, one might be inclined to assume that such activities exist. Even though we have already spoken of these phenomena in our investigation of psychological method, we want to return to this issue once again at this point.

It frequently happens that, while absorbed in some thought, we pay no attention to our environment. In these instances, even though the environment does not seem to produce any sensation in us, the results show that we have had sensations. Maudsley says:

> Let anyone take careful note of his dreams, he will find that
> many of the seemingly unfamiliar things with which his mind is
> then occupied, and which appear to be new and strange
> productions, are traceable to the unconscious appropriations
> of the day. There are other stories on record like that
> well-known one which Coleridge quotes of the servant girl who,
> in the ravings of fever, repeated long passages in the
> Hebrew language, which she did not understand, and could
> not repeat when well, but which, when living with a Clergyman,
> she had heard him read aloud. The remarkable memories of
> certain idiots, who, much deficient in or nearly destitute of
> intelligence, will repeat the longest stories with the greatest
> accuracy, testify also to this unconscious cerebral action; and
> the way in which the excitement of a great sorrow or some
> other cause, such as the last flicker of departing life, will
> sometimes call forth in idiots manifestations of mind of which
> they always seemed incapable, renders it certain that much is
> unconsciously taken up by them which cannot be uttered, but
> which leaves its relics in the mind.‡

Ulrici gives some other remarkable examples of related phenomena:

* *Physiology and Pathology of the Mind*, pp. 16 ff., 29 ff.
† P. 34.
‡ P. 25.

It happens very often that somebody speaks to us, but we are absentminded and, therefore, at the moment do not know what he is saying. A moment later, however, we collect ourselves, and then what we have heard comes to consciousness. We walk through a street without paying attention to the sign-boards we see, to the names and advertisements which are found on them, and are not able to mention any of these names immediately afterwards. Nevertheless, perhaps several days later, if we happen to come across one of these names elsewhere, we remember that we have read it on a sign-board. Consequently, we must have had as complete a visual sensation as any other of which we are directly conscious; otherwise, we obviously could not remember it. Likewise, we often remember several days later that we have made a mistake while writing or speaking, of which we were not aware, when we were writing. Even in these cases, I must have seen the misspelled word; I must have had a complete visual sensation of it. However, since while I was writing I paid attention only to the thoughts to be written and to the connection of the words expressing them, I did not notice the slip of the pen, i.e. the wrong letter.[6] Nevertheless, the sensory impression became an integral part of myself, and when afterwards I did no longer reflect upon the thoughts to be written, but on the words that were actually written, I become conscious of the given sensory change produced by the misspelled words.*

It is easy to recognize that these and similar arguments are incapable of establishing the existence of unconscious mental activity in our sense. The hypothesis of unconscious mental phenomena is not the only hypothesis on the basis of which these phenomena can be explained. In the case of the first and third example taken from Ulrici it is sufficient to assume that a sensation, accompanied by consciousness when it first occurred, is subsequently renewed in memory, and that upon this appearance there were certain associations and other mental activities connected with this phenomenon which some particular circumstances had inhibited the first time.[7] In

---

* *Gott und der Mensch*, I, 286.
[6] It may result from a change of attention that a part of the unitary consciousness is noticed at one time and not noticed at another. See above, Notes 1 and 3. Such an unnoticed part of consciousness is not yet unconscious in the sense of not being an object of secondary consciousness.
[7] Diverted attention can also belong among these hindrances. There is to

the one example, we did not connect the proper meaning with the words we heard; in the other example, we saw the misspelled word, but did not reflect in any way upon its conformity with the rules of orthography.* The case of the signboards is even simpler. It is based solely on the fact that not only the assimilation of an impression in memory, but also its actual reproduction are connected with certain conditions which are missing at the one time but are present at the other. The subsequent similar phenomenon aroused the earlier one according to a well-known law of the association of ideas, which obviously had not been effective as long as the antecedent condition was absent.

Something quite similar is true of the first example presented by Maudsley. Certain words, which the servant girl of whom he speaks could not remember at one time, came back to her memory of their own accord at another time, obviously under circumstances which included the antecedent conditions of association absent the first time. Even though these circumstances cannot be subjected to our analysis, we must assume that they were so favorable to the association in question that they overcame the disadvantage of a relatively weak preparation. From the fact that the servant girl did not understand the sense of the words which she was hearing, it certainly does not follow that she heard without being conscious of hearing. In the same way, it becomes evident that the phenomena of exceptional memories manifested by lunatics, either during or after their mental illness, do not allow us to draw any conclusion concerning the existence of unconscious mental phenomena.†

* There is a difference between not noticing "the mistake" and not noticing "the wrong letter." Ulrici has mistakenly identified the two.

† In the same work, pp. 35 ff., Maudsley speaks of the unconscious influence of certain internal stimuli, i.e. of the unconscious mental activity stemming from the influence of internal organs, e.g. the action of the sexual organs upon the brain. This matter can be settled in an analogous way on the basis of our previous remarks concerning the existence of an unconscious influence of external stimuli. The influence of these organs produces conscious sensations with which are linked, in the special case under discussion, vivid emotions that subsequently exert a very strong influence upon the entire mental life.

Lewes cites cases, not altogether rare, in which someone falls asleep during the sermon and awakens when it abruptly ends. According to Lewes, this would prove that he has had auditory sensations, but unconsciously, for otherwise he would know what was said. The answer which

be added to Brentano's arguments the distinction between implicit and explicit perception, which he later introduced himself. – See the Supplementary Essays and the Introduction, pp. 405 ff.

Speaking of the feelings of affection and love, we sometimes say that we become suddenly aware of them, after having nourished them for a long time.* The truth is that we were conscious of each individual act when we were performing it, but that we did not reflect upon it in a way that allowed us to recognize the similarity between the mental phenomenon in question and those which are commonly called by this name.

Often we also say that someone does not know himself what he wants, because after desiring something for a long time, he is annoyed when he gets it.† We overlook, however, that in his desire this person saw only the bright and not the dark side of the desired object, so that reality did not measure up to his expectations. Or could it also be that the very desire for change makes him want what is remote and reject what is present? In addition, there are undoubtedly other hypotheses which can adequately explain this fact.

It frequently happens that mere ideas or feelings, which are not accompanied by any conscious act of will, produce bodily movements. It was thought that we could infer from this fact the existence of unconscious acts of will directed toward these movements, since it is the will which produces outward effects.‡ It is not the least bit improbable, however, that such an effect is associated with other phenomena too.§

It would be tedious to pile up still more examples. Let me, there-

* Cp. Ulrici, p. 288.
† Cp. Hartmann, *Phil. der Unbewusstsein*, p. 216.
‡ Hartmann, p. 143.
§ Hartmann's arguments to the contrary (p. 93) are a perfect example of an arbitrary *a priori* speculation, in striking contrast to the promise he made in the introduction to follow scientific method.

we have given to the examples offered by Ulrici and Maudsley also applies to these cases. They prove that the sensation was present, but do not prove that it was unconsciously present. – Lewes also cites another case. One day in a restaurant he found a waiter who had fallen asleep in the midst of the noise. He called him in vain by his last name and by his first name. However, as soon as he uttered the word "waiter," he woke up. This entitles us to conclude that the waiter also heard the first calls, but not that such calls remained unconscious. The reason why the one call woke him up while the others did not, is that such a call was connected with associations, not just of ideas but also of feelings, which were strongly grounded in habit. And these, in spite of obstacles that were present in the sleeping condition, led to a powerful excitation of mental activities. This explanation also applies to the case of Admiral Codrington who, when he was a naval cadet, could be awakened from a deep sleep only by the word "signal" (Lewes, *Physiology of Common Life*, II).

fore, add only one remark. Even if we had to admit in certain cases that we are unable to understand a phenomenon without the hypothesis of the influence of unconscious mental phenomena, the argument would have little force as long as such inability can easily be explained on the basis of the deficiency of our knowledge of the area concerned. Hartmann really goes too far when he asserts* that the connection between the will and the movement which obeys it could not possibly be a mechanical one, and that it, consequently, presupposes intermediate mental phenomena which are unconscious, especially the unconscious idea of the location of the corresponding motor nerve endings in the brain. No prudent physiologist will support this claim. We can prove that part of this connection is mechanical. The possibility of proof ends only at the point where the field of brain-physiology, which is so far inaccessible, begins. Likewise, as we have had to acknowledge repeatedly, psychology itself is still in a very backward stage. It is, therefore, altogether conceivable that with fuller knowledge of psychological laws, it will be possible to trace back to conscious phenomena, as their sufficient cause, the phenomena which have been considered to be the result of unconscious mental activity.

5. As we have said, the second way in which we could attempt to prove the existence of unconscious mental acts is by making an inference from the cause to the effect. If a given fact involves a mental phenomenon as a necessary effect, we are entitled, in the absence of a conscious phenomenon, to assume the existence of an unconscious phenomenon.

Here, too, however, there are some conditions which cannot be ignored. To begin with, we must exclude the possibility that the mental phenomenon in question actually did appear in consciousness, but was then immediately forgotten. Furthermore, we must prove that the cause in this case is just like those in other cases. Finally, even though this point is implicit in the preceding ones, it is especially important for establishing the proof that the causes which prevented the accompanying consciousness in this case, and which were obviously not present in the other cases, did not also prevent the mental phenomenon, the existence of which is to be inferred, and, in general, that no special obstacle lay in the way of this phenomenon.

If we apply this criterion to the few proofs that have been advanced on the matter under discussion, we discover that not a single one of them has been successful. We want to prove this point in detail.

When a wave strikes the seashore, we hear the roaring of the surf,

* P. 56.

and are conscious of hearing. But when only one drop is set in motion we think that we hear no sound. Nevertheless, it is said, we must assume that in this case, too, we have an auditory sensation, for the motion of the wave is the simultaneous movement of its individual drops, and the sensation of the roaring wave can only be composed of the auditory sensations produced by the drops. We hear, but we hear unconsciously.*

The fallacy in this argument is obvious. It violates the second condition which we have laid down. The effect of a sum of forces is not only quantitatively, but very often also qualitatively different from the effect of its individual components. If the temperature drops to just above zero degrees it does not change water either partially or to a smaller degree into ice; and warming water to a temperature less than eighty degrees† does not lead to a gaseous state which is different only quantitatively from its ordinary gaseous state. So even if a strong physical stimulus produces an auditory sensation, a weaker one need not necessarily result in an auditory phenomenon which is only of lesser intensity.

The following attempted demonstration is similar. "We are not able," Ulrici says, "to perceive very small objects whose size does not amount to a twentieth part of a compositor's line. . . . Nevertheless, these objects must necessarily result in a stimulation of the optic nerve, and, consequently, in a sense impression. Larger objects, in fact, become visible only because each minimal point (invisible by itself) of an illuminated colored surface sends a ray of light into the eye which affects the nerves distributed over the retina. The stronger, noticeable and conscious visual sensation, therefore, is composed, so to speak, of a number of weak, perceptible sense impressions."‡ In this form, the inference to unconscious sensations on the basis of the above mentioned premises is invalid. Such an inference, however, could be formulated in a somewhat different manner. We could say that in many similar cases the intensity of the stimulation is apparently sufficiently large to produce a sensation. If observed through the microscope, the invisible often becomes visible. Nevertheless, in passing through the refracting lens, the light stimulus is not strengthened; on the contrary, it is weakened. In addition, on account of the dispersion of the stimulus on a greater surface area, the stimu-

* This argument goes back to Leibniz. Indeed, we could say that even Zeno of Elea touched upon this problem, although he made use of it in a different sense (Commentary of Simplicius on Aristotle's *Physics*, VII, 5).
† [Editor's note: Brentano is here using the Réaumur temperature scale on which the freezing point of water is zero degrees and the boiling point eighty degrees.]
‡ *Gott und der Mensch*, p. 294.

lation from each individual point must be lessened. This is supposed to make it certain, then, that even without the help of a microscope we must experience a color phenomenon which is actually more vivid and only somewhat less extended, but which nevertheless does not become an object of consciousness.

Even in this form the argument does not satisfy the second condition. Even though the microscope does not increase the intensity of the efficient cause, it does modify it at least in some way. So similar causes are not really present. We have no right to say that, since the intensity of the stimulation was no less in the one case than in the other, a sensation must have occurred. We can just as well suppose that the stimulation of a greater area of the retina fulfilled a necessary antecedent condition of the sensation which was absent before. Perhaps the lack of demonstrative force in this argument will become clearer if we take into consideration the third condition. Why is it that the sensation which, as we are told, although more narrowly limited spatially, instead of being less strong is actually stronger, could not enter into our consciousness? We are not able to advance any reason, and it may seem more difficult to understand how the limited stimulation of the retina should have hindered the formation of consciousness, on the hypothesis that there was a sensation, rather than having hindered the sensation itself.

Of great importance seems to be the following fact. Helmholtz* reports that in so-called after-images, he has often observed characteristics which he had not perceived while seeing the object. The same thing has often happened to me, too, and anyone can easily verify the facts by his own experience. In this case the stimulation was obviously very intense, otherwise it would not have produced an after-image. Likewise, we cannot say that the retina has not been stimulated on a sufficiently extended surface, since this would also have interfered with the appearance of the after-image. It seems certain, therefore, that there must have been a sensation of the particular characteristics in question. If, however, these characteristics remained unnoticed, it seems that we have to assume that an unconscious presentation has occurred.

This argument is far from being established with absolute certainty. It does not even satisfy the first of the three conditions which we have indicated. Who, in fact, can guarantee that the phenomenon in question was not actually accompanied by consciousness, only to be forgotten immediately? Our subsequent discussion of the influence of attention on the formation of association will show that this hypothesis is entirely plausible.[8] Furthermore, the second and

* *Physiologische Optik*, p. 337.   [8] See Note 7.

third conditions are not fulfilled either. The external stimulation was, of course, sufficiently strong in itself and sufficiently extended to produce a sensation. But were the necessary antecedent mental conditions also present? Assuming this to be certain, how is it that a *conscious* sensation did not occur? Because, we are told, attention was fully concentrated on something else. Is it not possible, however, that this complete absorption in another object could have prevented the sensation itself, just as easily as our consciousness of it? To this Ulrici replies that the after-image, being merely "the after-image of a definite original image, cannot possibly contain anything more or anything different from what is already contained in this original image, i.e. in the original sense impression. The characteristics which we observe in the after-image must have also existed, therefore, in the original image with even greater strength and clearness than in the after-image."* But anyone can see that he is grasping at a straw here. The whole support for his argument rests upon the term "after-image." This term, in fact, is not supposed to mean an imitation in the sense of being simply a copy of a pre-existing model;† it was probably chosen only to indicate temporal succession. The after-image makes its appearance noticeably later than the beam of light which stimulated the retina. The fact is that the actual cause of the so-called after-image is not the previous sensation but the persistence of the previous physical stimulation or of another physical process which follows it.‡ If we assume that because of a mental obstacle the original physical stimulus did not produce any sensation, it may not have been any less enduring on that account and it may be that its consequences are no less intense. Consequently, it is by no means impossible that we should perceive after-images or parts of after-images even though we had no sensation at the time that the beam of light stimulated the retina.

6. We come to the third class of possible attempted proofs. We said that the existence of unconscious mental phenomena may also be regarded as certain, if one can prove that the consciousness of conscious mental acts is a function of their own strength, and if it is because of this relationship that in some cases where the latter is a positive magnitude the former would have to be without any positive value.

The hypothesis that the strength of the consciousness of mental phenomena is a function of their strength is found, for example, in

* *Gott und der Mensch*, p. 304; cp. ibid., p. 285.
† When, after looking at a red surface, we see a green color, we cannot say that this is really a true copy.
‡ All physiologists agree on this point, even though there are many differences of opinion among them on other aspects of this subject.

Benecke.* According to him, consciousness occurs as soon as the intensity of a presentation reaches a certain level. No one, however, will assert that Benecke or anyone else has offered a passably adequate proof for the existence of a dependent proportional relation between the two intensities.† We may also assume that the inaccuracy of our psychological measurements, which we spoke of during our investigation of psychological method,‡ creates insurmountable obstacles to the exact determination of such a functional relation. Most people, however, tend simply to equate the strengths of conscious presentations with the strength of the presentation referring to them.

In this case, however, a special circumstance seems really to permit an exact and certain proof of the intensity relationship.

The intensity of the act of presentation is always equal to the intensity with which the object that is presented appears to us; in other words, it is equal to the intensity of the phenomenon which constitutes the content of the presentation. This may be taken to be self-evident, and thus psychologists and physiologists, almost without exception, either explicitly assert it or tacitly presuppose it. Hence we saw above§ that E. H. Weber and Fechner assume that the intensity of sensation is equal to the intensity with which the physical phenomenon appears in sensation. It is only on this condition that the law they established is a psychological law.

If this is true, if the intensity of the presentation is always equal to the intensity of the phenomenon which constitutes its content, it is clear that the intensity of the presentation of a presentation must also be equal to the intensity with which this latter presentation manifests itself. So it is simply a question of how the intensity which our own conscious presentations appear to have relates to their actual intensity.[9]

But there can be no doubt in this regard. Both intensities must be equal, if inner perception is indeed infallible. Just as inner perception cannot confuse seeing and hearing, neither can it mistake a strong

* *Lehrbuch der Psychologie*, 2nd ed., Sect. 57.

† In order to prevent any possible misunderstanding, I call attention once again to the fact that what Fechner calls an unconscious presentation is nothing but a more or less insufficient *disposition* to a presentation which is connected with a certain physical process, insofar as this process, through an increase in its intensity, would be accompanied by a presentation in the proper sense of the term. The threshold below which Fechner attributes negative values to the consciousness of sensation is at the same time the threshold of the sensation itself as a real mental act.

‡ Cp. Book One, Chap. IV, pp. 66 ff. above.

§ Pp. 66 ff.

[9] See *Untersuchungen zur Sinnespsychologie*.

auditory sensation for a faint one nor a faint for a strong one. So we come to the conclusion that the intensity of the presentation of every conscious presentation is equal to the intensity of that presentation.

From this we can in fact establish a mathematical relationship between these two intensities, namely, the simple relationship of complete equality. If, however, this relation, which is the simplest of all possible functional relations, shows us that a change in the intensity of the concomitant presentation is the necessary consequence of every increase and decrease in the intensity of the mental phenomenon it accompanies, this is a far cry from proving the existence of unconscious mental acts. It is so far from it, in fact, that we have to draw the opposite conclusion instead. There are no unconscious mental acts, for wherever there exists a mental act of greater or lesser intensity, it is necessary to attribute an equal intensity to the presentation which accompanies it and of which this act is the object. This seems to be the opinion of the great majority of psychologists, and, even among those psychologists whose words make it appear that they hold the opposite view, there are some whose opposition disappears and is transformed into full agreement as soon as we translate their statements into our own terminology.

There is yet a fourth way, however, which, according to some, proves not only the falsity, but also the absurdity, of the assumption that every mental activity is conscious. Before drawing our final conclusions, let us take a look at this type of argument, too.

7. Hearing as the presentation of a sound is a mental phenomenon and certainly one of the simplest examples of one. Nevertheless, if all mental phenomena are conscious, a simple act of hearing seems not to be possible without an infinite complication of mental states.

First of all, no mental phenomenon is possible without a correlative consciousness; along with the presentation of a sound we have a presentation of the presentation of this sound at the same time. We have, therefore, *two* presentations, and presentations of very different sorts at that. If we call the presentation of a sound "hearing," we have, in addition to the presentation of this sound, a presentation of the hearing, which is as different from hearing as hearing is from sound.

But this is not the end of it. If every mental phenomenon must be accompanied by consciousness, the presentation of hearing must also be accompanied by consciousness, just as the presentation of the sound is. Consequently, there must also be a presentation of it. In the hearer, therefore, there are three presentations: a presentation of sound, a presentation of the act of hearing, and a presentation of the presentation of this act. But this third presentation cannot be the last one. Since it too is conscious, it is present in the mind and in turn its presentation is also presented. In brief, the series will either be infinite or will terminate with an unconscious presentation. It follows that those who deny the existence of unconscious mental phenomena must admit an infinite number of mental activities in the simplest act of hearing.

It also seems self-evident that the sound must be contained by way of presentation not only in the act of hearing but also in the concomitant presentation of the hearing. In addition, the sound will be presented again for a third time in the presentation of the presentation of the act of hearing, while the act of hearing will only be presented for the second time. If this is the case, we have here a new ground for infinite complexity, inasmuch as the infinite series of phenomena is not made up of equally simple phenomena, but is a series of phenomena whose individual components themselves become more and more complex, *ad infinitum*.

This hypothesis seems to be very doubtful, in fact it is obviously absurd,* and no one will want to adhere to it. So how can we possibly persist in the denial of unconscious mental acts?

If we do not suppose the existence of an unconscious consciousness, there is only *one* hypothesis which seems to allow us to avoid the conclusion that there is an infinite complication of mental life. This hypothesis assumes that the act of hearing and its object are one and the same phenomenon, insofar as the former is thought to be directed upon itself as its own object. Then either "sound" and "hearing" would be merely two names for one and the same phenomenon, or the difference in their meaning might consist only in the fact that the term "sound" is used to designate the external cause, which formerly had usually been considered to be similar to the phenomenon within the person hearing and was therefore said to manifest itself in the act of hearing, while in fact it eludes our presentation.

Several English psychologists advocate such a view. In the previous chapter, we discussed a passage by Alexander Bain in which this philosopher fully identifies the act and the object of touch sensations, and indicates that the same relation of identity between the act and the object of the act applies to all the other types of sense-impressions. Certain remarks of John Stuart Mill's seem to reveal this same view.† But neither does this view seem to me to be true, nor if it were true, would it completely eliminate the difficulty. I claim that it is incorrect, because inner perception shows us with immediate evidence

* In recent times Herbart has touched upon these difficulties (*Psychologie als Wissenschaft*, Part Two, Sect. II, Chap. 5, No. 127; cp. ibid., Part One, Sect. I, Chap. 2, No. 27). In antiquity Aristotle has emphasized them (*De Anima*, III, 2), but did not regard them as insurmountable.

† Both in his work on the philosophy of Hamilton and in his notes to James Mill's *Analysis*.

that hearing has a content[10] different from itself, and which, in contradistinction to hearing, shares none of the characteristics of mental phenomena. This is why nobody understands the term "sound" to mean another act of hearing discoverable outside of us which, by means of its action on the ear, produces our hearing as a copy of itself. Likewise, no one understands it to mean a force, incapable of being present to our minds, which produces hearing, or else we would not speak of sounds which appear in imagination. On the contrary, this term refers to the phenomenon which constitutes the immanent object of our hearing, an object different from the act of hearing. And depending on whether or not we believe that it has a corresponding cause outside of us, we believe that a sound does or does not exist in the external world as well.

The occasions for the rise of this opinion, which so clearly contradicts inner experience and the judgement of every unprejudiced person, seems to lie in the fact that people formerly believed that when they were conscious of hearing they had, not only a presentation of a sound in addition to the presentation of hearing, but also an immediate knowledge of the existence of a sound in addition to immediate knowledge of the existence of hearing. It was thought that we perceive the sound with the same evidence as we perceive the hearing.[11] This belief was subsequently recognized to be false, since a sound is never contrasted with hearing as an external object which is perceptible by means of hearing. But people had become accustomed to thinking of hearing as a cognitive act and of the content of hearing as a real object, and since hearing was the only thing that proved to be real,[12] they came to regard hearing as its own object. This was an error in the opposite direction. Even if, in the act of hearing, nothing is perceived in the proper sense of the term but hearing itself, this does not make it any the less true that something else besides hearing itself is present within it as presented and constitutes its content.

Furthermore, even if this interpretation were correct, it would still be easy to prove that it cannot entirely eliminate the difficulty with which we are dealing. Even granting that the act of hearing has nothing but itself as its content, no one could assume the same thing of other mental acts, such as acts of memory and expectation, e.g. the remembrance of a past or the expectation of a future auditory experience, without being guilty of the most palpable absurdity.

[10] Content = object.

[11] See what was said in the Introduction on the subject of Husserl's later theory.

[12] Here *real* means the same as "actual" (*wirklich*) or "existing" (*seiend*), and not "thing-ish" (*dinglich*) or "substantival" (*wesenhaft*). See Introduction, p. 380.

John Stuart Mill himself says in a passage where he also makes known his views on sensation which we have rejected, "A sensation involves only this; but a remembrance of sensation . . . involves the suggestion and belief that a sensation, of which it is a copy or representation, actually existed in the past; and an expectation involves the belief, more or less positive, that a sensation or other feeling to which it directly refers, will exist in the future."* If this is true and undeniable, the same objection which was overcome in the case of hearing by identifying hearing and what is heard, looms up again in all its original strength in connection with the remembrance and expectation of hearing. If there are no unconscious mental phenomena, then, when I remember having heard something, in addition to the presentation of hearing I have a presentation of the present remembering of hearing, which is not identical with it. This last presentation, however, must also be conscious, and how would this be conceivable without the assumption of a third presentation which has the same relation to it as it has to the remembering? This third presentation, however, would likewise demand a fourth, and so on, *ad infinitum*. It seems impossible, therefore, that we can avoid assuming an infinite complexity of mental phenomena in a great number of very simple cases, if we consider every mental phenomenon conscious. In his work on Comte, while opposing Comte's assertion that the intellect cannot perceive its own acts, Mill says that the mind is able to comprehend more than *one* impression at the same time – in fact even a considerable number of impressions (no less than six, according to Hamilton). The mind, however, does not have the power to grasp an infinite number of presentations. Indeed, it would be absurd to ascribe such a power to it. So the assumption that there are unconscious mental phenomena seems to be unavoidable.

Still there is one thing which immediately makes us suspect that the difficulty may not be completely insoluble. In different epochs, great thinkers have encountered this difficulty, but only a few, because of it, have assumed the existence of unconscious mental activities. Aristotle, who first called attention to the problem, did not do so. Recently, Herbart inferred from it the necessity of the existence of unconscious presentations,† but he did so only after establishing the

* *An Examination of Sir William Hamilton's Philosophy*, Chap. 12.
† "Among the numerous masses of ideas, of which each successive member is apperceptive of the preceding one, or of which the third may take for its object the connection or the opposition of the first and the second, there must be one which is the last. *This highest apperception will not itself be apperceived further.*" *Psychologie als Wissenschaft*, Part Two, Sect. II, Chap. 5, No. 199.

existence of unconscious mental phenomena by means of other arguments. Besides, it is known that he all too readily finds merely apparent contradictions unresolvable. To my knowledge, the only important philosopher who seems to have been led to the assumption of unconscious mental activities by at least a similar route, was Thomas Aquinas. And his theory is such that we may doubt whether he gave his mature consideration to this question.*

* According to St. Thomas Aquinas, we are conscious of the sensations of the so-called five senses. The senses themselves, he believes, cannot, of course, perceive their own acts. That would imply a reflection upon their own acts, an action of the organs upon themselves, since St. Thomas considers sensations as functions of these organs. He considers such action impossible because a corporeal thing never acts upon itself to modify itself. According to St. Thomas, therefore, that which perceives the acts of the external senses is an inner sense faculty different from them, the *sensus communis* (*Summa Theologica*, P. I, Q. 78, A. 4, ad. 2; ibid., Q. 87, a. 3, obj. 3 and ad. 3). But this inner sense, like its corresponding object, is corporeal. It cannot, therefore, perceive its own activity. Since St. Thomas has not assumed still another new sense and another new organ, by which we could perceive the acts of the inner sense, it follows that, according to his doctrine, the perception of the sensory acts of the external senses will never be perceived, and consequently that, in the field of our senses, we immediately come upon unconscious mental activity. Undoubtedly, he could have easily added a second and third inner sense, but what would he have gained by this? Without the hypothesis of a really infinite number of senses and sense organs, which could not possibly be contained in a finite body, he could not sustain the universality of consciousness for all sensory acts, on the basis of his principles.

St. Thomas's theory of the consciousness of intellectual thinking is entirely different. The intellect (*intellectus*) is considered by him as immaterial and consequently capable of reflection upon itself. From this point of view, therefore, nothing prevents it from knowing its own acts. There arises, however, another difficulty: the intellect, as St. Thomas conceives it, cannot think more than *one* thought at a time. One potency never contains more than *one* act. St. Thomas extricates himself from this embarrassing position by asserting that the consciousness of a thought, rather than coexisting with the thought itself, follows it. In this way, according to him, if no act of thinking can remain unconscious, instead of a series of simultaneous acts we have a series of successive acts in which each act is related to a previous act. According to St. Thomas, therefore, we can admit without absurdity that the elements of this series multiply to infinity (*Summa Theologica*, P. I, Q. 87, A. 3, 2 and ad. 2). Actually this will never be the case. Thus, also here the last term of the series is an act of thinking which is and remains unconscious.

I want to point out quite briefly some essential difficulties of this theory. First of all, it is inconsistent for St. Thomas to give an entirely different theory for the consciousness of sensory activity and for the consciousness

It still seems, therefore, that there is a way out which allows us to avoid the conclusion that there is unconscious consciousness.

8. Let us, therefore, consider the matter once again and with the utmost precision.

There are undoubtedly occasions when we are conscious of a mental phenomenon while it is present in us; for example, while we have the presentation of a sound, we are conscious of having it. Now the question arises, in such a case, do we have several hetero-

---

of intellectual activity because, according to the testimony of inner experience, the two phenomena appear to be completely analogous. In addition, each of these two theories raises serious doubts. We are never supposed to be conscious that we are conscious of hearing, seeing, etc. Even this appears to be a difficult hypothesis. Another circumstance, however, proves even more clearly the impossibility of this conception. According to St. Thomas, the relation of the inner sense to its object is entirely identical with the relation of the external sense to the cause which produces a sensation. This is contradicted by the infallible evidence of inner perception, which is entirely absent in external perception. The inner perception of sensations could not possibly be immediately evident if it had for its object a state which is foreign to it, i.e. the state of an organ which is different from its own organ. Equally unsatisfactory is the theory of the consciousness of intellectual activity. According to this theory, we would be conscious only of past acts of thinking, never of the present act of thinking, an assertion which is not consistent with experience. If this were true, in the strict sense of the term we could not speak of an inner perception of our own thinking. Rather it would simply be a matter of some kind of memory which would relate to an immediately past act. It would follow, therefore, that here too the immediate infallible evidence of inner perception would be incomprehensible. In addition, how would we perceive the act of thinking? As present or past or undetermined as to time? Not as present, because perception would then be false. Not as undetermined, for otherwise it would not be a cognition of an individual act. Therefore, as past. This shows clearly that the perception of the act of thinking must be considered not only as something similar to memory, but as memory pure and simple. It would certainly be strange if we should subsequently have a recollection of something which we had not noticed when it was present.

Finally, let us remark that according to the Thomistic theory of the cognition of one's own intellectual acts there would exist not only some acts of which we will not be conscious even though we could be conscious of them, but also, just as in the case of sensations, acts of which we cannot possibly be conscious, unless we ascribe to the intellect an infinite power, an ability for an infinitely complicated thought process. "*Alius est actus,*" St. Thomas says, "*quo intellectus intelligit lapidem, et alius est actus, quo intelligit se intelligere lapidem; et sic deinde.*" The series of intellectual acts, therefore, becomes endlessly more complex in an increasing arithmetical progression.

geneous presentations or only a single one? Before answering this question we must become clear about whether we want to determine the number and the variety of presentations according to the number and variety of objects, or according to the number of mental acts in which the objects are presented. On the first alternative it is clear that we must say that in the case under consideration we would have several presentations and that they are of different kinds; so much so that one of them constitutes the content of another, while having a physical phenomenon as its own content. If this were true, the physical phenomenon must, to a certain extent, belong to the content of both of these presentations, to that of one as its explicit object, to that of the other as, so to speak, its implicit object. It would seem, therefore, as Aristotle also noted, to turn out that the physical phenomenon must be presented twice. Yet this is not the case. Rather, inner experience seems to prove undeniably that the presentation of the sound is connected with the presentation of the presentation of the sound in such a peculiarly intimate way that its very existence constitutes an intrinsic prerequisite for the existence of this presentation.

This suggests that there is a special connection between the object of inner presentation and the presentation itself, and that both belong to one and the same mental act. We must in fact assume this. Referring back to the example, we have to answer the question of whether there is more than one presentation affirmatively, if we determine them according to the number of objects; with the same certainty, however, we have to answer this question negatively if we determine these presentations according to the number of mental acts in which objects are presented. The presentation of the sound and the presentation of the presentation of the sound form a single mental phenomenon; it is only by considering it in its relation to two different objects, one of which is a physical phenomenon and the other a mental phenomenon, that we divide it conceptually into two presentations. In the same mental phenomenon in which the sound is present to our minds we simultaneously apprehend the mental phenomenon itself. What is more, we apprehend it in accordance with its dual nature insofar as it has the sound as content within it, and insofar as it has itself as content at the same time.*

---

* *De Anima*, III, 2, 425 b 12. "Since it is through sense that we are aware that we are seeing or hearing, it must be either by sight that we are aware of seeing, or by some sense other than sight. But the sense that gives us this new sensation must perceive both sight and its object, viz. color: so that either (1) there will be two senses both percipient of the same sensible object, or (2) the sense must be percipient of itself." [Engl. trans. J. A. Smith, in *The Works of Aristotle*, ed. W. D. Ross, Vol. III.]

We can say that the sound is the *primary object* of the *act* of hearing, and that the act of hearing itself is the *secondary object*. Temporally they both occur at the same time, but in the nature of the case, the sound is prior. A presentation of the sound without a presentation of the act of hearing would not be inconceivable, at least *a priori*, but a presentation of the act of hearing without a presentation of the sound would be an obvious contradiction. The act of hearing appears to be directed toward sound in the most proper sense of the term, and because of this it seems to apprehend itself incidentally and as something additional.

9. If this is correct it enables us to explain several remarkable phenomena and to answer the last objection against the hypothesis that all mental phenomena are conscious, as well as the other objections mentioned above.

Do we perceive the mental phenomena which exist within us? This question must be answered with an emphatic, "yes," for where would we have got the concepts of presentation and thought without such perception? On the other hand, it is obvious that we are not able to observe our present mental phenomena. But how can we explain this, if not by the fact that we are incapable of perceiving them? Previously, in fact, no other explanation seemed possible, but now we see the true reason clearly. The presentation which accompanies a mental act and refers to it is part of the object on which it is directed. If an *inner presentation* were ever to become inner observation, this observation would be directed upon itself. Even the defenders of inner observation, however, seem to consider this impossible. In arguing, against Comte, that it is possible to observe ourselves in the act of observing, John Stuart Mill appeals to our ability[13] to devote attention to *more than one thing* simultaneously.*

One observation is supposed to be capable of being directed upon another observation, but not upon itself. The truth is that something which is only the *secondary object of an act* can undoubtedly be an object of consciousness in this act, but cannot be an object of observation in it. Observation requires that one turn his attention to an object as a primary object.[14] Consequently, an act existing within us could only be observed by means of a second, simultaneous act directed toward it as its primary object. There just is no such accompanying inner presentation of a second act, however. Thus we see that no simultaneous observation of one's own act of observation or of any other of one's own mental acts is possible at all. We can ob-

* In his essay on *August Comte and Positivism*, Part I.
[13] Correcting a mistake in the first edition, which has "activity" here.
[14] On this point see Book One, Chap. 2, p. 29, together with the note, and the Introduction, pp. 405 ff.

serve the sounds we hear, but we cannot observe our hearing of the sounds, for the hearing itself is only apprehended concomitantly in the hearing of sounds. On the other hand, when we recall a previous act of hearing, we turn toward it as a primary object, and thus we sometimes turn toward it as observers. In this case, our act of remembering is the mental phenomenon which can be apprehended only secondarily.* The same holds true with regard to the perception of all other mental phenomena.

Thus, of the contradictory opinions which we have discussed above† – those of Comte, Maudsley and Lange on the one hand, and those of the great majority of psychologists on the other – the truth, as the saying goes, lies somewhere in between.

There is another question. When we have a presentation of a sound or another physical phenomenon and are conscious of this presentation, are we also conscious of this consciousness or not? Thomas Aquinas has denied this to a great extent. But any unbiased person will at least at first be inclined to answer this question affirmatively. He may begin to hesitate only when it is pointed out to him that in this case he would have to have a threefold consciousness, like three boxes, one inside the other, and that besides the first presentation and the presentation of the presentation he must also have a presentation of the presentation of the presentation. This hypothesis seems cumbersome and contrary to experience. The results of our investigation show how this conclusion is erroneously arrived at. These results show that the consciousness of the presentation of the sound clearly occurs together with the consciousness of this consciousness, for the consciousness which accompanies the presentation of the sound is a consciousness not so much of this presentation as of the whole mental act in which the sound is presented, and in which the consciousness itself exists concomitantly. Apart from the fact that it presents the physical phenomenon of sound, the mental act of hearing becomes at the same time its own object and content, taken as a whole.

In view of this, we can easily deal with the last attempt mentioned above to prove the existence of unconscious mental phenomena. An infinite complication of mental states was supposed to be entailed if every mental phenomenon were accompanied by a presentation

---

* This circumstance makes it more comprehensible how Thomas Aquinas could make the mistake of thinking of the consciousness which is concomitant with thinking as a consciousness which is subsequent to thinking, and regarding the consciousness of this consciousness as a third member of a series of reflexive acts in which each subsequent member refers to the one that precedes it.

† Book One, Chap. 2.

referring to it. And for a moment it seemed as if such an infinite complication was unavoidable. But if this opinion is so completely absurd, how can we explain the fact that almost everyone has espoused it, and that even among the philosophers who have accepted the existence of unconscious mental acts, very few have called attention to this absurdity? From the very beginning, then, we assumed that there had to be a way out of this impasse. And now we see clearly that this assumption was correct, and that it is truly unnecessary to infer this infinite complication. Far from having to absorb an infinite series of presentations which become more and more complicated, we see that the series ends with the second member.

10. The characteristic fusion of the accompanying presentation with its object, as we have described it, has indeed been recognized by the great majority of psychologists,* even though they have rarely discussed it in a thorough and precise way. And this was undoubtedly the reason that some did not see the difficulty and others were not disconcerted by it.

Aristotle is undoubtedly in the latter category. He pointed out the apparent necessity of an infinite series of mental states in almost the same way we did. But it did not occur to him to assume the existence of unconscious mental states on that account. On the contrary, he immediately draws the conclusion that a conscious mental phenomenon must involve consciousness of itself at the same time.†

He offers several explanations of this conception as it applies to sensations, but none of them is entirely satisfactory. It is quite certain, he says, that we perceive things in more than one way through sight, hearing, and so on. Through sight we perceive not only light but also darkness, through hearing not only sounds but silence, not only noise but stillness, the absence of any noise – but not in the same way. As has been proved, then, different types of perception are involved in sight, hearing, etc. So it is quite conceivable that through sight we perceive not only colors but also the act of seeing, through hearing not only sound but also the act of hearing, even though this last perception is not really an act of hearing. Furthermore, sound is immanently present in the act of hearing it and also in its sounding.‡ These two acts are related to each

---

* Very recently by Bergmann, *Grundlinien einer Theorie des Bewusstseins* (Berlin, 1870), Chaps. 1 and 2.

† *De Anima*, III, ii, 425 b 16–17. "Further, even if the sense which perceives sight were different from sight, we must either fall into an infinite regress, or we must somewhere assume a sense which is aware of itself." [Engl. trans. J. A. Smith.]

‡ [Translators' note: There is no really adequate English equivalent to the

other as action and passion. Therefore, in actuality they always exist simultaneously. We can only say that something actually produces a sound if there also exists a subject who actually hears this sound. Otherwise, we could only speak of the possibility of a sound's being produced. Sounding and hearing a sound, like an action and its corresponding passion generally, are actually one and the same thing; being conceptually correlative, they cannot be thought of except together in one and the same act.*

The comparison between the perception of the act of hearing and the perception of silence through hearing is not very much to the point. And calling the pair of concepts, hearing and sounding,

* *De Anima*, III, 2, 425 b 20–426 a 20. "It is clear therefore that 'to perceive by sight' has more than one meaning; for even when we are not *seeing*, it is by sight that we discriminate darkness from light, though not in the same way as we distinguish one color from another. Further, in a sense even that which sees is colored; for in each case the sense-organ is capable of receiving the sensible object without its matter. That is why even when the sensible objects are gone the sensings and imaginings continue to exist in the sense-organs.

"The activity of the sensible object and that of the percipient sense is one and the same activity, and yet the distinction between their being remains. Take as illustration actual sound and actual hearing; a man may have hearing and yet not be hearing, and that which has a sound is not always sounding. But when that which can hear is actively hearing and that which can sound is sounding, then the actual hearing and the actual sound are merged in one (these one might call respectively hearing and sounding).

"If it is true that the movement, both the acting and the being acted upon, is to be found in that which is acted upon, both the sound and the hearing so far as it is actual must be found in that which has the faculty of hearing; for it is in the passive factor that the actuality of the active or motive factor is realized; that is why that which causes movement may be at rest. . . . The same account applies to the other senses and their objects. For as the-acting-and-being-acted-upon is to be found in the passive, not in the active factor, so also the actuality of the sensible object and that of the sensitive subject are both realized in the latter. . . . Since the actualities of the sensible object and of the sensitive faculty are *one* actuality in spite of the difference between their modes of being, actual hearing and actual sounding appear and disappear from existence at one and the same moment, and so actual savor and actual tasting, etc., while as potentialities one of them may exist without the other." [Engl. trans. J. A. Smith.]

German expression "das Tönen des Tones." A particular example comes closer to reproducing in English the generic sense intended in German and in Aristotle's original Greek: A buzz buzzes and is heard; it is immanent in both the buzzing and the hearing.]

instances of action and passion is completely mistaken. The concept of sound is not a relative concept. If it were, the act of hearing would not be the secondary object of the mental act, but instead it would be the primary object along with the sound. And the same would be true in every other case, which is evidently contrary to Aristotle's own view.* Likewise, we could not think of anything except certain relations to ourselves and our thoughts, and this is undoubtedly false. But if Aristotle speaks, at the very least, inaccurately in this passage, elsewhere we find the correct view expressed by him with utmost clarity. Thus in the twelfth book of the *Metaphysics*, he says, "Knowledge, sensation, opinion and reflection seem always to relate to something else, but only incidentally to themselves."† Here it is apparent that his conception agrees entirely with our own and he undoubtedly had this conception in mind when he wrote the above quoted passage in which he rejected the infinite complication of mental activity as an unjustified inference. However, since he wanted here to make the peculiar union in one single act between the act of hearing and the perception of this act clear and vivid, and since he did not find suitable analogies for doing this, he simply happened to place this union in a false light.

It is easy to persuade ourselves that psychologists are almost universally inclined toward a similar viewpoint. John Stuart Mill,

---

* Otherwise he would admit that we see not only color but the act of seeing and he would not, insofar as the act of seeing apprehends itself, ascribe to the ὄψις a second kind of αἰσθάνεσθαι ("ἀλλ οὐχ ὡσαύτως").
† *Metaphysics*, XII, 9. Cp. also *Metaphysics* I, 7, 1072 b 20. Other passages give the impression that Aristotle, like Thomas Aquinas, admits a special inner sense for sensations and in this way was unfaithful to the theory that the sensation and the concomitant inner presentation are fused into *one* act. Indeed, it seems that his general theory of psychical faculties can be more easily reconciled with this sort of view. It is for this reason that in my *Psychologie des Aristoteles* I went along with the majority of his commentators and ascribed it to him. However, since the passage of *De Anima*, III, 2, speaks so clearly against it, and since it is highly unlikely that there is a contradiction among his different statements on this point, I adhere now to the conception presented here in the text. In his work, *Die Einheit des Seelenlebens aus den Principien der Aristotelischen Philosophie entwickelt* (Freiburg, 1873),[15] Herman Schell has attempted with a great deal of acumen to reconcile the statements which contradict this passage, and also to bring Aristotle's views on act and potency into accord with it. Cp. also below Book Two, Chap. 3, Sect. 5.
[15] H. Schell dedicated this work to his teacher Brentano. Later Schell became the leader of the German Modernism movement. His works were put on the Index: spiritual shock led to his premature death. He died in 1906.

whose diverging opinion on sensations we have already met and attempted to refute, expresses a conviction with regard to remembrances and expectations which is congruent with ours. He ascribes to them (and how could he do otherwise?), as their content, a phenomenon which is distinct from them, and thought to be earlier or later; but he believes that at the same time they are their own object, since in this regard he thinks they are in no way different from sensations. "In themselves," he says, "they are present feelings, states of present consciousness, and in that respect not distinguished from sensations."* If we recall Mill's doctrine concerning sensations, and especially the way in which, according to him, we are conscious of them, we see that he could not agree with us more clearly. Bain is undoubtedly of the same opinion. Lotze, too, believes that a consciousness of the mental phenomena which exist in us is given in the phenomena themselves. In fact, we may say that among all those who deny the existence of unconscious mental phenomena (in our sense of the term) no one holds a different opinion. Among them too is Ulrici who accordingly says explicitly that "all our sensations are simultaneously the soul's sensations of itself."† And even most of those who do not think all mental phenomena are conscious agree with us, as for example, Beneke who does not believe that the correlative consciousness which accompanies a mental phenomenon is added to it as a second, distinct act; rather, he believes that it exists along with the phenomenon itself, as a distinct mode and quality of it.‡ The universality of this conviction is obviously the reason that the fourth way of demonstrating the existence of unconscious mental phenomena has been adopted so rarely, and it confirms in a welcome manner the correctness of our analysis.

11. The characteristically intimate union of the mental act with the accompanying presentation which refers to it made it possible for us to refute the last type of attempt to prove the existence of unconscious mental acts. Let us see whether we can obtain further information from it.

We have already discussed the question of the existence of a functional relation between the intensity of conscious mental phenomena and the intensity of the accompanying presentations directed toward them. It was clear that the usual view was favorable to such a hypothesis, since whenever presentations of the presentations accompany them it is customary to attribute to them the same

---

* *An Examination of Sir William Hamilton's Philosophy*, Chap. 12.
† *Gott und der Mensch*, I, 284.
‡ *Lehrbuch der Psychologie*, 2nd ed., Sect. 57.

degree of intensity. A closer examination confirmed this opinion. Even though our line of argument was not very complicated, we still cannot believe that it represents the way in which the opinion is commonly formed. So we were not in a position at that point to explain the origin of this opinion. If I am not mistaken, we are now in a position to provide the missing explanation.

If we see a color and have a presentation of our act of seeing, the color which we see is also present in the presentation of this act. This color is the content of the presentation of the act of seeing, but it also belongs to the content of the seeing.*[16] Consequently, if the presentation of the act of seeing were more or less intense than the seeing itself, the color would be present to the mind with a different intensity than in the seeing. If, on the other hand, the color makes its appearance with the same intensity both insofar as it is seen and insofar as it belongs to the content of the presentation of the seeing of it, then the act of seeing and presentation of this act will be equal in intensity. This, then, gives us an obvious clue as to our judgement. We have recognized that the act of seeing and the presentation of this act are connected in such a way that the color, as the content of the act of seeing, contributes at the same time to the content of the presentation of the presentation of this act. The color, therefore, even though it is present to the mind both in the act of seeing and in the presentation of the seeing, is still presented only once.† It is self-evident, therefore, that there can be no question of a difference of intensity. This explains very simply the origin of the common belief, which now appears fully justified, that the act of seeing and the presentation of this act do not differ from each other in intensity. Consequently, if the strength of a conscious sensation or another conscious presentation increases or decreases, the strength of the accompanying inner presentation referring to it increases or decreases to the same degree, so that both phenomena always have the same degree of intensity.

12. Still there is an objection. If the intensity of the presentation of the act of hearing always increases and decreases to the same degree as the intensity of the hearing, it follows that, when the intensity of the act of hearing becomes zero, the intensity of the accompanying presentation will also become zero. The opposite, however, seems to be true. Otherwise how would we be able to perceive that we are *not* hearing as we do when noticing the rests in music and their lengths, and when noticing that complete silence – the cessation of all noise –

* Cp. above, Sect 8.
† Cp. above, Sect. 8.
[16] The color comes before the mind in *secondary* consciousness in *modo obliquo.*

has occurred! The presentation of non-hearing appears to be quite intense. Thus, it happens that the miller who sleeps peacefully through the clatter of the mill is awakened from his deepest sleep if the mill suddenly stops. The same phenomenon occurs in the case previously quoted from Lewes in which the listener who slept peacefully through the sermon awakened at its end, even before the noise of the congregation getting to its feet could wake him.

This objection may indeed cause some doubt for a moment, since it appears not merely to endanger the theory which we have just advocated, but actually seems to prove the existence of perceptions which do not have a positive object. The absence of hearing is obviously not a positive object. Upon closer examination, however, we do find an answer to this objection. If we have a presentation of a rest and of the length of the rest in a piece of music, the notes by which the rest is surrounded appear to us with their different temporal determinations. After being presented, as such, each sound continues to be before the mind for a certain time as past, and as past to a greater or lesser degree.[17] It is the magnitude of this difference which constitutes the so-called length of the rest. Thus we still have a presentation of notes just as we do when continuous music is present to our minds. It is just that notes of a certain intermediate temporal determination are not present. Since we do have a presentation of sounds, it is in no way surprising that it is accompanied by an equally intense presentation referring to it.

The perception of sudden silence is a similar but simpler phenomenon. A noise, which formerly appeared as present, appears now as immediately past, even if no noise appears as present. And the presentation of the noise which appeared as past is accompanied, according to our previous conclusions, by an equally intense presentation.

Perhaps the reply will be made that this explanation is not sufficient. As long as the mill continues to clatter, the miller has the presentation of a clattering which appears as immediately past, just as much as he would if the mill were beginning to stop. It is only that he also has a presentation which appears as present. Thus he has the presentation which, on our view, woke him up when the mill stopped, and another one besides. Consequently, we would still be without a cause which would really explain his awakening; and we will continue to be without one until we decide to admit a special perception of the absence of hearing. This situation is actually similar to that of a color which sometimes fills a larger space and sometimes

[17] On Brentano's theory of the origin of our direct perception of space, see "Zur Lehre von Raum und Zeit" and Kraus, *Franz Brentano*, p. 35. See also the Supplementary Essays.

a smaller one which is a part of the larger. Just as in the latter instance color appears more limited in space, the noise, upon stopping, appears more limited in time. In both instances, the image is changed, the contours are disturbed. Likewise, just as it can happen that the smaller colored surface can attract our attention, while it would not do so if it were more extended, something of the same sort can be true of noise. It will depend upon the particular associations which are bound up with these two phenomena. As soon as the wheel stops, the miller has the duty to do something about the interruption, although he can leave the mill to itself as long as the mechanism functions normally. So we can understand why the cessation of noise awakens him somewhat as we understand why the waiter in Lewes' case can be awakened more easily by calling him "waiter" than by any other name because it is by means of it that his services are usually requested.

We could discuss this issue more thoroughly, and in particular we could refer to the fact that the contour ordinarily draws attention to itself. The competition of visual fields offers so many striking examples of this fact. It seems better, however, to reserve this matter for later consideration.

13. Our previous conclusion, therefore, remains unchanged. If the strength of a conscious presentation increases and decreases, the strength of the accompanying presentation which refers to it increases and decreases to the same degree, and both phenomena always have the same level of intensity.

If correct, this conclusion not only refutes any possible attempt to prove the existence of unconscious presentations on the basis of the functional relation under discussion, but, as we have already indicated above, it can be regarded as a proof that there really are no unconscious presentations in our sense of the term. This, of course, does not yet show that all mental phenomena are accompanied, during their existence, by consciousness. There are other mental phenomena besides presentations – judgement and desire, for example. We have, nevertheless, taken an important step toward this conclusion.

And how will it be possible for us to supply the missing steps? Analogy could lead us to suppose that in the case of other conscious mental activities there is also a functional relation between their own intensity and the intensity of the accompanying consciousness which refers to them, indeed, the same relation of simple equality which we have demonstrated in the case of conscious presentation. But if by the intensity of a judgement we mean the degree of confidence[18] with

[18] Brentano later rejected the attempt to interpret degrees of conviction as levels of the judgement's intensity. (See *The Origin of our Knowledge of Right and Wrong*, p. 54.)

which it is made, experience teaches us that a weak opinion can be accompanied by a presentation which is just as strong as, if not stronger than, that which accompanies complete conviction, provided only that the presentation on which the opinion is based is quite strong. Upon further reflection, we shall easily recognize that we can in no way speak of an equality, nor of a greater or lesser intensity, of a presentation in comparison with the strength of a conviction, and that we are dealing here with differences which are in no way comparable.

Nevertheless, if it is true that the strength of the presentation of judgements cannot be compared with the degree of acceptance or rejection involved in the judgement, it is still certain that judgements have intensities which make comparisons possible. Just as the intensity of the presentation of an object is equal to the intensity with which the object appears in it, judgement also participates in the intensity of its content. The intensity of the presentation on which the judgement is based, is at the same time an intensity of judgement in the same sense. If we now compare this intensity with the intensity of the accompanying presentation which refers to the judgement, we can easily demonstrate, on the basis of the twofold procedure by means of which we proved the equality of the intensities of presentations and presentation of presentations, that the same relation is present in this case.[19] It emerges first as a consequence of the infallibility of inner perception, and is further confirmed by the fact that the presentation of the judgement appears to be connected with judgement in the same way as the presentations of presentations appear to be connected with these presentations. The content of judgement belongs not only to judgement itself, but also to its presentation without undergoing any kind of duplication. Consequently, there is no possibility left for a difference in intensity. What is true of judgement, however, is also true for the same reasons of any other kind of conscious mental activity.

The functional relation which we have discovered in the conscious presentation, between its intensity and the intensity of the inner presentation referring to it, may consequently be extended to the whole field of conscious mental phenomena. The accompanying phenomenon and the one it accompanies have the same intensity throughout and this proves that there never exists within us a mental phenomenon of which we have no presentation.

The question, "Is there unconscious consciousness?" in the sense in which we have formulated it, is, therefore, to be answered with a firm, "No."

[19] On Brentano's theory of intensity, see the *Untersuchungen zur Sinnespsychologie*.

III

Further Considerations Regarding Inner Consciousness

---

1. The investigations of the preceding chapter have revealed that every mental act is accompanied by a consciousness which refers to it. But a question now arises as to the complexity and nature of this accompanying consciousness.

Perhaps it would be well to clarify this question briefly.

As we explained earlier, we use the term "consciousness" to refer to any mental phenomenon, insofar as it has a content.[1] There are, however, different kinds of mental phenomena; as we have already mentioned, there are various ways of having something as content. Thus the question arises whether mental phenomena, when they are objects of consciousness, are consciously before the mind in one way or in several different ways, and if so, in which ways. Up to now, it has been shown only that we have presentations of them, and if they are in any way conscious, they must naturally be conscious in this way, since presentations are the foundations of all other mental phenomena. Our present problem is whether mental phenomena are merely objects of presentation or whether they can be in our consciousness in still other ways.

What is certain is that knowledge frequently accompanies mental phenomena. We think, we desire something, and know that we think and desire. But we only have knowledge when we make judgements. It is beyond doubt, therefore, that in many cases along with the mental act there exists within us not only a presentation which refers to it but also a judgement about it. We will now investigate whether there are cases in which such a judgement is not present.

2. No one who recalls our discussion of presentations will maintain

---

[1] Content = object.

that assuming that each mental phenomenon is the object of an accompanying cognition leads to an infinite complication of mental states and therefore would be by its very nature impossible. The characteristic fusion of consciousness and the object of consciousness is just as evident in cognition as it was there. Whenever a mental act is the object of an accompanying inner cognition, it contains itself in its entirety as presented and known, in addition to its reference to a primary object.

This alone makes possible the infallibility and immediate evidence of inner perception. If the cognition which accompanies a mental act were an act in its own right, a second act added on to the first one, if its relation to its object were simply that of an effect to its cause, similar to that which holds between a sensation and the physical stimulus which produces it, how could it be certain in and of itself? Indeed, how could we ever be sure of its infallibility at all?

It has often been said that an infallible check on perception would be possible if we were able to compare the content of the presentation with the real object. We cannot do this in so-called external perception because in this case only the presentation of the object but not the actual object exists within us.[2] External perception, therefore, is and always will be unreliable. On the other hand, we are absolutely certain of the veracity of inner perception, because in this case both the presentation and the real object of the presentation exist within us.

It is easy to recognize the error which is committed here. The comparison between the content of a presentation and a real object is not rendered possible because this object exists within us, but by the fact that it is known by us. A person could not recognize something within himself corresponding to his presentation, if he had no knowledge of that thing. The comparison, therefore, presupposes that we know with certainty the very object from which the certainty of knowledge is to be derived. This is contradictory in itself.[3]

The way in which Überweg justified his confidence in inner perception is just as unsatisfactory: "Inner perception or the immediate knowledge of mental acts and images," he says, "is able to apprehend its objects as they are in themselves with material truth. For inner perception results when the individual mental image is apprehended through association as an integral part of the totality of our mental images. . . . But the association of the individual image with others

[2] It would be less ambiguous if "object" were replaced by "thing."
[3] Cp. Alfred Kastil, *Jakob Friedrich Fries, Lehre von der unmittelbaren Erkenntnis* (Göttingen, 1912). The significance of these principles is not sufficiently appreciated. Again and again "epistemologists" take the path which is here proved to be impassable. See e.g. Kant's *Logik*.

cannot alter its content or form. It enters into this association just as it is. Accordingly, we are conscious of our presentations, thoughts, feelings, desires, and all the elements of our mental life and their connections, as they really are, and they really are just as we are conscious of them because in mental activities as such, being known to consciousness and existing are identical."*

It is clear, therefore, that Überweg does not claim that inner perception is guaranteed by comparing the content of the presentation and the real nature of the object. He believes that the perception of a mental act consists in its being combined with other acts. As a result of this combination the real act becomes a part of a cohesive whole which is formed out of the totality of real acts. It is this assimilation into the whole which constitutes the act's being perceived and known. It is necessarily perceived and known as it really is, since it is assimilated in its reality.

That would be all well and good if it were only true that a combination and a concatenation of real things, an integration of parts into a tightly connected whole, as for example of wheels, cylinders, plates and bars into the structure of a well-built machine, were the same thing as knowledge of these real things. In his history of philosophy Überweg reproached St. Anselm for confusing being thought with real being in his ontological argument. But he has made the same mistake himself, letting the actual existence of parts in a whole surreptitiously become existence in the sense in which we say of something known that it exists in the person who knows it.

These attempts to establish the infallibility of inner perception are, therefore, complete failures, and the same is true of any other attempt which might be suggested instead. The truth of inner perception cannot be proved in any way. But it has something more than proof; it is immediately evident. If anyone were to mount a skeptical attack against this ultimate foundation of cognition, he would find no other foundation upon which to erect an edifice of knowledge. Thus, there is no need to justify our confidence in inner perception. What is clearly needed instead is a theory about the relation between such perception and its object, which is compatible with its immediate evidence.[4] And as we have already said, such a theory is no longer possible, if perception and object are separated into two distinct mental acts, of which the one would be only an effect of the other, say. Descartes' well-known remark has already made this clear; for an infinitely powerful being, if it existed, would be able to produce the same effect as the object. So if that real unity, that peculiarly intimate

* *System der Logik*, 2nd ed., pp. 67 f.
[4] This part of epistemology thus answers the question: "How are evident perceptual judgements ever possible?"

connection which we have already discovered between the mental act and the accompanying presentation did not also exist between this same act and inner perception, it would be impossible for its cognition to be evident.

We can say that the force of this argument extends beyond the evidence of inner perception and it even serves to confirm the way in which the inner presentation is connected with its real object, a connection which we have already come to recognize in other ways. The cognition of a real object cannot be more intimately united with it than its presentation is, since presentation forms the basis of cognition. Not only does the same thing hold true of cognitions but for the same reasons. It is not surprising, therefore, that the psychologists (modern day as well as Aristotle) who, like ourselves, have thought that the presentation which accompanies a mental act is an accessory feature included in the act itself, have likewise believed that the accompanying cognition is contained in it, too.

3. Even though we have no need to fear the implication that psychical activity will become infinitely complex, another difficulty seems to stand in the way of the hypothesis that every mental act is accompanied by a cognition which refers to it. Every cognition is a judgement and every judgement, it is ordinarily said, consists in a predicate's being attributed to or denied of a subject. In the case of cognition through inner perception, the judgement is undoubtedly affirmative, but the predicate which is attributed to the subject would have to be existence, for what we perceive is that a mental act exists. Philosophers are not in agreement as to what the term "existence" really means, even though not only they, but any ordinary person, knows how to apply the term with confidence. But it does not seem difficult to see that it is a very general and hence a very abstract concept, even if it really was derived from experience and did not exist in us as an *a priori* concept prior to all experience (always an awkward assumption). Would it be conceivable, on the basis of what has been said, that the very first sensation a child has is accompanied not only by a presentation of the act of sensation, but also at the same time by a perception of this act? By a cognition that it exists? By a judgement which connects the concept of existence as predicate with the mental phenomenon as subject? I believe that everyone recognizes how improbable, indeed how impossible such a supposition is.

This argument would certainly be irrefutable, if the received theory of judgement were true. According to this theory, every judgement connects a plurality of concepts, and in particular the judgement which is expressed in the existential proposition adds the concept of existence to some subject-concept or other. Later on we shall prove generally that this conception is mistaken,* because a compounding of subject and predicate is not at all essential to the nature of judgement. The distinction between these two elements has to do, rather, with a commonly used form of linguistic expression. In cognition through inner perception we have before us in particular a judgement which quite obviously contradicts the usual view of psychologists and logicians. No one who pays attention[5] to what goes on within himself when he hears or sees and perceives his act of hearing or seeing could be mistaken about the fact that this judgement of inner perception does not consist in the connection of a mental act as subject with existence as predicate, but consists rather in the simple affirmation of the mental phenomenon which is present in inner consciousness. So this argument against the universal cognition of mental acts through inner consciousness turns out to be untenable, too.

4. Let us see if we can succeed in producing a positive proof for the universality of such an accompanying cognition.

We recall the procedure which we followed when we dealt with the question of whether every mental act is accompanied by a presentation referring to it. We showed that, with conscious mental phenomena, the intensity of the accompanying presentation increases and decreases to the same degree as the intensity of the act it accompanies (or the presentation on which the act is based), and is always on the same level with it. It follows that the accompanying presentation is absent only in those cases in which the act itself has been eliminated. With respect to the accompanying cognition, the proof does not seem to be so simple. In accord with our previous remarks, as a judgement, this cognition has two intensities: first, an intensity in the sense in which we say that presentations have an intensity; second, a kind of strength which is characteristic of judgement, i.e. the degree of conviction with which the judgement is made.[6] If one or the other fell to zero, there would be no judgement.

Our earlier investigations, however, have amply prepared us. We know that with regard to the first kind of intensity every judgement shares the level of intensity of the presentation on which it is based. The accompanying presentation loses all its intensity only in the case in which the object itself ceases to exist; consequently, as long

* Book Two, Chap. 7, Sect. 5 ff.

[5] This "paying attention" to what goes on within us must be understood to take place in memory, if there is to be no contradiction with what was said before on p. 128. The passage sounds as if a concurrent inner observation of the act of hearing were being maintained. See above and Introduction, p. 405 ff.

[6] See *Untersuchungen zur Sinnespsychologie*.

as the object is present, there will never be any reason for the cognition which accompanies the mental act to disappear.

[Therefore we still have to take into consideration only the strength which is characteristic of judgement, i.e. the degree of conviction. Here we find nothing which would resemble the functional relation which we discussed above. The degree of conviction which belongs to the accompanying cognition is in no way a function of the intensity of the act which it accompanies. Whether it is a question of a presentation, a judgement, a desire, or any other kind of mental phenomenon, the increase or decrease of its intensity does not affect the intensity of the conviction with which we know it. Nevertheless, the relations are such that they allow us to draw an undeniable conclusion. The strength of the conviction of the accompanying judgement which asserts the existence of the mental phenomenon is the same constant magnitude in every case. And this is not that small degree of acceptance which characterizes a weak and budding opinion; rather, it is the highest conceivable degree of conviction. Indeed, every inner perception is accompanied by this absolute conviction which is inherent in all types of immediately evident cognition. This relation, above all others, is what naturally lends support to the hypothesis of the universality of the accompanying cognition. If inner perception never occurs except with the highest degree of conviction, if, for this reason, inner perception never and under no circumstances shows a tendency to fade away, we may assert with certainty that inner perception will be absent only because of the possible absence of that other variable intensity of which we spoke above. This intensity, however, varies only as a function of such laws and in such a relationship with the intensity of the act it accompanies. That it decreases to zero only if this act itself completely disappears. We can assert, therefore, that the cognition which refers to the act will itself be absent only in this case.][7]* Every mental act, therefore, is accompanied by a twofold inner consciousness, by a presentation which refers to it and a judgement which refers to it, the so-called inner perception, which is an immediate, evident cognition of the act.

5. Experience shows that there exist in us not only a presentation and a judgement, but frequently a third kind of consciousness of the mental act, namely a feeling which refers to this act, pleasure or displeasure which we feel toward this act. Let us return to our old example: often the act of hearing a sound is obviously accompanied

* [Editor's note: This and several other passages have been bracketed by Kraus in order to indicate that Brentano later changed his views on the points discussed in these passages.]
[7] See the Supplementary Essays for Brentano's later views.

not only by a presentation and a cognition of this act of hearing, but by an emotion as well. It may be either pleasure, as when we hear a soft, pure young voice, or of displeasure, as when we hear the scratching of a violin badly played. On the basis of our previous discussions,* this feeling, too, has an object to which it refers. [This object is not the physical phenomenon of sound, but the mental phenomenon of hearing, for obviously it is not really the sound which is agreeable and pleasant or which torments us, but the hearing of the sound.] This feeling, consequently, also belongs to inner consciousness. Something similar occurs when we see beautiful or ugly colors, and in other cases.[8]

This accompanying feeling also turns out, when it appears on the scene, to form an integral part of the phenomenon which it accompanies, and to be contained in it just as the accompanying presentation and perception are. If the relation were different, the accompanying feeling would be a second mental act, which would again be accompanied by consciousness. But the presentation referring to it would necessarily contain not only this feeling itself, but also its content, the mental act to which it refers. This mental act, therefore, would be present twice: first by way of its own presentation of itself which belongs to it and is given in it, and secondly by way of the presentation of the feeling which belongs to the accompanying emotional act. Experience reveals nothing of the sort. On the contrary, it admits as possible only the hypothesis that, like inner presentation and perception, the inner feeling which accompanies hearing, seeing, and every other act of which we are conscious in this way, is fused with its object and is included within the object itself. Our previous analogous exposition spares us the task of clarifying these statements by means of a more detailed explanation.

On the other hand, perhaps it is worth while to point out the numerous and varied clues which point to the correctness of our conception.

We recall Hamilton's own peculiar view concerning the emotions of pleasure and displeasure. He believed that there is no relation of subject and object in them as there is in other mental phenomena. Subject and object are here so fused together that we can no longer speak of an object.† Certainly Hamilton had to have had some support in experience for his theory, even if he did not describe the phenomena quite correctly. Indeed, his error would be altogether incomprehensible if (in direct contradiction to his assertions about

* Book Two, Chap. I, Sect. 5.
† Cp. above, Book Two, Chap. 1, Sect. 5, pp. 89 ff.
[8] Brentano also modified these sentences within brackets. See the *Untersuchungen zur Sinnespsychologie* and the Supplementary Essays.

emotions), it were precisely the emotion which never fused with its object even in the sense in which this has been demonstrated of inner presentation and perception.

Furthermore we have seen above that in certain sensations the accompanying feeling of pleasure or displeasure has been confused not only with sensation itself, but even with the immanent object of sensation, i.e. with the physical phenomenon to which the act of sensation is referred as to its primary object. We found this to be true especially in connection with the pain and pleasure of the so-called sense of feeling. We say philosophers and non-philosophers alike fall into the same error here. This error, too, is undoubtedly a sign which calls attention to the intimate connection between the feeling and the act it accompanies.

Moreover, the concordant opinion of ancient and modern psychologists directly testifies to the relation which we have set forth. The most eminent English psychologists of the empiricist school hold that the pleasure or displeasure which accompanies a sensory act is contained in the act itself. This view, for example, is expressed by James Mill in his *Analysis of the Phenomena of the Human Mind,** and it is shared by Bain who distinguishes only two parts or two characteristics in sensation. There are, as he puts it, its intellectual character and its emotional character, by which he means the pleasure or displeasure which are associated with it. The younger Mill also supports the same view. Since he assumes it to be undoubtedly correct in most cases, he only raises the question, in a note to the work of his father mentioned above, whether in certain special cases the pleasure or displeasure which accompanies a sensation might perhaps constitute a separate reality, "rather than a particular aspect or quality of the sensation." After he has discussed what could give rise to such a divergent view where those particular sensations are concerned, he is still inclined to interpret them in the original way and he endeavors to eradicate any doubts on the subject.†

The same thing is true in Germany. Domrich, for example, in a work generally recognized to be of value, calls the feeling which accompanies a sensation "a quality of this sensation," using an expression very similar to Mill's. He conceives the relation in this way for all presentations accompanied by an emotion, calling the emotion "the way in which consciousness is aroused by the perception."‡ Nahlowsky, too, believes that the pleasure or displeasure

---

* *Analysis of the Phenomena of the Human Mind*, 2nd ed., Chap. 17, pp. 184 f.

† *Analysis of the Phenomena of the Human Mind*, 2nd ed., Chap. 17, p. 185, where he also gives an account of Bain's view.

‡ *Die psychischen Zustände*, pp. 16 f.

connected with a sensation is given in the sensation itself. He calls them the "tone of the sensation," but at the same time refuses to call them "emotions" because, in his opinion, they are entirely different from emotions properly so-called.* He was obviously led to this position by his desire to remain in agreement with the general principles of Herbart's doctrine on feelings. For even if Herbart and his school describe emotions as states of presentations, they nevertheless assert that emotions can only originate in a relation among several presentations. But since Nahlowsky was already well on his way toward freeing himself from Herbart in this area, it would have been better if he had given up the principle itself instead of making a distinction which is obviously untenable, and which brings him into opposition not only with all other psychologists, but with the leading Herbartians such as Drobish, Zimmerman, and others, as well. Wundt, too, rightly points out that more complicated emotions commonly arise out of the emotions which Nahlowsky would only consider "tones of sensations," which are the elementary factors of such complex emotions.† For this reason he uses the expressions "feeling-tone of sensation" and "sensory feeling" synonymously, but at the same time he states very explicitly that this sensory feeling is an "integral part" of sensation, "a third mode" which is added to the quality and intensity of sensation, insofar as every sensation is an "integral part of a conscious state."‡ Thus, Wundt, too, and perhaps even more than those mentioned above, is favorable to our view.

But these and other modern psychologists are not the only ones who incline toward this view. In antiquity, Aristotle had already anticipated it. In his *Nichomachean Ethics*, when he speaks of the pleasure which accompanies certain mental activities, he says that this pleasure contributes to the perfection of the act, not as a preparatory disposition, but as a formal cause; that it is added to the act in a way that perfects it; that it belongs to the act it accompanies in the way that maturity belongs to someone in the prime of life; that it is contained in the activity§ and that, as the perfection of the

---

* *Das Gefühlsleben*, Introduction. Expressions like Nahlowsky's are used by Volkmann, *Grundriss der Psychologie*, p. 55 and Waitz, *Psychologie als Naturwissenschaft*, p. 286.

† *Physiologische Psychologie*, p. 428.

‡ Pp. 436, 427.

§ *Nichomachean Ethics*, X, 4. Among other things he says: "Pleasure completes the activity not as the corresponding permanent state does by its immanence, but as an end which supervenes as the bloom of youth does on those in the flower of their age. So long, then, as both the intelligible or sensible object and the discriminating or contemplative faculty are as they should be, the pleasure will be involved in the activity."

act, it is specifically differentiated according to the act's specific difference.* All this shows unequivocally that this acute psychological observer agrees with our determinations.†

6. The question now arises whether this third mode of accompanying consciousness is like the other two in being connected with all mental acts.

Psychologists are divided on this issue. James Mill, for example, claims that there are neutral sensations, but at the same time recognizes that in every class of sensations we find sensations which are accompanied by pleasure or displeasure.‡ Indeed, all psychologists agree on this point. Some of them, however, go further. A. Bain,§ for example, and J. S. Mill are of the opinion that every sensation is accompanied by a feeling. With respect to those sensations which might not appear to be accompanied by feelings, Mill says, in his work on Hamilton: "Without being absolutely indifferent, they are not, in any absorbing degree, painful or pleasurable.¶

H. Spencer declares that, just as every emotion includes a cognition, every cognition includes an emotion.‖ Although he belongs to a different school, Hamilton is of the same opinion. According to him, every mental state is bound up with a feeling.** In Germany this view has many important adherents. Domrich, for example, says that emotions and feelings are not to be entirely separated from other mental phenomena. His investigations have convinced him that every sensation or presentation is accompanied by a concomitant feeling, even though the intensity of such feelings can certainly vary

---

* *Nich. Eth.*, X, 5.
† This undoubtedly corroborates our claim that Aristotle entertained an analogous view about the accompanying inner perception.
‡ *Analysis of the Phenomena of the Human Mind*, 2nd ed., II, Chap. 17, 185. Aristotle seems to have been of the same opinion. *Nich. Eth.* X, 4, 1174 b 20, shows that he admits there are feelings in every class of sensations. Indeed, he holds the same view with regard to all the other categories of mental activities, such as thinking (ibid.) and desire (ibid., 5, 2176 a 26). Yet *De Anima*, III, 7, 431 a 9, seems to show that he also admitted neutral sensations, even though the implication is not absolutely certain.
§ Bain believes that all sensations can be called feelings, since they all have a certain emotional character. It is strange, therefore, that besides pleasant and unpleasant emotions he admits emotions which are absolutely neutral, such as surprise (*Mental Science*, 3rd ed. pp. 215, 217). J. S. Mill's conception is undoubtedly more correct.
¶ *An Examination of Sir William Hamilton's Philosophy*, Chap. 13.
‖ Cp. Ribot, *Psychologie Anglaise Contemporaine*, p. 195.
** *Lectures on Metaphysics*, I, pp. 188 f.; II, pp. 433 f.

greatly.* Lotze is almost even more explicit. He says in his *Microcosmus* that

> We must above all wean ourselves from the habit of looking
> on the feelings as subsidiary events that sometimes occur
> in the succession of our internal states, while the latter for the
> most part consist of an indifferent series of painless and
> pleasureless changes. . . . Whatever stimulations, then, the soul
> may undergo, from each one we must expect an impression
> of pain or pleasure, and more accurate self-scrutiny, so far as it
> can recognize the washed-out colours of these impressions,
> confirms our conjecture, unable as it is to find any
> manifestation of our mental activity not accompanied by some
> feeling. The colours are indeed washed-out in the mature mind,
> in contrast to the preponderant interest which we bestow on
> particular ends of our personal endeavours, and deliberate
> attention is needed to detect them, just as microscopic
> examination is necessary to trace the regular formation of
> invisible objects, which the unassisted eye is wont carelessly
> to overlook. To each simple sensation, each colour, each tone,
> corresponds originally a special degree of pain or pleasure; but,
> accustomed as we are to note these impressions only in their
> significance as marks of objects, whose import and notion are of
> consequence to us, we observe the worth of these simple objects
> only when we throw ourselves with concentrated attention into
> their content. Every form of composition of the manifold
> produces in us, along with a perception, a slight impression
> of its agreement with the usages of our own development, and it
> is these often obscure feelings that give to each several object its
> special complexion for each several temperament. . . . Even
> the simplest and apparently driest notions are never quite
> destitute of this attendant feeling; we cannot grasp the
> conception of unity without experiencing a pleasant
> satisfaction that is part of its content, or that of antagonism
> without participating in the pain of conflictive opposition; we
> cannot observe in things or evolve within ourselves such conceptions
> as *rest, motion, equilibrium*, without throwing ourselves into them
> with all our living strength, and having a feeling of the kind
> and degree of resistance or assistance which they might bring
> to bear on us. A considerable part of our higher human culture
> is the result of this pervading presence of feelings.†

As we have said, many other psychologists share this same conviction, so it at least approaches the truth when Horwicz says, "that

* *Die psychologische Zustände*, p. 163.
† *Microcosmus*, I, 242 f.

all sensations are more or less characterized by tone, i.e. are pleasant or unpleasant, and that none of them is entirely without tone, is acknowledged by all psychologists nowadays."*

Even in this connection, however, there arise difficulties. One could object that the hypothesis that every mental activity is accompanied by pleasure or displeasure would necessarily lead to an infinite complexity of simultaneous acts, since pleasure and displeasure are themselves mental activities. But our previous discussion should have circumvented such objections. On the other hand, another objection remains to be considered.

Wundt, even though he classifies pleasure and displeasure as sensation to a very great extent, nonetheless thinks it is impossible for every sensation to be accompanied by a feeling. He reasons as follows: "We characterize the sensory feeling as agreeable or disagreeable, as a feeling of pleasure or displeasure. Pleasure and displeasure, however, are opposite states which change into one another through a neutral point. This implies that there must exist sensations which lack tone, i.e. which are not accompanied by a sensory feeling." If we grant the truth of the premises, it would follow that it certainly is possible for there to be sensation without an accompanying feeling. It would in no way follow, however, that such a sensation has ever really existed even for a short time. Wundt himself admits this when he continues, "Since the relation of sensations to consciousness is continually fluctuating, in general, this neutral point always corresponds to nothing but a passing state of mind from which a transition to feelings of pleasure or displeasure easily ensues. For this very reason every sensation must be regarded as associated with a certain degree of feeling."† I myself am very doubtful whether even the premises of this argument can be established, and whether the neutral sensations which occur between decidedly pleasant and decidedly unpleasant sensations should not rather be described (in accord with John Stuart Mill) as sensations which contain a mixture of pleasure and displeasure such that neither of them is predominant over the other. The chief argument which Wundt can advance in support of his conception is the dependence of the accompanying feeling of intensity. If we eliminate the influence exerted by the connectedness of our presentations upon the feelings accompanying each sensation, experience shows us, according to Wundt, that every sensation of moderate intensity is accompanied by a feeling of pleasure, and every sensation of very great intensity by a feeling of pain. He adds that in the case of a very weak sensation the

* *Psychologische Analysen*, I, 239.
† *Physiologische Psychologie*, p. 426.

pleasure is slight and at first increases as the sensation itself increases. Then it reaches a maximum and a turning point. Beyond this point, the feeling of pleasure decreases rapidly and, after passing through a neutral point, changes into displeasure. As a result of further, continuous, increase in the stimulation which corresponds to the sensation this displeasure may attain an infinite magnitude. If this theory is correct, we should be able to verify it especially in the case of the higher senses, since they can be investigated with the greatest possible degree of accuracy. It cannot be denied that a certain faint feeling of pleasure is connected with a faint sensation of light and that this feeling of pleasure increases considerably as the light shines with more vivid color, but that if the brightness exceeds a certain degree a feeling of displeasure arises. When we look directly at the sun this displeasure becomes an intolerable pain. At first sight, therefore, all evidence seems to confirm Wundt's interpretation. On a more careful study of the facts, however, this impression vanishes immediately. Is that extreme pain, which Wundt believes we may describe as infinite, really associated with the sensation of light? Wundt himself has to deny this. He says, rather, that this sensation has a quality which differs in no way from the qualities of other similarly painful sensations caused by means of other sensory nerves.* But how can this be? Has a color been transformed gradually into an absolutely heterogenous quality through an increase in the intensity of the sensation? This transformation seems as inconceivable as a gradual metamorphosis of a color into a sound. The truth is that experience teaches us something entirely different. When the sensation of light becomes so intense as to produce a feeling of displeasure, we find the visual phenomenon itself no less beautiful. The sight of the sun or of electric light enchants us, even though pain is associated with it. There arises in us a conflict of desires insofar as we would like to avoid the pain, and yet not turn our eyes away from such a beautiful sight. In this case, therefore, we have a mixed feeling, or rather two

---

* *Physiologische Psychologie*, p. 433. Wundt says that the extreme feeling of displeasure "no longer exhibits any qualitative differentiation," and he explains this by the fact that the sensations have been completely fused into the feeling of displeasure. This comment is difficult to understand, for, in view of his whole theory of feeling (cp. pp. 426, 427), we can hardly believe that he has intended to assert that the elements of which "the sensation exists in and for itself" have been completely eliminated. Nevertheless, if this were his opinion, he would have committed the same error for which we have previously reproached other psychologists, when we showed that feeling is based necessarily upon a presentation. The conjectures which we have advanced, then, concerning the reasons underlying this error would be confirmed. (See above, Book Two, Chap. I, Sect. 3.)

different feelings, connected with two sensations, simultaneously transmitted by the same nerves, but no less distinct or less heterogeneous on that account. It is for this reason that the displeasure seems similar to the pains which are usually caused by the so-called nerves of feeling. This displeasure has nothing in common with the displeasure which, for example, is usually produced by a faded gray color, either by itself or in connection with other phenomena. Only the pleasure appears as an increased delight such as the sight of colors grants. With each further increase of the stimulation both the pleasure and the pain seem to me to grow simultaneously, but obviously in very different proportions. At first, the beauty of the sight may make us disregard the unpleasantness of the second sensation; soon, however, the pain becomes so great that beauty no longer entices us and we are governed only by the desire to avoid the pain. In that event what happens is that we characterize the sensation simply as disagreeable, even though, as long as there remains any trace of color at all, we will never call it ugly. So the phenomena which seemed most to confirm Wundt's theory, seem, upon closer analysis, most to refute it. What we have said of the feelings associated with visual sensations applies also to those associated with the other senses. Indeed, it is even more difficult there to isolate one sensation from another. Olfactory sensations, for example, are not merely what we would, strictly speaking, call odors. Others result from the excitation of sensory nerves and still others are connected with the lungs or the stomach, such as those which we experience in connection with the phenomena that we are accustomed to calling fresh or stale odors, or, again, with those we call nauseous. Thus, we may assume – and the assumption seems to be entirely probable – that these phenomena involve a mixture of pleasant and unpleasant feelings, instead of a truly neutral state of sensation standing midway between feelings of pleasure and feelings of displeasure.

Thus, it is not correct to say that we must assume from the outset the existence of neutral mental activities in addition to those which are accompanied by feelings. But are we yet in a position to produce a positive proof that this third kind of inner consciousness is no less universal than those previously considered?

Of course, we recall the procedure we followed earlier. We explained the universality of accompanying presentations on the basis of the functional relation between their intensities and the intensities of the phenomena they accompany. Could we, perhaps, explain the universality of accompanying feelings in the same manner? It is not difficult to see that this is impossible. Feelings, like judgements, possess two kinds of intensity: one which is shared by the underlying presentation and the other which belongs exclusively to them.

151

In inner perception, we found that while the first kind of intensity varied with the intensity of the perceived act, the particular intensity of the conviction always remained the same. The situation is different in the case of inner feelings. It is certain – and we already touched upon this point in our earlier discussions – that the intensity peculiar to the feeling, i.e. the degree of pleasure and displeasure, depends upon the intensity of the pleasant or unpleasant phenomenon. The intensity of inner perception is always equal to the intensity of the felt act and the same is true of the intensity which is shared by the inner feeling and its underlying presentation, but this is not true of the intensity which is peculiar to the inner feeling. Indeed, it even appears that the same mental phenomenon, the same sensation, for example, arouses entirely different feelings under different circumstances; that it is sometimes more pleasing and sometimes less; and even that the same sensation sometimes causes pleasure and sometimes causes displeasure. When we play the scale up or down we hear the same notes, but with different feelings. Moreover, these differences become more numerous and distinct when we change the order of the notes. If a note fits with the melodic context it seems pleasant; if it does not, it will be accompanied by an unpleasant feeling no matter how resonant it may otherwise be.[9] If a melody is played in another key, each note gives the same feeling as the note which it replaces. The feeling which it produces, however, is entirely different from the feeling which was associated with it when it was first played. The same thing occurs in the case of colors. We say that there are certain colors that go well together and there are others of which the opposite is true. While the former, whether seen simultaneously or in succession, produce an especially pleasant effect, the latter, under the same circumstances, offend our eye. We shall speak later on of the phenomena of simultaneous contrast in which a color, even though absolutely unchanged in its appearance, is taken to be another color.[10] What is also noteworthy in this case is the feeling which accompanies the sensation of color changes. When we transpose a melody from one key to another, every note is accompanied by a feeling related to the feeling we previously had for the note which formerly occupied the corresponding place. Similarly. we find that a color which is confused with another is accompanied

[9] This shows that these feelings do not have the "sound" as their object but are evoked as "redundancies" by the concomitant arousal of certain sensations belonging to the "*Spürsinn*".

[10] Brentano rejected Helmholtz's explanation of simultaneous contrast very early and adopted Hering's. He himself devised stereoptic experiments to refute the doctrine of illusions of judgement, and communicated them to Hering for his use.

by a feeling related to the feeling which that color usually arouses. If, for example, we see a gray color as rose-red or as green, this color appears to be extraordinarily improved in appearance and acquires all of the characteristic attractiveness which distinguishes the color phenomenon concerned. This much, therefore, is evident: even though it cannot be denied that the intensity of the accompanying feeling is dependent upon the intensity of the mental phenomenon which it accompanies, nevertheless, this is not the only factor upon which this intensity depends. Many other conditions should be taken into consideration; it is possible that some of these conditions are as yet absolutely unknown, and that the amount of influence which others have cannot yet be precisely measured. We can see, then, that the universality of accompanying feelings cannot be proved in this way.

Consequently, we see ourselves turning to simple experience, for this path, which was not open to us when we were dealing with inner presentation and inner perception, has been paved for us by our earlier discussions. As long as it had not been established that every mental act is perceived by us, simple induction could give us no assurance that this or that kind of consciousness always accompanies our mental activities. It would have been clearly ridiculous to investigate whether in the sphere of our inner perception there existed an act which escaped our inner perception. Now, however, we know that all our mental activities are within the sphere of our perception and we have every right, therefore, to pose the question: does inner perception reveal only activities with which inner feeling is connected, or does it also reveal exceptions to this?

So distinguished a psychologist as Lotze found no exceptions, and, as we saw, many other prominent psychologists join him in this view. If we examine Wundt's statements, we see clearly that he found no mental activity unaccompanied by feeling. It is only through deductive arguments that he acquired the conviction that there had to be exceptions. Consequently, if we can show that this deduction hardly rests upon sound foundations, we may expect that even from this quarter the opposition to the hypothesis that accompanying feelings are universal will cease, and the hypothesis will find welcome support from this new and valuable testimony.

7. Let us review the investigations of this and the preceding chapter and briefly summarize their results.

Every mental act is conscious; it includes within it a consciousness of itself. Therefore, every mental act, no matter how simple, has a double object, a primary and a secondary object. The simplest act, for example the act of hearing, has as its primary object the sound, and for its secondary object, itself, the mental phenomenon in which the sound is heard. Consciousness of this secondary object is three-fold: it involves a presentation of it, a cognition of it and a feeling toward it. Consequently, every mental act, even the simplest has four different aspects under which it may be considered. It may be considered as a presentation of its primary object, as when the act in which we perceive a sound is considered as an act of hearing; however, it may also be considered as a presentation of itself, as a cognition of itself, and as a feeling toward itself. In addition, in these four respects combined, it is the object of its self-presentation, of its self-cognition, and (so to speak) of its self-feeling. Thus, without any further complication and multiplication of entities, not only is the self-presentation presented, the self-cognition is known as well as presented, and the self-feeling is felt as well as known and presented.[11]

The intensity of the presentation of the secondary object is always equal to the intensity of the presentation of the primary object. The same thing is true of the intensity of the accompanying judgement and feeling, insofar as they are based on a presentation.

[The intensity characteristic of the cognition of the secondary object, the strength of the conviction with which it is perceived, is invariable; it is always the highest conceivable.]

By contrast, the intensity characteristic of the accompanying feeling, the degree of pleasure or displeasure, does not exhibit a similar regularity. It is neither constant, as is the strength of the conviction in inner perception, nor does it increase or decrease in regular proportion to increases and decreases in the intensity of the presentation. It depends upon the intensity of this presentation, but at the same time it depends upon many other factors as well, which will be the subject of a later inquiry insofar as we can give any account of their influence. Original differences in aptitudes, difference in acquired dispositions, differences in the connection with other phenomena serve here, along with the intensity and quality of the primary object and diversity of references to it, to make this area one of the most varied and diversified fields of investigation.

---

[11] In order to correct Sections 5, 6 and 7, see *Untersuchungen zur Sinnespsychologie*. It has become usual to ignore most of what Brentano wrote after 1874. Thus many scientists still have Brentano teaching that "every mental activity is also object of an emotional reference included within it," though later on he expressed the opposite opinion repeatedly.

IV

On the Unity of Consciousness

---

1. Our investigation has shown that wherever there is mental activity there is a certain multiplicity and complexity. Even in the simplest mental state a double object is immanently present.[1] At least one of these objects is conscious in more than one way: it is not simply the object of a presentation but of a judgement and [a feeling] as well. But this lack of simplicity was not a lack of unity. The consciousness of the primary object and the consciousness of the secondary object are not each a distinct phenomenon but two aspects of one and the same unitary phenomenon;[2] nor did the fact that the secondary object enters into our consciousness in various ways eliminate the unity of consciousness. We interpreted them, and had to interpret them, as parts of a unified real being.[3]

In reality, such a simple state never occurs. It frequently happens, instead, that we have a rather large number of objects before our minds simultaneously, with which we enter into many diverse relations of consciousness. The question remains whether with such a large number of mental phenomena there is still a real unity which encompasses them all. Are these phenomena all parts of a really unitary whole, or are we confronted here with a multiplicity of things, so that the totality of mental states must be regarded as a collective reality, as a group of phenomena, each of which is a thing in its own right or belongs to a particular thing?[4]

[1] That is to say, we have something as our primary object and at the same time the mentally active subject has himself as object, as someone who is mentally active.

[2] I.e. one and the same unitary act.

[3] At any rate, that is, as one and the same substantive entity (*Realen*). See Supplementary Essay II.

[4] The following passage in brackets could be dropped without causing any harm; it, too, contradicts Brentano's later theory. In my opinion, two ideas have been mixed up here: 1. The question, whether a number of substantive entities does not still fall under the concept of a substantive

[I believe that the question has been stated clearly. Nevertheless, since misunderstandings are very common in this area, I shall offer some short explanatory observations. It is impossible for something to be one real thing and a multiplicity of real things at the same time. This was asserted by Aristotle* and since then it has been insisted upon repeatedly, and rightly so. We can, of course, group together a multiplicity of objects and call their sum by *one* name, as when we say "herd" or "the plant world." The objects thus grouped, however, are not thereby *one* thing. What the name designates is not a thing, but what we might call a *collective*. A city, indeed each house in a city, each room in the house, the floor of each room, which is composed of many boards, are also examples of collectives. Perhaps the boards themselves are collectives composed of many elements, whether points, or invisible atoms or larger units. It is not our concern here to investigate this question. One thing, however, is certain: without some real unities there would be no multiplicities, without things there would be no collectives.†

* *Metaphysics*, Z, 16.
† It hardly needs to be mentioned that the extension of the term "collective" as we use it is different from what it has in the grammarian's sense of the term, and the reason for this is obvious.[5]
[5] Grammar does not call a plank a collective any more than it does an atom, which is a collective according to contemporary opinion.

---

entity. Aristotle answered this question in the negative and the *Psychology* of 1874 agrees with him. But later on Brentano emphatically opposed this doctrine. (See the Introduction, the Supplementary Essays and Brentano's *Aristoteles und seine Weltanschauung*.) 2. The second question, which it seems to me is not adequately separated from this one, is whether a "unitary thing in and of itself" can also be a *number of things existing in and of themselves*. It is obvious and self-evident that this must be denied as an absurdity. On the other hand, one *thing in and of itself* can have parts which are not "things in and of themselves." Brentano called them "divisives." A half, a quarter, and so on, of a continuum, which we are capable of distinguishing in it, are "divisives" of this kind, for example. After they have been separated, they are "things in and of themselves" and constitute a collective thing in and of itself. – Now at that time Brentano also included the *attributes, accidents* of a unitary thing under the term *divisive*, as if what they involved had to do with parts, while in fact the substance is included in the accident as a part. Now then Brentano asks whether our mental states are parts of a collective or whether they are divisives, the following alternatives are intended: "Are they many things existing in and of themselves (a *collective*, or something which like a continuum can be *interpreted* as a collective of many things, not existing in and of themselves), or are they *attributes, properties* of one and the same thing?"

Nevertheless, even though it is clear and obvious at the outset that one thing can never be a multiplicity of things, this does not mean that no multiplicity can be distinguished in it. Unity and simplicity – Aristotle again has already emphasized this point* – are concepts which are not interchangeable. Even if one real thing cannot be a multiplicity of real things, it can nevertheless contain a multiplicity of parts. A clear example of this is found in those relatively uncomplicated mental states discussed in the preceding chapter. That to which the primary and the diversified secondary consciousness belonged was one thing, but obviously not an utterly simple thing. Naturally, just as we can use one term to cover a number of things taken together, we can also consider each part of a thing as something in itself and call it by its own name. But just as in the first case the object to which the term is applied is not a thing, but a mere collective, the object will not be a thing in this case either. So, for want of a commonly used unequivocal term (since the term "part" is also applied to real things when they are in collectives) we shall call this a divisive.]

We can now re-formulate the question in a more concise form: in the case of more complex mental states, do we have to assume a collective of things, or, does the totality of mental phenomena, in the most complex states just as in the simplest, form *one* thing in which we can distinguish divisives as parts?

2. Instead of the relatively simple state involved in the presentation of a sound or a color, two kinds of complication are possible. On the one hand, we can be conscious of the same primary object in different ways, as for example when we not only think of an object, but desire it as well. And secondly, an even greater complexity can arise from the fact that our mental activity can be directed toward more than one primary object, as for example, when we see and hear at the same time. Both kinds of complexity can also occur simultaneously, thus producing an even more complex mental state. It is clear, however, that what we decide about this case depends upon our decisions about the cases in which there is only one kind of complexity. If neither of the two kinds of complexity does away with real unity, then the two taken together will not destroy it either, and the mental phenomena which are simultaneously present in our consciousness will always constitute such a unity.

This hypothesis has its difficulties. If our simultaneous mental acts were never anything but divisives of one and the same unitary thing, how could they be independent of one another? Yet this is the case; they do not appear to be connected with one another either

* *Metaphysics*, A, 7.

when they come into being or when they cease to be. Either seeing or hearing can take place without the other one, and, if they do occur at the same time, the one can stop while the other one continues. In this case of complexity, the mental acts are mutually independent; in other cases there is at least a partial independence. I can only desire something when and while I have a presentation of it, but I can have a presentation of it without desiring it. It may happen that I think of something long before I begin to desire it, and subsequently my desire may cease or even change into aversion while my thought remains directed toward this same object.

Furthermore, if we compare the relation between simultaneous acts of seeing and hearing with the relation which we have previously considered between the different forms of inner consciousness, we see immediately and unmistakably that the latter is an incomparably more intimate relation. With seeing and hearing there is nothing like the reciprocal interrelationship that we find among the [three] aspects[6] of inner consciousness, where each one has each of the others as its object. If seeing and hearing, like the [three] forms of inner consciousness, were part of the same real unity, then we should expect differences in the intimacy of the connection to be impossible. For it is obvious that nothing can be more of a unity than that which is really one by nature. Consequently it appears that the totality of a complex mental state must be thought of as a collective.

Nevertheless, there is some support for the view that even in this case the real unity is not replaced by a multiplicity. In particular, it seems impossible to conceive of the complexity which arises when we are conscious of one and the same primary object in different ways, collectively, as an aggregate of several things – a complexity, for example, such as occurs when something is thought of and loved at the same time. It seems to us immediately absurd that something should be loved without being the object of a presentation,[7] and we are right to view this as a contradiction, because, as we have previously shown, every other mode of consciousness is based upon a presentation and includes a presentation in it.* If the presentation and the love were two separate acts, each a thing in its own right, and if one were only by chance the cause of the other, then it would be possible for this cause to be replaced by another, so that we could love something of which we have no presentation. Therefore in every

* Book Two, Chap. I, Sect. 3.
[6] According to the corrected theory, it is often a matter of only two factors.
[7] The impossibility of love not based on a presentation is also self-evident from the concepts involved, according to Brentano – a law of mind which is not obtained by induction.

case the love and the presentation of the object loved must belong to the same real unity. If we did assume, nevertheless, that the presentation must be a thing in its own right because it can continue after the love ceases, we would then have to say that when we loved the object it was presented twice, which is incorrect and contrary to experience.

Even when we turn our attention simultaneously toward several different primary objects, for example when we see and hear at the same time, there are reasons which can be adduced in favor of saying that both phenomena belong to the same real unity. We do compare colors which we see with sounds which we hear; indeed, this happens every time we recognize that they are different phenomena. How would this presentation of their difference be possible if the presentations of color and sound belonged to a different reality? Should we attribute it to the presentation of color or to the presentation of sound, or to both of them taken together, or to some third thing? Obviously neither to the presentation of color nor to the presentation of sound taken separately, because each of them excludes one of the two objects which are compared; nor, for the very same reason, to a third reality, unless we admit that the presentations of color and sound are repeated and united in it, Should we, therefore, attribute such a presentation to both of them taken together? But anyone can see that this, too, would be a ridiculous hypothesis. In fact, it would be like saying that, of course, neither a blind man nor a deaf man could compare colors with sounds, but if one sees and the other hears, the two together can recognize the relationship. And why does this seem so absurd? Because the cognition which compares them is a real objective unity, but when we combine the acts of the blind man and the deaf man, we always get a mere collective and never a unitary real thing.[8] Obviously, it makes no difference whether the blind man and the deaf man are far apart or near one another. If they lived together permanently in the same house, indeed, even if they had grown up together as inseparably as Siamese twins or even more so it would not increase the possibility of the hypothesis one bit.[9] Only if sound and color are presented jointly, in one and the same reality, is it conceivable that they can be compared with one another. Not only do we make comparisons among different primary objects, but they also enter into our thoughts and desires in many other relations. We figure out means to ends and develop elaborate plans; if we divided the individual components of our thoughts into a multiplicity of things, all these arrangements and combinations would disintegrate into a multiplicity or rather into

[8] The subject with its manifold references is a thing with many attributes.
[9] I.e. it is true not only of a collective but of a continuum as well that it is never a unitary substantive entity. See note 4.

nothingness. Does not the desire for the means include the desire for the end, and, therefore, does it not contain the presentation of the end along with that of the means? Does not the unitary act of choice necessarily contain the presentation of the objects of choice and of the motives which support this or that object?[10] All this is so evident that it would be superfluous to say anything further about it.

The same thing emerges when we consider the inner aspect of consciousness. When someone thinks of and desires something, or when he thinks of several primary objects at the same time, he is conscious not only of the different activities, but also of their simultaneity. When someone hears a melody, he recognizes that he has a presentation of one note as occurring now and of other notes as having already occurred. When a person is aware of seeing and hearing, he is also aware that he is doing both at the same time. Now if we find the perception of seeing in one thing and the perception of hearing in another, in which of these things do we find the perception of their simultaneity?[11] Obviously, in neither of them. It is clear, rather, that the inner cognition of one and the inner cognition of the other must belong to the same real unity. And from our previous investigations we know that what applies to the inner cognition of mental activities also applies to these activities themselves. Consequently, it seems that we are justified in concluding that neither kind of complexity can ever prevent us from regarding the totality of our mental activities as a real unity.

The last view is unquestionably the correct one, and the arguments which we have advanced in favor of it can in no way be refuted. And the arguments opposing it lose their force completely when we clarify the real point of the question.

It is not a question of whether simultaneous mental activities are all really identical. In opposition to conceptual identity, two things have real identity, if one is the other. Thus everyone is really identical with himself. By contrast, different men are conceptually identical in

---

[10] Here too it is a matter of an *a priori* self-evident law.

[11] "Perception of simultaneity" is to be understood to mean "knowledge of simultaneity." To say that two events are *simultaneous* means that they are *not temporally distinguished*, and nothing else. I know that two occurrences are simultaneous, i.e. not temporally distinguished, if I perceive them both in the present mode and know that I do so. So we should not really speak of perceiving simultaneity but of the fact that two events are perceived with the same temporal mode (present mode). This comment is important in connection with erroneous interpretations of the concept of simultaneity. See my article in *Logos, Naturwissenschaftliche Zeitschrift*, V, 67/68 (1919/20), and Brentano in *Kantstudien*, XXV and the Supplementary Essays.

that they are, of course, men, but this is not real identity. In this connection, it does not matter whether that which is called identical in the real sense is a thing, a divisive, a collective, or a privation or whatever; we say, for example, that blindness is a defect, and a herd is a group of animals of the same species. In the case under consideration, as we have already said, there is no question of real identity. And it is clear that such real identity never holds between our concurrent mental activities, and that it will never be found between the diverse aspects of the simplest mental acts which were differentiated earlier. The perception of hearing is not identical with the feeling we have toward hearing. They are divisives of the same reality, but this does not make them really identical with it and thus with one another.[12] A real thing, which, together with other things, comprises a collective, is not identical with this collective nor with other things which belong to it – it would never occur to anyone to say that the army is a soldier or that one soldier is another soldier. Likewise, a divisive, which I *distinguish* as a part in a real thing, cannot be called identical with this thing and hence with the other divisives which can be distinguished in it. A divisive never stands in a relation of real identity with another which has been distinguished from it, for if it did it would not be another divisive but the same one. But they do both belong to *one* real entity. And it is this common membership in *one* real thing which constitutes the unity about which we are speaking.

If by these observations we have removed the danger of confusion to which this terminology, inherited from the Scholastics, might easily lead, the answers to the counter-arguments emerge immediately.

It was said that nothing can be more of a unity than that which is really one. If, then, the totality of our simultaneous activities were a real unity, it could not be the case that the connection between some of them is less intimate than the connection between others, especially between the different modes of inner consciousness. We have here

---

[12] If someone sees and hears or has a presentation of and desires something at the same time, and knows that he does so, then these "divisives" are attributes of one and the same substantive entity. To put it more precisely, they are *accidents* or *modes* of one and the same reality; they are distinct as modes or accidents, but they are identical in terms of their *substance*. It is the *modes* or *accidents* which are the *whole*, since they include within themselves the substance (the subsisting entity) as a common part. The expression "divisive" is consequently inappropriate and was no longer applied by Brentano at a later period. See Kraus, *Franz Brentano*, p. 53. "Divisive" does not designate a unitary concept at all, since both the parts of a continuum and the diverse accidents of a substance fall under it. See Note 4 above.

before our eyes an example of the confusion we warned against above. The relation of real identity is necessarily always the same wherever it is actually present; it does not matter whether it is a thing, a collective, a divisive, or what it is that is called identical with itself. Nothing is more identical with itself than anything else. But this is not true of the relation between the parts which belong to a real unity. [If there really are small unitary things such as those which have been called atoms, the relationship which holds between the various attributes of these atoms is different from the relationship which holds between the various quantitative parts which the invisibly small bodies still contain as divisives. It is said that the quantitative parts of such an atom cannot be separated from it, and that some of its qualities cannot be lost. But there are other qualities of which this is obviously not true, even though they cannot be considered as things in their own right either. An atom, for example, passes from rest to motion. Motion itself is not a real thing in its own right; if it were it would be conceivable that it could continue to exist apart from the atom. I do not mean to presuppose in any way that the truth of the atomic theory has been established, nor do I want to consider the relations among the different properties of atoms as an example drawn from reality. My aim is simply to show, on the basis of a popular hypothesis, that when we are dealing with parts which belong to one and the same reality, we can *conceive* them to be connected with one another in many ways and with greater or lesser intimacy.][13] It is possible, therefore, that between the different parts which we distinguish in the totality of our mental states, the ways of being united are very different, even though they are all divisives of the same unitary thing.

[13] The entire passage from the words "If there really are small unitary things" to the words "or lesser intimacy" could be omitted without disturbing the sense. It serves as illustration but Brentano would have made various corrections if he had prepared a second edition himself. In the first place, according to his later theory, a physical body, no matter how small it may be, is never truly a "unitary thing." Leibniz is still correct here; every continuum, and therefore every physical object, is a thing, rather, which can be thought to consist of many, indeed as many as you please – only not infinitely many – finite things. (See Kraus, *Franz Brentano*, p. 46.) Every part of a continuum is a thing, only it is no *thing in and of itself*, though it can become a thing in and of itself – by being separated. It is to be called a "divisive," then, in an entirely different sense from the divisives which were referred to as such above, those which were identical in terms of their substance (like seeing and hearing which are encompassed by the same consciousness and belong to the same individual). See the previous note. Finally, rest and motion are not attributes of physical bodies in the sense of accidents.

The act of hearing is certainly more intimately connected with the [triple] consciousness of hearing than it is with the simultaneous act of seeing. Insofar as the presentation and perception of hearing undergo no changes which are not dependent on the act of hearing, while the concomitant feelings also change because of other factors, we could say that even here there are different degrees of intimacy within the unity. We could likewise claim that the connection between two activities directed toward the same primary object, of which one is based upon the other, as desire is based upon the corresponding presentation, is a more intimate one than the connection between activities which have to do with different primary objects. The simultaneous presentations of the words of a sentence which I have just heard appear more intimately connected[14] than the simultaneous sensations of different senses; and we could point out many other differences of intimacy in the union between concurrent mental activities. The fact that there are such differences is in itself worth noticing and may be important in many respects, especially in connection with the laws of the association of ideas. It is clear, however, that we cannot derive from it any valid *objection* to the assertion that all ideas belong to one and the same real unity.

Thus the second argument against the real unity of more complex mental states has been disposed of.

The first argument, based upon the independent appearance and persistence of certain mental activities, is also implicitly refuted. That which is really identical cannot undergo any separation, since this would mean something being separated from itself. But that which belongs as a distinct part, along with others, to a real whole may cease to be, while the other parts continue, without there being any contradiction.[15]

3. Our investigations lead to the following conclusion: the totality of our mental life, as complex as it may be, always forms a real unity. This is the well-known fact of the *unity of consciousness* which is generally regarded as one of the most important tenets of psychology.

Frequently, however, this tenet has been misunderstood both by its supporters and its opponents. In contrast with them, we intend to articulate once again, in clear and precise terms, what the unity of consciousness is, and what it is not.

The unity of consciousness, as we know with evidence through

[14] This "more intimate relationship" later gave occasion for talk of a "Gestalt quality" in connection with sentences. See Oskar Kraus, in *Logos*, V, 69.

[15] Brentano later deepened his studies on the various relations of parts and presented them in detail.

inner perception, consists in the fact that all mental phenomena which occur within us simultaneously such as seeing and hearing, thinking, judging and reasoning, loving and hating, desiring and shunning, etc., no matter how different they may be, all belong to one unitary reality only if they are inwardly perceived as existing together. They constitute phenomenal parts of a mental phenomenon, the elements of which are neither distinct things nor parts of distinct things but belong to a real unity. This is the necessary condition for the unity of consciousness, and no further conditions are required.

First of all, when we teach the unity of consciousness, we do not maintain in any way that different groups of mental phenomena, which do not belong to one and the same reality, can never be connected with one and the same connected physical body. We find such a relation in corals where countless little animals appear to have a common bodily life in one and the same stem. The simultaneous mental phenomena of one little animal and another do not form a real unity. But there is also no inner perception which apprehends their simultaneous existence. Consequently, it would in no way run counter to our definition if there were another self besides me present within my body, as though my body were possessed by one of those evil spirits whose exorcisms are so frequently reported in the Scriptures. There would be no real unity between the consciousness of this spirit and my consciousness, but then I would not directly apprehend its mental phenomena in inner perception along with my own, either.[16] The same would apply if, somewhat as Leibniz believed, my body were really nothing but an immense number of monads, i.e. of genuinely distinct substances each with a certain mental life of its own. My inner perception would not extend beyond myself, the dominant monad. Whether such a theory is true or false, at any rate it does not conflict with the unity of consciousness, as it is revealed to us by inner perception.

Furthermore, the unity of consciousness does not mean that consciousness, as it is in reality, excludes every plurality of parts of any kind. On the contrary, we have already seen that what inner perception reveals to us can be differentiated into a variety of activities, and inner perception is infallible. Herbart, of course, was of the opinion that a thing must be simple. According to him, only a collection of things can have a multiplicity of parts; a non-simple being would be a contradiction, and the Law of Contradiction must be upheld under all conditions. We fully agree with Herbart on this last point. A person who questions the Law of Contradiction in any

[16] Modern studies of so-called "possession" and the so-called split personality confirm that all of the pertinent phenomena belong to the same substantive self.

way and in any connection would be turning his arguments against something which is immediately evident and thus more certain than any proof. But exactly the same is true of the facts of our inner perception. Herbart's great error, and Kant's before him, was to affirm the phenomena of inner perception and to make them the basis for their investigations in just the same way that they did those phenomena toward which so-called external perception is directed, i.e. to view them as mere appearances which point to real beings and not as things which are themselves real.* If Herbart had conceived mental phenomena as real beings, the incompatibility of his metaphysical theory with the facts of inner perception would have called his attention here and elsewhere, to certain gaps and quivocations in his proofs and it would not have required someone else's acumen to show that the contradictions he insisted on were merely apparent contradictions.† In asserting the real unity of consciousness, therefore, we do not thereby in any way assert that consciousness is an absolutely simple reality. We only assert that the parts which can be distinguished in it are to be regarded as mere divisives of a real unity.

It would also be going too far to say that if the unity of consciousness does not require simplicity, it is only compatible with a plurality of parts which are inseparable from one another. On the contrary, as revealed by experience, we have seen that some of our activities often cease while others persist, that some of them change while others undergo no change.

Furthermore, it is necessary to emphasize that the unity of consciousness does not exclude either a plurality of quantitative parts or spatial extension (or an analogue thereof). It is certain that inner perception does not show us any extension; there is a difference,

---

* According to Herbart, the being which mental phenomena point to is the soul, i.e. a simple real substance with a simple quality which, in contrast to other simple real substances, is self-maintaining. What appears to us as a presentation in reality is nothing but such a process of self-maintenance. Consequently, the plurality of presentations which we perceive in us does not allow us to postulate in any way a plurality of properties and parts of any kind in our true being. At least this seems to be the way in which Herbart's doctrine must be interpreted in order to eliminate the most glaring contradictions between his metaphysics and his psychology. Or should we perhaps assume that Herbart believed that our presentations are nothing but processes of self-maintenance which remain unchanged in spite of all threats of disturbance, but that nevertheless they are what they appear to us? In this case Herbart would either have been guilty of the most obvious contradiction or would have denied in the most categorical manner the evidence of inner perception.

† Cp. Trendelenburg, *Historische Beitrage zur Philosophie*, II, 313 ff.

however, between not showing something and showing that something does not exist.[17] Otherwise, we would have to say that the judge judged fairly who, as the story goes, acquitted a man charged with using offensive language because the plaintiff only promised to produce five witnesses who had heard the insult, while the defendant promised to bring in one hundred who had not heard it. Of course it is certain that we cannot conceive of the mental activities which belong to the unity of consciousness as *quantitatively divided* every which way. It is not possible for seeing to occur in *one* quantitative part of our consciousness while the inner presentation, perception or pleasure which accompanies the act of seeing occurs in a quantitatively different part of consciousness.[18] This would contradict all we have heard about the particularly intimate connection and close union of these phenomena. It is likewise clear that a presentation is never contained in one quantitative part of our consciousness, while the judgement or desire directed upon the object of this presentation are contained in another part. In this case, there would be no presentation as the basis of the judgement and the desire, as inner perception shows that there is. On the other hand, we do not as yet have any reason to contest the view that perhaps one presentation is extended, or that different presentations may exist, in something analogous to a spatial way, alongside one another, etc.[19]

If you cut a worm into pieces, each section often shows the most unequivocal signs of voluntary movement, and, consequently, of feeling and presentation. Some people, including Aristotle, have explained this by saying that when the animal's body is cut up, its soul is, so to speak, cut up too. The unitary consciousness of the dissected animal, therefore, must have been in some sense spatially extended. Others have rejected this view in favor of the view that there were already several different souls in the worm before it was dissected – a different one in each different section.[20] We will not investigate here to what extent the latter succeeded in making their view plausible. We shall pay some attention to this question in a much later passage of this work.*

Suffice it to say at this point that if, as some people have actually done, we wanted to invoke the fact of the unity of consciousness

* [Editor's note: Brentano meant to return to this question in Book VI, of the *Psychology*, which was never written.]
[17] See above, p. 87.
[18] This thought, completed in the following sentence, is decisive.
[19] Later investigations were supposed to show that these hypotheses are excluded.
[20] Many modern animal psychologists and biologists deny that these brainless creatures have any consciousness.

against the older theory, this argument would not of itself be the least bit decisive against it. We have seen that the unity of consciousness is compatible with a plurality of activities which are in no way inseparably bound together. A plurality of separable quantitative parts, therefore, would not contradict such a theory.[21]

Just as the unity of consciousness does not exclude a plurality of parts, it does not exclude their diversity. It is not necessary that the parts be all of one kind, but only that they belong to the same real unity. We have already discovered that our consciousness taken as a whole encompasses not only a number of mental activities, but activities of very different kinds – not just presentations, but feeling as well. Unity is not the same as simplicity, nor is it the same as homogeneity of its parts. So far, at least, there is nothing to prevent someone, who wanted to consider our set of mental activities as extended in space, from assuming that their quantitative parts are homogeneous and reveal themselves as such in our mental phenomena. We do not wish to assert that this or any similar hypothesis is true, but if it should prove to be true, it would in no way be decisive against our theory of the unity of consciousness. We saw, in fact, that this unity encompasses a plurality of parts, in any case, which are related to one another in a variety of ways.

Finally, the unity of consciousness does not imply that the mental phenomena which we ordinarily refer to as our past mental activities, were parts of the same real thing that encompasses our present mental phenomena. One thing is beyond any doubt: just as inner perception shows us directly only one really unitary group of mental phenomena, memory, too, reveals to us directly only one such group of phenomena for each moment of the past. Of the other simultaneous mental phenomena memory gives up only a sort of indirect acquaintance by showing us that there is knowledge of these phenomena within the group we are concerned with, just as the group of phenomena revealed by inner perception can also contain the belief in the existence of other groups. Memory, then, reveals directly no more than *one* temporally continuous series of groups, each of which is only interrupted now and then by a gap. On further reflection, we sometimes succeed in filling these gaps, too. The continuity of the series also means that the successive groups bear a certain kinship to one another. It may be perfect similarity with only a temporal difference, or there may be a difference which increases

---

[21] See Kraus, *Franz Brentano*, p. 54, on the question of the soul. The unity of consciousness is compatible with a "multiplicity" of its parts, i.e. of the attributes, states, modes of one and the same subsistent *unitary* thing, but a *physical body* is always a *multiple thing* and this also holds true of the atom or electron.

167

gradually through infinitesimal gradations, for it is inconceivable that a continual modification should at any moment contain a leap of finite magnitude or a transition to a completely heterogeneous phenomenon. The fact is that even after the most violent sudden changes, a relationship between the earlier and the later phases reveals itself. Thus, in the phase immediately following the occurrence of a relatively great change, memory reveals a consciousness of the contrast between the new state and the preceding one. And we may even say generally acts of memory, which often refer back to members of the series in the distant past, never refer to a group of phenomena which does *not* belong to the series. The last member of the series forms the group which we apprehend directly in inner perception. We usually call this chain of mental phenomena our past life. Just as we say, "I see," "I hear," "I want," when seeing, hearing and wanting are revealed in inner perception, we also say, "I saw," "I heard," "I wanted," when the same phenomena appear directly in memory. Therefore, we generally consider the phenomena which memory directly reveals to us as activities known through inner perception. It is easy to understand the tendency toward such a conception in view of the character of these memory phenomena which we have described in some of its most essential features. But we cannot yet claim that it is self-evident that the same real unity which contains our present mental phenomena also really previously encompassed those which we usually call "our past." Nor are any of the proofs by means of which we established the real unity of present mental phenomena applicable here. Of course our present acts of memory must belong to the same reality as the rest of our present mental acts. But the content of an act of memory is not the act of memory itself. And what is our guarantee that the memory and its content are to be ascribed to the same substantive unity, if they are not identical? If the knowledge provided by memory were immediately evident, we could draw this conclusion, as we do in the case of inner perception. But memory is notorious for lacking evidence and is even subject to many deceptions. It remains an open question, then, for the moment, whether the continued existence of the self is the persistence of one and the same unitary reality or simply a succession of different realities linked together in such a way that, so to speak, each subsequent reality takes the place of the reality which preceded it. Consequently, the belief that the self is a corporeal organ which forms the substrate of continuous substantial changes would not contradict our previous statements, provided that whoever might hold such a belief admits that the impressions experienced by such an organ exert an influence upon the way in which it renews itself. Thus, just as a wound leaves a scar, the past

168

mental phenomenon would leave as an after-effect a trace of itself and with it the possibility of a recollection. The unity of the self in its past and present existence, therefore, would then be no different from that of a flowing stream in which one wave follows another and imitates its movement. The only hypothesis that would have to be excluded by those who wished to consider an organ as the bearer of consciousness would be the atomistic hypothesis that looks upon every organ as a multiplicity of things. At best the only value that they could ascribe to this hypothesis would be to view it as some kind of regulative principle for inquiries in the field of natural science, as Du Bois-Reymond did in his talk at the natural scientists' convention in Leipzig.*

4. The doctrine of the unity of consciousness, as outlined here, has a more modest content than that which has often been assigned to it. For this reason it has been really and completely proved in the preceding discussion. And it has shown itself to be safe from every objection even though not only those arguments mentioned above but others as well have been raised against it.

C. Ludwig, in his physiology textbook, declares that the real unity of our mental phenomena runs into a "completely insoluble difficulty." "As we have already noted repeatedly," he says, "there are never any reasons which can induce us to assume an essential difference between the sensory and motor nerve fibers. And if there is no such difference, how can we explain the dissimilarity in the effects of the reciprocal action of homogeneous nerves and of a homogeneous soul? This difficulty reminds us at least to bear in mind that what we call the soul is a very complicated structure made up of different parts which are intimately connected with one another, so that the states of one part are easily communicated to the whole."†

Let us assume that this argument of Ludwig's is convincing and forcibly drives home the conclusion with which it ends. The real unity of consciousness, as we have explained it, would not thereby be refuted in any way. If this unity had quantitative and heterogeneous parts and were a very complicated structure, it would satisfy Ludwig's requirements.[22] Of course, such an assumption could be challenged as an impossibility on the basis of the atomistic hypothesis.[23] But no matter how much may be said for this hypothesis, its

---

* *Ueber die Grenzen der Naturerkenntnis*, 1872.

† *Lehrbuch der Physiologie des Menschen*, I, 606.

[22] A truly unitary thing cannot have any quantitative parts in the sense of extended parts. See the preceding note and Brentano's later works on the theory of the soul.

[23] Because as a consequence of this, the organism and the brain in particular must be a collective.

probability may not be asserted in the face of the evident character of inner facts.

Still more, Ludwig speaks of states being communicated from individual parts to the whole, i.e. to the rest of the parts taken altogether. Every part, therefore, will have the same states as the others. Thus every part will see, hear, etc., even if *one* part is chiefly stimulated by light and the other by sound. Now even if the whole were a collective and only the parts were real unities, each of these parts would nevertheless contain a group of mental activities in its own right, as we apprehend them through inner perception. It would not be necessary, therefore, that our inner perception should extend beyond one real unity. Indeed, this is not even likely, because it would only exhibit the same set to us repeatedly. On Ludwig's view, then, the situation would be only that besides our unitary consciousness, there are several others in the same body exactly like it. Again, this would not contradict the unity of consciousness in our sense of the term.

But perhaps the argument itself is not as cogent as Ludwig believes. He asserts that no essential difference has yet been discovered in the nerve fibers. Are we thereby certain that no difference will ever be discovered? Moreover, can we assert with confidence that differences which appear insignificant in other respects are not perhaps "essential" with regard to sensations? Recently some physiologists have claimed that there were no essential differences in the ganglia, and that consequently the differences of the external organs should be considered as the sole basis for the differences observed in sensations.* Whether or not it is admissible, this hypo-

---

* Wundt, *Physiologische Psychologie*, Chap. 5, pp. 173 ff., and Chap. 9, pp. 345 ff. "It is highly probable," says Wundt, "that the principle of functional indifference, to the extent to which it is admitted with regard to the nerve fibers, must likewise be extended to their central endings. The differences which are found in the latter are no greater than those exhibited by the different kinds of nerves. In addition, when different nerve endings become entangled during the healing process, we can subsequently release motor reactions by stimulating sensory fibers. This experimental phenomenon implies numerous reciprocal substitutions among central nerve extremities as closely equivalent facts. Obviously, by transferring in this manner the seat of specific functions to the central nervous system, we have simply resorted to the artifice of relegating such a seat to a sphere which was still sufficiently unknown in order to risk any hypothesis of our own choosing" (p. 347). Wundt's own explanation of these facts, however, contains a contradiction. On the one hand, Wundt begins with the premise that the physical similarity of nerves (indeed, of nerve endings) is too great to enable us to consider their difference as the reason for the specific function. But on the other hand he concludes that the reason for the specific

thesis shows the uncertainty of the argument. In fact, if it is inadmissible, it shows, in terms of an example, how physiological differences can escape our observation or appear insignificant and nevertheless be of great importance. Finally, it would be conceivable that the differences in the central structures to which the sensory nerves lead really determine the differences between visual and auditory sensations, but only in the way in which we would ascribe the cause of these differences to the nerves themselves, if they turned out to be strikingly different, namely as links in a chain that leads still further.

Like many others, A. Lange claims that the phenomena of division by which animals can often be split in two and the opposite phenomena of the fusion of two animals into one are incompatible with the unity of consciousness. "The *Radiopods*," he says, "the descendants of the *Vorticella*, often approach each other, and attach themselves intimately to one another. At the point of contact there occurs first a flattening and then a complete fusion. A similar process of copulation occurs in the *Gregarines*. Siebold found that even a worm, the Diplozoon, is formed through the fusion of two Diporpea."*

We have already pointed out that the phenomena of division, even if they should compel us to admit the splitting of a group of mental phenomena into several quantitative parts, would prove nothing contrary to the unity of consciousness, since it does not require either the simplicity or the indivisibility of consciousness.[24] For the same reason, the phenomena of fusion cannot be used as evidence against this unity. Similarly, if we attributed memory to these lower animals, and admitted that each of the two animals resulting from division remembered the life of the dissected animal, so that now the same consciousness would exist in two things,† this would not be an objection to the unity of consciousness in our sense of the term. Of

---

* *History of Materialism*, iii, 41.
† [Translators' note: Both the original edition of 1874 and the 1924 edition read "Qualitäten" here, but in Brentano's copy of the first edition, now at Brown University, this has been corrected to "Realitäten," presumably by Brentano.]
[24] The unity of consciousness admits only such parts of the subject-consciousness as are related as accidents (modes) to the accidentally modified subject (substance) or as those modes are to each other.

---

function is actually to be found in a difference of nerves, namely a difference acquired through habit.

course, if we have asserted that the mental activities revealed directly by memory always belong to the same reality as those which are apprehended in inner perception, we would have to conclude that two groups of phenomena belong to the same reality, and simultaneously that they should be conceived as two distinct realities, which is contradictory. Our assertion, however, was restricted to activities belonging to the present group of mental phenomena, so these contradictory conclusions cannot be derived from it. And if we assumed that the single animal resulting from the fusion of several animals has memories of a previous double life, this would not contradict the unity of consciousness either. In this case, memory would indeed directly reveal a plurality of simultaneously existing real mental unities, but the horizon of inner perception would never extend beyond the boundaries of a single real unity.

It is odd that Lange maintains, on the one hand, that certain facts contradict the unity of consciousness, and, on the other, recognizes that a group of mental activities such as we find within ourselves is inconceivable without real unity. Thus he submits to a contradiction reminiscent of Kant's antinomies, which he resolves as a true disciple of that philosopher by ascribing only phenomenal truth to the contradictory appearances. In order to avoid the contradiction between unity and plurality, we must assume, according to him, that neither unity nor plurality exist in reality but that both concepts are only subjective constructs of our thinking. "The only salvation . . . consists in regarding the opposition of manifoldness and unity as a consequence of our organisation, in supposing that in the world of things in themselves it is resolved in some way unknown to us, or rather does not exist there. In this way we escape the inmost ground of the contradiction, which lies in the assumption of absolute unities, which are nowhere given to us. If we conceive all unity as relative (namely to our thinking and to just this or that particular act of thinking), if we see in unity only the combination of our thought, we have indeed not embraced the inmost nature of things, but we have certainly made possible the consistency of the scientific view." (In other words, despite the contradictions which come to light, we can confidently carry on the investigation by regarding them as merely phenomenal contradictions, in no way pertaining to reality.) "It fares ill indeed with the absolute unity of self-consciousness, but it is not a misfortune to get rid of a favourite idea for some thousand years."*

Of course the unity of consciousness would fare ill if the phenomena of inner perception too had only phenomenal truth. Not even

* *History of Materialism*, iii, 37.

the existence of consciousness would be assured. But we have already pointed out repeatedly that Kant and Lange, who follows him here, are on the wrong track. It is an out and out contradiction to attribute a mere phenomenal truth both to inner and outer perception, as Kant does, for the phenomenal truth of physical phenomena requires the real truth of mental phenomena. If mental phenomena did not exist in reality, neither physical nor mental phenomena would even exist as phenomena.[25] The contradiction, then, cannot be removed in this way. On the other hand, we have already seen that the phenomena invoked by Lange can very easily be reconciled with the fact of the unity of consciousness, provided that we understand it correctly.

Lange also places special emphasis upon yet another phenomenon. "Relative unity," he says, "occurs amongst the lower animals very remarkably in those polyps which possess a common stem, on which there appears by gemmation a mass of creatures, which in a certain sense are to be regarded as independent, but in another sense only as organs of the entire stem. We are led to the supposition that in these beings even the voluntary movements are partly general, partly special in their nature; that the sensations of all these semi-independent stems stand related to each other, and yet have their separate operation, as well. Vogt is quite right when he calls the controversy as to the individuality of these beings a controversy over the Kaiser's beard. 'There occur gradual transitions. The individualisation step by step increases.'"* It is true that the mental activities in a polypary cannot be conceived as a real unity. But is it supposed to be necessary, therefore, to conceive of them as a transition between unity and plurality, as something which is no longer one but not yet many? I see no reasons which compel us to assume this something-in-between which is so full of contradictions and prevents us from assuming a plurality of real mental unities in the same stem. Lange's statement that in polyps "the voluntary movements are partly general, partly special in their nature" is only the correct interpretation of the phenomena in the sense in which it could also be said of a large number of human beings who belong to a city or a nation. As Lotze pertinently remarks, in such a colony of creatures, each individual consciousness is independent of the others in exercising the meagre expressions of vital activity which are possible to it. All these consciousnesses are, however, "by their mutual connection subject in common to many external influences."† And these commonly experienced influences may produce the simultaneous excitation of certain desires and activities which harmonize with each other. Thus we are faced with no contradictory

---

* *History of Materialism*, iii, 41. † *Microcosmus*, I, 153.
[25] See Kraus, *Franz Brentano*, p. 28.

concepts which would compel us to sacrifice our confidence in inner experience and in the conclusions we draw from it by means of reliable analogies.

Lange concedes that, if we want to assume that mental phenomena as revealed by inner consciousness are real, we would have to conceive of them as a real unity. C. Ludwig, however, denies this and rejects the psychologists' arguments for the unity of consciousness as invalid. Perhaps it is not superfluous to discuss briefly this eminent physiologist's attack on the arguments in support of the unity of consciousness, to the extent to which we ourselves find them compelling, having previously discussed his attack against the unity itself.

Ludwig reproduces these arguments in the following way. The hypothesis that sensation, will and thought processes belong to a real unity "is believed to be justified," he says, "because consciousness asserts that the same thing simply fulfills three special functions." This is not expressed very clearly, but what follows seems to indicate that Ludwig wants to say that people have tried to prove the unity by arguing that one and the same consciousness is conscious of these three separate functions. For, turning to criticism, he continues, "But this fact seems to be meaningless unless we are told what position consciousness occupies in relation to the three functions, since they could be thought to fall within it without being identical with it." The meaning of this statement is obviously that we can only conclude from this fact that the three functions belong to *one* real unity if we presuppose that in order for them to be perceived by consciousness, they must belong to the same real unity to which that consciousness belongs. For then the law that two things which are identical with a third are identical with one another applies. But Ludwig thinks that that presupposition is unjustified. If it is true of other perceptions, e.g. visual perceptions, that we perceive something which does not belong to the same real unity as the perception itself, why could the same thing not take place with inner perceptions, i.e. in the perceptions of mental functions? "Even dream phenomena," he adds, "enhance the probability of such a view, because in dreams our own sensations and presentations appear to us as sensations and presentations which are absolutely external, as shown, for example, by the fact that we direct questions to them."*

If we think back to our earlier discussion, we see immediately that this formulation of the argument for the unity of consciousness is very incomplete. For example, there is no mention at all of the fact that will is necessarily based upon presentation, being altogether

* *Physiologie der Menschen*, I, 605 f.

inconceivable without it, even though it is precisely this circumstance which constitutes a striking proof of the unity of these two activities. In addition, he gives an inexact presentation of the facts when he speaks as if the assumption that the inner perception of a mental activity and this activity itself belong to the same real unity is entirely arbitrary. As we have seen, many facts require this assumption, in particular the fact that without it the evidence of inner perception would be impossible. In reality, therefore, we have already provided the proof Ludwig demands that the mental function perceived in inner consciousness and this consciousness itself must belong to the same real unity. Finally, we may say that Ludwig's reference to dream phenomena which is supposed to make it probable that sensations and presentations do not belong to the same reality as the consciousness which accompanies them, is completely beside the point.

In the first place, it is certainly odd to conclude that because our sensations and presentations appear in dreams to be external, they probably are. If this were the case, we could conclude with equal justification that, since they appear to us as trees, houses and people (to whom, according to Ludwig, we often address questions), these sensations and presentations probably are trees, houses and people. Yet we ordinarily distinguish dreaming from waking on the basis of the fact that the former presents to us a false picture of reality, and intermixes an element of truth only now and then. So the presupposition upon which Ludwig bases the conclusion that, since in dreams our presentations and sensations appear to us as external realities, they probably *are* something external, is wholly unacceptable.

Not only is the major premise false, but the minor premise as well. It is not true that our presentations and sensations appear to us in dreams as "absolutely external," if we understand presentations to be acts of presenting and sensations to be acts of sensing. Of course these terms, as such, can also be used in a different sense, in which "presentation" means not only the act of presenting but also the object which is presented, and "sensation" means not only the act of sensing, but also the object which is sensed.[26] In our case, however, we are dealing with mental activities. These activities appear to us to be inner activities both in dreams and in waking life; and with regard to them there is no deception even in dreams. It is true that in dreams we have presentations of colors and sounds and various other forms, that we are afraid, get angry, feel pleased and experience other emotions. But that which these mental activities refer to as their content and which really does appear to be external is, in

[26] Many psychologists and epistemologists are still guilty of this confusion today.

actuality, no more outside of us than in us. It is mere appearance,[27] just as the physical phenomena which appear to us in waking life really correspond to no reality although people often assume the opposite. We have already seen how the psychologists, after having seen this existence of the apparent external world to be a mistake, regarded the act of sensation as the reality concerned and to be directed upon itself because they were in the habit of conceiving the objects of sensation to be real.* In a somewhat similar way, it seems, Ludwig has come to mistake the acts of sensation and presentation which take place in dreams for the objects which appear in them. The equivocation of the terms "presentation" and "sensation" may have played a role in concealing his mistake from him. Someone might argue in the following way: what appears to us in dreams as something external does not actually exist outside of us; therefore, it exists only as something present to our minds; therefore, it is nothing but our presentations and like all our presentations belongs to our mental activities; therefore, in dreams our mental activities appear to us as something external.[28] But this argument contains an obvious fallacy of equivocation, the word "presentation" being used first in the sense of the object presented, and then in the sense of the act of presenting it.

We see then that Ludwig is no more fortunate when he tries to undermine the proofs for the unity of consciousness than he was when he tried unsuccessfully to establish the opposite view. All other objections against the unity of consciousness can be rejected just as easily as the attacks of Ludwig and Lange. Since the errors are essentially the same as those which we have encountered in these two eminent thinkers, it would be unprofitable for us to consider each one in detail.

The fact of the unity of consciousness, as we have explained it, must, then, be considered to be indubitably certain.†

* Cp. Book Two, Chap. II, Sect. 5.

† We use the term "unity of consciousness" in several senses, just as we do the term "consciousness." In fact, the differences in meaning are even more numerous in this case, because, not only does the word "consciousness" vary, but "unity" does too, being used sometimes to refer to the object instead of the subject. Thus some people understood it to mean the fact that one can only pay attention to and consistently follow only *one* train of thought at a time, that we can truly occupy ourselves with only one thing at a time. We will deal with the unity of consciousness in this sense later on, since, so interpreted, it is very closely connected with the laws of the association of ideas.

[27] See p. 92 above.

[28] Those who make sensation in the sense of what is sensed a substantive component of our consciousness argue in a similar way.

V

A Survey of the Principal Attempts to Classify Mental Phenomena

1. We now come to an investigation which is not only of great importance in itself, but important for all our subsequent investigations as well. For scientific study must have classification and order, and these may not be arbitrary. They ought, as far as possible, to be natural, and they are natural when they correspond to a classification of their subject-matter which is as natural as possible.

We shall encounter divisions and subdivisions among mental phenomena just as we do elsewhere. But first of all we will have to deal with the determination of the most general classes.

The first classifications, as is generally the case in the area of psychology, went hand in hand with the progressive development of language. Language contains more general and less general expressions for phenomena belonging to the inner sphere, and the earliest works of poetry show that even before the beginning of Greek philosophy people drew essentially the same distinctions which we draw in everyday life even today. But before Socrates stimulated interest in definition, with which scientific classification is very intimately connected, philosophers had made no attempts worth mentioning to set up a fundamental classification of mental phenomena.

Plato quite probably deserves the credit for having pioneered in this area. He distinguished three basic classes of mental phenomena, or rather, as he put it, three parts of the soul, each of which includes particular activities, namely, the *appetitive*, the *spirited*, and the *rational* parts of the soul.* As we have already remarked in

---

* The Greek expressions are τὸ ἐπιθυμητικόν, τὸ θυμοειδές, and τὸ λογιστικόν.

passing,* these three parts corresponded to the three main classes
Plato distinguished in the state, the class of workers, which included
shepherds, farmers, artisans, merchants, and others; the class of
guardians or warriors; and the ruling class. The three main ethnic
groups were also supposed to be distinguished in terms of the
relative preponderance of the same three parts of the soul. There were
the soft Southerners (Phoenicians and Egyptians) who sought the
pleasures of wealth; the brave but uncultured northern Barbarians;
and the culture-loving Greeks.

Just as he has used his classification to define the essential differences of the various directions of man's endeavors, Plato seems to
have taken such differences into account when setting it up. He found
in man a conflict of opposites, first between the demands of reason
and physical desires, but also between physical desires themselves. In
the latter case, the opposition between the violent and surging
passion, which rages in the face of pain and death, and the soft
inclination toward pleasure, which retreats from every pain, appeared
to him especially striking and just as great as the opposition between
rational and irrational desires. So he believed that three parts of the
soul should be recognized and distinguished in terms of their location, too. The rational part was supposed to reside in the head, the
spirited part in the heart, and the appetitive part in the abdomen.†
The first resides in the head in such a way that it is separable from
the body and immortal; and only the other two are attached to it
and bound to it in their existence. Plato also believed that these parts
differed in that they may each be present in a wider or narrower
sphere of living beings. Of all the living things on earth, only man
was supposed to possess the rational part. He was supposed to share
the spirited part with animals, and the appetitive part with animals
and plants alike.

It is easy to see that this classification is imperfect. It is rooted
entirely in ethical considerations. The fact that one of the parts of
the soul is described as rational does not contradict this statement

---

* Book One, Chap. 2, Sect. 7.
† Democritus had believed that thought was located in the brain and
anger in the heart. Desire he placed in the liver. There would seem to be
only an insignificant difference between this conception and the subsequent
Platonic doctrine. Nothing, however, makes it seem probable to suppose
that Democritus wished to reduce the totality of mental activities to these
three parts. On the contrary, according to the logic of his system, he had
to conceive each organ as endowed with special mental activities. This
seems to be indicated by a passage in Plutarch. (*Plac.*, IV, 4, 3.) So we
cannot say that an attempt to give a basic classification of mental phenomena had already been made by Democritus.

because both Socrates and Plato regarded virtue as knowledge. Difficulties arise as soon as we wish to determine to which part a given activity belongs. It seems, for example, that sensory perception must be assigned to both the appetitive and the spirited parts and in certain passages Plato gives the impression of placing it, along with other kinds of knowledge, in the rational part.* In addition, the allegedly successful applications that Plato makes of his classification, which he hoped would confirm it, only serve to reveal its weakness anew. Hardly anyone these days would be inclined to agree with Plato in thinking that the three classes, workers, guardians, and rulers, exhaust the main vocational activities in a society. Neither art nor science has an appropriate place in this classification. But experience shows us so clearly the difference in aptitudes for theoretical and practical achievements that we must recognize that the abilities of the scientific thinker involve a kind of perfection wholly different from that which is involved in the ability to rule. Apart from that, having a philosopher as ruler, which Plato envisioned as ideal, would constitute a great danger to the freedom of science and thus to its unhampered progress.

Nevertheless, the Platonic classification contained the seeds of the classification which Aristotle substituted for it, and which, being incomparably more important than Plato's classification, has been authoritative for thousands of years.

2. We find in Aristotle three basic classifications of mental phenomena. Two of these classifications, however, are so similar in their structure that we may look upon them as *one*.

First of all, he draws a distinction among mental phenomena by considering some of them as activities of the *central organ* and the others as incorporeal, hence as phenomena of the mortal and immortal parts of the soul, respectively.

Then he distinguishes them, in terms of their wider or narrower extension, into activities *common to all animals* and *activities* which are *peculiarly human*. On Aristotle's view this turns out to be a threefold classification because, as we have seen above, he had a broader concept of the soul than we do, and so he attributes souls to plants, too. Thus he enumerates a vegetative, a sensitive, and a rational part of the soul. The first, which includes in itself the phenomena of nutrition, growth, and reproduction, is supposed to be common to all living beings, including plants. The second, which embraces the senses, the imagination and other related phenomena, including affective states, is, according to him, specifically animal. Finally, he believes that the third part, which comprises the higher faculties

* Cp. Zeller's comments in his *Philosophie der Griechen*, II.

of thought and will, is, among earthly living things, characteristic exclusively of man. But, as a result of the way the concept of psychical activities was later narrowed, the first of the three now falls entirely outside the sphere of these activities. In the modern sense of the term, therefore, Aristotle divides mental activities into only two groups by means of this classification: activities which are common to all animals and activities which are specifically human. The elements of this classification coincide with those of the first. Their order, however, is determined by the degree to which their existence is general.

Another classification given by Aristotle divides mental phenomena, in our sense,* into *thought* and *desire*, νοῦς and ὄρεξις, in their broadest sense. This classification cuts across the preceding one in the form that we are now concerned with it. In the class of thought, in fact, Aristotle includes not only the highest activities of the intellect, such as abstraction, making universal judgements, and scientific inference, but also sense perception, imagination, memory and expectation based on experience.† In the class of desire we find both high aspirations and strivings as well as the lowest drives, and along with them all feelings and affective states – in short, all mental phenomena which are not included in the first group.

If we inquire why Aristotle united in this classification those phenomena that he had separated in his first classification, it is easy to see that he was led to do this by a certain similarity between sensual presentation and appearance, and intellectual and conceptual presentation and affirmation. The same similarity is apparent between the lower appetites and higher aspirations. To use an expression we have already borrowed from the Scholastics, he discovered the same mode of intentional inexistence in both cases.‡ On the basis of this

* See *De Anima*, III, 9, 10.

† Wundt charges those who maintain that there is a similarity between sensation and higher cognition with "logicism." If this reproach were well founded, it would apply to Aristotle, too. How is it, then, that Descartes professed the very same doctrine? Indeed, how is it that many others, who completely denied universal concepts, chose to class the relevant activities of thought under sensory activities? This was an error, to be sure, but it would be no less serious a mistake to ignore what is common to sensation and intellectual thought processes. [Note of 1911.]

‡ This expression had been misunderstood in that some people thought it had to do with intention and the pursuit of a goal. In view of this, I might have done better to avoid it altogether. Instead of the term "intentional" the Scholastics very frequently used the expression "objective." This has to do with the fact that something is an object for the mentally active subject, and, as such, is present in some manner in his consciousness, whether it is merely thought of or also desired, shunned, etc. I preferred

principle he put activities that had been united by his first classification into different classes. For the reference to the object is
different in thought and in desire. And it is precisely this that
differentiates the two classes for Aristotle. He did not believe that
they are directed toward different objects, but that they are directed
toward the same object in different ways. He said clearly, both in his
treatise *On the Soul* and in his *Metaphysics* that thought and desire
have the same object. It is first present in the faculty of thought and
there the desire stirs.* So the first classification was based upon
differences in the bearers of mental phenomena and the extent to
which they are distributed over a wider or narrower range of beings
endowed with mental faculties; the second is based upon differences
in their mode of reference to the immanent object. The order of the
succession of the member classes is determined by the relative
independence of the phenomena.† Presentations belong to the first
class, but a presentation is the necessary antecedent condition of any
desire.

3. An essentially Aristotelian classification remained dominant
throughout the Middle Ages; indeed its influence extends into modern times.

When Wolff divides the faculties of the soul first into *higher* and
lower faculties, then into the faculties of *cognition* and *desire*, and
makes these two classifications cut across one another, it is easy to
see that this schema corresponds in essence to the two Aristotelian
classifications.

In England, too, at least the latter classification has held sway for a
long time. It is basic to Hume's inquiries, and both Reid and Brown
introduced only insignificant and by no means auspicious changes.
Reid drew a distinction between the intellectual and active‡ faculties

---

* *De Anima*, III, 10. *Metaphysics*, XII, 7.
† See the passages cited above.
‡ Aristotle had also considered the appetite as the principle of voluntary
movements (*De Anima*, III, 10).

---

the expression "intentional" because I thought there would be an even
greater danger of being misunderstood if I had described the object of
thought as "objectively existing," for modern-day thinkers use this
expression to refer to what really exists as opposed to "mere subjective
appearances." [1911.][1]

[1] Brentano added this note to the 1911 edition. This common characteristic is also overlooked by all those who deny the intentional character of
sensation – those who ascribe it to the idea of Jupiter, for example, but
deny it of the sensation of blue. See Introduction to *Psychology from an
Empirical Standpoint*, p. 395.

of the mind and Brown at first opposed sensations, as *"external affections,"* to all other affective states which he considered as *"internal affections,"* and then divided the latter group into *"intellectual states of mind"* and *"emotions."* The last class embraces all the phenomena included by Aristotle in his concept of ὄρεξις.

4. A classification which was more significant in its divergences and more enduring in its influence and which is even today generally considered a step forward in the classification of mental phenomena, was set up in the second half of the last century by Tetens and Mendelssohn. They divided mental activities into three coordinated classes and assumed for each of them a special mental faculty. Tetens called these three fundamental faculties *feeling, understanding* and the *power to act* (will);* Mendelssohn characterized them as the *faculty of cognition,* the *faculty of feeling, or approbation* ("by which we feel pleasure or pain at something") and the *faculty of desire.*† Kant, a contemporary of theirs, adopted this classification in his own way.‡ He called the three faculties of the soul the *cognitive faculty,* the *feeling of pleasure and pain,* and the *faculty of desire,* and made them the basis of the classification of his critical philosophy. His *Critique of Pure Reason* deals with the cognitive faculty insofar as it contains the principles of knowledge itself; the *Critique of Judgement* with the cognitive faculty insofar as it contains the principles of feeling; and the *Critique of Practical Reason* with the cognitive faculty insofar as it contains the principles of desire. This is chiefly responsible for the classification's having become so influential and widespread that it is almost universally dominant even today.

Kant considers the classification of mental activities into cognition, feeling and will to be fundamental because he believes that none of these three classes is capable of being derived from the others or of being reduced along with any other class to a third class which is their common root.§ The differences between knowing and feeling are too great, he thinks, for such a thing to seem conceivable. Even if pleasure and pain always presuppose knowledge, knowledge is simply not a feeling and a feeling is not knowledge. Similarly, desire reveals

---

* *Ueber die menschliche Natur,* I, Versuch X, 625 (published 1777).

† In a comment on the faculties of cognition, feeling and desire, which dates from 1776, although it was first published in his *Gesammelte Schriften* (IV, 122 ff.); and in *Morgenstunden,* Lecture VII (*Gesammelte Schriften* II, p. 295), which appeared in 1785.

‡ Cp. J. B. Meyer, *Kants Psychologie,* pp. 41 ff.

§ "All faculties or capacities of the soul can be reduced to three, which do not admit of any further derivation from a common ground: the faculty of knowledge, the feeling of pleasure and pain, and the faculty of desire." (*Critique of Judgement,* Intro. III.)

itself to be completely different from either knowledge or feeling. In fact, every desire, not just an explicit act of will, but also an impotent wish and even the yearning for what is known to be impossible,* he says, is a striving for the realization of an object, while knowledge merely apprehends and judges the object, and the feeling of pleasure and pain does not relate to the object at all, but only to the subject, since it is the basis in itself for maintaining its own existence in the subject.†

Kant says little to substantiate and justify his classification. But later on many philosophers such as Carus, Weiss and Krug, who reverted to a twofold classification of faculties of cognition and endeavor, criticized Kant's view and also tried to show that it was impossible from the outset. Then others undertook to defend and develop the ideas which Kant had only outlined. This was particularly true of Sir William Hamilton.

The attacks against Kant's view were indeed peculiar. Krug argued that the faculties of presentation and endeavor should be considered as two different faculties, only because the activity of our mind exhibits a twofold direction, one inward and the other outward. For this reason, the activities of the mind should be divided into immanent or theoretical, and transeunt or practical. It would be impossible to add a third class because such a class would have to have a direction which would be neither inward nor outward, which is inconceivable.

Hamilton had no difficulty in pointing out the vacuity of this type of reasoning. Why, he asks with Biunde, should we not say instead that we must envisage in the same soul three kinds of activities, "an

* *Critique of Judgement*, Intro. III.
† In a section of his treatise *On Philosophy in General*, in which he deals with "The System of all the Faculties of the Human Mind," Kant presents his theory and justifies it more fully than in any other place. He says that certain philosophers have tried to prove that the difference between the cognitive faculty, the feeling of pleasure and pain, and the faculty of desire is merely apparent and have tried to reduce all the faculties to that of cognition. But it was all in vain. "For there is always a great difference between ideas insofar as they, from the point of view of their relation to the object and the unity of consciousness of this object, belong to cognition. The same is true of their objective relation when we consider them on the one hand as the cause of the reality of this object and thus attribute them to the faculty of appetite, and on the other as the cause of their relation to the subject, when they serve as foundation for their own existence, and thus consider them in their relation with the *feeling of pleasure*. This feeling certainly neither is nor produces any knowledge, even though the latter may indeed be presupposed as its fundamental determination' (Kants *Werke*, Rosenkranz ed., I, 586 ff.).

ineunt, an immanent, and a transeunt?"* In fact, by this somewhat cavalier way of proceeding we could arrive at a classification which, in its three parts, would agree well enough with what Kant said of cognition, feeling, and desire, in the above quoted passage.

Hamilton, however, does not confine himself to refuting the attack. He also attempts to offer a positive proof of the necessity for assuming that feelings form a distinct class. To this end he shows that there are certain states of consciousness which can be classified neither as a thought nor as a desire. Such are the emotions which we experience when reading the story of Leonidas' death at Thermopylae, or hearing the following verse in a famous old ballad:

> For Widdington my soul is sad,
> That ever he slain should be,
> For when his legs were stricken off,
> He kneeled and fought on his knee.

Such emotions are not mere processes of thought, nor can they be called acts of will or desire. Still they are mental phenomena, and consequently it is necessary to add to the two classes a third which we could designate, with Kant, as that of feeling.†

It is easy to see that this argument is inadequate. It could be that the terms "will" and "desire," taken in their ordinary usage are too narrow to cover all mental phenomena other than the phenomena of thought. Perhaps there is no appropriate term for these phenomena in our ordinary language, and still the phenomena which we call desires and those we call feelings together constitute a single broad class of mental phenomena which is naturally coordinated with the phenomena of thought. A true justification of the classification is impossible without stating the principles of classification. Hamilton does not hesitate to offer such a principle in another passage, agreeing with Kant that the three classes are for phenomena of different faculties of the soul which cannot be derived from one another.

Descartes, Leibniz, Spinoza, Wolff, Platner and other philosophers, he says, thought that they had to regard the faculty of presentation as the fundamental faculty of the mind from which all the others are derived, because the knowledge involved in inner consciousness accompanies all phenomena. But this is incorrect. "These philosophers did not observe that, although pleasure and pain – although desire and volition, are only as they are known to be; yet, in these modifications, a quality, a phenomenon of mind, absolutely new, has been superadded, which was never involved in, and could, therefore, never have been evolved out of, the mere faculty of knowledge. The

* *Lectures on Metaphysics*, II, 423.
† *Lectures on Metaphysics*, II, 420.

faculty of knowledge is certainly the first in order, inasmuch as it is the *conditio sine qua non* of the others; and we are able to conceive a being possessed of the power of recognizing existence, and yet wholly void of all feeling of pain and pleasure, and of all powers of desire and volition. On the other hand, we are wholly unable to conceive a being possessed of feeling and desire, and, at the same time, without a knowledge of any object upon which his affections may be employed, and without a consciousness of these affections themselves.

"We can further conceive a being possessed of knowledge and feeling alone – a being endowed with the power of recognizing objects, of enjoying the exercise, and of grieving at the restraint, of his activity, and yet devoid of that faculty of voluntary agency – of that conation, which is possessed by man. To such a being would belong feelings of pain and pleasure, but neither desire nor will, properly so-called. On the other hand, however, we cannot possibly conceive the existence of a voluntary activity independently of all feelings; for voluntary conation is a faculty which can only be determined to energy through a pain or pleasure, through an estimate of the relative worth of objects."*

This justification of the classification with respect to the principle, number, kind and order of the member-classes may be regarded as an extension of Kant's comments to the same effect.

Let us now hear from Lotze, who, in opposition to Herbart's new attempt to do away with all plurality of faculties, undertook a thoroughgoing defense of Kant's tripartite classification in his *Medizinische Psychologie* and even more in his *Microcosmus*.

"The older psychology," Lotze says, "was confident that Feeling and Will contain peculiar elements, arising neither from the nature of Ideation nor from the general character of Consciousness, in which all three take part; they were accordingly coordinated with the faculty of Cognition (of Ideation) as two equally original capacities, and more recent conceptions do not seem to be successful in refuting the grounds on which this triad of original faculties was based. We could not indeed wish to maintain that ideation, feeling, and will share between them the realm of the soul, as three independent series of development springing from distinct roots, each growing on unconnected with the others, and coming in contact with the others in varied action and reaction only in the final ramifications of their branching growth. It is too obvious from observation that, in general, incidents in the train of ideas form the points of junction of the feelings, and that from these, from pain and pleasure, are evolved motions of desire and aversion. And yet this evident connection does

* *Lectures on Metaphysics*, I, 187; cp. II, 431.

185

not dispose of the question whether here the preceding event does indeed give rise by its own energy to that which immediately succeeds, as its full and complete efficient cause, or whether it only draws the latter after it, as an exciting occasion, from acting partly with the extraneous force of a silently cooperative condition that eludes our notice. . . .

"A comparison of these mental phenomena forces us, if we are not mistaken, to adopt the latter hypothesis. If we look on the soul as a merely cognitive existence, we shall, in no situation – however peculiar – into which it may be brought by the exercise of that activity, discover any sufficient reason why it should depart from that mode of manifesting itself and develop feelings of pain and pleasure. Of course it may seem, on the contrary, that there is nothing so self-evident as that unreconciled antagonism between different ideas, whose contrariety does violence to the soul, causes it pain, from which must spring an effort after recovery and improvement. But this seems so to us only because we are more than cognitive beings; the necessity of this sequence is apparent not in itself, but from the invariable use and wont of our internal experience, where we have long been accustomed to it as an inevitable matter of fact. This alone makes it possible for us to overlook that in truth between each preceding and each subsequent link in the series there is a gap, which we can fill up only by bringing in some as yet unobserved condition. Apart from this experience, the merely cognitive soul would find in itself no reason for regarding an internal change – even were it one fraught with risk to the continuance of its existence – otherwise than with the indifferent keenness of scrutiny with which it would look upon any other conflict of forces; further, should a feeling, arising from other sources, set itself alongside of the perception, the merely feeling soul would yet even in the intensest pain find in itself neither reason nor capacity for going on to an effort after alteration; it would suffer, without being roused to will. Now this is not so, and in order that it should not be so, the capacity of feeling pleasure and pain must be originally inherent in the soul; also the separate events of the train of ideas, reacting on the nature of the soul, do not produce the capacity, but only rouse it to utterance; moreover, whatever feelings may sway the soul, they do not beget effort, they only become motives for a power of volition which they find existing in the soul, but which, were it absent, they could never inspire. . . .

"These three primitive powers would thus stand as progressive grades of capacity and the manifestation of the one set free the energy of the next."*

* *Microcosmus*, I, 177 ff.

Lotze carried this explanation, justification, and defense of the Kantian classification even further. The passage quoted above, however, is enough to show us that the way he conceives the principle and established the trichotomy of faculties and their order agrees with that of Hamilton. Indeed, neither of them does more than extend Kant's ideas.

Yet the principle employed by Kant in his fundamental classification and adopted by both Hamilton and Lotze as well as by many others, does not seem very appropriate for the determination of the fundamental classes. I say this not because I accept Herbart's opinion on the matter, but rather for an opposite reason.

If two phenomena are to be ascribed to two different basic classes just because the capacity for the one cannot be inferred *a priori* from the capacity for the other, we would have to distinguish not only presentation from feeling and desire as Kant, Hamilton, and Lotze do, but we would also have to distinguish sight from taste and even seeing red from seeing blue, as phenomena belonging to distinct fundamental classes.

With respect to sight and taste what I have just said is evident. There are, in fact, numerous species of lower animals which possess the sense of taste without sight. But as I have said, the same thing applies to seeing red and seeing blue. An obvious proof of this is provided by the phenomenon of red-blindness or Daltonism, as it is called.*

These considerations show beyond any doubt that the capacity for perceiving one color cannot be inferred from the presence of the capacity for perceiving another color. In fact, if we were limited to seeing only blue and yellow, we would never have the slightest

* [Editor's note: The remainder of this paragraph, as it appeared in the 1874 edition, was omitted from the 1911 and 1924 editions. The text was as follows: "Someone who is red-blind sees only the intermediate colors in the spectrum, while more strongly or weakly refracted light rays such as red and violet escape him. There are also kinds of light rays, as is well-known, that even the normal eye is incapable of seeing, namely those which are more strongly refracted than red and more weakly refracted than violet. We obtain knowledge of them only through their chemical effects and their effect on temperature, as well as through experiments in which we succeed in transforming a prismatic color into another which is more strongly or more weakly refracted. We also transform light rays which are invisible to us into visible ones in this way. It is obvious that there is nothing against our assuming that with eyes or a sense of vision different from our own, a more extended scale of colors would be possible, one which would also sense the kinds of light we cannot and which would relate to ours, then, as they do to the eyes and visual sense of the red-blind person."]

187

notion of red.[2] For this reason, even John Stuart Mill looks upon the appearance of every single color as an ultimate underivable fact.*

Now anyone can see that it would be absurd to assign to different fundamental classes the presentations of red and of other particular species of color as phenomena dependent upon different original faculties which are incapable of being derived from one another. We are thus forced to the conclusion that this principle of classification is in no way appropriate for determining the fundamental classes of mental phenomena. If it were, however, we would obviously have to distinguish not only thought, feeling, and volition, but an incomparably greater number of fundamental classes of mental phenomena as well.

It is certainly somewhat awkward to claim that Kant and the eminent men who followed him in advocating a threefold classification did not take sufficient account of the principle which guided them in their classification. Besides, we find that Kant's predecessors, Tetens and Mendelssohn, had already appealed to the underivability of the faculties to justify their fundamental classification. Nevertheless, if we bear in mind the disparity between the alleged basis of this classification and its structure, we cannot avoid the assumption that all these thinkers were guided, more or less unconsciously, by entirely different motives. And there are unmistakable signs of this to be found in their own statements.

What really prompted Kant to divide mental activities into his three classes was, I believe, their similarity or difference when looked at from a point of view similar to that adopted by Aristotle when he distinguished between thinking and desire. The passage of his treatise on philosophy in general which we have quoted above clearly places the distinction between *knowing* and *desiring* in a difference in their reference to the object, while the distinctive characteristic of *feeling* is sought in the fact that it does not have such a reference, since this mental phenomenon only refers to the subject.†
This, then, was the important difference, from which, of course, the mutual underivability may follow. But it in itself is a cleft which cuts more deeply than mutual underivability – a cleft which does not exist in this way in the other instances in which we are forced to assume distinct original faculties.

We find the same thing in Hamilton. If we ask him why he

---

* *A System of Logic*, Book III, Chap. 14, Sect. 2.
† See above, p. 183 note †.
[2] The first edition reads, "In fact, if we were limited to seeing green, we would never have the slightest notion of yellow." So in 1874 Brentano took green to be a simple color. He abandoned this view later and combated it energetically in his *Untersuchungen zur Sinnespsychologie*.

characterizes feeling and volition as phenomena of particular original faculties and considers it impossible to explain them by means of *one* fundamental faculty, he gives the following answer in the second book of his *Lectures on Metaphysics*. He says he does this because in these phenomena consciousness reveals to us certain other qualities which are neither explicitly nor implicitly included in the phenomena of knowledge itself, though knowledge is always mixed in with them because of inner perception.

"The characters by which these three classes are reciprocally discriminated are the following. – In the phaenomena of Cognition, consciousness distinguishes an object known from the subject knowing. . . .

"In the phaenomena of Feeling, – the phaenomena of Pleasure and Pain, – on the contrary, consciousness does not place the mental modification or state before itself; it does not contemplate it apart, – as separate from itself, – but is, as it were, fused into one. The peculiarity of Feeling, therefore, is that there is nothing but what is subjectively subjective," an expression which we have already mentioned once before.[3] "In the phaenomena of Conation, – the phaenomena of Desire and Will, – there is, as in those of Cognition, an object, and this object is also an object of knowledge. . . . But though both cognition and conation bear relation to an object, they are discriminated by the difference of this relation itself. In cognition, there exists no want; and the object, whether objective or subjective, is not sought for, nor avoided; whereas in conation, there is a want, and a tendency supposed which results in an endeavor, either to obtain the object, when the cognitive faculties represent it as fitted to afford the fruition of the want; or to ward off the object, if these faculties represent it as calculated to frustrate the tendency of its accomplishment."*

This passage from Hamilton seems almost like a paraphrased commentary of Kant's remark mentioned earlier. It is in essential agreement with it and all it does is state the case more clearly and completely. Clearly, when we go to the heart of the matter, Hamilton classified mental phenomena into different fundamental classes from the point of view of intentional inexistence, just as Aristotle did. According to Hamilton, in certain mental phenomena there is no intentional inexistence of an object at all; he places feelings in this category. But on his view even those which have an intentionally inexisting object are supposed to exhibit a fundamental difference in the way the object inexists, and thus they fall into two groups, thought and volition.

* *Lectures on Metaphysics*, II, 431 ff.
[3] See above, I, pp. 89 ff., and *Untersuchungen zur Sinnespsychologie*, p. 120.

Finally, in the case of Lotze, there are plenty of indications that there was a factor more important than the mere underivability of the faculties which made him view the three classes, presentation, feeling, and volition, as different basic classes of mental phenomena. It was only because the Herbartian school had denied this underivability that he emphasized this point. The fact that there are more than three faculties of the soul which are not derivable from one another does not escape Lotze; rather, he regards the ability to see and the ability to hear as different elementary abilities, just as we do. And we find this fact mentioned precisely when he discusses the three basic classes.* Why then did he assign presentation of sound and colors in the same fundamental class? And why was he not influenced in his classification by other differences, especially in the domain of feeling, whose similar underivability is easy to prove? The decisive factor must have been the perception of an especially profound difference existing between these three classes, but which is not similarly found in other cases in which derivation is impossible. After what we have discovered in Kant and Hamilton, we may suspect from the outset that it was a differentiation of mental activities with respect to their reference to an object which led Lotze, too, to consider the three classes as the most distinct and as the basic classes of mental phenomena.

All that remains to be investigated, then, is whether it really is a good idea to adopt this point of view when making a fundamental classification of mental activities, and whether the threefold division into thought, feeling and volition really coincides with and exhausts the fundamental differences revealed by mental phenomena in this connection. We shall deal with this point when, after completing our survey of previous attempts at a classification, we have to decide our own views on the matter.

5. As we have already remarked, the division of consciousness into presentation, feeling, and will has been very generally accepted in recent times. Even Herbart and his school have adopted it, and, in their treatises on empirical psychology, Herbartians make it the basis of the order they impose upon their material, just as others do. What is different about them is that they do not consider the two latter classes to be separate original faculties; rather, they want to derive them from the first class – an attempt which is obviously futile, as we have already remarked on several occasions.

6. Among the representatives of the empirical school in England, which is opposed, to a certain extent, to Hamilton's school, Alexander Bain has likewise set up his own threefold division using similar terms. He distinguishes first, thought, intellect or cognition;

* *Microcosmus*, I, 177 ff.

second, feeling; and third and last, volition or the will. Thus it would seem that here, too, we encounter the same classification, and Bain himself points to this similarity as a confirmation of his view.

Yet, if we examine the explanation which Bain gives of the three parts of his classification, we notice that his use of the same expressions conceals a considerable difference in ideas. By "volition" or "will" Bain understands something entirely different from what the German psychologists, and Hamilton, usually designate by this term. He uses it to mean "the effect produced by mental phenomena." So at the beginning of his voluminous work on the senses and the intellect he declares that volition or the will embraces *all of our activity* insofar as it is controlled by our feelings.* Further on he explains this concept in the following way:

"All beings," he says, "recognized as possessing mind cannot only feel, but also act. The putting forth of force to attain some end marks a mental nature. *Eating, running, flying, sowing, building, speaking* – are operations rising above the play of feeling. They all originate in some feelings to be satisfied *which give them the character of proper mental actions.* When an animal *tears, masticates,* and *swallows its food, hunts its prey,* or *flees from danger,* the stimulus or support of the activity is furnished by its sensations or feelings. To this feeling-prompted activity we give the name volition."†

We would not call eating, walking, speaking, and the like, acts of will, but only effects of an act of will. Kant, of course, sometimes speaks of desire as though he thought of it as the production of the desired object. In his *Critique of Practical Reason* he defined the faculty of desire as "the power [a being has] of causing, through its ideas, the reality of the objects of these ideas."‡ But I will never believe that he meant to call eating or walking a desire; everything indicates, rather, that he was merely expressing his ideas in an inappropriate way.§ Bain is another matter. His statements above force us to admit that he actually did use the term "will" in a deviant sense. What he says immediately afterwards confirms this interpretation. He tries to establish the difference between what he calls "volition" and the natural forces of wind, water, gravity, gunpowder, etc., as well as unconscious physiological functions such as

---

* *The Senses and The Intellect*, p. 2.
† *The Senses and the Intellect*, p. 4. Cp. *Mental and Moral Science*, p. 2.
‡ *Critique of Practical Reason*, Preface. See *Critique of Judgement*, Intro., III, and the note and passages from his treatise on philosophy in general cited above, p. 183 note †.
§ Otherwise he would not have counted every wish and longing a desire (which Bain does not do), nor would he have placed freedom in the faculty of desire.

the circulation of the blood. He obviously would not have done this if he had not understood "volition" to mean not so much an inner mental phenomenon as a (physical) effect of mental phenomena, hence a physiological or, if you wish, a psychophysical phenomenon.

Basically, then, Bain's classification of mental phenomena agrees more with the Aristotelian twofold division into thought and desire (with which a voluntary movement is connected under certain circumstances) than with the later threefold division into presentation, feeling and desire. What we call desire and will, Bain classifies as feeling. And for him, feeling and will seem to constitute *one* single class. He further broadened the domain of feeling in still another area by including sensations in its sphere, which, according to most modern thinkers and Aristotle himself, should be ascribed to the first class.

In addition to this classification, Bain has still another classification which cuts across this one. He divides mental phenomena into primitive phenomena and those which emerge from primitive phenomena as development takes place. In the first class he includes sensations, desires resulting from the needs of the organism, and instincts, by which he means actions which are carried out without having been learned or practiced. He makes this dichotomy, in preference to all other classifications, the basis of his arrangement of the material in the later editions of his great psychological work as well as in his compendium. Bain seems to have been prompted to this dichotomy by Herbert Spencer, in whom a similar division of mental phenomena into primitive and more developed phenomena may be discerned, just as the idea of evolution generally dominates all others in his *Principles of Psychology*. Spencer divides the more developed mental activities into cognitive (memory, reason) and affective (desire, will), and thinks that both classes have their origin in primitive phenomena. Thus we could perhaps say that, there is a second classification that cuts across the first and which, in its arrangement is reminiscent of the Aristotelian distinction between νοῦς and ὄρεξις.*

7. With this we can bring to a close our survey of the principal attempts at classification. If we take account of the principles we found applied in them, we discover four different viewpoints. Three of these we had already encountered in Aristotle. He had divided mental activities, first according to whether or not he believed them to be linked with the body; then according to whether or not he thought they were common to men and animals or were exclusively

* Cp. Ribot, *Psychologie Anglaise Contemporaine* (Paris, 1870), p. 191, a work that contains a very nice survey of Spencer's psychological views in particular.

human; and finally according to their different modes of intentional inexistence, or, to put it another way, according to differences in their modes of consciousness. The last principle of classification has been used most frequently and in all periods. In addition to these three, there is the principle used in Bain's second classification which divides mental phenomena into primitive phenomena and phenomena which develop out of them.

In the following investigations, we shall try to come to a decision of our own with respect to both the principle and the structure of the basic classification.

VI

Classification of Mental Activities into Presentations, Judgements, and Phenomena of Love and Hate

---

1. To what principles must we adhere in the fundamental classification of mental phenomena? Obviously to the same ones that are taken into consideration in other cases of classification, and the natural sciences offer us many outstanding examples of their application.

A scientific classification should be such that it arranges the objects in a manner favorable to research. To this end, it must be natural, that is to say, it must unite into a single class objects closely related by nature, and it must separate into different classes objects which are relatively distant by nature. Thus classification is only possible when there is a certain amount of knowledge of the objects to be classified, and it is the fundamental rule of classification that it should proceed from a study of the objects to be classified and not from an *a priori* construction. Krug committed this error when he argued from the outset that mental activities had to be of two types, those directed inward from without, and those directed outward from within. Horwicz, too, violated this principle when, as we saw earlier,* instead of striving to confirm or to correct the usual classification by a more precise study of mental phenomena themselves, he jumped to the conclusion, on the basis of physiological observations which revealed the opposition between sensory and motor nerves, that a similar opposition between thought and desire extends throughout the whole mental realm. In view of the backward state of their science, it is easy to understand why psychologists might be

---

* Book One, Chap. 3, Sect. 5.

194

glad to acquire an appropriate classification supported by investigations of something other than mental phenomena. But if the natural procedure is still impracticable, no other procedure can offer us any hope of approaching our goal. On the other hand, if we allow ourselves to be guided by the psychological knowledge which has been attained so far, we shall at least pave the way for the best ultimate classification, even though it may be impossible as yet to establish it. For here, as in other fields, the classification and knowledge of characteristics and laws will mutually perfect one another as the science develops further.[1]

2. All the attempts at classification which were discussed in the previous chapter deserve our approval insofar as they proceed from the study of mental phenomena. Their authors were also aware of the fact that the structure must be in conformity with nature, for they let themselves be guided by the independence of certain phenomena from others or their radical dissimilarity. Of course this is not to say that they were not misled in their efforts by this imperfect knowledge of the psychological sphere. In any case, some of these attempted classifications are less valuable than others both because their basis is still subject to dispute, and because the advantages which they seemed to hold for research were lost as a result of special difficulties.

Let us clarify these statements with specific examples.

Aristotle divided mental phenomena into those common to man and animals and those which are peculiar to man. From the standpoint of the Aristotelian theory, this classification appears to have many advantages. For Aristotle believed that certain faculties of the soul were the exclusive property of man and were immaterial, whereas he held that the faculties which are common to all animals are faculties of a bodily organ. Consequently, supposing that the Aristotelian theories are correct, this classification divides into two groups phenomena which occur in isolation from others in nature, too. And the fact that the latter are functions of an organ, while the former are not, allows us to assume the existence of important common characteristics and laws in each of these two classes of phenomena. But the Aristotelian theories on the basis of which this classification suggests itself are highly controversial. Many deny the claim that intellectual powers belong exclusively to men as opposed to animals; and in general people are unable to agree as to which mental phenomena are common to men and animals and which are

[1] The purely descriptive or "phenomenological" point of view already is prevalent in Brentano's thinking here. This is why I said that it was historically incorrect to trace the distinction between descriptive and genetic psychology back to Hering, who drew it only for the area of *sensations*.

not. While Descartes denies all mental activity to animals, other not unimportant scholars allow the higher classes of animals to share with us all kinds of simpler mental phenomena. They believe that there is only a difference of degree between our activities and the activities of those animals, and they are of the opinion that all the differences between animal behavior and ours can be adequately explained by this fact. If Aristotle, in particular, believes that animals lack the capacity for general, abstract concepts, Locke certainly agrees with him, but from various other sides opposition arises to the idea that this constitutes a fundamental difference between the mental endowment of men and animals. Some consider it a proven fact that animals, too, have general concepts; others, Berkeley in the vanguard, deny that even men have them.

Even though the study of reflexes has inclined many modern thinkers toward Descartes' view, it will trouble us even less. For even now reputable thinkers representing otherwise divergent schools of thought profess the opposite point of view. The followers of Berkeley in particular have become numerous in England and are beginning to gain ground on the Continent as well. Now if there were really no qualitative difference, so to speak, between the mental endowment of men and animals, the classification of mental phenomena into phenomena common to all animals and phenomena peculiar to man would obviously lose much of its importance. In any case, the conflicting views and the difficulty of resolving them prevents us from using this as the fundamental classification for the organization of our material.

Besides that, the main advantage which this classification at best could offer to research, i.e. the study of one sphere of our mental phenomena in isolation, is essentially limited by the fact that we have only indirect insight into the mental life of animals. This fact as well as the desire to make no unproved assumptions, are the reasons why Aristotle himself did not use it as the fundamental classification in his systematic treatise on the soul.

Bain, as we have heard, divided mental phenomena into elementary phenomena and the phenomena which develop from them. Here, too, the first class encompasses phenomena which occur in nature independently of the others. But again something holds true here, which is similar to what we have just seen, namely, that where these phenomena do occur independently, they are not directly observable by us. In addition, it is no small difficulty to arrive at a confident opinion concerning the nature of the first beginnings of mental life. When, in later years, a physical stimulus produces a sensation, acquired dispositions can exert a powerful transforming influence upon such a sensation.[2] And in fact, we find that this field is one of the principal areas of controversy today. Consequently, no matter how much we must take Bain's viewpoint into consideration in determining the organization of our investigations, we will do better to choose a different criterion for our fundamental classification.

Of the classifications which we have considered there still remain those which have as their basis of classification the different relations that mental activities have to their immanent objects. or their different kinds of intentional inexistence. Aristotle preferred this point of of view to all others for arranging the material. In later periods, thinkers holding the most diverse views have, more or less consciously, inclined toward this point of view more frequently than any other for the fundamental classification of mental phenomena. Nothing distinguishes mental phenomena from physical phenomena more than the fact that something is immanent as an object in them.[3] For this reason it is easy to understand that the fundamental differences in the way something exists in them as an object constitute the principal class differences among mental phenomena. The more psychology has developed, the more it has discovered that the properties and laws common to each group of mental phenomena are more closely connected with fundamental differences in the way the phenomena refer to an object than with any other difference. And if the classifications mentioned earlier were open to the objection that a large part of their usefulness was lost because of the observer's position, the classification in question is free from such a limitation on its value. Thus, many quite different considerations lead us to make use of the same principle for our fundamental classification as well.

3. But how many and which fundamental classes must we distinguish? We saw that there is no unanimity among psychologists on this question. Aristotle distinguished two fundamental classes, thought and appetite. Most modern authors instead prefer a trichotomy of presentation, feeling and will (or whatever they choose to call them).

To state our view at the outset, we, too, maintain that three main classes of mental phenomena must be distinguished, and distinguished according to the different ways in which they refer to their

[2] The greatest difficulties in the psychology of sensation and the so-called *theory of perception* stem from this.
[3] Although Husserl remarks, in *Logical Investigations*, II, 856, that, according to Brentano, mental phenomena are "adequately" characterized as objects of inner perception, this and other passages show clearly that nothing characterizes them as certainly as the "having-of-something-objectively."

content. But my three classes are not the same as those which are usually proposed. In the absence of more appropriate expressions we designate the first by the term "presentation," the second by the term "judgement," and the third by the terms "emotion," "interest," or "love."[4]

None of these is such that it cannot be misunderstood; on the contrary, each of them is often used in a more restricted sense than the one in which I use it. Our vocabulary, however, provides us with no unitary expressions which coincide better with the concepts. And, although it is somewhat hazardous to use expressions with variable meaning in definitions of such great importance, especially when using them in a wider sense than usual, it still seems to me better than introducing completely new and unfamiliar terms.

We have already explained what we mean by "presentation." We speak of a presentation whenever something appears to us. When we see something, a color is presented; when we hear something, a sound; when we imagine something, a fantasy image.[5] In view of the generality with which we use this term it can be said that it is impossible for conscious activity to refer in any way to something which is not presented.* When I hear and understand a word that names something, I have a presentation of what that word designates; and generally speaking the purpose of such words is to evoke presentations.†

By "judgement" we mean, in accordance with common philosophical usage, acceptance (as true) or rejection (as false). We have already noted, however, that such acceptance or rejection also occurs

* Book Two, Chap. I, Sect. 3.

† Meyer in *Kants Psychologie*, Bergmann in *Vom Bewusstsein*, Wundt in *Physiologische Psychologie*, and others use the concept of presentation in a much more restricted sense, while Herbart and Lotze, for example, use it in the same way we do. We can apply here what we have previously said with regard to the term "consciousness" (Book Two, Chap. II, Sect. 1). The best thing to do would be to use this term in such a way as to fill a gap in our terminology as best we can. While we have other expressions for less general classes, we have no other expressions for our first fundamental class. Consequently, the use of the term "presentation" in this very general sense seems called for.

[4] In the notes to *The Origin of Our Knowledge of Right and Wrong*, Brentano shows that Descartes preceded him in this threefold division. Descartes distinguished: *ideae, iudicia, voluntates*.

[5] In connection with this, see Book Two, Chap. I, note 2. We do not see "landscapes," "boxes" and so on, but extended color-patches. In the *Untersuchungen zur Sinnespsychologie*, Brentano shows that we not only have a presentation of the color, the sound, etc., but also have a blind belief in them.

in cases in which many people would not use the term "judgement," as, for example, in the perception of mental acts and in remembering. But of course we will not hesitate to include these cases, too, in the class of judgement.

The lack of a single appropriate expression is felt most strongly in the case of the third class, whose phenomena we designated as "emotions," as "phenomena of interest" or as "phenomena of love." In our view this class is said to include all mental phenomena which are not included in the first two classes. But the term "emotion" is usually understood to mean only affects which are connected with noticeable physical agitation. Everybody would call anger, anxiety and passionate desire emotions; but in the general way in which we use the word, it also applies to all wishes, decisions and intentions. Yet Kant, at least, used the word (*Gemüt*) in an even broader sense than ours, since he characterizes every mental faculty, even that of knowledge, as a faculty of emotion.

Likewise, the term "interest" is usually used only to designate certain acts which belong to the class we are describing, namely, those in which curiosity or inquisitiveness are aroused. Yet it is not inappropriate to describe every pleasure or displeasure in something as interest, and every wish, every voluntary decision is an act of taking an interest in something, too.

Strictly speaking, instead of the simple term "love" I should have used the expression "love or hate" to characterize the third class. In the interest of brevity I have used just one of the two words, only because we do the same thing in other instances; for example, we say a judgement is an act by means of which we hold something to be true, or we speak of the phenomena of desire in the broad sense of the term* yet we always think of these expressions as meaning the opposite as well. But even apart from this, some people will perhaps criticize me for using this term in too broad a sense. And it is certain that the word "love" does not, in each of its senses, cover the entire area. In fact, in one sense we say that we love our friend and in another that we love wine; I love my friend in that I wish him well, but I love wine in that I desire it as something good and drink it with pleasure. Now I believe that in every act which belongs to this third class something is loved, or, more strictly speaking, loved or hated, in the sense in which we used the word in the second case above. Just as every judgement takes an object to be true or false, in an analogous way every phenomenon which belongs to this class takes an object to be good or bad. In subsequent discussions, we shall explain

* Kant has followed the same procedure by calling one of his three fundamental faculties the appetitive faculty and Aristotle by employing the term ὄρεξις [appetite] to designate one of his fundamental classes.

this point in more detail, and, hopefully, establish it beyond doubt.[6]

4. If we compare our trichotomy with that which has been dominant in psychology since Kant, we discover that it differs in two respects. It divides into two fundamental classes the phenomena which until now have been united in the first class; and it combines the phenomena of the last two classes into one. In each of these respects we shall have to justify our position.

But how are such justifications to be achieved? Is there anything we can do besides appeal to inner experience which teaches us that the relation of consciousness to its object is either exactly the same or similar in one set of cases and a radically different one in the other? It would seem that no other means is available. Inner experience is clearly the only arbiter which can resolve disputes about the sameness or difference of intentional reference. But each of our opponents cites his own inner experience, too. And whose experience should take precedence?

Still, the difficulty here is no different than in many other cases. People make errors in observation, too, whether through oversight or because characteristics which are inferred or otherwise attained through reasoning are mixed up with or confused with what has been observed.[7] But if others call our attention to this point, we recognize, especially by observing a second time, the errors we made. We will have to follow the same procedure here, in the hope of winning the assent of our opponents and reaching complete agreement on this important question.

But if inherited and deep-rooted prejudices accompany errors in observation, experience shows us and psychology explains the fact that this makes it much more difficult to recognize one's error. In such an event it is not enough merely to contradict the received opinion and to recommend that new observations be made. Nor is it enough to call attention to the points at which the errors in the observation you wish to correct occur, and to contrast these errors with the true state of affairs. What we have to do instead is at the same time direct our attention to related characteristics, especially those which are universally accepted but which contradict the alleged observation. Finally, we must try to discover not only the error, but also the cause of the error.

If this procedure is ever called for, it is called for in this case. In the next chapter we shall try to give a careful justification along these lines of our separation of presentation and judgement, and in the following chapter we shall do the same for our combination of feeling and will.

[6] See *The Origin of Our Knowledge of Right and Wrong.*
[7] See Supplementary Essay XII, note 3.

VII

Presentation and Judgement: Two Different Fundamental Classes

1. When we say that presentation and judgement are two different fundamental classes of mental phenomena, we mean, in accord with our preceding remarks, that they are two entirely different ways of being conscious of an object. This is not to deny that every judgement presupposes a presentation. On the contrary, we maintain that every object which is judged enters into consciousness in two ways: as an object of presentation and as an object of affirmation or denial. This relation, then, is similar to the one which most philosophers – Kant as well as Aristotle – have rightly assumed, as we have seen, to hold between presentation and desire. Nothing is an object of desire which is not an object of presentation; but desire constitutes a second, entirely new and distinctive type of reference to the object, a second entirely new way in which it enters into consciousness. It is also true that nothing is an object of judgement which is not an object of presentation, and we maintain that when the object of presentation becomes the object of an affirmative or negative judgement, our consciousness enters into a completely new kind of relationship with the object. This object is present in consciousness in a twofold way, first as an object of presentation, then as an object held to be true or denied, just as when someone desires an object, the object is immanent both as presented and as desired at the same time.[1]

This, we maintain, is revealed clearly to us by inner perception and the attentive observation of the phenomena of judgement in memory.

2. The true relation between judgement and presentation has, to be sure, been generally misunderstood despite this fact. And so I must expect my position to meet with the greatest suspicion at first, even

[1] It is not that the object is contained in consciousness in duplicate, but that one is concerned with the thing in a twofold way.

though I say nothing which is not confirmed by the testimony of inner perception.

Even if you refuse to admit that in judgement there is, in addition to presentation, a second and radically different way in which consciousness refers to the object,[2] it is not and cannot be denied that there is some difference between the one state and the other. Perhaps a closer examination of where the difference between judgement and presentation might really lie, if it is not interpreted in our way, may make our opponents more inclined to accept our view, by showing that there is no reasonably acceptable alternative.

If a second, distinctive mode of referring to an object were not present, in addition to the presentation, in judgement, then the way in which the object of judgement is in one's consciousness is essentially the same as the way in which the object of presentation is in consciousness. So the difference between them could be made out only in one of two ways: it could either be a difference in content, i.e. a difference between the objects to which presentation and judgement refer, or a difference in the fullness with which we have the same content* before the mind in mere presentation and in judgement. For there certainly is an intrinsic difference between the kind of thought which we call presentation and the kind of thought which we call judgement.

Bain, of course, had the unfortunate idea of looking for the difference between presenting and judging not in the activities of thought themselves, but in the consequences stemming from them. Because we let something influence our actions and volition in a special way when we judge it to be true as opposed to merely having a presentation of it, he thought that the difference between holding something to be true and mere presentation simply consists in this influence upon the will. The presentation which exerts such an influence becomes, by virtue of the very fact that it exerts it, a belief. I have called this theory unfortunate. And, indeed, why is it

---

* The way in which I use the term "content" here, a usage which I retain in this edition in the interest of reproducing the original text faithfully, is hardly to be recommended. It differs from its usual use, for no one would say that the judgement, "God exists", has the same content as the judgement, "God does not exist", just because they have the same object. In the remarks appended to the present edition, I have used the term in its ordinary sense and not in the unusual sense in which it was used here. [1911.][3]

[2] This formulation expresses Brentano's theory better than it does to say, as above, that the object is present in consciousness in a twofold way.

[3] The word "content" is often used in this way, which Brentano has rejected, but not in a consistent manner.

that the one presentation of an object has such an influence on behaviour while the other does not? Just to raise the question is enough to show very clearly the oversight of which Bain is guilty. There would be no special consequences, if there were no special basis for them in the nature of the thought process. Rather than making the assumption of an intrinsic difference between mere presentation and judgement unnecessary, the difference in consequences emphatically points up this intrinsic difference. When challenged by John Stuart Mill,* Bain himself acknowledged that the position he had advocated in his major work on the emotions and the will† as well as in the first editions of his compendium of psychology was mistaken, and he repudiated the opinion in a concluding note to the third edition.‡

The elder Mill§ and, more recently, Herbert Spencer,¶ have committed a similar error. These two philosophers are of the opinion that the presentation of the union of two characteristics is accompanied by belief when an inseparable association is formed between these two characteristics in consciousness, i.e. when the habit of presenting two characteristics together has become so strong that the presentation of one invariably and irresistibly calls the other into consciousness and becomes connected with it. Belief, they tell us, is nothing more than this inseparable association. We will not inquire at this point whether it really is true that whenever a certain combination of characteristics is affirmed as true, an inseparable association really exists between them, and whenever such an association is formed, the combination is really held to be true. Even if we assume that both of these claims are correct, it is still easy to see that this definition of the distinction between judgement and presentation will not do, because if this were the only difference between the judgement and the corresponding presentation, then both, considered in themselves, would be exactly the same act of thought. The habit of thinking about two characteristics joined together is not itself a thought or a particular characteristic of a thought, but a disposition which manifests itself only in its consequences. And the impossibility of thinking about one of the two characteristics without thinking about the other one is not a thought or a particular characteristic of a thought either.

* In a note to *Analysis of the Phenomena of the Human Mind*, by James Mill, 2nd ed., I, 402.
† *The Emotions and the Will.*
‡ *Mental and Moral Science*, 3rd ed. (London, 1872), note on the chapter on belief, Appendix, p. 100.
§ *Analysis of the Phenomena of the Human Mind*, Chap. XI.
¶ *Principles of Psychology*, 2nd ed. (London and Edinburgh, 1870), I. See also the note by John Stuart Mill mentioned above.

On the contrary, according to the views of these philosophers, it is only this disposition to a particularly high degree. If this disposition only manifests itself in the fact that the combination of characteristics is thought of without exception, but is still thought of in exactly the same way as it was before the acquisition of this disposition, it is clear that, as we said, there is no intrinsic difference between the earlier thought, which was a mere presentation, and the later thought, which is supposed to be a belief. But if the disposition turns out to have influence in still another way, so that after it has been acquired it modifies the thought of the combination and confers upon it a new, special characteristic, then we have to say that it is this quality rather than the inseparable association by which it is produced that constitutes the real difference between holding something to be true and mere presentation. That is why I said that James Mill's and Herbert Spencer's error is related to Bain's. For, just as Bain confused a distinctive feature of the consequences with the intrinsic property of holding a thing to be true, the elder Mill and Spencer proposed as a distinctive feature of this sort of thought process a characteristic which, at best, they could only have called the possible cause of its distinctive character.

3. This much, then, is certain: the difference between presentation and judgement must be an intrinsic difference between the one kind of thought and the other. And if this is true, then what we said above is too, namely, that those who reject our view of judgement can only seek the difference between judgement and mere presentation in one of two things: either in a difference in the objects which are thought, or in a difference in the fullness with which these objects are thought. Let us take up the second of these two hypotheses first.

When it comes to a difference in the fullness of two mental activities which are alike in the way in which they refer to their object, as well as in the content to which they refer, it can only be a difference in the intensity of the two acts. The question to be investigated, therefore, is just this: does the distinctive character of judgement, as opposed to presentation, consist in the fact that in judgement the content is thought of with a greater intensity, so that a presentation of an object might attain the status of a judgement simply by increasing in intensity? It is self-evident that such a position cannot be correct. On this view, judgement would merely be a more intense presentation and presentation a weaker judgement. But to be an object of presentation is not to be an object of judgement no matter how clear and distinct and vivid it is, and a judgement, no matter how little confidence we have in it, is not merely a presentation. Of course a person may take to be true something which appears to him with feverish vividness in his imagination just as he does something he sees,[4] and perhaps he would not have done this if the impression had been less strong. But even if in certain cases the act of taking something to be true coincides with the greater intensity of a presentation, the presentation is not, on that account, itself a judgement. That is why the error in question may disappear, while the vividness of the presentation persists. And in other cases we are firmly convinced of the truth of something, even though the content of the judgement is anything but vivid. Finally, if the affirmation of an object were an intense presentation, how would we conceive of the negation of the same object?

It would doubtless be unprofitable to spend any more time combating a hypothesis which, it is clear from the outset, very few people would be inclined to defend. Instead, let us see if we can show that the other alternative, which might seem more plausible to those who reject our view, is impossible.

4. It is a very common opinion that judgement consists in a combination or separation that takes place in the realm of presentation. The affirmative judgement and, in a somewhat modified way, the negative judgement are usually characterized, in contrast with mere presentations, as compound or associative thought processes. Interpreted in this way, the difference between judgement and mere presentation would really be nothing but a difference between the content of a judgement[5] and the content of a presentation.

If a certain kind of union or relationship between two properties were thought, this thought would be a judgement, while every thought which had no such relationship as its content would have to be called a mere presentation.

But this view, too, is untenable.

If we assume it is true that the content of a judgement always consists in a certain kind of combination of several characteristics, we would surely be able to distinguish judgements from some presentations, but by no means from all. For it obviously does happen that an act of thought which is merely a presentation has for its content a combination of characteristics which is completely similar, indeed perfectly identical to that which in another case constitutes the object of a judgement. If I say, "A tree is green," green combined with tree forms the content of my judgement. But someone could ask me, "Is any tree red?" Not being too well acquainted with the vegetative realm, and forgetful of the colors of leaves in autumn, I might withhold all judgement on the matter. Nonetheless, I do understand the question, and so I must have a presentation of a red tree. Red combined with tree, just like green above, would form

---

[4] Compare p. 136 above.   [5] See note 3 to this chapter.

the content of a presentation not accompanied by any judgement. And someone who had only seen trees with red leaves and had never seen one with green would, when questioned about green trees, probably have as the content of this presentation not just a similar combination of characteristics, but the very same one which formed the content of my judgement.

James Mill and Herbert Spencer obviously knew this, for in their definition of the distinctive nature of judgement they did not limit themselves to saying, as most others do, that the content of judgement is a certain kind of combination of presented attributes; they added another condition – that an inseparable association must exist between them. Even Bain deemed it necessary to add a special determining factor, namely the influence of thought upon action. Their error was only that they did not attempt to complete their theories by citing some intrinsic property of judgement. They proposed instead differences in dispositions or consequences. John Stuart Mill was more fortunate. He placed great emphasis on this point, and in general, came closer than any other philosopher to a correct appraisal of the difference between presentation and judgement.

"It is," he says in his *Logic*, "of course, true that . . . when we judge that gold is yellow . . . we must have the idea of gold and the idea of yellow, and these two ideas must be brought together in our mind. But in the first place, it is evident that this is only part of what takes place; for we may put two ideas together without any act of belief; as when we merely imagine something, such as a golden mountain; or when we actually disbelieve: for in order even to disbelieve that Mahomet was an apostle of God, we must put the idea of Mahomet and that of an apostle of God together. To determine what it is that happens in the case of assent or dissent besides putting two ideas together, is one of the most intricate of metaphysical problems."*

In his critical notes to James Mill's *Analysis of the Phenomena of the Human Mind*, he goes into the matter more thoroughly. In the chapter on predication he argues against a view that would regard assertion as the expression of a certain ordering of ideas and would similarly regard a term as the expression of a single idea. He says that the characteristic difference between an assertion and any other form of speech is, rather, that it not only brings a certain object to mind, it also *asserts* something about this object; it not only calls forth a presentation of a certain sequence of ideas, it also calls forth a belief in them, indicating that this order is an actual fact.† He

* *A System of Logic*, Book I, Chap. 5, 1.
† "The characteristic difference between a predication and any other form of speech is that it does not merely bring to mind a certain object . . .; it asserts something respecting it. . . . Whatever view we adopt of the

comes back to this point again and again both in this chapter* and in subsequent ones, as, for example, in the chapter on memory, where he states that in addition to the idea of a thing and the idea of the fact that I have seen it, there must also be the belief that I have seen it.† It is in a lengthy note in the chapter on belief, however, that he discusses most extensively the specific nature of judgement as opposed to presentation. He shows clearly, once again, that judgement cannot be resolved into mere presentation, and that it cannot be made up of a simple combination of presentations. On the contrary, he says, we must recognize that it is impossible to derive the one phenomenon from the other, and we must regard the difference between presentation and judgement as an ultimate and primitive fact. At the end of a rather lengthy discussion he asks himself, "What, in short, is the difference *to our minds* between thinking of a reality and representing to ourselves an imaginary picture? I confess that I can perceive no escape from the opinion that the distinction is ultimate and primordial."‡ We see then that John Stuart Mill recognizes a difference here analogous to that which Kant and others have asserted between thinking and feeling. Expressed in their terminology, Mill's statement would amount to saying that for presentation and belief, or, as we would say, presentation and judgement, two different fundamental faculties must be assumed. In our terminology, however, his theory says that presentation and judgement are two entirely different kinds of reference to a content, two radically different ways of being conscious of an object.

Thus, as we said, even if we assume that a combination or separation of presented attributes really takes place in every judgement – and, in fact, John Stuart Mill was of this opinion§ – it does not

---

* *Analysis*, I, 187, note 55. † *Analysis*, I, Chap. X, 329, note 91.
‡ *Analysis*, I, 412.
§ This view is expressed both in his *Logic*, where he discusses the content of judgement (Book I, Chap. 5), and in his notes on the above-mentioned work of his father. For example, he says, "I think it is true that every assertion, every object of Belief, – everything that can be true or false,

---

psychological nature of belief, it is necessary to distinguish between the mere suggestion to the mind of a certain order among sensations or ideas – such as takes place when we think of the alphabet, or the numeration table – and the indication that this order is an actual fact which is occurring, or which has occurred once or oftener, or which, in certain definite circumstances, always occurs; which are the things indicated as true by an affirmative predication, and as false by a negative one." *Analysis of the Phenomena of the Human Mind*, 2nd ed., Chap. IV, Sect. 4, I, 162 ff., note 48.

follow that the essential property of judgemental thought, as opposed to mere presentation, consists in this. Such a characteristic would distinguish judgement from some presentations, but not from absolutely all of them. So this characteristic would not render superfluous the assumption of another and more characteristic property such as the one we affirm – a difference in modes of consciousness.

5. But there is still more. It is not even correct to say that there is a combination or separation of presented attributes in all judgements. Affirmation and denial are no more always directed toward combinations or connections than desires or aversions are. A single feature which is the object of a presentation can be affirmed or denied, too.

When we say, "A exists," this sentence is not, as many people have believed and still do, a predication in which existence as predicate is combined with "A" as subject. The object affirmed is not the combination of an attribute "existence" with "A" but "A" itself. By the same token, when we say, "A does not exist," there is no predication of the existence of "A" in a negative way – no denial of the conjunction of an attribute "existence" with "A." On the contrary, "A" is the object we deny.

By way of further clarification, I call attention to the fact that when someone affirms a whole, in so doing he affirms each part of the whole as well. So whenever someone affirms a combination of attributes he simultaneously affirms each particular element of the combination. In affirming the existence of a learned man, i.e. the combination of a man and the attribute "learned," he affirms the existence of a man in so doing. Let us apply this to the judgement, "A exists." If the judgement consisted in affirming the combination of an attribute "existence" with A, then it would include the affirmation of each individual element in the combination, and hence would include the affirmation of A. So we do not avoid the assumption of a simple affirmation of A. But in what way does this simple affirmation of A differ from the affirmation of the combination of A and the attribute "existence" which is supposed to be expressed by the sentence, "A exists."? Obviously it does not differ at all. So we see that the affirmation of A constitutes the true and complete sense of this proposition, and that A alone is the object of the judgement.

Let us now examine the proposition "A does not exist," in the

---

that can be an object of assent or dissent – is some order of sensation or ideas: some coexistence or succession of sensations or ideas actually experienced, or supposed to be capable of being experienced." I, Chap. IV, 162, note 48.

same way. Perhaps the consideration of this proposition will make the truth of our position even more evident. When someone affirms a whole, he also affirms, in so doing, each part of this whole, but it is not true that when someone denies a whole he is denying each individual part of this whole. If we deny the existence of blue and white swans, we do not thereby implicitly deny that there are white swans. And this is quite natural, for if even *one* part is false, the whole cannot be true. So when a person denies a combination of attributes, in so doing he in no way denies every single attribute which is an element in the combination. For example, if someone denies the existence of a learned bird, i.e. denies the combination of a bird with the attribute "learned," he does not thereby deny that a bird or learning exists in reality. Now, let us apply this to our case. If the judgement, "A does not exist," were the denial of a combination of an attribute "existence" with "A," then A would not be being denied in any way. But it is impossible that anybody should hold such a view, for it is clear that this is precisely the sense of the proposition. Hence A alone is the object of this negative judgement.

6. That predication is not the essence of every judgement emerges quite clearly from the fact that all perceptions are judgements, whether they are instances of knowledge or just mistaken affirmations. We have already touched upon this point when speaking of the various aspects of inner consciousness.* And this is not denied by those thinkers who hold that every judgement consists in a conjunction of subject and predicate. John Stuart Mill, for example, recognizes it explicitly both in the passage quoted above and elsewhere. In that passage, he adds that it is no more difficult to hold, as he does, that the difference between the affirmation of a reality and the presentation of a figment of the imagination is ultimate and primordial than it is to hold the difference between a sensation and an idea† to be primordial. It seems to be nothing but another aspect of the same difference.‡ But it is hard to think of anything more obvious and unmistakable than the fact that a perception is not a conjunction of a concept of the subject and a concept of a predicate, nor does it refer to such a conjunction. Rather, the object of an *inner*

* Book Two, Chap. 3, Sect. 1 ff.
† In Hume's sense. See above, Book One, Chap. 1, Sect. 2.
‡ He adds "There is no more difficulty in holding it to be so, than in holding the difference between a sensation and an idea to be primordial. It seems almost another aspect of the same difference." Likewise he says in the course of the same treatise, "The difference [between recognizing something as a reality in nature, and regarding it as a mere thought of our own] presents itself in its most elementary form in the distinction between a sensation and an idea." *Analysis*, p. 419.

perception is simply a mental phenomenon, and the object of an *external* perception is simply a physical phenomenon, a sound, odor, or the like.[6] We have here, then, a very obvious proof of the truth of our assertion.

Or should some doubts be raised about this, too? Because we say not only that we perceive a color, a sound, an act of seeing, an act of hearing, but also that we perceive the existence of an act of seeing or of an act of hearing, someone might be led to believe that perception, too, consists in the affirmation of the conjunction of the attribute "existence" with the phenomenon in question. Such a misunderstanding of obvious facts seems to me almost inconceivable. The untenability of such an opinion, however, will again emerge with supreme clarity from a discussion of the concept of existence. Some philosophers have held that this concept cannot be derived from experience. Therefore we shall have to go over this aspect of it in connection with our study of so-called innate ideas. And when we do, we will find that this concept undoubtedly is derived from experience, but from *inner* experience, and we acquire it only with reference to judgement.[7] So the concept of existence could not have been the predicate of our first judgement any more than the concept of judgement could have been. Thus, in this way, too, we come to recognize that at least the first perception, the one which was present in the first mental phenomenon, could not possibly have consisted of such a predication.

In the last (eighth) edition of his *Logic*, John Stuart Mill defines the concept "existence" in the following way. Existence, he says, means arousing or being able to arouse some (however many) sensations or other states of consciousness. Although I do not agree with it entirely, this definition is nevertheless sufficient to show very clearly the impossibility of the concept "existence" having been used as the predicate of a judgement in our first sensation. For this definition agrees with the one whose truth we hope to demonstrate insofar as it could only have been derived with respect to mental activities which, if the theory we are opposing were true, would themselves presuppose the concept of "existence" and employ it as something already given.

7. The fact that not all judgements refer to a conjunction of pre-

---

[6] See Book Two, Chap. 1, note 2, and Kraus's Introduction.

[7] The most fundamental exposition of this theory in relation to conflicting ones is contained in Anton Marty's *Gesammelte Schriften*, II, 1, 187, and in his *Untersuchungen zur Grundlegung einer allgemeinene Grammatik und Sprach-philosophie* (Halle, 1908). In Supplementary Essay IX, Brentano goes on to show that the word "existence" is not an independent part of speech.

sented attributes and that predicating one concept of another is not a vital element in judgement is a truth that philosophers have usually, but not always, failed to recognize. In his critique of the ontological argument for the existence of God, Kant made the pertinent remark that in an existential proposition, i.e. in a proposition of the form "A exists," existence "is not a real predicate, i.e. a concept of something which can be added to the concept of a thing." "It is," he says, "only the positing of a thing or of certain determinations, as existing in themselves." But now, instead of saying that the existential proposition is not a categorical proposition at all, neither an analytical one in the Kantian sense, i.e. one in which the predicate is included in the subject, nor a synthetic one, in which the subject does not contain the predicate,* Kant allowed himself to be misled into classifying it as a synthetic proposition. For he thought that just as the "is" of the copula usually places two concepts in a relationship to each other, the "is" of the existential proposition places "the object in a relationship to my concept." "The object," he says, "is added synthetically to my concept."†

This half-way measure was unclear and contradictory. Herbart put an end to it by clearly distinguishing existential propositions from categorical proposition as a special distinct kind.‡ Other philosophers have sided with him on this point, not only his numerous disciples, but also, to a certain extent, those who, like Trendelenburg, usually polemicize against the Herbartian school.§

---

* I am using Kant's own definitions here, too, even though (as will emerge from the following investigations) they are not really appropriate to the judgements in question. This does not prevent them from providing an adequate characterization because they agree with the commonly held view of judgements.

† That Kant included existential propositions among categorical judgements can be inferred from his failure to make special mention of them in connection with the relation of judgement.

In the Middle Ages, St. Thomas came as close as Kant to the truth, remarkably enough by reflecting upon the same proposition, "God exists." According to him, the "is" is not a real predicate but merely a sign of affirmation (*Summa Theologica*, P. I, Q. 3, A. 4 ad 2). But he, too, considered this proposition categorical (see passage cited) and believes that the judgement contains a comparison of our presentation with its object, which, in his opinion, is true of every judgement (Q. 16, A. 2). We have already seen that this is impossible (Cp. Book II, Chap. 3, Sect. 2, p. 139).

‡ On this matter compare Drobisch, *Logic*, 3rd ed., p. 61.

§ *Logische Untersuchungen*, 2nd ed., II, 208. See also the passage he quotes from Schleiermacher (II, 214, note 1). Suggestions of the correct view of existential propositions can be found as far back as Aristotle.

But this is not all. Even though not all philosophers admit as yet the truth of our interpretation of the existential proposition, all without exception now grant another truth from which our view can be rigorously deduced. Even those who misconstrue the nature of the "is" and "is not" in the existential proposition, have a perfectly correct view of the nature of the "is" and "is not" which are added to a subject and predicate as copula. Even if they believe that the "is" and "is not" of the existential proposition signify something in and of themselves, i.e. that they add the presentation of the predicate "existence" to the presentation of the subject and connect them together, they recognize nevertheless that the copula has no meaning in and of itself, since it merely makes the expression of a presentation into the expression of an affirmative or negative judgement. Let us hear, for example, from John Stuart Mill, who is our opponent on the subject of the interpretation of existential propositions. He says, "A predicate and a subject are all that is necessarily required to make up a proposition; but as we cannot conclude from merely seeing two names put together, that they are a predicate and a subject, that is, that one of them is intended to be affirmed or denied of the other, it is necessary that there should be some mode or form of indicating that such is the intention; some sign to distinguish a predication from any other kind of discourse. . . . This

---

Yet he seems not to have attained complete clarity about them. In his *Metaphysics* (IX, 10) he teaches that, since truth consists in an agreement of thought with reality, the knowledge of simple objects, in opposition to other kinds of knowledge, must not be a conjunction or separation of attributes, but a simple act of thinking, a perception (he calls it a contact, θιγεῖν). In *De Interpretatione* (Chap. 3) he clearly states that the "being" of the copula does not in itself signify anything, as a name does, but simply completes the expression of a judgement, and he never distinguished the "being" of the existential proposition from this "being" of the copula as something essentially different, as something which has meaning in itself. Zeller is correct in stating, "Nowhere does Aristotle say that every judgement, even the existential judgement, logically considered, consists of three elements." And he points out that, on the contrary, there is much to lead us to believe that Aristotle held the opposite view (Eduard Zeller, *Aristotle and the earlier Peripatetics*, trans. B. F. C. Costelloe and J. H. Muirhead, London, 1897, I, 231, note 2). If this is true, Aristotle's view would not be inferior to the commonly accepted later logical doctrine, as Zeller seems to think. On the contrary, here, as in many other places, Aristotle has anticipated a more correct point of view. (Cp. also Thomas Aquinas' reproduction of Aristotle's doctrine in *Summa Theologica*, P. I, Q. 85, A. 5.)

function is commonly fulfilled by the word *is*, when an affirmation is intended; *is not*, when a negation; or by some other part of the verb *to be*. The word which thus serves the purpose of predication is called . . . the copula."* Subsequently, he explicitly draws attention to the difference between the "is" or "is not" of the copula and that which includes the concept of existence in its meaning. This doctrine, however, is not characteristic of John Stuart Mill alone, but is shared by all those who oppose our conception of the existential proposition. Not only logicians, but grammarians and lexicographers as well advocate it.† And John Stuart Mill is very much mistaken when he credits James Mill with being the first to have developed this interpretation clearly.‡ He could have found it expressed in exactly the same way in the Port Royal Logic, for example.§

Well then – all we need is this admission from our opponents with regard to the copula to draw the necessary conclusion that no additional function can be ascribed to the "is" and "is not" of the existential proposition either.[8] For it can be shown with utmost clarity that every categorical proposition can be translated without any change of meaning into an existential proposition, and in that event the "is" or "is not" of the existential proposition takes the place of the copula.[9]

I want to prove this with some examples.

The categorical proposition, "Some man is sick," means the

---

* *A System of Logic*, Book I, Chap. 4, Sect. 1.

† Cp. for example, Heyses, *Wörterbuch der Deutschen Sprache*.

‡ *A System of Logic*, Book I, Chap. 4, Sect. I.

§ Antoine Arnauld and Pierre Nicole, *Logique ou l'Art de Penser*, Part II, Chap. 3.

[8] That is to say, no function other than that of a dependently meaningful ("synsemantic") sign can be ascribed to it.

[9] The four kinds of categorical propositions cannot be "translated" into existential propositions without any change in meaning, as emerges from Supplementary Essay IX. For one thing, a double judgement may be logically equivalent to an existential proposition, but it is *psychologically* different. Brentano did not recognize until later (see *The Origin of our Knowledge of Right and Wrong* (pp. 58–59 and 107) that in addition to thetic judgements of the form, "A is," "A is not," there are also synthetic (truly predicative) judgements of the form "A is B," "A is not B." They are to be regarded as double judgements, in which a judgement about the predicate is constructed upon a judgement about the subject. In view of these later statements, one should not ascribe to Brentano *all* the doctrines in the *Psychology* of 1874, as is unfortunately done in recent – even the most recent – works on the history of philosophy.

same as the existential proposition, "A sick man exists," or, "There is a sick man."

The categorical proposition, "No stone is living," means the same as the existential proposition, "A living stone does not exist," or "There is no living stone."

The categorical proposition, "All men are mortal," means the same as the existential proposition, "An immortal man does not exist," or "There is no immortal man."*

The categorical proposition, "Some man is not learned," means the same as the existential proposition, "An unlearned man exists," or "There is an unlearned man."

Because the four examples I have chosen illustrate all four classes of categorical propositions usually distinguished by logicians,† this represents a general proof of the possibility of transforming verbally categorical propositions into existential propositions. Furthermore, it is clear that the "is" or "is not" of the existential proposition is merely equivalent to the copula, so they are not predicates and have no meaning at all in and of themselves.

But is our reduction of the four types of categorical propositions to existential propositions really correct?[10] Herbart himself, whose doctrine we have previously invoked in support of our point of view, might object to such a reduction, since his conception of categorical propositions is completely different from ours. He believes that every categorical proposition expresses a hypothetical judgement, and that the predicate can be ascribed to, or denied of the subject only on a certain assumption, namely the assumption that the subject exists. It is precisely on this point that he bases his argument that the existential proposition cannot be interpreted as a categorical proposition.‡ We believe, on the contrary, that the categorical proposition corresponds to a judgement which can be expressed just as well in the existential form, and that the truly affirmative categorical propositions contain within them the affirma-

* Logic usually considers the judgements, "All men are mortal," and "No man is immortal," to be equipollent (cp. Überweg, *Logic*, 2nd ed., Part V, Sect. 96, p. 235); the truth is that they are identical.

† The particular affirmative, universal negative, the (mistakenly) so-called universal affirmative and the particular negative. In truth, as is clearly indicated by our reduction of these propositions to the existential form, no affirmative judgement is universal (for we would then have to call a judgement about an individual universal) and no negative judgement is particular.

‡ Cp. Drobisch, *Logik*, 3rd ed., pp. 59 ff.

[10] Brentano himself takes up this question again in Supplementary Essay IX. See Alfred Kastil's introduction to Anton Marty's *Gesammelte Schriften*, II, Part 1.

tion of the subject.*[11] But as much as we agree with Herbart's view concerning the "being" of existential propositions, we cannot say that we agree with his derivation of it. This seems to us a perfect example of Aristotle's remark that mistaken premises may lead to a true conclusion. It is an unreasonable, an impossible expectation to ask us to believe that the proposition, "Some man is walking," or the one introduced above, "Some man is sick," contains the tacit presupposition "If, indeed, there is a man." Similarly, it is not only incorrect, it is not even remotely plausible that the proposition, "Some man is not learned" contains the same presupposition. In the proposition, "No stone is living," I have no idea what the restriction, "If, indeed, there is a stone," is supposed to mean. Even if there were no stones, it would still be just as true that there is no living stone, as it is now when there are stones.[12] It is only in the example, "All men are mortal," i.e. in the so-called universal affirmative proposition, that such a limiting condition has a certain appearance of plausibility. This proposition seems to assert the conjunction of "man" and "mortal." The conjunction clearly does not exist if no man exists. And yet the existence of a man cannot be deduced

* Truly affirmative propositions are, as was pointed out in a previous note, the so-called particular affirmative and particular negative propositions. The truly negative propositions, among which are included the universal affirmative propositions, obviously do not contain the affirmation of the subject, since they really do not affirm anything, but merely deny something. We have explained earlier why they do not also contain the denial of the subject (p. 209).

[11] They include the affirmation of the subject's existence and are consequently double judgements, i.e. the subject is affirmed as existent and then something is ascribed to or denied of the affirmed subject.

[12] In Supplementary Essay IX, p. 291, Brentano himself remarks that no consideration has been given to apodictic judgements. That is also true of this polemic against Herbart. If one takes apodictic judgements into account, it emerges that the addition of "if there are any stones" can very well be meaningful. Take the example, "No stone is transparent"; if, following Brentano, this is translated as "There are no transparent stones," the sentence is true *if there are no stones*, for in that case there are neither stones that are transparent nor stones that are not. But if we say, "No stone is transparent, if there are any stones" = "If there are any stones, none of them are transparent," the sentence is also untrue if there are no stones. For here, under the hypothetical clothing, is hidden the apodictic negative thought that transparent stones are impossible and this is false whether there are any stones or not. – Leaving apodictic judgements out of account has given rise to unjustified criticisms. We should note that negative judgements cannot be studied successfully without investigating apodictic-evident judgements, for nothing but evident apodictic negative judgements create universal certainty.

from the proposition, "All men are mortal." This proposition, therefore, seems to affirm the conjunction of man and mortal, only on the assumption that a man exists. Yet a glance at the existential proposition which is equivalent to the categorical proposition solves the whole difficulty. It shows that the proposition is not really an affirmation, but a denial, so something similar to what we just said about the proposition, "No stone is living," holds true of it.[13]

[13] Here, too, Brentano understands the proposition assertorically, but it can also be understood apodictically, and the latter case has not been taken into consideration here. Understood as a mathematical law, the proposition, "All triangles have an angle sum of two right angles" ("The triangle has an angle sum of two right angles.") is a negative-apodictic proposition; it can also be expressed hypothetically: "If there are triangles, they have an angle sum of two right angles." – It is obvious that Herbart has very much the same idea when he says in his *Lehrbuch zur Einleitung in die Philosophie*, Sect. 52, that "the judgement, 'the square circle is impossible,' certainly does not include the idea that the square circle exists, but means that *if* a square circle is thought of, the concept of impossibility must be added on to it in thought." Brentano's theory comes very close to the Herbartian one here, except that according to Brentano it is not that "the concept of impossibility must be added," but that the square circle is denied apodictically (i.e. in the mode of impossibility). When we are dealing with the proposition, "All men are mortal" (alternatively, "Man is mortal"), must we first of all decide whether we wish to express an assertoric or an apodictic denial? It is obvious that as a rule we intend a natural law, and are therefore thinking of an apodictic denial, and this can also be expressed by means of the hypothetical form, "If there are men, they are mortal." But if we understand "All men are mortal" assertorically to mean the mere denial of immortal men, this proposition is true if there are no men. But on this latter presupposition the assertoric proposition "Mortal men do not exist" is also true. On the other hand, the proposition, "There can be no immortal men," i.e. the apodictic denial, remains true whether there are men or not. For just this reason the hypothetical formulation – "If there are men, they are mortal," i.e. "I do not know whether there are men or not, but one thing I do know, there can be no men who are immortal" – also remains true.

In many cases, nevertheless, when we are concerned with sentences involving "all" we do add on in thought a positive existential affirmation. In the proposition, "All men are mortal," for example, there is an affirmation of men as well. But the linguistic expression is such that only from the context can we see what is really meant. As a rule, mathematical propositions do not include existential affirmation. In my opinion, then, Brentano's opposition to Herbart is only partially justified, i.e. with regard to truly predicative (categorical) judgements of the form I and O.

I say that as a rule mathematical judgements do not include any existential affirmation. But of course it should be admitted that the existence of denumerable things or three-dimensional physical objects is generally presupposed and that interest in the three-dimensional Euclidean geometry depends primarily on this presupposition.

It is strange that the negative character of all so-called laws, especially mathematical ones, is still generally ignored, in spite of Brentano's irrefutable arguments. Kant, however, came close to recognizing it: "The above proposition (that a triangle has three angles) does not say that the angles are necessary absolutely, but that *under the condition* of a triangle being there (being given), the angles are also necessary (within it)." (*Critique of Pure Reason*, Transcendental Dialectic, Chap. 3, Sect. 4.) And now should we not finally claim some insight into the fact that the notorious law of identity – A is A – can mean nothing but that on the condition that there is an A, it is A, so that it is nothing but a linguistic form of the law of contradiction?! An A which is not A cannot exist. (See O. Kraus, "Das a priori bei Kant" in *Hochschulwissen*, I, No. 4 (1924), 144.)

There is one conclusion to draw from what has been set forth in my introduction: Brentano gives *a priorism* all of its rights. By his clear insight into the negative character of all of our apodictic (*a priori*) self-evident judgements, by his theory that all affirmative judgements with universal "subject matter (Materie)" are "particular," all negative ones "universal," Brentano clears away age-old obstacles to the progress of epistemology. Let us consider for example the "universal affirmative" proposition, "All triangles have an angle sum of two right angles." (Anyone who holds that this proposition is not deducible *a priori* may choose another mathematical proposition which does plainly appear to him to have universal validity.) Other philosophers, too, have already seen a "double negation" in the little word "all," so that instead of this we could also say: "No triangle which does not have an angle sum of two right angles exists." Others, as we have said, have clothed it in hypothetical form. "If there are triangles, they must have an angle sum of two right angles." Both formulations move in the direction of Brentano's thesis: The proposition expressed in a linguistically affirmative form is not at all affirmative as far as its meaning is concerned; the affirmation belongs to syntax, to the "constructive inner linguistic form." Its true meaning is *negative*. According to the reform attempted in the "descriptive psychology" of 1874 the proposition is synonymous (correctly: logically equivalent) with the proposition: "A triangle which does not have an angle sum of two right angles does not exist"; schematically: "S – non P does not exist."

But if one takes account of the apodictic character, it must mean: "S – Non P is impossible (cannot exist)." "A triangle which does not have an angle sum of two right angles is impossible." The words "is impossible," "cannot exist," indicate the apodictic character of the proposition. The supplementary essays to the *Classification* correct the theory in that, as is now demonstrated, the transformation into existential propositions does not take place without any change of meaning, as Brentano said originally. The thoughts are psychologically distinct, but logically equivalent.

217

Besides, when I have here attacked Herbart's theory that all categorical propositions are hypothetical propositions, I have done so only to justify my translations of them into existential propositions, and not because such a reduction would be impossible if Herbart were correct. On the contrary, what I have said of categorical propositions is equally true of hypothetical propositions; they, too, can all be clothed in the existential form, and it turns out that they are all purely negative assertions. An example will suffice to show how the same judgement, without the least modification, can be expressed equally well in the form of a hypothetical proposition, a categorical proposition, and an existential proposition. The proposition, "If a man behaves badly, he harms himself," is a hypothetical proposition. As far as its meaning is concerned, it is the same as the categorical proposition, "All men who behave badly harm themselves." And this, in turn, has no other meaning than that of the existential proposition, "A man who behaves badly and does not do harm to himself does not exist," or to use a more felicitous expression, "There is no such thing as a man who behaves badly and does not harm himself."[14] In view of the clumsiness of the expression in its existential form, it is easy to see why language has found other syntactical expressions. But the difference between the three types of proposition is merely a difference in linguistic expression, although the famed philosopher of Königsberg was misled by such differences into assuming fundamental differences of judgement and basing special *a priori* categories upon these "relations of judgements."[15]

The reducibility of categorical propositions, indeed the reducibility of all propositions which express a judgement, to existential propositions is therefore indubitable.* And this conclusion serves

[14] There is no disputing the fact that the proposition's meaning is negative, but in the present case its apodictic character also comes out distinctly: "There can be no man who behaves badly and who does not harm himself."

[15] Kant's table of functions of judgement includes "Categorical, Hypothetical, Disjunctive" under the title "Relation." This throws linguistic and objective differences together in confusion. Sigwart criticizes it too. See also Marty, *Gesammelte Schriften*, II, Part 1, 280, and Supplementary Essay IX. Leibniz had already treated the disjunctive and hypothetical forms as linguistic differences. On these so-called "categories," see my Introduction, p. 389 and my article, "Das a priori bei Kant" in *Hochschulwissen*, Vol. I, No. 4 (1924), 141 ff., and my lecture on Kant, *Hochschulwissen*, Vol. I, No. 7.

* There are still certain cases in which such a reducibility can be attacked on the basis of special considerations. Although I do not wish to interrupt the course of the discussion in the text on their account (for many readers will not be particularly disturbed by them to begin with), it does seem to me to be a good idea at least to consider them in a note. In the passage of

John Stuart Mill's *Logic* in which he tries to make clear the difference between the "is" of the copula and the "is" of the existential proposition, which, in his opinion comprises the concept of existence, he cites, for purposes of elucidation, the proposition, "A centaur is a poetic fiction." This, he says, could not possibly assert existence since, on the contrary, the proposition expressly asserts that the subject has no real existence (Book I, Chap. 4, Sect. 1). On another occasion he cites the proposition "Jupiter is a Non-ens," for a similar purpose. These are, in fact, propositions of a kind such that the possibility of reducing them to existential propositions does seem to be minimal. In correspondence with Mill I once raised the question of existential propositions, and in particular, I maintained, against the view that the "is" of the existential proposition has the relation to that of the copula which Mill believed it to have, that it was possible to reduce every proposition to an existential proposition. In his reply Mill persisted in his old view. And although he did not expressly contradict the reducibility of all other assertions to existential ones which I had set forth, I nevertheless suspected that I may not have made this point of my demonstration sufficiently clear to him. For that reason I went back again to this question and discussed the examples in his *Logic* specifically. Since I have just found a rough draft of that letter among my papers, I will reproduce this little discussion here verbatim. "It might not be unhelpful," I wrote, "if I demonstrate the possibility of such a reduction with specific reference to a proposition which you present in your logic as an example meant, so to speak, to prove the opposite. The proposition, 'A centaur is a poetic fiction,' does not imply, as you rightly point out, that a centaur exists, rather it implies the opposite. But if it is true, it does imply that something else exists, namely a poetic fiction which combines part of a horse with part of a human body in a particular way. If there were no poetic fictions and if there were no centaurs *imaginatively created* by poets, the proposition would be false. In fact the sentence means just that, 'There is a poetic fiction which conceives the upper parts of the human body joined to the body and legs of a horse,' or (which comes to the same thing), 'There exists a centaur *imaginatively created by the poets*.'[16] The same thing is true when I say, 'Jupiter is a Non-ens,' which is to say that he is something which exists merely in the imagination but not in reality. The truth of the proposition does not require that there be a Jupiter, but it does require that there be something else. If there were not *something which existed merely in one's thought*, the proposition would not be true. The specific reason people are inclined to doubt the reducibility of propositions such as 'The centaur is a fiction,' to existential propositions lies, it seems to me, in a relation between their predicate and their subject which has been previously overlooked by logicians. Just as adjectives ordinarily enrich the concept of the substantive to which they are added with new attributes, so do predicates, but sometimes they add something which modifies the subject. The former holds true, for example, when I say, 'A man is learned,' the latter when I say, 'A man is dead.' A learned man is a man, but a dead man is not. So the proposition, 'A

[16] More correctly expressed: "There is a poet imagining a centaur."

219

dead man exists,' does not presuppose the existence of a man in order to be true, but merely the existence of a *dead* man. Similarly, the proposition, 'A centaur is a fiction,' does not presuppose that there is a centaur, but only that there is an imagined centaur, i.e. the fiction of a centaur...." Perhaps this will serve to remove whatever doubt anyone could have been entertaining. As for Mill, it turned out that such clarification had not been necessary at all, for he wrote to me on February 6, 1873, "You did not, as you seem to suppose, fail to convince me of the invariable convertibility of all categorical affirmative propositions into predications of existence. [He means affirmative existential propositions, which obviously I had not characterized as "predications of existence".] The suggestion was new to me, but I at once saw its truth when pointed out. It is not on that point that our difference hinges. . . ." Even though Mill admitted the reducibility of all categorical propositions to existential propositions, he held fast to his earlier opinion that "is" and "is not" contain within them the concept of the predicate "existence." This is clearly indicated in the passage from his letter quoted above, and he stated it even more emphatically in what followed. How he could continue to maintain his theory of the copula at the same time, he did not reveal. If he had been consistent he would have given that up and would have had to make some essential modifications in parts of his *Logic* as well (as, for example, Book I, Chap. 5, Sect. 5). I had hoped, after receiving an invitation to join him in Avignon in the early summer, that we could come to an understanding on this and other questions pending between us more easily in oral discussions, so I did not press the point further. But his sudden death thwarted my hopes. [Editor's note: There are eleven letters from Mill to Brentano to be published in the forthcoming edition of *The Later Letters of John Stuart Mill (1849–1873)*, eds F. E. Mineka and D. N. Lindley, in *The Collected Works of John Stuart Mill* (University of Toronto Press, Toronto, 1963–), Nos. 1709, 1726, 1734, 1739, 1741, 1746, 1752, 1767, 1774, 1789 and 1802.]

I only want to add one short remark to my debate with Mill. Propositions of the sort, "A man is dead," are not, in the true sense of the word, categorical, because "dead" is not an attribute, but, as we remarked, entails a modification of the subject. What would we say about the categorical syllogism, "All men are living creatures; Some man is dead; Therefore, some living creature is dead." If the minor premise were a true categorical proposition, it would be a valid syllogism of the third figure. If we wished to assume with Kant that there are different classes of "relation" of judgement which correspond with these different forms of assertion, here again we would have to make new "transcendental" discoveries. The truth is, however, that such exceptional forms of assertion are easily dealt with, since the existential proposition, "There is a dead man," means absolutely the same thing as "A man is dead." And so I hope that people will finally, once and for all, stop confusing linguistic differences with differences in thought.[17]

[17] Except for Marty, scarcely anyone has sufficiently brought out the importance of this note on "modifying predicates" for logic and the

in two ways to refute the erroneous opinion of those who assert that the essential difference between judgement and presentation consists in the fact that judgements have as their content a conjunction of attributes. For one thing, when we reduce categorical propositions to existential propositions, the "is" of the latter replaces the copula and is thus shown not to involve a predicate any more than it does. Further, it is quite obvious that the compounding of several elements, believed to be so essential for the universal and specific nature of judgements, the combination of subject and predicate, of antecedent and consequent, etc., is in fact nothing but a matter of linguistic expression.

If this had been recognized from the beginning, probably no one would ever have thought of distinguishing presentations from judgements on the grounds that the content of the former is a simple and the content of the latter a compound idea. In fact, with regard to content, there is not the slightest difference between them. The same object is present to consciousness whether a person affirms it, denies it, or is uncertain about it; in the last case it is merely presented,[18] in the first two cases it is simultaneously presented and affirmed or denied. And every object which is the content of a presentation can also become, in the appropriate circumstances, the content of a judgement.

8. Once again let us quickly review the most essential phases in the course of our investigation. We said that, even if one does not admit that the difference between presentation and judgement is analogous to that between presentation and desire, i.e. a difference in the mode of relation to the object, no one denies that there must be *some difference* between them. This difference, however, could not possibly be merely an external one, i.e. a difference in causes or results. Rather, if we exclude a difference in the mode of reference, there are only two ways in which we can conceive of it: either as a difference in *what* is thought, or as a difference *in the intensity with which* it is thought. We examined both hypotheses. The second proved immediately untenable. But the first one, which may have been more attractive at first, also proved, upon closer examination,

---

[18] To be more complete one should add that in such a case in addition to having a presentation of the object, the person desires to know something about it.

---

philosophy of language. On the other hand it is to be observed that according to the Supplementary Essays the linguistic transformation of I and O statements into existential propositions results in psychologically different but logically equivalent propositions.

to be untenable. Though it is still a very widely held opinion that a presentation refers to a simple object and a judgement to a complex one, to a combination or separation, we have proved both that mere presentations also have compound objects as their content and judgements simple ones. We have shown that the combination of subject and predicate and other similar connections are in no way part of the essence of judgement. We based this claim on a consideration of affirmative as well as negative existential propositions. We confirmed it by reference to our perceptions, especially our initial perceptions, and finally by means of the reduction of categorical and, indeed, all types of assertion, to existential propositions.[19] What constitutes the distinctive feature of judgement as opposed to presentation can no more be a difference in content than it can be a difference in intensity. Nothing remains, then, but to think of the distinctive feature of judgement as a particular kind of relation to the immanent object, as we have done.

9. I believe that the discussion just completed confirms our thesis – so much so as to allay all doubts on the matter. Nevertheless, because of the fundamental importance of this question, we will elucidate the difference between presentation and judgement again, from another point of view. For many other things besides the mere impossibility of finding an alternative account point to the truth which, we claim, is immediately given in inner experience.

To this end, let us compare the relation between presentation and judgement with the relation between two other classes of phenomena where the fundamental difference in their relation to their object is beyond question, namely the relation between presentation and the phenomena of love or hate. As certain as it is that an object which is at the same time presented and loved or presented and hated is intentionally in consciousness in two different ways, it is just as certain that the same thing holds true of an object which is simultaneously presented and affirmed, or presented and denied. All of the circumstances in the two cases are analogous and all show that if a fundamentally different mode of consciousness has been added to the first mode in the one case, it has been added in the other as well.

Let us consider this in detail.

Among presentations we find no contraries[20] other than those of the objects which are contained in them. Insofar as warm and cold,

[19] This reduction, as the Supplementary Essays show, never takes place without some change of meaning. It is to be regarded as a logical artifice making for greater simplicity.

[20] Even if there are no contraries, there are still different modes. See Supplementary Essay III.

light and dark, higher and lower pitch, etc., constitute contraries, we can say that the presentation of the one is opposed to that of the other. But in the entire realm of these mental activities there is no other sense in which there are any contraries at all.

When love or hate enter in, there arises an entirely different kind of opposition. This opposition is not an opposition of objects, for the same object can be loved or hated; it is, rather, an opposition between references to an object. This is certainly a clear indication that we are here dealing with a class of phenomena in which the nature of the reference to the object is entirely different from what it is in presentations.

An entirely analogous opposition manifests itself unmistakably in the domain of mental phenomena when we affirm or deny the object which is presented instead of directing love or hatred toward it.

Furthermore,* in presentations the only intensity involved is the greater or lesser sharpness and vividness of the phenomenon.

When love and hate enter in, however, a new kind of intensity is introduced – a greater or lesser degree of energy, vehemence or moderation in the strength of these feelings.

In an altogether analogous manner, we also find an entirely new kind of intensity when judgement is added to presentation. For it is obvious that the greater or lesser degree of certainty in conviction or opinion is more closely related to the differences in the intensity of love than to differences in the strength of presentations.

Furthermore, there is *no virtue, no wickedness, no knowledge, no error* in presentations. All this is intrinsically foreign to it; at best, it is only by homonymy that we may call presentations morally good or bad, true or false. For example, a presentation is called bad because anyone who loved the object presented would sin, and false, because anyone who affirmed the object presented would err; or because the danger of such a love or of such an affirmation is implied in the presentation.†

The sphere of love and hate reveals, then, a wholly new kind of perfection and imperfection, not the slightest trace of which is revealed in the sphere of presentations. As love and hate are added to the phenomena of presentation, moral good and evil enter into the realm of mental activity – at least they often do so, and in cases where a responsible mental being is concerned.

Even here something similar holds true of judgement, for the other kind of perfection and imperfection, which is completely new and

* Compare the following with the discussion in the Appendix (VI) and my *Untersuchungen zur Sinnespsychologie*, to which I refer there.

† Compare, in my treatise *Von der mannigfachen Beduetung des Seienden nach Aristoteles*, pp. 31 ff., what Aristotle remarked about this.

of such great importance, and which, as we have said, is entirely absent in mere presentation, is the property of the domain of judgement. Just as love and hate are virtue and wickedness, affirmation or denial are knowledge or error.[21]

Finally, one last point. Even though they are not independent of the laws governing the succession of presentations, love and hate, as a special class of phenomena with a fundamentally different mode of consciousness, are subject to *special laws of succession and development*, which, above all, constitute the main psychological foundation of ethics. Very frequently an object is loved or hated on account of another, while it, in and of itself, would move us in neither way, or, perhaps, would arouse only the opposite emotion in us. And love, once transferred in this manner, often becomes permanently attached to the new object without regard to its origin.

In this respect, too, we find an absolutely analogous fact in judgements. Here, too, besides the general laws governing the succession of presentations whose influence in the domain of judgement must not be overlooked, we find special laws, which are particularly valid for judgements, and which bear the same relation to logic as the laws of love and hate do to ethics. Just as *one* love arises from another according to special laws, so *one* judgement follows from another according to special laws.

John Stuart Mill is right, then, when he says in his *Logic*: "In respect to Belief, psychologists will always have to inquire what beliefs we have by direct consciousness, and according to what laws one belief produces another; what are the laws in virtue of which one thing is recognized by the mind, either rightly or erroneously, as evidence of another thing. In regard to Desire, they will have to examine what objects we desire naturally, and by what causes we are made to desire things originally indifferent or even disagreeable to us; and so forth."* Accordingly, in his notes to James Mill's *Analysis* he rejects not only the author's view and Herbert Spencer's as well, that belief consists in a close and inseparable association of ideas, but he also denies that belief is founded entirely upon the laws of association of ideas, which those two thinkers had necessarily to assume. He says, "If belief is only an inseparable association, belief is a matter of habit and accident, and not of reason. Assuredly an association, however close, between two ideas, is not a sufficient *ground* of belief; is not *evidence* that the corresponding facts are united in external nature. The theory seems to annihilate all distinc-

* *A System of Logic*, Book VI, Chap. 4, Sect. 3.
[21] What is meant is this: just as love and hate can be justified or unjustified, so can affirmation and negation, in an analogous way.

tion between the belief of the wise, which is regulated by evidence, and conforms to the real succession and coexistence of the facts of the universe, and the belief of fools, which is mechanically produced by any accidental association that suggests the idea of a succession or coexistence to the mind: a belief aptly characterized by the popular expression, believing a thing because they have taken it into their heads."*

It would be superfluous to dwell further on a point which is sufficiently clear and, with only rare exceptions, is recognized by all thinkers. Subsequent discussions will throw further light upon what we have just said about the special laws of judgements and emotions.†

Our conclusion, therefore, is this: from the analogy of all the accompanying relationships, it becomes apparent once again that if there is a fundamental difference in reference to the object between presentation and love, and in general between any two different mental phenomena, we must assume that such a fundamental difference exists between judgement and presentation.

10. To summarize briefly, the arguments in support of this truth are as follows: firstly, inner experience directly reveals the difference in the references to their content which we assert of presentation and judgement. Secondly, if this were not the distinction between them, there would be no difference between them at all. Neither the hypothesis of a difference of intensity, nor the hypothesis of a different content for judgement as opposed to mere presentation is tenable. Thirdly, if we compare the distinction between presentation and judgement with other instances of differences among mental acts, we find in it all of the characteristics which are present in the other cases in which consciousness refers to an object in wholly different ways, and not a single one is missing. Consequently, if we do not affirm such a difference here, we cannot affirm one in any other case within the mental realm.

11. There remains *one* more difficulty for us to solve. Besides showing the error in the commonly held view, we must also show the reason for such an error.

There was, it seems to me, a twofold reason for this error. One reason was *psychological*, which is to say there is a mental fact which favors such a deception; the second, *linguistic*.

The psychological reason seems to me pre-eminently to lie in the fact that every act of consciousness, however simple it may be, as for example the act in which a sound is the object of my presentation, contains simultaneously a presentation and a judgement, a cognition.

* *Analysis*, I, Chap. XI, 407, note 108.
† Books IV and V (never published). [Note of 1911.]

This is the cognition of the mental phenomenon in inner consciousness, the universality of which we have demonstrated above.*[22] This circumstance, having led some thinkers to subsume all mental phenomena under the concept of cognition as though they were in a single class, has induced others to include at least presentation and judgement in the same class because they never occur separately, while they establish distinct new classes only for phenomena which, like feelings and strivings, are added on in particular cases.

To substantiate this remark, I need only recall a passage from Hamilton's *Lectures* already quoted above: "It is evident that every mental phenomena is either an act of knowledge, or only possible through an act of knowledge, for consciousness is a knowledge – a phenomenon of cognition; and, on this principle, many philosophers – as Descartes, Leibniz, Spinoza, Wolff, Platner, and others – have been led to regard the knowing, or representative faculty, as they called it – the faculty of cognition, as the fundamental power of the mind from which all others are derivative. To this the answer is easy. These philosophers did not observe that, although pleasure and pain – although desire and volition, are only as they are known to be; yet in these modifications, a quality, a phenomenon of mind, absolutely new, has been superadded, which was never involved in, and could, therefore, never have been evolved out of, the mere faculty of knowledge. The faculty of knowledge is certainly the first in order, inasmuch as it is the *conditio sine qua non* of the others...."†

We see that because no mental phenomenon is possible unless it is accompanied by inner cognition, Hamilton believes that knowledge precedes all other mental phenomena, and, since he groups knowledge and presentation in the same class, he distinguishes separate classes only for feeling and striving. But in fact it is not correct to say that knowledge is the primary mental act. It is, to be sure, present in all mental acts, and therefore in the first one, but only secondarily. The primary object of the act is not always known (if it were we could never judge falsely) and not even always judged (if it were there would be no questions or inquiries about it), but often, and in the simplest acts, it is merely presented.[23] Moreover, even with regard to the secondary object, knowledge, in a way, constitutes

---

* Book Two, Chap. 3. [Note of 1911.]

† *Lectures on Metaphysics*, I, 187.

[22] There is also the fact that every sensation involves a belief in what is sensed.

[23] The proof does not seem to be quite rigorous. For even if the primary "object" is always an object of judgement, as is actually the case with belief in sense-qualities, doubt in the judgement's correctness can arise subsequently.

only the second factor, since like every judgement, it presupposes a presentation of the object judged. It is this presentation, then, which is prior, if not temporally, at least in the nature of things.

By arguing in the same way as Hamilton did for the primacy of cognition, one could also argue that feelings are primary, and as a consequence of this they, too, might be confused with presentations and judgements. For, as we have seen, there are feelings which occur as secondary phenomena in every mental act, too.* The reason that this universality of feeling has not led, or at least has not led as frequently as the universality of the accompanying inner perception, to a similar misconception, is that on the one hand, the universal presence of feeling has not been as generally recognized, and, on the other, certain presentations leave us at least relatively indifferent, and the same presentation is accompanied by different, even opposite feelings, at different times.† Inner perception, on the contrary, exists always and invariably in consciousness with the same fullness of conviction, and if its intensity does vary, it varies in proportion to the variations in intensity of the phenomena it accompanies.‡

This, then, is what I have called the psychological reason for the error under discussion.

12. In addition, there is, as we have said, a linguistic reason.

We cannot expect that relations which led even acute thinkers into error would not have had an influence upon ordinary opinions as well. It is from these, however, that the language of the people develops. Consequently, we must expect as a matter of course that among the terms used in everyday life to designate mental activities there is one which is applicable both to presentation and judgement, but to no other phenomenon, and which groups the two together in one single broader class. This is in fact the case. We call both presentations and judgements thoughts equally well; we cannot, however, apply the same expression to a feeling or a volition, without doing violence to the language.²⁴ We also find terms which are used this way in foreign languages, both ancient and modern.

No one who knows the history of scientific endeavor will contradict me when I say that this has had a detrimental influence. If very distinguished modern philosophers have succumbed to the fallacy of equivocation time and time again, how could they have failed to

---

* See Book Two, Chap. 3, Sect. 6. See also the discussions in the Supplementary Essays and my *Untersuchungen zur Sinnespsychologie* to which they refer. [Note of 1911.]

† See again Book Two, Chap. 3, Sect. 6. [Note of 1911.]

‡ See Book Two, Chap. 3, Sect. 4.

²⁴ Descartes included these as well under "cogitatio." See *The Origin of our Knowledge of Right and Wrong*, p. 50.

have been misled by a similarity of terms in the classification of a realm of phenomena? In his *History of the Inductive Sciences*, Whewell gives us abundant examples of this and related errors, for just as it has often led to combining things which have no likeness, language has also led to separating them when there is no difference. The Scholastics were not the only ones to base distinctions upon mere words. It is very natural, therefore, for the homonymy of the term "thinking" to have exerted a detrimental influence in our case.

13. But undoubtedly another peculiarity of linguistic expression has made knowledge of the true relationship even more difficult. It can be said that the expression of a judgement is usually a sentence, a combination of several words, and this is easily understood from our point of view, too. It has to do with the fact that every judgement is based on a presentation and that affirmative and negative judgements agree with regard to the content to which they refer, since the negative judgement merely denies the object which the corresponding affirmative judgement affirms. Although the expression of judgement is the chief end of linguistic communication, this very fact strongly suggests that the simplest form of expression, the individual word, should not be used by itself for this purpose. But if it were used by itself as the expression of the presentation on which both members of the pair of judgements are based, and if a double form of flexion or two kinds of stereotyped little words (such as "is" and "is not") were then added in order to express the judgements, this simple device would save one's memory half the effort, for the same word would be used in both the affirmative and the corresponding negative judgements. Besides that, by omitting these supplementary signs you have the advantage of possessing a pure and isolated expression for another class of phenomena, presentations. Since presentations form the basis for desire and feeling, too, such an expression could perform further admirable functions in questions, exclamations, commands, etc.

It was inevitable, therefore, that, long before the beginnings of genuine scientific inquiry, the expression of a judgement had become a composite of several distinguishable elements.

Accordingly, the view arose that judgement itself must also be a composite, and, of course, since the majority of words are names and names express presentations – a composite of presentations.* And once this was established, we seemed to have a characteristic which distinguished judgement from presentation, and no one felt called upon to investigate further whether this could be the whole

* For an illustration of this compare the first chapter of Aristotle's *De Interpretatione*.

difference between them, or even whether the difference between them could possibly be understood in this way.

Taking all this into account, we can explain quite well why the true relationship between two fundamentally different classes of mental phenomena remained concealed for such a long time.

14. Meanwhile, this false root naturally put forth various erroneous offshoots which branched out further and extended not only into the domain of psychology, but into those of metaphysics and logic as well. The ontological argument for the existence of God is but one of their fruits.[25] The fierce disputes in which the Medieval schools engaged concerning *essentia* and *esse*, indeed, concerning the *esse essentiae* and the *esse existentiae*, are testimony to the convulsive efforts by which an energetic intellectual power strove to master this indigestible element. Thomas, Scotus, Ockham, Suarez – all ardently took part in this fight; each one was correct in his polemics, but none in his positive assertions. The question always turns on whether the existence of a being is the same or a different reality than the being itself. Scotus, Ockham, Suarez rightly deny that it is a different reality (which is very much to Scotus's credit, especially; in fact in his case it should be regarded as nothing less than a miracle). But as a consequence they fall into the error of thinking that the existence of a thing belongs to the essence of the thing itself, and they regard it as the thing's most general concept. Here the Thomists' opposition was correct, although their criticism did not touch upon the real weak point, but was based primarily on the foundation of erroneous assumptions which were held in common. How, they cried, could the existence of a thing be its most general concept? – This is impossible! – Then its existence would follow from its definition, and consequently the existence of a creature would be just as self-evident and antecedently necessary as the existence of the Creator Himself. The only thing which follows from the definition of a created being is that it is not contradictory and hence is possible. The essence of a creature, therefore, is its mere possibility, and every actual creature is composed of two parts, a real possibility and a real actuality. The one is asserted of the other in the existential proposition, and they are related to one another somewhat as Aristotle's matter and form are related in physical objects. The boundaries of possibility are naturally also those of the reality encompassed in it. Thus existence, which in itself is something limitless and all embracing, is limited in the creature. It is different in the case of God. He is that which exists necessarily in itself, upon which everything accidental depends.

[25] What is meant is the Cartesian form of the ontological argument and not St. Anselm's argument. See p. 208 above and especially Anton Marty, *Untersuchungen*, pp. 344, 346 ff., 386, 482.

He is thus not composed of possibility and actuality. His essence is His existence; the claim that He does not exist is a contradiction. And for this very reason He is infinite. Encompassed by no possibility, His existence is unlimited; He is, therefore, the epitome of all reality and perfection.

These are high-flying speculations, but they will no longer carry anyone aloft with them. What is remarkable is that an eminent thinker, as St. Thomas Aquinas undoubtedly was, really believed that he had demonstrated the infinite perfection of the first cause of the world by means of such a proof. After this, I do not need to refer the reader to well-known examples from modern metaphysics, which would make it just as clear what a tragic influence has been exerted by mistaken views about judgement and things that are closely connected with it.*

15. In logic, too, the failure to understand the essence of judgement necessarily engendered further errors. I have thought through the consequences of that idea from this point of view, and have found that it leads to nothing less than a complete overthrow, and at the same time, a reconstruction of elementary logic.[26] Everything then becomes simpler, clearer, and more exact. I shall only show the contrast between the rules of this reformed logic and those of traditional logic in a few examples, since a complete exposition and justification would, of course, detain us too long and would lead us too far away from our theme.†

I replace the old rules of the categorical syllogism with the following three main rules, which can be directly applied to each figure, and which are perfectly sufficient by themselves for testing any syllogism:

* Their effect upon Kant's transcendental philosophy was mentioned above.

† In preparation for my lectures on logic which I gave during the winter of 1870–71 at the University of Würzburg, I systematically and completely worked out an elementary logic built upon this new basis. Because it was greeted with interest not only by my students but also by those of my colleagues in philosophy to whom I communicated it, I intend to revise and publish it after I complete the publication of my *Psychology*. The rules that I give here by way of example will receive, along with others, the careful justification which the reader is certainly entitled to demand of someone who opposes the whole tradition which has gone on in logic since Aristotle. Besides, many readers may perhaps see for themselves the necessary connection between this and the views about the nature of judgement which have been presented. (Compare Franz Hillebrand, *Die neuen Theorien der Kategorischen Schlüsse*, Vienna, 1891.) [Note of 1911.]

[26] One cannot speak of a complete overthrow, but of a radical and simplifying reform. See Supplementary Essay IX.

(1) *Every categorical syllogism includes four terms, two of which are opposed to each other, and the other two appear twice.*

(2) *If the conclusion is negative, then each of the premises has in common with it its quality and one of its terms.*

(3) *If the conclusion is affirmative, then the one premise has the same quality and an identical term, and the other has the opposite quality and an opposite term.*

These are rules which a logician of the old school could not possibly hear without being horrified. Each syllogism is said to have four terms, yet he has always condemned the *quarternio terminorum* as a fallacy.* Negative conclusions are said to have purely negative premises, yet he has always taught that nothing can follow from two negative premises. Even among the premises of an affirmative conclusion we say there is a negative judgement, while the traditional logician would swear that this conclusion invariably demands two affirmative premises. Indeed, there is no longer any room for a categorical conclusion derived from two affirmative premises; yet he has always insisted in his lectures that affirmative premises are best and he calls it a *pejor pars* when a negative premise is adjoined to an affirmative one. Lastly, no mention is made in these new rules of "universal" and "particular" premises; yet he always has these expressions on the tip of his tongue, so to speak. And have his old rules not shown themselves to be so well-adapted for the testing of syllogisms that, in turn, the thousands of inferences measured by their criteria are themselves now proof and confirmation of them? Shall we no longer admit as valid the famous syllogism "All men are mortal. Caius is a man. Therefore, Caius is mortal," and all those like it? – This seems an impossibly unreasonable demand.

Actually, the situation is not as bad as all that. The errors out of which the old rules of syllogistic theory arose consisted in a misconception of the nature of judgement as concerns both their content and their form. So, when the rules were consistently adhered

---

* Very recently an English logician, Boole, has also rightly recognized that many categorical syllogisms have four terms, of which two are in opposition to one another. Others have subscribed to his view, and even Bain, who reports at length on Boole's contributions to syllogistic in his own *Logic*, makes known his agreement in no uncertain terms (I, 205). Although Boole simply places these syllogisms with four terms alongside the syllogisms with three terms, instead of recognizing the *quarternio terminorum* as the general rule, and although his entire method of derivation bears no resemblance to my own, it was still of interest to me as a sign that across the Channel, too, people are beginning to have their doubts about the law that there must be three terms in a syllogism.

to in their application, the harmful effects of the errors generally cancelled each other out.* Among all the inferences which were declared valid according to such old rules, only those in four modes were improperly deduced. On the other hand, however, a not insignificant number of valid modes were overlooked.†

* While saying, for example, as a result of a misunderstanding of propositions, that three terms were necessary for a valid categorical syllogism, logicians were led by this same misunderstanding to see in particular arguments only three terms, while in reality there were four.

† The English logicians mentioned before have already recognized this point. The four invalid modes, of which I speak are *Darapti* and *Felapton*, in the third figure, and *Bamalip* and *Fesapo*, in the fourth.[27]

[27] As Hillebrand showed in *Die neuen theorien der Kategorischen Schlusse* (Vienna, 1891) Darapti, Felapton, Bamalip, and Fesapo, can be justified if one, for example, admits an affirmative judgement into the premises in Darapti. Moreover, Brentano himself wrote the following in a letter to Marty on April 15, 1876: "I read a note from Leyden about my reform of logic in *Mind* yesterday. It was written by someone called Land and was not very friendly. The matter is set forth as if what I offer is only an arbitrary change in terminology. But contradicting this, a few lines later a polemic is raised against the reducibility of categorical propositions to existential ones. Every categorical proposition, it is maintained, presupposes the existence of a subject in the real or in an imaginary world. (This "or" is dubious.) The author grants that if this were not the case my rejection of Darapti, Bamalip, etc. would be correct. *Conversely, I must admit that if the existence of the subject is already presupposed to be true (i.e. to be already known and indisputable), these arguments are correct.*

"But what is actually the case with the argument, 'All devils have been damned by God, All devils are spirits, Some spirits have been damned by God?' The major and minor premises follow from the definition of devil. No one can assert the conclusion who does not believe in Hell. . . .'"

In other words, if we add to the premises the further thought, "There are devils," the inference is correct, but no one who does not believe in Hell and devils can draw a conclusion by Darapti in this case. So, two years after the publication of the *Psychology*, Brentano completed his theory and showed how to construct a bridge to scholastic logic: by means of the insight that when expressions like "all men," "the men," "man" are used, the linguistic expression is equivocal: sometimes *purely* negative, sometimes, however, with an affirmative presupposition. Anyone who adds the premise, "There are devils," to the above argument, is making a formally correct inference, i.e. the truth of the *three* premises cannot be combined with the falsity [Translators' note: Correcting an obvious error in the German text, which reads "*Richtigkeit*" here] of the conclusion. But Scholastic logic knows nothing of three premises. Couturat has called our attention to the fact that Leibniz attempted a similar criticism of Scholastic logic. (See Willy Freitag in *Archiv für die gesamte Psychologie*, Vol. 38, 140, and the memoir by Stumpf in my book, *Franz Brentano*, p. 107 n.)

The consequences were more harmful in the case of the theory of so-called immediate inferences. Traditional logic not only asserted, as the true rule for the conversion of syllogisms, that every categorical proposition is simply convertible (provided we are clear about the true subject and the true predicate), but according to the old rules, many conversions were regarded as valid which were not truly valid, and vice versa. The same applied to so-called inferences by subalternation and opposition.* Besides, when we compare critically the old rules with one another we find, strangely enough, that they sometimes contradict themselves, so that what is valid according to one rule is invalid according to another.

16. I shall, however, leave to a future revision of my logic the task of verifying and developing this in detail.† We are less concerned here with the harmful consequences which the misconception of the nature of judgement has had on logic or metaphysics than with those which have resulted for psychology itself. Because of the relation between psychology and logic they have undoubtedly added a new obstacle to its fruitful development as well. It is fair to say that up until now psychology has improperly neglected the investigation of the laws of the origin of judgement. This occurred because presentation and judgement were always grouped together in one class as "thinking" so that people believed that when they had investigated

* The conversion of a universal affirmative proposition into a particular affirmative proposition is inadmissible; the usual inferences by subalternation are never valid; likewise, among inferences by opposition, those which are drawn from the falsity of contraries or the truth of sub-contraries are never valid.[28]

† See the work of Franz Hillebrand mentioned above, which has since been published. This book deals more thoroughly with what I have touched on here. [Note of 1911.] [Editor's note: Brentano's logic has been published posthumously as *Die Lehre vom richtigen Urteil*, ed. Franziska Mayer-Hillebrand. Bern, 1956.]

[28] The conclusions drawn by subalternation (I from A and O from E) can be correct only if they are interpreted as conclusions drawn from *two* premises; for example, "Some S is P" can be correctly inferred from "All S's are P" only if we think "There are S's," and "No S is not P." "No S is P" implies "Some S is not P" only under the presupposition that we think of the judgement, "S's exist"; an additional so-called *conversio per accidens* then follows from this inference by means of so-called *conversio simplex* of the conclusion.

Inferences *ad contrariam propositionem* are also correct only on the presupposition that S exists, hence as inferences from two premises. The same thing holds of the arguments by opposition, which Brentano cites.

Contraposition is based primarily on equating the affirmation of so-called *Privativa* and *Negativa* with making certain negative judgements obtained by subalternation and conversion.

the laws of the succession of ideas, what was essential for judgement had already been done. As eminent a psychologist as Lotze himself says, "When, for instance, we find judgement and imagination placed . . . alongside one another, we must unhesitatingly grant that these two do not form part of the original mental stock, but are capabilities developed in the advance of life, the one slowly, the other quickly. We must at the same time acknowledge that to explain their growth *nothing is needed beyond the laws of association. . . .*"* This statement shows that the reason for this great neglect lies in the faulty classification which Lotze borrowed from Kant.

John Stuart Mill's judgement on this matter was better. In the passages quoted above we saw that he laid great stress upon the unavoidable necessity of a specific investigation of the laws of judgement. He considered it absolutely insufficient merely to derive them from the laws of the succession of ideas. Nevertheless, in spite of his otherwise correct views on the nature of judgement, he always held that the conjunction of ideas, the combination of subject and predicate, was essential to it. And this prevented him from seeing with sufficient clarity the nature of judgement as a distinct class of mental phenomena equal to the other fundamental classes. And so it happened that not even Bain, who was so close to Mill, took advantage of the hint he gave in order to fill a great yawning gap in psychology.

The phrase which the Scholastics inherited from Aristotle, *parvus error in principio maximus in fine*, is thus confirmed on every side, in the present case.

---

* *Microcosmus*, trans. E. Hamilton and E. E. Constance Jones (Edinburgh, 1885), I, 176.

VIII

Feeling and Will United into a Single Fundamental Class

1. After it has been established that presentation and judgement are distinct basic classes, we must still justify our second departure from the traditional classification. Just as we separate presentation and judgement, we unite feeling and will.

This is not as much of an innovation as the previous point was, for, from Aristotle down to Tetens, Mendelssohn, and Kant, it has been generally assumed that there was just *one* basic class for feeling and striving. Among present day psychological authorities, we have seen that Herbert Spencer distinguishes only two areas of mental life, a cognitive one and an affective one. But in view of the importance of the question, we should not let this keep us from establishing and supporting our theory with the same care, making use of all the resources at our disposal.

We shall proceed in the same way here as we did in our study of the relationship between presentation and judgement. We appeal, then, above all, to the testimony of immediate experience. Inner perception, we say, reveals the absence of a fundamental distinction in this case, as clearly as it revealed the presence of one in the other case. Here it reveals an essential agreement in the kind of reference to an object, while there it revealed a thoroughgoing difference.

If the remaining mental phenomena – those we are now considering – really revealed a radical difference similar to the one between presentation and judgement, if by their very nature there was indeed a sharp boundary line between feeling and striving, we might make errors in our definitions of the distinctive nature of each of the two classes, but the demarcation of the groups, the specification of which phenomenon belongs to which group, would certainly be an easy task. Even if someone is completely unclear about the nature of judgement, he can still say without hesitation that "man" expresses

235

a mere presentation and, "There are men," expresses a judgement. The same holds true throughout the entire range of mental acts covered by the two kinds of thought. But the question of what counts as a feeling and what as a desire, a volition, or a striving is quite another matter. To be quite truthful, I, at least, do not know where the boundary between the two classes is really supposed to lie. There are other phenomena which have an intermediate position between feelings of pleasure and pain, and what is usually called willing or striving. The distance between the two extremes may appear great, but if you take the intermediate states into consideration, if you always compare the phenomena which are adjacent to one another, there is no gap to be found in the entire sequence – the transitions take place very gradually.

Consider the following series, for example: sadness – yearning for the absent good – hope that it will be ours – the desire to bring it about – the courage to make the attempt – the decision to act. The one extreme is a feeling, the other an act of will; and they may seem to be quite remote from one another.[1] But if we attend to the

---

[1] Ehrenfels objected to this series on this ground: "sorrow" contains a "hate" while a "love" was dominant in the "yearning," with the result that a discontinuity appears in the series. But one can also begin the series with yearning, which is also generally taken to be a feeling. Brentano does not offer a detailed analysis of emotions in this passage; one should look to the *Untersuchungen zur Sinnespsychologie* for supplemental material. Here Brentano also goes into the analysis of affective sensations and "redundancies," those more or less intensive "sensations of feeling" which are characteristic of both human and animal emotional life, while animals have no share in our non-sensual emotional acts of valuation. The unity of our entire emotional life propounded by Brentano encounters more general agreement today, especially on the part of psychiatrists.

Complexity is greatest in this area, and here, too, language is an untrustworthy guide. For example, if one says, "I am sorry that A does not exist," there lies hidden within this statement:

1. I love A.
2. I judge: "A does not exist."
3. The consciousness of this combination is unpleasant to me.
4. Associated with this are sensual redundancies, namely unpleasant feelings (i.e. sensations which belong to what Brentano called the *Spürsinn*, which are unpleasant to us. See *Untersuchungen*.)

Or similarly: I am sorry that A exists.

1. I hate A.
2. I believe that A exists. [Translators' note: Correcting an error in the German text, which here reads "*Ich glaube, A sei nicht.*"]
3. and 4. As in the preceding example.

The same thing holds, *mutatis mutandis*, for "I am glad that A exists (does not exist)."

intermediate members and compare only the adjacent ones, we find the closest connections and almost imperceptible transitions throughout. – If we wished to classify them as feelings or strivings, to which of the two basic classes should we assign each case? – We say, "I feel yearning," "I feel hope," "I feel a desire to bring this about for myself," "I feel courageous enough to attempt this," – the only thing which no one would say is that he feels a decision. Perhaps, then, this is the boundary line and all the intermediate elements should be classified as feelings. If we permit ordinary language to settle the matter for us, we shall, of course, judge in this way. And, in fact, it may at least be true that sadness at being deprived of something is related to the desire to possess it in the same way that the denial of an object is related to the affirmation of its non-existence. But is there not already a germ of the striving lying unnoticed in the yearning, which germinates when one hopes, and blooms when one thinks of possibly doing something oneself, when one wishes to act and then has the courage to do so, until finally the desire overcomes both the aversion to any sacrifice involved and the wish to reflect any longer, and it ripens into a decision? – Surely, if we still wish to divide this series of phenomena into a number of basic classes at all, we can no more group its intermediate members together with the first one, call them *feelings*, and contrast them with the last one, than we can group them with the last member and contrast them with the first under the heading of the *will* or *striving*. Instead, nothing is left but to consider each phenomenon a special class in itself. But in that event, I believe, it will be unmistakable to everyone that the distinctions between these classes are not as deep and incisive as that between presentation and judgement, or that between them and all other mental phenomena. The character of the data given in inner consciousness compels us, then, to extend one unified fundamental class over the entire range of feeling and striving.*

* It is interesting and instructive to observe the psychologists' futile efforts to establish a firm boundary line between feeling and will or striving. They contradict ordinary linguistic usage, one contradicts the other, and not infrequently they even contradict themselves. Kant even assigns the hopeless longing for something which is known to be impossible to the faculty of desire, and I have no doubt that he would have classified remorse in the same way, too. But this does not agree with ordinary language – for we do speak of a feeling of longing – any more than it agrees with his definition of the faculty of desire as "the faculty by which one causes, by means of his presentations, the reality of the objects of those presentations." (See above, p. 189.) Hamilton is surprised at the confusion which, he acknowledges, is so prevalent concerning the phenomena of the two

classes, since he thinks it is so easy to determine the natural boundary between them (*Lectures on Metaphysics*, II, 433). But his repeated attempts to define it precisely show that it is no easy matter. He decides, as we have already heard, that feelings are objectless in the full sense of the word, that they are "subjective" (II, 432; cp. above, p. 189), while acts of striving are all directed toward an object. It should be remarked that this would be a simple and easily applicable criterion. But as surely as this would have to be the case if the definition were to correspond to the distinctive character of the phenomena, Hamilton could not, in view of its incorrectness, make it work. Everyone would say that phenomena such as joy and sorrow, which are most decidedly feelings, seem to have an object. So then Hamilton draws yet another distinction, although not without contradicting the first one, perhaps. "Pain and pleasure," he says, "as feelings, belong exclusively to the present; whereas conation has reference only to the future, for conation is a longing – a striving, either to maintain the continuance of the present state, or to exchange it for another." (II, 433.) These definitions do not involve the same error as the previous ones, namely that there is, in fact, no mental phenomenon which corresponds to one of them. That, however, is the only thing which can be said for them. For distinguishing between the two areas on the basis of present and future is as incomplete as it is arbitrary. It is incomplete, for how are we to classify those emotions such as remorse and gratitude which refer neither to the present nor the future, but to the past? – We would have to make a third class for them. But incompleteness would be the lesser evil; much worse is the arbitrariness with which mental phenomena that are very intimately related would be separated into different classes, depending upon the various temporal position of their objects. Thus, for example, the mental phenomena ordinarily called wishes are sometimes wishes for something future, sometimes for something in the present and sometimes for something past. I wish to see you often, I wish that I were a rich man, I wished I had not done that – these are examples from each of the three periods of time. And although the last two wishes are fruitless and have no prospect of fulfilment, they still preserve the general character of wishing, as Kant, Hamilton's principal authority, recognized. It can even happen that when someone wishes that his brother has arrived safely in America, his wish refers to something which is past, without referring to something obviously impossible. Should we view these mental states as related by nothing more than the fact that language unites them under the common term wishes? Should we separate them from one another, classifying some of them with acts of will, and others with pleasure and pain, and still others with the class which we are going to establish for those with past objects? I believe that no one could help but see how unjustifiable and unnatural such a procedure would be. Thus, this attempt at defining a boundary between feeling and will has come to grief, too. It is not surprising, then, to find that Hamilton shares the confusion between feeling and striving for which he rebuked others. When you hear the definitions he gives for specific phenomena, it is often hard to make out which phenomena he wants to assign to which of

2. If the phenomena of both feeling and will are in the same basic class, then, according to the principle of classification we have adopted, the two forms of consciousness must be essentially related as regards the way they refer to something. But what is the common characteristic in the ways in which they refer to their objects? If our viewpoint is correct, the answer to this question, too, must be given by inner experience. And it does indeed provide an answer, thus supplying an even more direct proof that the ultimate class has unity.

Just as the general nature of judgement consists in the affirmation or denial of a fact, we learn from the testimony of inner experience that the general character of the area now under consideration consists in a certain acceptance or rejection – not in the same sense, but in an analogous one. If something can become the content of a judgement in that it can be accepted as true or rejected as false, it can also become the object of a phenomenon belonging to the third basic class, in that it can be agreeable (in the broadest sense of the word) as something good, or disagreeable as something bad. Here we are concerned with an object's value or lack thereof, while in the other case we were concerned with its truth or falsity.

I do not believe that anyone will understand me to mean that phenomena belonging to this class are cognitive acts by which we perceive the goodness or badness, value or disvalue of certain objects. Still, in order to make such an interpretation absolutely impossible, I explicitly note that this would be a complete mis-understanding of my real meaning. In the first place, that would mean that I viewed these phenomena as judgements; but in fact I separate them off as a separate class. Secondly, it would mean that I would be assuming quite generally that this class of phenomena presupposes presentations of good and bad, value and disvalue. This is so far from being the case, that instead I shall show that such presentations can stem only from inner perception of these pheno-mena.[2] Our presentations of truth and falsity, too, presuppose and

[2] See *The Origin of our Knowledge of Right and Wrong*.

his two basic classes. He defines vanity as "the wish to please others from the desire of being respected by them," and assigns it – to feelings (II, 519). And he does the same with remorse and shame, i.e. "the fear and sorrow at incurring [the] disrespect [of others]" (II, 519), as if their direction upon an object and their reference to something which is not present were not perfectly obvious – the one in and of itself and the other from the definition that Hamilton gives. This complete failure on the part of such a distinguished philosopher, confirms, I believe, in a striking way, what I have said about the lack of any clear-cut, natural boundary between the two allegedly basic classes.

are acquired by reflection upon judgements, as no one would doubt. If we say that every affirmative judgement is an act of taking something to be true, and every negative judgement an act of taking something to be false, this does not mean that the former consists in predicating truth of what is taken to be true and the latter in predicating falsity of what is taken to be false. Our previous discussions have shown, rather, that what the expressions denote is a particular kind of intentional reception of an object, a distinctive kind of mental reference to a content of consciousness. The only correct interpretation is that anyone who takes something to be true will not only affirm the object, but, when asked whether the object is to be affirmed, will also affirm the object's to-be-affirmedness, i.e. its truth (which is all that is meant by this barbarous expression).[3] The expression, "to take something to be true," may be connected with this. The expression, "to take something to be false," will receive an analogous explication.

Similarly, then, the expressions which we used in an analogous manner, "to be agreeable as good," and "to be disagreeable as bad," do not mean that in the phenomena of this class goodness is ascribed to something which is agreeable as good, or badness to something which is disagreeable as bad. Rather, they, too, denote a distinctive way in which the mental act refers to a content. And here the only correct interpretation is that a person whose consciousness is directed toward a content in such a way will, as a consequence, give an affirmative answer to the question of whether the object is of such a kind that it can enter into this sort of relation, which simply means ascribing goodness or badness, value or disvalue to it.[4]

A phenomenon belonging to this class is not a judgement. ("This is something to be loved," or "This is something to be hated," would be judgements about goodness or badness.) It is, rather, an act of love or hate. In the sense of the explanations just given, I now repeat, without fear of being misunderstood, that the relationship between the goodness and badness, value and disvalue of objects, and the phenomena belonging to this class, is analogous to that which obtains between truth and falsity and judgements. And it is this character-

---

[3] The object's "to-be-affirmedness" is nothing but what Brentano's older school calls the judgement-content, the state of affairs (*Sachverhalt*), the objective, or the like (analogously, the "to-be-deniedness" in the case of negative judgement). Brentano rejects these concepts in Supplementary Essays III through IX.
[4] According to Brentano's later theory, "goodness, badness, value, disvalue" are not independently meaningful words, either. Supplementary Essay IX deals with this more extensively, as does my book, *Franz Brentano*, and *The Origin of our Knowledge of Right and Wrong*.

istic reference to the object which, I maintain, reveals itself in an equally direct and evident way in desire and will, as well as in everything that we called feeling or emotion, through inner perception.

3. As far as striving, desiring and willing are concerned, what I say can be regarded as generally recognized. Let us hear from one of the most prominent and influential defenders of the fundamental separation of feeling from will.

Lotze, in opposing those who interpret willing as a kind of knowing and say that "I will" is merely a confident "I shall," locates the essence of will in an act of approval or disapproval, i.e. in an act of finding something to be good or finding something to be bad. "Perhaps," he says, "the mere assurance that I shall *act* may be tantamount to the knowing of my volition, but then the notion of acting must include the peculiar element of approval, permission, or intention, that makes the will such. . . ."* And again, against those who would understand volition as a certain power to produce effects, he says, "The approval through which our will adopts as its own the resolution offered to it by the pressing motives of the train of ideas, or the disapproval with which it rejects it, would be conceivable even if it neither possessed the slightest power of interfering, for determination and alteration, with the course of mental events."* What is this approval or disapproval Lotze is speaking of? It is clear that he does not mean finding something good or bad in the sense of a practical judgement, since he assigns judgements to the class of presentations, as we saw. What else could he be maintaining, then, but that the essence of will consists in a particular relation of the mental activity to the object as good or bad?

Similarly, we could cite passages from Kant and Mendelssohn, the principal founders of the usual threefold classification, which support the view that such a reference to the object as good or bad constitutes the basic character of any desire.† But we prefer to go back to antiquity, so as to combine the ancient psychology's testimony with that of the modern.

Aristotle speaks on this subject with a clarity that leaves nothing to be desired. He takes "good" and "desirable" to be synonymous. "The object of desire" (τὸ ὀρεκτόν), he says in his books on the soul, "is either the good or the apparent good." And at the beginning of his ethics he declares, "Every action and every choice seems to aim at some good and for this reason the good has rightly been described

---

* *Microcosmus*, trans. E. Hamilton and E. E. Constance Jones (Edinburgh, 1885), I, 257.
† Cp. Mendelssohn, *Gesammelte Schriften*, IV, 122 ff.

as that at which all things aim."* For this reason he identifies the
final cause with the good.† The same doctrine was then preserved
throughout the Middle Ages. Thomas Aquinas teaches very clearly
that just as thought is related to an object as knowable, so desire is
related to an object as good. So it could happen that one and the
same thing could be the object of quite heterogeneous mental
activities.‡⁵

We can see from these examples that, with regard to striving and
willing, the most eminent thinkers of various periods agree in
acknowledging the empirical fact that we have asserted, even
though they may not all have evaluated its significance in the same
way.

4. Let us turn to the other phenomena involved, namely pleasure and
pain, which are the ones most commonly separated, as feelings, from
the will. Is it true that here, too, inner experience clearly reveals this
distinctive way of referring to a content, this "agreeable as good,"
or "disagreeable as bad," as the basic characteristic of the phenomena? Is it also clear that these phenomena have to do with the
value and lack of value of their objects in a manner analogous to
that in which judgements have to do with truth and falsity? – As far
as I am concerned, this seems no less obvious in the case of feelings
than it does in the case of desire.

But because it is possible to believe that there is a prejudice at
work here causing me to misinterpret the phenomena, I shall appeal
once again to the testimony of others. First of all, let us hear from
Lotze in this connection. "If it was an original peculiarity of mind,"
he says in *Microcosmus*,§ "not only to undergo changes, but to
apprehend them as presented in thought, it no less originally belongs
to it, not merely to present them to itself, but also to become aware
of their value for itself in terms of pain and pleasure." And immediately below he makes a similar assertion, "the soul . . in pleasure
becomes conscious of this exercise of its power as of an enhanced
value in its existence. . . . " And he repeats these ideas even more
often, holding them equally firmly in connection with both higher
and lower feelings. In his opinion, the genuine core of the sensual
drive is "always . . . a feeling that in pain or pleasure discloses to us

---

* *On The Soul*, III, 10. *Nichomachean Ethics*, I, 1. *Metaphysics*, XII, 7.
Compare also *Rhetoric*, I, 6.
† *Metaphysics*, XII, 10 and elsewhere.
‡ Cp., for example, *Summa Theologica*, P. I, Q. 80, A. 1 ad 2.
§ I, 240.
⁵ On this point, see Alfred Kastil: "Die Frage nach der Erkenntnis des
Guten Bei Aristotles und Thomas von Aquine," *Sitzungsberichte der
kaiserlichen Akademie der Wissenschaften* (Vienna, 1900).

the value of a bodily state perhaps not rising to conscious clearness.''*
"And the moral principles of each age were always sanctioned by
the soul otherwise than were the truths of cognition, they too were
dictates of an appreciative feeling."†

I do not venture to offer a completely confident account of how
Lotze conceives of the sensing of value in feeling, but it is certain
that he did not view the feeling itself as the cognition of a value. This
is clear not only from particular statements,‡ but also because if he

---

* *Microcosmus*, I, 255.　　　　† *Microcosmus*, I, 247.

‡ In the passage just quoted he contrasts approval through feeling as
"another kind of approval," with affirmation of a truth. And at I, 241, he
says that with regard to feelings of pleasure or pain, our consciousness
never doubts that feelings of pleasure and pain can be interpreted as some
unknown favouring influence or disturbance. The approval, then, only
follows the feeling, even if it follows right on its heels. – If we ask, however, why those feelings are always interpreted in that way, Lotze does
not give us, it seems to me, a wholly satisfactory answer. It does not appear
to be his view that the presentation of pleasure without the sort of accompanying benefit which, according to him, we take it to signify, would be a
contradiction. What, then, is the source of this necessity or this insurmountable inclination? – We, from our point of view, can, I believe,
answer the question. When one performs a mental act which belongs to
the third basic class of mental phenomena, he ascribes value to its object
as a result of this act (see above, page 241) with the same necessity with
which he ascribes truth or falsity to the object of an affirmative or negative
judgement as a result of this judgement. And this holds for pleasure and
pain, too. Thus, if we have a bodily sensation accompanied by pleasure,
we ascribe a value to the sensation, and to this extent the process is
obviously necessary. But right away we will have to go further. Since
we, for example, have noted that pleasant sensations depend upon certain
physical processes, they, too, will necessarily come to be of value to us
because of their consequences. And because of the special laws which we
will later have to establish for this area of mental phenomena, it will turn
out that they will gradually become objects of our love and value, even
without regard for their consequences. It can even come to the point
where we attribute advantages to them which we do not have the slightest
rational basis for assuming, as when we say, for example, without any
experience to that effect, that good-tasting foods are healthier – ascribing
this good quality to them because of their pleasant taste. Indeed, according
to folk superstition, gold is supposed to be an effective remedy for
illness, just because it has often proved to be valuable and useful in other
ways. Nevertheless, in the case in question there are, in addition, specific
facts of experience which make it clear that there is a very extensive
connection between pleasure and organic betterment. And this provides a
more reasonable basis for supposing that the same thing might hold true
in this particular case. And this may, if not always, at least as a rule,
reinforce the motives already mentioned and work in conjunction with them.

had he would have included it in his first class. On such a theory, it would appear that the expression can be defended in only *one* way, namely in accordance with our view. It is also worth noting that Lotze does not merely say that feeling senses value and the lack thereof, and relate it in this way to the object as good and bad. He also uses the term "approval," in this connection – the very same term he had previously used in order to identify the "peculiar element . . . that makes the will such." Conversely, on another occasion he uses the phrase *"herzliche Teilnahme,"* an expression which is ordinarily applied to phenomena of pleasure and pain, for "will." How could this transposition of the most characteristic terms from one area to the other be anything but involuntary yet significant testimony to the essential affinity in the way both kinds of phenomena refer to their objects – testimony in favor of their being united in a *single* basic class?

Hamilton – for we do not wish to leave out this great defender of a separate status for feelings – using expressions exactly like Lotze's, calls "pleasure and pain" "an estimate of the relative worth of objects."* We must leave it to Hamilton himself to reconcile this with what he taught us about the "subjectively subjective" character of feelings. Such statements, which plainly acknowledge that feelings refer to their objects as good or bad, recur elsewhere in Hamilton, indeed they occur very frequently.*

Finally, Kant, in his *Critique of Judgement* calls both feeling and desire *liking*, just at the point where he wants to separate them, only the one is disinterested liking and the other practical. When this is examined more closely, it comes down to the fact that in feeling one has an interest only in the presentation of an object, while in desire one has an interest in its existence. And this distinction would be done away with, too, if it should be shown that what Kant calls feeling in this case is really directed to the presentation itself as its object. But in an earlier work Kant says precisely that, "It is in our own time that we have first begun to have insight into the fact that the capacity of representing the true is knowledge but the capacity of experiencing the good is feeling, and the two must not be confused with one another."†

The significance of such testimony from the lips of our most distinguished opponents certainly cannot be denied. And here, too, there are opinions from periods long past which are in agreement

---

* See *Lectures on Metaphysics*, II, 434 ff., and especially 436, Nos. 3 and 4.
† "Enquiry concerning the clarity of the principles of natural theology and ethics," Kant, *Gesammelte Schriften*, II; reprinted in *Selected Precritical Writings*, trans. G. B. Kerford and D. E. Walford (Manchester and New York, 1968).

with these modern views.* Our historical survey has taught us how incorrect it is to say, as Kant did, that it was not until his time that a special faculty, which refers to something as good, was first set alongside the faculty which is directed on something as true. Earlier psychology, insofar and as long as it was dominated by Aristotle, distinguished between thought and desire in this sense. In desire – so broad a sense was attached to the term – were included feelings of pleasure and pain and anything at all which is not presentative or judgemental thought. What chiefly interests us here in connection with our question is that this involved the recognition that the relation to the object as good or bad, which we assert to be the universal and essential basic characteristic of feelings, is no less present in feelings than it is in desire and will. Aristotle's statements about the relation of accompanying pleasure to the perfection of the act, found in the *Nichomachean Ethics*, which we referred to in our study of consciousness, show the same thing. So do some passages in his *Rhetoric*.† The Peripatetic School in the Middle Ages upholds the same view in a most unambiguous fashion. This is especially true of Thomas Aquinas in his interesting doctrine of how emotions are connected.‡

Ordinary language also indicates that pleasure and pain involve a reference to an object which is essentially akin to the will's. It is fond of taking expressions which were first applied in the one area and transposing them to the other. We call what we enjoy pleasant and what gives us pain unpleasant, but we also speak of something

---

* Herbart gives some further testimony in favor of saying that feeling and will agree in character – although he does it most involuntarily, to be sure. If one asks psychologists for the origin of the boundary between feeling and desire, he says, "their explanations go around in a circle. . . ." Maass, in his work on feelings (p. 39, the first part) defines feeling in terms of desire ("a feeling is *pleasant* insofar as it is desired for its own sake"), but all the same, in his work on the passions he says it is a well-known law of nature to desire what is presented as good and to shun what is presented as bad. So then the question arises, *what is good* and *what is bad*? To which we are given the answer: our sensory nature presents as good what affects us *pleasantly*, and so on. That brings us around full circle. – In his *Grundriss der Erfahrungsseelenlehre*, Hoffbauer begins his chapter on the faculties of feeling and desire in this way: "We are conscious of many states which we strive to produce; these we call *pleasant*. Certain presentations make us strive to realize their objects; these we call desires," etc. Here the very same basis, striving, is given for both feeling and desire. (*Lehrbuch der Psychologie*, V, II, Part 1, Chap. 4, Sect. 96.)
† See above Book Two, Chap. 3, Sect. 6 and Aristotle's *Rhetoric*, I, 11, esp. 1370 a 16; II, 4, 1381 a 6.
‡ *Summa Theologica*, P. II, 1, Q. 26 ff.

being "my pleasure" or say "It is a pleasure to do something," where this has to do with the will. It is obvious that *"Placet,"* in the sense of approval, was extended from the area of feeling to that of acts of will in the same way. It is just as clear that the verb "to please" has undergone the same process in "Do as you please," or "What is your pleasure?" and so on. Even the word *"Lust"* ("pleasure") itself becomes unmistakably a designation for an attitude of will in the question, *"Hast du Lust?"* ("Would you like to?"). *"Unwillen"* ("indignation"), on the other hand, is hardly something which can be called will at all, although that is the etymology of the word; and there is no denying that *"Widerwillen,"* as a designation of certain phenomena of disgust or loathing, has become the name of a feeling.

But language does more than just extend the names of certain phenomena from one area to the other. In the expressions "love" and "hate" it possesses designations which are quite properly applicable to any phenomenon in the entire range. For even if they are less commonly used in this case or that, one still understands what is meant when they are used and sees that they have not been severed from their real meaning. The only thing to be said against using them in such cases is that linguistic usage ordinarily prefers more specific designations. For the truth is that, in a sense usually, though not exclusively attached to them, they are expressions that characterize the kind of reference to an object which is generally distinctive of our third class.

The juxtaposition of *"Lust and Liebe,"* *"lieb und leid"* and so on, shows how the expression "Liebe" is used to refer to the most diverse feelings. And when we say *"lieblich"* or *"hässlich,"* do we not simply mean a phenomenon which arouses pleasure or displeasure? On the other hand, expressions such as *"es beliebt mir,"* *"tue was dir lieb ist,"* clearly refer to phenomena of will. The sentence, "He has a preference (*Vorliebe*) for scientific work," expresses something which some people might call a feeling while others might consider it an habitual disposition of the will. Just the same, I shall leave it to others to decide whether better reasons can be adduced in the case of terms such as *"Missliebig,"* *"unliebsam,"* *"Liebling,"* (including *"Lieblingspferd,"* and *"Lieblingstudium"*), for including love, the phenomenon in question, in the area which they call feelings or in that which they refer to as will. As far as I am concerned, I believe that it, as the more general expression, encompasses both areas in these particular cases.

A person who yearns for something, would love to have it; someone who is sad about something finds what he is sad about unlovely; someone who is happy about something loves the fact that it is so;

and a person who wants to do something, likes to do it, if not for its own sake, at least for the sake of one or another of its consequences, and so on. The acts just mentioned are not things which merely exist alongside love, they are acts of love themselves. It is clear, then, that "to be good" and "to be something to be loved in some way" mean the same thing, as do, "to be bad" and "to be something to be hated in some way." It is also clear that we are justified in having chosen the word "love" to cover both love and its opposite, which, as we noted previously, is customarily done in the case of desire and will.

As a result of our discussion, we may say, then, that inner experience clearly reveals the unity of the basic class of feeling and will. It does so by showing us that there is never any sharply drawn boundary between them and that they are distinguished from other mental phenomena by a common characteristic of their reference to a content. The things said about them by philosophers of the most diverse persuasions, even those who divide them into two basic classes, give clear indications of this common characteristic and confirm, as does ordinary language, the correctness of our description of these inner phenomena.

5. Let us continue with our plan of inquiry.

When we were concerned with proving that presentation and judgement are two distinct basic classes, we were not satisfied with merely invoking the direct testimony of experience. Instead, we also showed that the great difference which undeniably exists between these two kinds of phenomena is to be determined entirely according to the different ways in which they refer to their objects. Apart from this distinction, every judgement would coincide with a presentation and vice versa. We will now pose the same question in connection with feeling and will. If someone recognized no difference between the way a feeling of pleasure or pain refers to its object and the way a volition does, would he perhaps be able to name some other thing which constitutes the differentiating factor between them? Would all the differences between them then be settled? – Surely this is not the case.

We have previously seen that there is a continuum of mental states between the feeling of a pleasure or pain, and the will in the strictest sense of the term – in-between states, as it were. And we do not really know on which side they belong when we distinguish between the areas of feeling and will. Yearning, hope, courage, and other phenomena belong to this group. Surely no one will claim that any of these classes is of the sort that, apart from any peculiarity in its way of referring to an object, no differences exist between them. Distinctive properties of the presentations and judgements on which

they are based serve to differentiate one from the other, and, therefore, people, both in ancient and in modern times, have been guided
by such distinctions in their attempts to define the boundaries
between them. This was true of Aristotle in his *Rhetoric* and in his
Nichomachean Ethics. Others, for instance, Cicero, in the fourth
book of his *Tusculanae Quaestiones*, followed his example. Later on
we discover similar attempts in Church Fathers such as Gregory of
Nyssa, Augustine, and others, and to a very high degree in the
Medieval period in Thomas Aquinas' *Prima Secundae*. Again in the
modern period, we encounter such attempts in Descartes' *Treatise on
the Passions*, in the third part of Spinoza's *Ethics* (definitely the best
part of the entire work), and also in Hume, Hartley, James Mill,
and so on, up to the present time.

Of course such definitions which were meant to differentiate each
individual class, not only from some other class, but from *all* other
classes, could not always ignore the opposition which pervades this
area in the same way that affirmation and denial pervade the area of
judgement. And they also had to take account of differences in the
intensity of the phenomena. But in fact this is all that is necessary,
and this, together with the resources mentioned above, is entirely
sufficient for the definition of any class concept which belongs to this
area. It obviously goes without saying that this does not mean that
every attempt made with their help has actually been successful.

Lotze, who follows this same method of definition in his *Medizinische Psychologie* when defining the various classes he assigns to
feeling, refrains from any such attempt in connection with the
distinctive character of will, for he holds that it must necessarily
fail. "It is in vain . . . to deny the reality of volition, as vain as it
would be to endeavour by lengthy explanations to make plain its
simple nature, which is only to be known directly through
experience."*

This is consistent with his point of view,† but it does not seem to
me to be true at all. Every act of will shares the common character
of our third basic class, and, therefore, anyone who calls the willed
object something which someone loves (*was jemand lieb ist*), has to

---

* *Microcosmus*, I, 257.
† Kant and Hamilton, to be sure, did not draw this conclusion; but, on
the one hand, they were not very successful in their attempts, and on the
other hand, to the extent that they did succeed, they themselves merely
bear witness to the incorrectness of their basic idea that there is a fundamental distinction between the classes. This is true of Kant when he
contrasts satisfaction of the will, i.e. satisfaction taken in the existence of
something, with the satisfaction of feeling, i.e. disinterested satisfaction
which is content with the mere presentation (see above, p. 237).

some extent already characterized the nature of volitional activity and in a very general way. If we then specify the particular nature of the content and the distinctive character of the presentation and judgement on which the act of will is based, these complete the original characterization and make an exact definition of it in much the same way as they do in other cases where a class of feelings is being defined. Every act of will has to do with an action we believe to be in our power and with a good which is expected to result from the act of will itself.[6] Aristotle touched on these specifications when he called what is capable of being chosen a good which can be attained through action. James Mill and Alexander Bain give a more detailed analysis of particular conditions which are determined by the presentations and judgements upon which the phenomena are based. Even if we should find that there are objections to be made to one or another of these analyses, anyone who pays close attention to them will, I believe, be convinced that the will really can be defined in a similar way and with similar means as particular classes of feelings can, and that the will is not as indescribably simple as Lotze claimed.*

6. When we say that the will can be defined by adding specifications of this kind to the general concept of love, we do not mean that someone who has never himself experienced the specific phenomenon could attain complete clarity concerning it merely from the definition. This is by no means the case. In this connection there is a great difference between defining the will and defining a particular class of judgements by citing the kind of content toward which they are affirmatively or negatively directed. Anyone who has ever made an affirmative and negative judgement at all can bring any other judgement vividly to mind as soon as he knows what it is that the judgement is affirmatively or negatively directed toward.[7] On the other hand, no matter how often a person has engaged in activities of love and hate at various levels of intensity, if he had never specifically willed anything, he could never obtain a complete idea of the distinctive nature of the phenomenon from any statement of the distinctive characteristic of will in the respects mentioned. If Lotze had wanted to say only this much, we would declare ourselves to be in complete agreement with him.

* We shall have to go into this question in detail in Book Five. [This Book was never completed.]
[6] See below, Sect. 10.
[7] It is obvious that this is what is meant: we can conceive of any other affirmative or negative judgement about "any object you please," as soon as we have once made a judgement. On the other hand we could not have any idea of an apodictic judgement, if all our thoughts had been assertoric.

But we have said nothing which is not equally true of other specific classes which usually come under the heading of feelings, for each of them, too, manifests a distinctive hue, to use one of Lotze's own expressions. It would be impossible for someone who had only experienced feelings of joy and sorrow to become perfectly clear about the distinctive inherent character of hope or fear merely from their definitions. The same thing is even true of the various kinds of joy or pleasure; the enjoyment of a good conscience, the pleasure of being agreeably warm, the joy of looking at a beautiful painting, and the pleasure taken in a delicious meal differ from each other not only quantitatively, but qualitatively. And without having had the specific experience, no specification of the object could produce an idea which corresponds perfectly to that object.

Because of these qualitative differences, one will, of course, have to admit that within the area of love there are still distinctions in the manner in which objects are referred to. But this is not to say that the phenomena of love are not also encompassed by the unity of the same basic class. On the contrary, there is an essential kinship and agreement between qualitatively different phenomena of love just as there is between qualitatively different colors. The analogy with the area of judgement also makes this clear. There, too, there are many different ways of referring to an object; first and foremost, we should regard the distinction between affirmation and negation as such a difference.* It is correct to call them qualitatively different.

Still, the unity of one and the same basic class extends over both, since they are alike in their general character, and their separation, though it too is part of their nature, does not even begin to approach the fundamental significance of the distinction between presentation and judgement. Exactly the same thing is true in the present case. If anything, it is even more obvious that the qualitative differences between particular kinds of love cannot be taken into consideration, in a basic classification of mental phenomena, than it is that the qualitative differences between judgements should not be taken into account in such a classification. If they were, the ultimate classes would become extraordinarily numerous, or rather downright innumerable, particularly since anything which becomes associated with an object of love or hate becomes an object of love or hate itself, and usually the phenomenon changes its hue in the process. Also, the narrow limits of each of these ultimate classes would be contrary to the whole purpose of a first and fundamental classification.

* We might also think here of the difference between evident and non-evident, apodictic and merely assertoric judgements, and others as well. [Note of 1911.]

For that reason, even those who take the area which we include within the bounds of *one* basic class, and divide it into several classes, do not take all of these differences into account in their classification. They distinguish only two classes, feeling and will. They disregard all of the various shades of love and hate in the area they call will, and the still more numerous ones in the area of feelings. They recognize in practice in by far the larger number of cases, then, that such subordinate distinctions do not justify a division into different basic classes. And if our explanation is correct, they thereby admit in principle that their differentiation between feeling and will is to be rejected, too.

7. We come now to a third set of considerations which will confirm our thesis that feeling and will belong to *one* natural basic class.

When we were concerned with establishing the fundamental difference between presentation and judgement, we showed how all the circumstances point to the fact that what differentiates one phenomenon from another is a basic difference in the way they relate to their content. When judgement is added to presentation, we find an entirely new kind of contrast, an entirely new kind of intensity, an entirely new kind of perfection and imperfection, and an entirely new kind of law governing their generation and succession. At that time, it was also shown that the class of love and hate, taken as a whole, distinguished itself in the same thoroughgoing way from presentation and judgement, through its characteristic properties. If, within this class itself, there were still another fundamental distinction in the way an object is referred to, we could expect that here, too, the one area would manifest its distinctness from the other in each of the respects cited and in a similar manner.

But this is not at all the case.

In the first place it is easy to convince oneself of the fact that there are never any differences in contrast within the area of feeling and will which would make the one pair as different from the other as the contrast between love and hate is different from that between affirmation and denial. Even if we compare joy and sorrow with willing for and against something, we see that in both cases it is fundamentally the same contrast – that of being liked and being disliked, of being pleasing and being displeasing – which confronts us. Of course it appears to be somewhat modified in each of the two cases, corresponding to the phenomena's various different hues, but the difference is no greater than that between joy and sorrow, hope and fear, courage and cowardice, desire and aversion, and many others which are found in this class.

The same thing is true with regard to intensity. The whole class is clearly distinguished by a special kind of intensity. As we remarked before, there is no comparison between differences in degree of certainty and differences in the degree of love or hate. Indeed it would be quite ridiculous for someone to say, "This is twice as probable to me as that is dear." But the same thing is never true within the class itself. We can compare differences in the degree of love or hate with one another just as we can compare different levels of conviction in affirmation and denial. Just as there is no difficulty in saying that I affirm one thing with greater certainty than I deny something else, I can also say that I love one thing more than I hate another.[8] And we can determine not only that the intensity of opposites is relatively greater or lesser, but also that the intensities of pleasure and desire and volition and intention are greater or lesser in relation to one another. The pleasure that I take in this is greater than the desire I have for that; my desire to see him again is not as strong as my intention to make him aware of my disapproval, and so on.

Something similar is apparent in connection with *perfection* and *imperfection*. We saw that there is neither virtue nor moral evil, neither knowledge nor error in presentations. We get the latter when we have phenomena of judgement; the former, as we have seen, are found exclusively in the area of love and hate. Might it perhaps turn out that they are found in only one of the two classes into which this area has been divided, in the will, but not in the feelings? – It is easy to see that this is not the case, but that there are morally good and morally bad feelings just as there are morally good and morally bad acts of will, as, for example, compassion, gratitude, courage, envy, pleasure at the misfortune of others, cowardly fear, etc. Because of the previously mentioned absence of a clear line of demarcation, I really do not know to what extent each particular example might be more correctly classified in the domain of will; but if even one of them is a feeling, it will do for our purposes.* Nor

---

[8] Later on, Brentano conceived of such differences of degree, not as comparative valuations within love and hate having different degrees of intensity, but as differences in a particular species of emotional activity, i.e., "preference." Preference is a "relative valuing," which is described in greater detail in *The Origin of our Knowledge of Right and Wrong*, and in Supplementary Essay V. Preferences are of special importance for value theory, including the economic theory of value. See Kraus, "Grundlagen der Werttheorie," in Frischeisen-Köhler's *Jahrbücher der Philosophie* (Berlin, 1914), and *Zur Theorie des Wertes: eine Benthamstudie* (Halle, 1901).

* It is true that we usually use the terms virtue and wickedness in too narrow a sense to be able to say of every act of love or hate that it is virtuous or wicked. Only certain outstanding acts, acts in which some-

252

can it be said that virtue and wickedness are common to both classes but that there is another special new class of perfection and imperfection in the will, in addition. So far, at least, no one has, to my knowledge, identified any such class.

Let us turn to the last point of comparison, the *laws* governing the succession of phenomena.

Although judgements are in no way independent of the laws governing the sequence of presentations, there are additional special laws for them, incapable of being derived from those governing presentations. We have already noted that these laws constitute the principal psychological foundations of logic. We said then that something similar is true of love and hate. The fact is that these phenomena are independent neither of the laws governing the sequence of presentations nor of the laws governing the way in which judgements are generated and follow one another; yet they, too, exhibit special underivable laws which govern their succession and development, laws which constitute the psychological foundations of ethics.[10]

Let us now ask what the situation is with respect to these laws. Might it be the case that they are restricted exclusively to the will? Or is it, at least, that only a part of them governs both feelings and acts of will, while another part, distinguished by some special new characteristic, applies exclusively to the phenomena of will? – Neither of these two possibilities is correct; on the contrary, in one case one act of will results from another, in just the same way that one act of joy or sorrow results from another in another case. I am

---

thing is loved that is truly worthy of being loved, or in which something is hated that is truly worthy of being hated, are honored with the name virtue. Similarly, we only give the name wickedness to certain especially conspicuous acts in which the opposite attitudes occur. Acts of love and hate in which the proper attitude occurs obviously, as a matter of course, are not called virtuous. Perhaps we could show how these concepts could be extended so they would have completely general applicability. But it will suffice here to have demonstrated that as they are commonly used, they, at least, give no support to the customary distinction between feeling and will.[9]

[9] The essence of the theory which appears in *The Origin of our Knowledge of Right and Wrong* comes out very clearly in this note.

[10] According to Brentano, the psychological foundations of logic and ethics – not the only foundations, since both disciplines extend their roots into other areas as well – are constituted in part by descriptive facts and laws (of an a *priori* character) and in part by genetic laws having an empirical-inductive nature. See Eisenmeier, *Die zentrale Stellung der Psychologie* (Halle, 1911). See also p. 230 above and the Introduction.

glad or troubled about one object for the sake of another, although ordinarily it would have left me unmoved. In the same way, I desire and will one thing on account of another, though ordinarily I would not have wanted it. It is also true that a pleasure which we enjoy habitually arouses a stronger desire when we are deprived of it, and, vice-versa, a pleasure that occurs after a longer period of desire is thereby heightened and intensified.

But how? – We say that essentially the same laws apply to the area of feeling and the area of will, yet the greatest contrast that exists anywhere in the whole realm of psychology seems to lie precisely here. For the will, as distinguished from all other classes, is supposed to be the realm of freedom. And even if this does not completely remove it from any influence of laws, it certainly removes it from their control, such as exists in the other areas. So we seem to have before us a strong argument in favor of the conventional division between feeling and will.

It is well known that freedom of the will, on which this objection is based, has long been the subject of heated conflict, into which we shall not enter until later.* But I believe we are already in a position to refute the argument without anticipating our future result in any way. Let us suppose that there is complete freedom in the area of will, so that in the same specific case it is possible to will something, not to will it, or to will the opposite. This certainly does not exist throughout the entire area, but only where different ways of acting – or at least acting and not acting – can each be regarded as a good in its own way. The most important advocates of free will have always explicitly acknowledged this.[11] But, although it may be less distinctly stated, it is just as unmistakably their conviction that there are also free acts among the mental activities which cannot be called acts of will and which are ordinarily called feelings. The pangs of remorse over an earlier transgression, malicious pleasure, and many other phenomena of joy and sorrow are thought to be no less free than a resolution to change one's life and the intention of harming someone.

---

* This was intended for Book Five. [Editor's note: The topic is dealt with, however, in Brentano's *Grundlegung und Aufbau der Ethik*, the English edition of which is *The Foundation and Construction of Ethics*, trans. Elizabeth H. Schneewind, Routledge & Kegan Paul, 1973.]

[11] When Brentano wrote the *Psychologie des Aristoteles*, he was still an indeterminist. Later he recognized the falsity of a theory which violates the law of universal necessity. Therefore he agreed with Alfred Kastil, who proved Aristotle's determinism in his *Die Lehre von der Willensfreiheit bei Aristoteles* (Vienna, 1900), as Kraus did later on in *Die Lehre von Lob, Tadel und Strafe bei Aristoteles* (Halle, 1905). See *The Origin of our Knowledge of Right and Wrong*, Appendix (VI).

Some people, indeed, believe the feelings involved in a contemplative love of God to be more worthy than the charitable exercise of the will in the service of one's neighbor, and they do so even though they only speak of worthiness and unworthiness in relation to free acts. If, despite this, people only speak of freedom of the *will*, this was connected in ancient philosophy, as we have seen, with an expanded use of the term, which covered both feeling and will in the narrower sense. Among modern philosophers, however, it is often connected with the other unclarities which are involved in their investigations. Even Locke never got completely clear about the distinction between being able to perform an action or to forbear, depending on whether one wills it or not, and the possibility of willing it or not willing it under the same circumstances.[12] It is certain, then, that if there is freedom in the area of love and hate at all, it does not range over acts of will alone, but extends equally to certain acts of feeling. It is also certain, on the other hand, that we can no more call every act of will free than we can every act of feeling. This suffices to show that the cleft between feeling and will is not widened by acknowledging the existence of freedom, and that this gives no support to the traditional classification.

8. We have now completed the third part of our prescribed course of inquiry. We have followed essentially the same path in examining the relationship between feeling and desire that we followed before when we were proving the fundamental difference between presentation and judgements. But this time, at each step, our observations have been just the opposite.

Let us briefly summarize these results.

Firstly, inner experience showed us that there is never any sharp boundary between feeling and will. We found that all mental phenomena which are not presentations or judgements are all alike in the way in which they refer to their content, and they can all be called phenomena of love and hate in an unequivocal sense.

---

[12] What is involved is the following distinction: The person willing is free insofar as he has the power to realize what he wills as a consequence of his willing (*actus imperatus voluntatis*). This sort of freedom in the sense of the power of the will, in which the will comes into consideration as a cause, is quite compatible with the fact that the will (*actus elicitus voluntatis*) of the person willing is itself caused or produced. It is compatible then with non-freedom in the sense of determination. The will need not be free from causality in order to be free in the sense of being a force, indeed, it would not be a force if it were. Ethical freedom is not, then, to be understood to mean unqualified freedom from causes but freedom from causes determinative of spurious decisions. See *The Origin of our Knowledge of Right and Wrong*.

Secondly, although it was impossible to cite any distinction between presentation and judgement at all when it was denied that there was a difference in the kind of reference, we have seen that quite the opposite is true in the area of love and hate. Here each particular class can be defined in terms of the special phenomena on which it is based, with the aid of the contrast between love and hate and their differences in intensity.[13]

And finally, thirdly, we have seen that no variation in circumstances, which usually occurs when there is a difference in the kind of consciousness, is to be found in feeling and will.

So we may consider the unity of our third class to have been fully demonstrated. All that remains is for us to show here, as we did earlier in connection with presentation and judgement, the reasons which prompted the misunderstanding of the true situation.

9. The causes of the illusion seem to me to have been threefold: *psychological*, *linguistic*, and, if we may call them that, *historical*, i.e. causes which arose from psychology's previous mistakes on other questions.

Let us consider first of all the most prominent *psychological* reasons.

We saw earlier how the phenomena of inner consciousness are fused with their objects in a characteristic way. The inner perception is included within the act it perceives, and in the same way the inner feeling which accompanies an act is itself a part of its object.[14] This made it easy to confuse the special way in which it is connected with its object with the special way in which it intentionally refers to it, and to treat the phenomena of love and hate which belong to inner consciousness, as a *separate* basic class.

If we recall what Kant said about the difference between feeling and desire, I believe we shall see clear traces of a connection between his theory and the distinction just mentioned. He said that the faculty of desire has an "objective reference," while the feeling refers "merely to the subject."*

In Hamilton this fact comes out even more strikingly, to the extent that he enlarges upon the separateness of feeling from striving in great detail. And definitions which are otherwise very difficult to reconcile with one another do consistently point to the fact that when he talked about the class of feelings, it was mainly the phenomena of feeling which belong to inner consciousness that he had in mind. His definition of feeling as something which belongs

* See above, p. 183 note †.

[13] What are meant are differences in value ("superiorities"). See note 8 above.

[14] See p. 153 and Supplementary Essay II.

exclusively to the present is vindicated, and his characterization of feeling as "subjectively subjective" at least becomes intelligible. The study of the origin of feelings in the second volume of his lectures is also in perfect agreement with such an interpretation.*

But why is it that if the special connection between inner phenomena and their objects leads to a distinction between two fundamental classes in this case, the same thing did not happen in the area of cognition? Why do we not separate inner perception from every other cognition as a particular, basically different way of referring? – The answer to this is easy. We have seen how one of the peculiar features of our third class is that it includes a number of varieties which differ from each other more than particular classes of judgement do. Here, then, it was much easier to fail to see that the kind of reference had a generally consistent character than it was in connection with the phenomena of cognition. The same circumstance which could give rise to the mistake in one case, proved to be no temptation in the other case.

10. In addition to the one which has been cited, there is still another psychological reason for the error. As we recall, Kant and his followers maintained that the underivability of the phenomena of will from those of feeling favored the fundamental difference between these two classes. It is unquestionably true that the phenomena of will cannot be derived from any other mental phenomena. And I do not mean by this just that the particular shade of volitional activity can only be known through specific experience, for that is something which is equally true of other individual classes of love and of hate. The particular hue which hope has as compared with pleasure of ownership, the particular tone of higher spiritual pleasure as opposed to the lower bodily pleasures are also underivable. Something else is responsible for the fact that the will in particular appears to be especially incapable of derivation, and brings about the inclination to interpret the will as the activity of a special primitive faculty.

Every volition or striving in the strict sense refers to an action. It is not simply a desire for something to happen but a desire for something to happen as a result of the desire itself. An act of will is impossible for someone who does not yet know, or at least suspect, that certain phenomena of love and desire directly or indirectly bring about the loved object.

But how is one supposed to acquire such knowledge or such a suspicion? – It cannot be acquired from the nature of phenomena of love, whether they are phenomena of pleasure or pain, or desire

* *Lectures on Metaphysics*, II, pp. 436 ff. See also Lotze, *Microcosmus*, I, 240 ff. and elsewhere.

or fear, or any others. The only possibility left, then, is either to assume that it is innate, or that one draws on experience for it, as we do for other knowledge about relations of forces. The first alternative would obviously be the assumption of a quite extraordinary fact, which is the last thing that would admit of derivation. But the second alternative, which is certainly incomparably more probable at the outset, clearly presupposes a special range of experiences and the existence and actual exercise of a special kind of power to which these experiences refer. Consequently the power of certain phenomena of love to realize the objects toward which they are directed is a pre-condition of volition. And it is this which, in some way, first gives us the ability to will, even if we do not consider the capacity to act as the faculty of will itself, as Bain did. Now because this power to express and actively practice love and desire is completely different from the capacity for love and desire itself, it seems to be no more derivable from them than from the faculty of knowledge, in fact it seems much less so. And so the capacity for will and striving naturally appears to be a faculty that is especially incapable of derivation, although the impossibility of its derivation is not based on the fact that the relevant phenomena themselves are fundamentally different in character from the other phenomena of love.

On the contrary, a closer examination will reveal that this discloses a new sign of kinship between the phenomena of will and other phenomena of love and desire. If volition presupposes that one has experienced the influence of phenomena of love bringing forth the loved object, then it obviously presupposes that phenomena of love which cannot be called volitions also prove to be efficacious in a manner similar to the way in which the will is, though perhaps to a lesser degree. For if such an influence were exclusively connected with the will, we would be involved in a disastrous circle. The will would presuppose experience of the will, while that in turn naturally also presupposes the will. It is another matter if the mere desire for certain events results in their occurrence; then, it can be repeated with the modification which our knowledge of this relationship of forces brings about, which is to say, as an act of will.[15]

[15] On this point, see Anton Marty, *Ursprung der Sprache* (Würzburg, 1875), p. 34. According to this book, the will can be considered a love which is motivated by love or hate toward something. In the first case, what I love is that something should begin or continue to be as a result of my love. In the second case, it is that something should cease to be or be prevented from being as an effect of my love. The motive of this love which makes its appearance as an act of will is love in the one case, hate in the other.

These suggestions will have to suffice until later when we shall take up the problem of the origin of will in detail.*

If a statement of Kant's about the distinctive character of feelings, which we considered earlier, led us to recognize the connection between his classification and the fact that certain phenomena of love belong to inner consciousness, there are quite a few others which point very clearly to the relationships we have just considered. Indeed, Kant defined the faculty of desire as "the capacity of one's ideas to bring the objects of those ideas into existence." In the same passage in which he speaks of ideas referring "merely to the subject," with regard to which they are "considered in relation to the feeling of pleasure," he speaks of another "objective relationship which is counted part of the faculty of desire, because it is at the same time considered to be the cause of the reality of this object." But now the boundary between the two classes which emerges if the inner phenomena of love are grouped together as feelings and contrasted with all others, does not coincide at all with the one we get when we separate the act of striving for an object (which presupposes that the relation of forces we have discussed is known) from all other phenomena of love. This is why we find in Kant that curious claim that any wish, even if it were recognized to be impossible, for example the wish to have wings, is an aspiration to attain what is wished for and includes the idea of our desire's causal efficacy.†
This is a desperate attempt to bring the boundary line that the one set of considerations requires into harmony with the other one. Others have preferred to extend the class of feelings further, right up to the limits of volition in the strict sense, and still others have ascribed more or less considerable portions of the intermediate area to each of the two classes – hence the uncertainty we have encountered concerning the boundary line.

11. We said that there were *linguistic* factors in addition to the psychological ones that stem from the characteristic nature of the phenomena themselves.

Aristotle, who correctly recognized the unity of our third fundamental class, designated it, as we have heard, by the term "appetite" (ὄρεξις). The expression was not well chosen,‡ for nothing is farther

---

* [Editor's note: As Brentano meant to do in Book Five. See, however, *The Foundation and Construction of Ethics*.]

† *Critique of Judgement*, Intro, III, note.

‡ Aristotle probably arrived at it in an attempt to find a term for a more generalized combination of θυμός and λογισμός, which appear in Plato's classification along with ἐπιθυμία. This is one more sign of the truth of our earlier remark that Aristotle's basic divisions generally developed from the Platonic ones. The connection is undeniable from other aspects, as well.

from ordinary linguistic usage than to call joy an appetite. But this did not stop the Middle Ages from allowing themselves to be guided by the authority of "The Philosopher" and his translators in this as in so many other respects, and designating the capacity for all of the acts belonging to this class as the *"facultas appetendi."** Later on Wolff took over the Scholastic expressions when he distinguished between his cognitive and appetitive faculties. Now since in actual use the term "appetite" has much too narrow a meaning for it to be able to encompass all mental phenomena other than thinking, this gave rise to the idea that there are phenomena which are not included in the classes set up so far, and so a new class must be coordinated with these phenomena. A passage from Hamilton which we quoted earlier† shows that this situation really did have an influence on people.

12. But we said that the mistake concerning the unity of this class of mental phenomena had a third kind of cause as well; *errors committed in earlier inquiries* have had a detrimental effect.

The principal error which we have in mind here is the fact that people regarded presentation and judgement as phenomena belonging to the same basic class. The Three Ideas (the title with which they are often honored), the *True*, the *Good*, and the *Beautiful* had been discovered; and they seemed to be coordinated with one another. People believed that they had to be related to three coordinated, fundamentally different sides of our mental life. The Idea of the True was attributed to the cognitive faculty, the Idea of the Good to the appetitive faculty; so the third faculty, that of feelings, was a welcome discovery, for the Idea of the Beautiful could then be the share attributed to it. As early as Mendelssohn there is talk of the True, the Good and the Beautiful, when he speaks of the three faculties of the soul. And later advocates of a similar threefold division reproach Kant for having limited the feeling of pleasure and pain "onesidedly to the esthetic judgement of taste," and for having "considered the appetitive faculty not as a pure psychological power, but in relation to the ideal of the Good, which it is supposed to serve."‡

A more detailed investigation of whether the apportionment of the True, the Good and the Beautiful to the three classes of the cognitive, appetitive and affective faculties is really justified will raise many doubts indeed.

---

* Only in isolated instances are there signs of emancipation, as for example when Thomas Aquinas uses the expression *"amare"* as the most general name for this class in the *Summa Theologica*, P. I, Q. 37, A. 1 and frequently elsewhere.

† *Lectures on Metaphysics*, II, 420; cp. above, Chap. 1, Sect. 4.

‡ J. B. Meyer, *Kants Psychologie*, p. 120.

We earlier quoted a passage from Lotze, in which this thinker, who himself divides will and feeling into two basic faculties, designates "the fundamental moral principles of each age" as "dictates of an appreciative feeling." In fact, Herbart ascribed all of ethics to aesthetics, the former being one particular branch, the latter the more general theoretical science.* So in his view the ideal of the Good threatens to be swallowed up completely by that of the Beautiful, or at least it is subordinated to the more comprehensive idea as one of its special forms.

Others have made the opposite attempt, they have subordinated the concept of the Beautiful to the concept of the Good. This is true, for example of Thomas Aquinas, when he says that the Good is that which pleases and the Beautiful that the appearance of which pleases.† Here, to begin with, the appearance of the Beautiful is regarded as something good, and then naturally that which calls forth the appearance is also good, in view of that fact. In fact, Beauty in this sense should, no doubt, be called a good, but the same thing must also be said of truth; and consequently the character of desirability seems to be common to all three. Indeed, we could not think of it in any other way, if only because we are dealing here with three ideals.

It is necessary, then, to interpret this triad of the *Beautiful*, the *True*, and the *Good*, in a somewhat different fashion. In so doing, it will emerge that they are related to three aspects of our mental life; not, however, to knowledge, feeling and will, but to the triad that *we* have distinguished in the three basic classes of mental phenomena.

Each of the basic classes of mental phenomena has its own particular kind of perfection. This perfection makes itself known in the inner feeling, which, as we saw, accompanies every act. Inherent in the most perfect acts in each fundamental class there is, so to speak, a noble pleasure. The highest perfection of the activity of presentation lies in the contemplation of the beautiful, whether this is reinforced by the influence of the object, or independent of such influence.

---

* Ultimately even Adam Smith does too (if Kant is correct) when he says that the Beautiful is that which arouses disinterested pleasure. Indeed, long before them Augustine said "*Honestum voco intelligibilem pulchritudinem, quam spiritualem nos proprie dicimus.*" (83Q. Q. quaest. 30, near the beginning.)

† *De ratione boni est quod in eo quietetur appetitus. Sed ad rationem pulchri pertinet quod in ejus aspectu seu cognitione quietetur appetitus. . . . Pulchrum addit supra bonum quendam ordinem ad vim cognoscitivam; ita quod bonum dicatur id quod simpliciter complacet appetitui; pulchrum autem dicatur id cujus ipsa apprehensio placet.* (*Summa Theologica*, P. II, I, Q. 27. A. 1 ad 3.)

The highest pleasure which we can find in presentation as such is associated with this. The highest perfection of the activity of judgement lies in the knowledge of the truth; we naturally find this perfection most of all in the knowledge of those truths which reveal to us, more than others do, a rich fullness of being. This is the case, for example, when we grasp a law which (like the law of gravitation) explains a wide range of phenomena at a single stroke. For that reason, knowledge is a joy and good in and for itself, apart from all of the practical uses it has. "All men by nature desire to know," says the great philosopher who tasted the joys of knowledge more than many others. And again, he says, "intellectual contemplation is sweetest and best."* The highest perfection of the activity of *love*, finally, lies in being able to rise freely to higher goods, unhampered by consideration of one's own pleasure and profit; in giving oneself, in a spirit of self-sacrifice, to that which, because of its perfection, is more and above all else worthy of love; in the exercise of virtue or the love of the good for its own sake according to the degree of its perfection. It is the pleasure inherent in noble acts and above all in noble love which corresponds to this perfection, as the joy in knowledge and in the contemplation of the beautiful correspond to the perfection of the other two sides of consciousness. The *Ideal of Ideals* consists in the unity of all Truth, Goodness and Beauty, i.e. in a being whose presentation is a manifestation of infinite beauty, revealing in it and in its infinite and surpassing archetypes every conceivable finite beauty; a being whose *knowledge* is a disclosure of infinite truth, disclosing in it as in its ultimate and universal principle of explanation all finite truth; and a being whose *love* loves the infinite all-encompassing good and, in it, all else which shares in a finite way in its perfection. That, I say, is the Ideal of all Ideals. And the greatest bliss of all would be the threefold enjoyment of this threefold unity, in which the infinite beauty is beheld and in the beholding is recognized through itself as necessary and infinite truth, and as infinite loving kindness becomes manifest, is loved with total and necessary devotion as the infinite good. This is the promise of blessedness which is offered in Christianity, in the most perfect religion that has appeared in history. And the greatest of the pagan thinkers, especially the divinely inspired Plato, are in agreement with it in hoping for such blissful happiness.[16]

* Aristotle, *Metaphysics*, I, 1; XII, 7.
[16] When Brentano wrote the *Psychology*, he had been inwardly separated from positive Christianity for some years. On April 11, 1873, he had resigned from the priesthood; his formal withdrawal from the Church was only completed on the occasion of his marriage in 1880. He ceased to belong to any confessional group. The statements in my book, *Franz*

We see that if you agree with us in denying that feeling is a basic class, and if you just go on to adopt our basic classification, then the triad of Ideals, the Beautiful, the True, and the Good, can well be defined in terms of the system of mental faculties. Indeed, this is the only way in which it becomes fully intelligible, and even in Kant there is no dearth of statements testifying to the fact that only by relating the beautiful to the activity of presentation in the way we have done do we put it in its proper place. Of the many passages available in various writings of his, I will here mention only one or two. In the *Critique of Judgement* Kant says, "When the form of an object . . . is, in the mere act of reflecting upon it, without regard to any concept to be obtained from it, estimated as the ground of a pleasure in the representation of such an Object, then this pleasure is also judged to be combined necessarily with the representation of it, and so not merely for the subject apprehending this form, but for all in general who pass judgement. The object is then called beautiful; and the faculty of judging by means of such a pleasure (and so also with universal validity) is called taste."* In the *Metaphysical Elements of Justice* (1797) he repeats once again that there is a pleasure which is not associated with any desire for the object at all, but with *the mere presentation* one forms of an object, and remarks, "The pleasure which is not necessarily connected with the desire for an object, which is thus basically not a pleasure in the existence of the object of presentation, but attaches *merely to the presentation alone* could be called mere contemplative pleasure or inactive enjoyment. Feeling of the latter kind of pleasure we call taste."†

Our assertion holds good, then, i.e. the assertion that the failure to

---

* Kant's *Critique of Judgement*, trans. James Creed Meredith (Oxford, 1952). Intro. VII, p. 31.

† *Metaphysische Ansfansgründe der Rechtslehre*, Chap. 1. Translated as *The Metaphysical Elements of Justice, Part I of the Metaphysics of Morals*, by John Ladd (New York, 1965). Thomas Aquinas, who, like the Peripatetic School in general, shared with Kant the mistake of combining presentation and judgement into the same basic class, also offers support, in the passage cited above (p. 261 note †), for the connection between the Beautiful and presentation. Elsewhere he says, "*Bonum proprie respicit appetitum. . . . Pulchrum autem respicit vim cognoscitivam: pulchra enim dicuntur, quae visa placent.*" *Summa Theologica*, P. I, Q. 5, A. 4 ad 1.

Brentano (Munich, 1919), which seem to place his withdrawal from the Church in 1873, should have been corrected in this respect.

See the posthumous book, *Die Lehre Jesu und ihre bleibende Bedeutung*, edited by A. Kastil (Leipzig, 1922), *The Origin of our Knowledge of Right and Wrong*, and my book on Brentano.

recognize the fundamental difference between presentation and judgements prepared the way for the acceptance of another fundamental differentiation which does not really exist. In this way, the first mistake which we encountered in the classification of mental phenomena made an important contribution to the second. It appears as though this situation has not been the least troublesome factor involved.

In addition, the new error was naturally also furthered by the lack of clarity concerning the true principle of classification. We have already spoken of that and can therefore spare ourselves any further discussion at present.

Whatever else may have contributed to the fact that feeling and will were thought to be two different basic classes of mental phenomena, I believe that we have assembled, in the foregoing inquiry, the chief factors which gave rise to the mistake. They are so diverse and important, it is no wonder that many distinguished thinkers permitted themselves to be misled by them. I hope, then, that as a result of our exposition, the last doubt about the thesis which we have defended, that feeling and will belong together, will have disappeared. But then our whole fundamental classification seems to be absolutely assured. For this reason, therefore, we may consider it established that mental phenomena exhibit no more and no less than a threefold fundamental difference in their reference to a content, or, as we might put it, in their mode of consciousness, and that, in view of this, they fall into three basic classes; the class of *presentations*, the class of *judgements*, and the class of the *phenomena of love and hate*.

IX

Comparison of the Three Basic Classes with the Threefold Phenomena of Inner Consciousness. Determination of their Natural Order

1. The three basic classes we have established, presentation, judgement and love, remind us of a triad of phenomena we discovered earlier. We saw that the inner consciousness which accompanies every mental phenomenon includes a presentation, a cognition and a feeling, all directed toward that phenomenon. It is obvious that each of these elements corresponds to one of the three classes of mental activities which have now emerged.

This shows us that phenomena of the three fundamental classes are most intimately intertwined. For it is not possible to conceive of a more intimate connection than that between the three elements of inner consciousness.[1]

Furthermore, we know that the three classes are of the utmost universality; there is no mental act in which all three are not present. There is a certain ubiquity pertaining to each class in all of our conscious life.

As we noted previously, however, it does not follow from this that they are derivable from one another. Each total state of consciousness shows that a capacity for each of the three kinds of activity is present. But it is conceivable without contradiction that there might be a form of mental life which is missing one or even two of these kinds of mental activity and lacks all capacity for them as well. By the same token, there is still a difference between those mental acts which are called in a relative sense mere acts of presentation and

[1] See Supplementary Essay II.

those of which this is not the case, insofar as the primary object of an act is sometimes merely presented, sometimes also affirmed or denied, and sometimes simultaneously loved or hated in some way. In the latter cases, strings which had only, so to speak, resonated in the first case are now struck directly.

The fact only testifies to the universal significance of each of the three classes, then, and this testimony is certainly welcome when we are concerned with questions about the fundamental character of the classes. The usual threefold division into knowledge, feeling and will cannot appeal to it in the same way. Hamilton also claimed complete universality for volition, to be sure, probably because he realized the significance of the situation. "In our philosophical systems," he says, "they may stand separated from each other in books and chapters; – in nature they are interwoven. In every, even the simplest, modification of mind, knowledge, feeling, and desire or will, go to constitute the mental state," and so on.* But for anyone who analyzes the concept of will there can be no doubt but that Hamilton is claiming something which is impossible for his third class. A volition, as we said before, only becomes possible through the idea of one's own causal efficacy. This indicates the altogether less general character of this class concept, and it proves in particular how far it is from being applicable to a primitive activity.

We see, then, that our classification has an advantage over the usual one in this respect, too, although I would not like to say that this is as decisive in its significance as some of the results of our earlier discussions are.

2. There is still just *one* more question which remains to be answered and we have already prepared the way for our decision in the previous investigations, in fact we have anticipated it to a certain extent. It is the question of the natural order of the three classes.

Here, as everywhere, the relative independence, simplicity and universality of the classes must determine their order.

On this principle it is clear that presentation deserves the primary place, for it is the simplest of the three phenomena, while judgement and love always include a presentation within them.

It is likewise the most independent of the three, since it is the foundation for the others, and, for exactly the same reason, it is the most universal. I do not say this because I want to deny that judgement and love are also represented in some way in every mental state. On the contrary, we have explicitly stressed this. But we have at the same time noted a certain difference as regards their universality, insofar as the only way in which the primary object is neces-

* *Lectures on Metaphysics*, I, 188. Later (II, 433) he repeats the same idea once more, but no longer with the same confidence.

sarily and universally present in consciousness is with the kind of intentional inherence peculiar to presentations. We can conceive, without contradiction, of a being which has no capacity for judgement or love, equipped with nothing but the capacity for presentation, but we cannot conceive of it the other way around. Furthermore, the laws governing the succession of presentations for a psychological fiction such as this could be the same as some of the laws which manifest their influence on our mental life now.

For similar reasons, judgement is entitled to the second place. For, after presentation, judgement is the simplest class. It is based only on presentation, and not on the phenomena of love and hate. The idea of a being which combined the activities of presentation and judgement without any stirring of love or hate involves no contradiction. And we are in a position to add to those laws we spoke of, which govern the sequence of presentations, a certain range of special laws governing judgement, which still leave phenomena of love entirely out of account. But when we consider those phenomena in relation to judgement, it is a different matter. It is certainly not necessary that someone believe that a thing exists or is even capable of existing, in order for him to love it, but, nonetheless, every act of love is loving the existence of something.[2] And one love would never arouse another, one thing would never be loved for the sake of another, unless there were a belief in certain connections between the one and the other which played some part. An act of love will be one of joy on some occasions, sorrow on others, or hope or fear or any number of other forms, depending upon what judgement is made concerning the existence or non-existence, probability or improbability of the object loved. In fact, then, it seems inconceivable that a being should be endowed with the capacity for love and hate without possessing that of judgement. And it is equally impossible to set up any law governing the sequence of this kind of phenomena which completely leaves out the phenomenon of judgement. With regard to independence, to simplicity, and, for the very same reason, to universality, then, this class comes after the class of judgement. In universality this is true, of course, only in the sense in which a difference in universality can also be spoken of between presentation and judgement.

We can see from what has been said how completely mistaken as to the true relationship of the facts those people are who consider will to be the most basic of all mental phenomena – something

[2] This is not true of those emotional acts which arise from their concepts and which Brentano calls "experienced as being correct" ("als richtig characterisiert"). See *The Origin of our Knowledge of Right and Wrong*, the Introduction and Appendix.

which is frequently done even in our own time. It is not just presentation that is obviously a prerequisite for the will. The discussion just conducted shows that judgement precedes love and hate generally and, all the more, the relatively late phenomena of the will. Those philosophers thus turn the natural order precisely around.

We shall base the special investigations which follow upon the natural classification we have discovered and upon the natural order of its members as well. We shall discuss the laws governing presentations first, then those of judgements, and finally those of love and hate. Of course, it will be impossible completely to avoid glancing ahead while we are considering the earlier classes, since we have only claimed, and only could claim, that they are independent in a limited and relative sense. The will exerts a dominating influence not only in the external world, but also in the inner realm of presentations; and feelings, too, influence the course our presentations follow. It is equally well known that men often believe something to be true because it flatters their vanity or is otherwise in accord with their wishes.[3] Even the most natural classification is still somewhat artificial, and the same is true of the most natural order of its members. When Comte set up a serial order for all theoretical disciplines in his famous hierarchy of sciences, Herbert Spencer opposed it with his doctrine of the "consensus" of all sciences, which forbade us to say that one is prior to the other. Perhaps this claim went too far, but Comte himself had admitted that his gradation was not absolute, and that even the earlier sciences are supported and advanced in many ways by the later ones.

[3] For just this reason there are also certain ethical rules which belong in logic. See above, Book Two, Chap. 8, note 10.

APPENDIX TO
THE CLASSIFICATION OF MENTAL PHENOMENA

(Prepared for the 1911 Edition)

Supplementary Remarks Intended to Explain and Defend, as well as to Correct and Expand upon the Theory

---

I   *Mental Reference as Distinguished from Relation in the Strict Sense*

What is characteristic of every mental activity is, as I believe I have shown, the reference to something as an object.[1] In this respect, every mental activity seems to be something relational. And in fact, where Aristotle enumerates the various main classes of his category of πρός τι (relation) he mentions mental reference. But he does not hesitate to call attention to something which differentiates this class from the others. In other relations both terms – both the fundament and the terminus – are real, but here only the first term – the fundament – is real.[2]

Let us clarify his meaning a little! If I take something relative (*ein Relativ*) from among the broad class of comparative relations, something larger or smaller for example, then, if the larger thing exists, the smaller one must exist too. If one house is larger than another house, the other house must also exist and have a size.[3] Something

---

[1] "Activity" is to be understood simply in the sense of an event, not in the sense of action. See above, Note 3 to Chapter 6: In every act of consciousness I have something as an object. "To have something as an object" = "being conscious of something." "Object" is *not an independently meaningful word in this usage*, but an expression which is only dependently meaningful (*synsemantic*). This should be carefully noted, for it is almost universally overlooked. See Introduction, p. 370.

[2] Most members of Brentano's school, following Locke and earlier writers, distinguish two fundaments in every relation, instead of a fundament and a terminus.

[3] Brentano later excluded so-called comparative relations from relatives, as being "*denominationes mere extrinsecae*." See Kraus, *Franz Brentano*, p. 44 and the Introduction, p. 378.

like what is true of relations of similarity and difference holds true for relations of cause and effect. For there to be such a relation, both the thing that causes and the thing that is caused must exist. That which acts only does so as long as that which is acted upon is acted upon. There is no causation without temporal contact. And whatever is in temporal contact with something shares a temporal boundary with it, just as whenever things are in spatial contact they share a spatial boundary. As long as the causal influence lasts there is a temporal coincidence of that which causes and that which is caused for just that length of time.

It is entirely different with mental reference. If someone thinks of something, the one who is thinking must certainly exist, but the object of his thinking need not exist at all.[4] In fact, if he is denying something, the existence of the object is precisely what is excluded whenever his denial is correct. So the only thing which is required by mental reference is the person thinking. The terminus of the so-called relation does not need to exist in reality at all.[5] For this reason, one could doubt whether we really are dealing with something relational here, and not, rather, with something somewhat similar to something relational in a certain respect, which might, therefore, better be called "quasi-relational" ("*Relativliches*"). The similarity consists in the fact that, like someone who is thinking of a relation in the proper sense, someone who is thinking of a mental activity is, in a certain way, thinking of two objects[6] at the same time, one of them *in recto*, as it were, and the other *in obliquo*. If I think of someone who loves flowers, then the person who loves flowers is the object I am thinking of *in recto*,[7] but the flowers are what I am

[4] More precisely, what should be said here is this: "The one doing the thinking must exist, but what he has as his object need not exist at all," for "thinking of something" means "having something as an object" and *insofar* as I have something as my object it does not exist. It is possible for something to exist and for me to have it as object besides, i.e. have it present to my mind; but it may also be that I have something as my object, i.e. have it present to my mind, which does not exist, indeed cannot exist. *For the sake of brevity, here and frequently elsewhere Brentano says "the object" instead of "what I have as my object."* But this is misleading, for *"object" is not an independently meaningful word*, by itself it signifies no concept. Only the phrase, "I have something as my object" has any meaning by itself; it means that I have something present to my mind.

[5] The "terminus" of the so-called mental relation is that with which I am mentally concerned, or what I have as an object. Sometimes it exists (is, has being), sometimes it does not.

[6] A better way to express that would be to say he is thinking of two things (two *Realia*). Compare note 5 above.

[7] More clearly: *"then I have the person who loves flowers as my object."*

thinking of *in obliquo*. That, however, is similar to the case in which I am thinking of someone who is taller than Caius. The taller person is thought of *in recto*, Caius *in obliquo*.

I am not unmindful that some people nowadays, in opposition to Aristotle, deny that both things must exist in order for something to be larger or smaller than another thing. For example, a group of three would be smaller than a trillion, whether or not there is a trillion. So the difference of which I spoke seems to be done away with. Indeed, it would be turned into its very opposite if we were to accept, too, the further claim which many have fallen into, that a group of three would still be less than a trillion even if neither the three nor the trillion existed. For it is essential, if there is to be a mental reference, that the person who is mentally referring to the object exist, even if the existence of the object is not essential.[8] But how could a group of three still be smaller than a trillion, if it is no longer even a group of three? And indeed it is a group of three only as long as it exists. Just as a cube ceases to exist when it has been transformed into a ball, it also ceases to have six square sides and to be a cube. We see, then, that we have before us a fallacy of equivocation. Someone who says that three is less than a trillion is not positively asserting the existence of a relation. He is saying, rather, that if there is a group of three and a group of a trillion, that relation must exist between them; in other words there could be no case in which three and a trillion exist without having that* relation.[9]

Nor may we appeal to cases in which we say that a grandson is taller than his grandfather was, when the grandfather does not exist along with the grandson. Here too the statement does not say that the grandson is taller than the grandfather. For if this were so, then every time a younger man grows taller than an older man, at the moment when the former reaches his height, it could not only be said that he is now as tall as the other, but that he is both taller and shorter as well. But that is absurd; what is true is simply that, as we express it, he is taller than the other man was, and shorter than he

* [Translators' note: Reading "jene" for "jede."]
[8] More clearly: "even if the thing I have as object need not exist . . .".
[9] See above, Book Two, Chap. 7, note 13, on apodictic judgements. The failure to recognize the negative character of mathematical-geometrical propositions, as well as the failure to recognize their *a priori* nature, has been ruinous to modern epistemology.

The expression, "the person who loves flowers is the object of which I am thinking *in recto*" could be misunderstood as if something was being predicated of the person who likes flowers. But it is being said of me that I have him as object, i.e. I have him present to my mind.

273

will be. This means only that if the younger man were still the size he had been earlier, or had already reached the size he is going to reach, the older man would not be the same size as he, but would be taller or shorter than he.

It is also the same when I say, "Titus is taller than Caius believes he is." There is no genuine relation of size in this case, even if there is some other kind of comparative relation between the size he has and the size he is judged to have. And it is easily seen that the distinctive character of mental reference plays a part in it. Kant says on one occasion that a hundred real dollars is not a single dollar more than a hundred imaginary dollars. But the truth is that a hundred imaginary dollars is not just one but a full hundred dollars less than a hundred dollars; or, rather, that because it is not a sum of money at all, and indeed does not exist at all, it cannot stand in any quantitative relation which holds between sums of money to the real hundred dollars, whether it be a relation of equal to equal, or larger to smaller, or smaller to larger.

I do not wish to bring this discussion of mental reference to a close without having given a word of consideration to the view that there is a distinction between "being" and "existing." According to this view both are to be taken in a very peculiar sense. Namely, a person might be led to say that if someone is mentally referring to an object, the object really always has being just as much as he does, even if it does not always exist as he does.

Perhaps none of the advocates of this view has yet gone quite so far. But in any case many of them say of the red and the blue we see, the sounds we hear, and other objects of sensation which according to science do not exist, that although, of course, they do not exist, they nevertheless have being. And if we think general concepts, they maintain that the universals which are our objects have being as universals, although they do not exist.[10]

I confess that I am unable to make any sense of this distinction between being and existence. As far as universals are concerned, the assumption that they have being is just as absurd as the assumption that they exist, for it leads to contradictions. And the law of contradiction not only denies that the same thing can both exist and not exist at the same time but also that the same thing can be and not

---

[10] The "mental inexistence of the object" is often revived in another form by the very ones who first rejected it. Thus one speaks of "pseudo-existence, subsistence, real component of consciousness, ideal entity, ideal existence as opposed to real existence." I can make "the seven regular solids," or this or that number my object, but from this fact it does not follow that these objects can be said to exist, or to subsist, or to *be* in any way. It is always only I, the one who is thinking of them, who exists.

be at the same time. What would it be to think of a triangle in general subsisting by itself? – Obviously it would be to think of something to which everything common to all individual triangles would pertain, but nothing which is true of one triangle and not of another. Therefore we would have to deny of this triangle in general subsisting by itself that it is right-angled, and that it is acute-angled, and likewise that it is obtuse-angled, from which it must follow that it is not right-angled nor acute-angled nor obtuse-angled. But this very claim is contradictory to the nature of the triangle in general, since, generally speaking, there can be no triangle which is not right- nor acute- nor obtuse-angled. For it holds of every individual triangle that it possesses specific and individuating differences, even if these differences vary from triangle to triangle. Accordingly, it must also be true of the triangle in general subsisting by itself that it possesses specific and individuating differences. But to admit that and still to maintain its universality and its freedom from all individual differences would be a contradiction, than which no more flagrant example could be imagined.[11] – But that it is impossible to make use of that distinction – of which I can make no rational sense – between being and existence for mental reference generally is already quite well enough proved by our earlier reference to those cases in which an object[12] of presentation is at the same time an object of our correct denial.*

II *On Mental Reference to Something as a Secondary Object*

When we said that reference to something as object is that which is most characteristic of mental activity, this should not be interpreted as though "mental activity" and "reference to something as object" mean exactly the same thing. Just the opposite is already clearly apparent from what we have said about every mental activity relating to itself as object, not, however, primarily, but secondarily or, as Aristotle, by whom the fact had already been noticed, puts it,

---

* In the foregoing discussion I have adhered to Aristotle's usage with respect to the term "relation," but I gladly acknowledge that this is by no means required. If anyone wishes to speak of relations to past and future things, because what was and what will be, as opposed to what never is, belong to the realm of actuality in a certain sense, it would be foolish to engage in a verbal dispute with him.

[11] Locke's proof, which is here defended against recent attacks, calls to mind the Aristotelian one, on which Brentano reports in *Aristoteles und seine Weltanschauung* (Leipzig, 1911), p. 36.

[12] This should say: a thing which we are thinking of.

"incidentally" ("nebenbei").* In a single mental activity, then, there is always a plurality of references and a plurality of objects.[1]

As I have already emphasized in my *Psychology from an Empirical Standpoint*, however, for the secondary object of mental activity one does not have to think of any particular one of these references, as for example the reference to the primary object. It is easy to see that this would lead to an infinite regress, for there would have to be a third reference, which would have the secondary reference as object, a fourth, which would have the additional third one as object, and so on. The secondary object is not a reference but a mental activity, or, more strictly speaking, the mentally active subject, in which the secondary reference is included along with the primary one. Although now no infinite regress of mental references ἐν παρέργῳ can arise, it does not follow that mental activity is to be conceived as something simple. Even when mental references have the same object,[2] they can still be different if the modes of reference are different. This is what we find to be the case with mental references ἐν παρέργῳ. We have distinguished three fundamental classes of modes: presentation, judgement and relations of feeling. It is obvious that in mental references ἐν παρέργῳ the mode of presentation is never absent, for it is the prerequisite of the others. Judgement, however, is no more absent than presentation is, and, in fact, an evident affirmation is always present. In addition, it is very generally believed that there is a so-called "feeling-tone" ("Gefühlston") in every mental activity which is as much as to say that just as every mental activity is the object of a presentation included within it and of a judgement included within it, it is also the object of an emotional reference included within it. I myself adopted this view in *Psychology from an Empirical Standpoint*. Since then, however, I have abandoned it and I now believe that even among sensations there are many cases in which there is no emotional reference, and so no pleasure or displeasure, contained within it. Indeed, I believe the entire broad classes of visual and aural sensation to be completely free of affective character. This does not rule out the fact that very lively affects of pleasure and pain ordinarily accompany them in various ways determined by laws. On this point, see my *Untersuchungen zur Sinnespsychologie*.

The fact that the mentally active subject has himself as object of a secondary reference regardless of what else he refers to as his

* ἐν παρέργῳ.
[1] In view of note 4 to I, above, it would be more to the point to say: "We always have a number of references and a number of things as object."
[2] Unambiguously, "when they have the same substantive thing as object," and likewise on a number of other occasions.

primary object, is of great importance. As a result of this fact, there are no statements about primary objects which do not include several assertions. If I say, for example, "God exists," I am at the same time attesting to the fact that I judge that God exists. Or if I say, "There is no God" this includes the fact that I deny that there is one. It is very good to notice this when one is making a psychological analysis of judgements, for as a result of this, it will often emerge, if one proceeds with the proper care, that the objects of judgement and of the presentations on which they are based are quite different from what people commonly imagine them to be. A good part of them will prove to be objects of the references given ἐν παρέργῳ, which are determinately compounded with the primary objects in a distinctive manner.

It does not seem superfluous to add some further remarks to what has been said, so as to avoid misunderstanding, and as a defense against the obvious objections which are actually raised quite frequently.

Not everything which is apprehended is apprehended explicitly and distinctly. Many things are apprehended only implicitly and confusedly. I believe I have demonstrated in my *Untersuchungen zur Sinnespsychologie* that the notes combined in a chord and the color-elements of a compound color are always really apprehended, but often not distinguished. The dispute about the simplicity or complexity of phenomenal green, which still goes on today, is related to this fact. Indeed, I believe I have shown that the differences in intensity of sensible objects are to be derived from differences in phenomenal thickness. Sensible space is alternatively full and empty in one place and in another,[3] but the individual full and empty places are not clearly differentiated. If this is true of physical phenomena, something analogous is true of the mental activity which refers to it. Thus we have in this case, and in many others elsewhere, mental activities which are not explicitly perceived in all of their parts. Inner perception is, rather, confused, and although this imperfection does not limit the degree to which it is evident, it has nevertheless given rise to various errors. And these themselves have again led some psychologists to dispute the fact that inner perception is evident and even to question the correctness of saying that inner perception is universally valid.

[3] Unambiguously: "*I see* a sensory space alternatively full and empty in one place and another," for the sensory space does not *exist* and consequently it is not alternatively full and empty. *This remark is a truism for Brentano*, but the numerous misunderstandings which have been connected with his theory of "external perception" justify these many notes and repetitions.

Others have been led to the same erroneous viewpoint by assuming right away that all presentations and all judgements which refer to a mental activity are acts of inner perception. But this is not correct; the mental as well as the physical can become a primary object. This is, for example, quite undeniable when we form a clear conception of the inner mental life of someone else, something we do in many cases even with animals. We know or suspect that they have sensations and think and will in certain ways which more or less agree or contrast with our ways of sensing, thinking, and desiring. Quite similarly, we often imagine that we ourselves would be mentally active in such and such a way in given circumstances, and we are also often convinced that we really shall feel and will in such and such a way or have felt and willed that way. In such cases there is always an inner perception, to be sure, but it is not a perception of those of our mental acts just named; it is a perception of another act which is now actually occurring and which is directed toward the others as its primary object.

All memories and expectations that refer to our own mental experiences have these experiences as their primary objects, and have themselves only as their secondary object or a part thereof.

This gives me the means to defend myself against a charge which has been made against me. Exception has been taken to my saying that inner perception cannot become inner observation but that we do often observe later on in memory what was earlier perceived in inner perception. Against this it has been alleged that memory is only a weaker repetition of the mental act we remember. But it can easily be seen that this is not the case; otherwise by remembering an earlier mistake one would be making the mistake again, and someone who is ashamed of an earlier sinful act of will would sin again. My own earlier mental activity which I remember does not make its appearance as secondary object ἐν παρέργῳ, but as primary object, just as when I believe someone else is having an idea or is otherwise mentally active.

III   *On the Modes of Presentation*

When I designated presentation, judgement, and emotional attitude as the three basic classes of mental reference, I meant that they were capable of still more various subdivisions. In fact we have already shown such subdivisions in the basic class of judgement when we pointed out the contrast between affirmation and denial, and in the basic class of emotional attitudes in the contrast between love and hate. But it is also true of the basic class of presentations that the way of referring is generally the same but is differentiated into particular modes. And just as two judgements are different in kind despite the fact that they have the same object if the one judgement affirms what the other denies, the same thing is frequently also true of two presentations despite the sameness of their objects.

When I wrote my *Psychology from an Empirical Standpoint*, this had not yet become obvious to me, or at least not entirely so. As a result there are many things that I not only have to expand upon but also to correct.

Above all we must designate temporal differences as modes of presentation. Anyone who considered past, present, and future as differences in objects[1] would be just as mistaken as someone who looked upon existence and non-existence as real attributes. If we hear a series of sounds in a conversation or in a melody, or if we watch a physical object which is in motion or is changing color, the same sound, the same individual spatially and qualitatively defined colored thing,[2] appears to us first as present, then more and more as past, while new things appear as present, whose presentation then undergoes the same modal alteration. Anyone who took these differences to be differences of the objects involved – somewhat as spatial differences undoubtedly are when I have a presentation of something more to the right or more to the left in my field of vision – would be unable to do justice to the great difference which exists between space and time. As far as space is concerned, we can assume without absurdity that there are non-spatial things too: spirits without length, breadth, and depth and without really being in one place or another. In the same way we can assume topoids of four and more dimensions, in which the fourth dimension is supposed to be added to length, breadth, and depth analogously as in the physical thing depth is added to breadth and breadth to length; and the same would hold of every further dimension in relation to its predecessors – a very familiar idea in modern geometry, on the other hand, it would be simply absurd for someone to set up a hypothesis according to which something might exist and yet not be present and contemporary with everything else which exists, in that

[1] That is to say, anyone who believed that what is involved in intuitively given temporal differences are differences in the things he has before his mind, would be mistaken. Brentano calls such differences "differences in the object" for short. See the Introduction.

[2] In accord with Brentano's later studies, we should say here "specifically the same sound," "specifically the same color" and strike out "individual." Intuitive perception does not reveal to us anything individual, because the spatial factor enters into appearance merely as something relative, not as completely defined. See the Introduction and Supplementary Essay XVI below.

either it has no analogy with the present, or it endures or changes in a chronoid of more than one dimension.[3] Just as no judgement can fail to have a qualitative mode, and we can confidently assert this for all beings which make judgements, no presentation could fail to have a temporal mode. And we can assert this without being rash, not only of man and beast but of any being whatsoever that has presentations. It holds true with the same certainty as the principle that there can be no presentation without an object.

This point, which is of the utmost importance, has the most far-reaching consequences, and I shall go into it in greater detail on another occasion. At that time I shall also go into the question of whether it may not be true that we must assume a continuous succession of real differences for everything which has temporal duration, in addition to the continuous series of temporal differences with which it is to be conceived. These differences, being wholly transcendent, would not be given in any of our concrete intuitions.

I will not leave entirely unmentioned, though, the fact that it is impossible to have a presentation of something with a general temporal mode, as though a thing might appear indeterminately as past, future or still more indeterminately as sometime or other actual. This is just as unfeasible as judging with an indeterminate qualitative mode, i.e. judging but neither affirming nor denying. I do not wish to go further into the explanation of why it appears to be feasible, at the present time.

It hardly need be remarked explicitly that the question of what is meant by time can in no way be reduced to the question of what serves as the basis of our measurement of temporal quantities and intervals, whether it be by rational assessment or by habitual or originally instinctive estimation.[4] The latter too is of great psychological interest and leads the investigator to teleological factors similar to those which are found in blind trust in memory, habitual expectation, and many natural inclinations and antipathies. It is not these questions, however, but only the first and preeminently important one, with which we must concern ourselves here.

Another important point of view from which differences in mode of presentation are to be discussed has already been mentioned. It is the standpoint from which we differentiate the *modus rectus* and

[3] See the treatise on time and space, published posthumously in *Kantstudien* XXV, 1921, and further Supplementary Essay XVI below.

[4] In 1911 Brentano had not yet become aware of the confusions between time and the measurement of time committed by the relativity-theorists; this warning is all the more interesting. See my book, *Offene Briefe an H. Albert Einstein und Max von Laue über die gedanklichen Grundlagen der speziellen und allgemeinen Relativitätstheorie* (Vienna, 1925).

modus obliquus. The first, of course, is never absent when we are actively thinking. The second is present along with it, however, whenever we are thinking of something which has mental reference or of something relative in the strict sense. Besides the mentally active subject, which I think of *in recto*, I always think of his object, too; besides the fundament of the relation, which I think of *in recto*, I also think of the terminus *in obliquo*. And the *modus obliquus* itself is not really one *single* mode; it is differentiated in various ways. It is one mode when it has to do with a quantitative relation, another when it has to do with a causal relation, another when it has to do with mental reference to an object; in fact, it is one mode when this mental reference is a mere presentation or a judgement, and a different one depending upon whether it is an affirmative or negative judgement, and so on and so on.

IV   *On Attributive Combination of Presentations*
in recto *and* in obliquo

It is well known that our presentations of objects which are not entirely simple are sometimes more and sometimes less distinct.[1] As often as we have a rather distinct presentation of such objects, the presentational reference is a complex one and is clear in the Cartesian sense in a complex way. As it has to do with the whole, so it also has to do with the parts individually, which then appear to be united in a determinate way. This is the case, for example, when I distinguish a red patch as colored, as red, as spatial, as located here, as triangular, etc., and think of it as characterized by all of these attributes. One of them then appears as something which is united with the others in a determinate way. Every presentational reference to an attribute has a particular object, which, since the attributes are determined, forms along with the others the intuitively (*anschaulich*) presented unitary whole.

But we have the further ability to unite the most diverse objects by identifying them with one another whether they are compatible with each other in reality or not, and we thus arrive at an integral object[2] which has attributive, but not intuitive unity. For example, I am capable of thinking in this way of a round square, a white stallion which is black, and a red which is blue. I can also have a presentation of the same attribute identified with itself, as for example, a white

---

[1] More precisely: "It is well known that we can have things as objects sometimes more and sometimes less distinctly."
[2] "Integral presentation" could replace "integral object" here. See the last sentence of this section.

napkin, whereupon the identification of the thing leads to an equivalent of the attribute itself. It is easy to see that it can also happen that attributes which can be united in an intuitive way such as a certain color and shape, are united not in an intuitive way but merely in an attributive way.

I have already explained at length in my *Psychology* that someone who makes an attributive identification of two qualities in presentation is not yet making a judgement which predicates one of them or the other. But, as is obvious to anyone who reflects on what has been pointed out previously about secondary reference, this is not to say that there is no judgement whatsoever in this case. Indeed, it might even turn out upon closer investigation that whenever we have a distinct presentation we are related to ourselves in a certain way as negatively judging, since we know that the mental reference to one part is different from the mental reference to another part.

It is plain that a clarification of the presentation can come about through an analysis of its object both *in recto* and *in obliquo*. And those free identifications which are possible *in recto* are just as possible *in obliquo*. In addition, something which is thought of *in recto* can be identified with an object thought of *in obliquo*, as for example when I have a presentation *in recto* of flowers and of a flower-lover who wants these flowers, in which case flowers are thought of both *in recto* and *in obliquo* and are identified with one another. If I am thinking of a green tree, I am thinking of the tree *in recto* and of the green *in recto* and I identify the two presentationally. If, on the other hand, I think, as they say, of a non-green tree, the process seems a much more complicated one. For Aristotle, at least, denied that a negative could be an object. And if it is really impossible, as I have no doubt that it is, nothing is left but to assume that we are thinking of a tree, of which it is correct to deny that it is green, so that we are then dealing with a case of identification *in obliquo*.[3] We shall

[3] The objection might be made: Brentano speaks of thinking of a tree of which something is rightly denied. But now according to Brentano himself one can never "deny something of something" without affirming the existence of the thing of which something is denied. Whether positive or negative predication (*Zuerkennung* or *Aberkennung*) is involved, not only should the subject of the predication concerned be present to the mind, but its existence should be affirmed. Reply: *If we think of a tree of which it is rightly denied that it is green*, we are not denying something of something, we are not even making a predicative judgement, i.e. a negative predicative judgement (*negativ-absprechendes Urteil*). But we are thinking of a tree *modo recto* and we are thinking of someone making a synthetic judgement, someone who rightly denies green of a tree which is indirectly thought of as the subject of the denial we are thinking of, and we identify the two trees which are (directly or indirectly) present to our mind. In order to

return to this point later. Leibniz has already emphasized the fact that denial as such is nothing negative and therefore there is no objection to making it an object of presentation as there was to making something non-green an object.

V On the Modifications in Judgement and Attitude Brought about by the Modes of Presentation

Like the differences in objects of presentations, differences in their modes have importance not merely for presentations themselves, but for judgmental and emotional references as well, since these are based upon presentations.

This clearly holds true of the temporal mode. If I judge that a tree

---

think of the tree as "subject of a judgement of negative predication (*eines absprechendes Urteils*), we must think of someone making a predicative judgement in this way. For this reason, Marty used to say 'S Non P' is present to our mind in 'reflection on predicative judgements.'" See Essay IX, which discusses the form S Non P. The form S Non P is the symbol of identification *in obliquo* in the case of "non-green tree." These analyses are extremely important for logic and for the understanding of language. Perhaps it will serve to make the theory of attributive combination of presentation more intelligible to add the following: if I think of someone who wants flowers, I have the person with this desire as my object, i.e. *modo recto*, but I am thinking of the flowers indirectly (Essay I). In this case we speak of what is "desired as such." In place of the sentence, "There is someone who wants flowers," we can also say "There are desired flowers *as desired*." For these two equivalent assertions to be true, it is not necessary for there to be any flowers but only someone who thinks of them and desires them. Something desired as desired *exists* no more than something thought of as thought of. On the other hand, if I say, "There are desired flowers," without any further addition, I am saying the same as if I say, "There are flowers which are desired." This assertion means that there are flowers and that someone desires them. This is a case where the judgement is based on an "attributive combination of presentations *in obliquo*," namely "flowers which are loved," "loved flowers." In this case I have flowers as object directly and at the same time I have them as object in *modo obliquo*, namely as what the flower lover I am thinking of has as his object, and I combine these two presentations in an attributively identifying way to form the idea of "flowers loved by a flower lover." (In analogy with non-green tree.) The Cartesian Port Royal logic treats the following as a complex inference: *La loi divine oblige d'honorer les rois. Louis XIV est roi. Donc la loi divine oblige d'honorer Louis XIV.* The analysis of this inference and its premises cannot be carried out without the *modus obliquus* or identification *in obliquo*.

exists, and that a tree did exist, I am making an affirmative judgement in both cases, but with a different mode of affirmation. Just as the object of the presentation, "tree," distinguishes not only the presentation, but the judgement, so does the presentation's temporal mode; it makes a temporal distinction in the judgement as well. Something similar is true when I wish for something for the past or for the future. Both are acts of love, but they are temporally differentiated, as are the presentations on which they are based.

It is easily seen that this occurs without the mediation of a temporal judgement. The wish for the present or for the future includes neither the belief that the object wished for exists or will exist, nor the denial of this. I do not hesitate to emphasize this point explicitly, because the special relevance of the conjugation of the verb to temporal differences could incline people to believe that the temporal modes have to do with differences which primarily concern judgement and which are not equally relevant to presentation. For the verb is that linguistic form whose special function is to complete the expression of a judgement.

In connection with the difference between *modus rectus* and *modus obliquus*, it is true that judgements and emotional attitudes are based only on presentations *in modo recto* and not on presentations *in modo obliquo* all by themselves, for, of course, the latter never exist all by themselves but only together with the *modus rectus* in a mental act. If I think of someone who is denying something or even if I know of someone who is denying something, I do not deny this myself any more than I cause something when I think of a cause that produces that thing, even though the indirect object and the particular *modus obliquus* with which my thought is directed to it are not irrelevant to the content of my judgement; it is as a result of them that judgement is directed on one object rather than another.

When Meinong subjected the case in which one says, "Locke taught that there are no innate ideas," to psychological analysis, he saw quite correctly that the person who makes this statement is not maintaining that there are no innate ideas. But instead of saying, as we do, that in this case the person is thinking *in recto* of Locke denying innate ideas and affirming this, and referring by way of presentation to the innate ideas *in obliquo* but with a double mode,[1] he says that there we are dealing with a fourth basic class of references to an object. A class which stands between presentation and judgement and corresponds to the traditional expression in the language,

---

[1] It is a double mode because the "ideas" are both presented and affirmed. See p. 281.

"supposing." It is easy to show that he is laboring under a complicated delusion here.[2]

The *modus obliquus* of a presentation is surely different when we
are thinking of someone affirming or denying an object from what it
is when we are thinking of someone merely thinking of it. But something similar is also true in the case when we are thinking of someone
loving or hating the object. It is no more necessary to speak of a
special basic class of mental references in the first case than it is in
the second, or else to be consistent, we would have to do this even
when we think of an effect *in obliquo* while thinking of its cause *in
recto*. Rather, it is clear that this is a matter concerning subordinate
forms of the indirect mode of presentation, which then, of course,
take on significance for judgements based on the presentation with
modus rectus, as we have already remarked.

Furthermore, no one who knows the German language will grant
that Meinong is using the word "annehmen" ("supposing") here
in one of its heretofore ordinary meanings. As Meinong uses it, we
could often suppose two contradictory things at the same time, as
for example when we say, "Locke says that Descartes is mistaken in
teaching that there are innate ideas." For in this case we would be
supposing that someone is mistaken when he teaches that there are
innate ideas, and supposing that there are innate ideas, all at the
same time. To avoid this Meinong would have to set up a new basic
class for these second order indirect references, which would be
related to his "supposing" as his "supposing" is related to
judgement.

"Supposing" is often used as a synonym for "affirming" and in
particular for "agreeing," in cases where someone else has expressed
a claim. Often, and in especially numerous cases, it refers to a still
more complicated mental process, namely purposely holding on to
an idea as if you had made a judgement about something,[3] in order
to investigate what other judgements or practical decisions you would
be led to by thinking in a rational manner. Just as I can analyze an
object without affirming it, I can also make clear to myself the
consequences to which a judgement must lead, merely by thinking
of a person making the judgement and not affirming such a person.
Someone who proceeds hypothetically proceeds, although he does
not have knowledge, exactly analogously to the way in which he
would proceed if he did have knowledge. Hence even that which
truly corresponds to the term "supposing," does not involve a special

[2] See Anton Marty, "Über Annahmen," *Gesammelte Schriften*, Vol. II,
Part 2, 3 ff.
[3] Vaihinger's *Philosophie des Als Ob* (1911), deals very extensively with
this heuristic fiction.

basic class but, rather, a combination of several mental activities which have already been specified.*

VI   On the Impossibility of Ascribing Intensity to Every Mental Reference and in Particular the Impossibility of Understanding Degrees of Conviction and Preference as Differences of Intensity

When I undertook to prove in my *Psychology* that in presentation and judgement we have to do with two different basic classes of mental reference to the object, I supported my view by citing the incomparability of the degree of intensity of these two ways of referring, since at the time I followed the received opinion, according to which degrees of conviction were to be understood as differences in intensity. But this opinion, as I have now seen, is a mistaken one. I refer the reader to my *Untersuchungen zur Sinnespsychologie* in this connection. There I show too that the degree of preference and the will's degree of determination are not at all comparable to the degrees of intensity of a sensation. And I show in general that the view that every mental reference exhibits intensity in the strict sense must be given up since we even find presentations (as for example that of the number "three" in general) without intensity. Consider two persons who are distinguished by the fact that one judges something affirmatively and has no doubts about it whatsoever, while the other believes it to be merely probable. The latter does not make the same judgement as the former but with a lesser degree of intensity. Rather, the one who judges with probability makes a judgement (actually he makes several judgements differentiated in content), which refers only *in obliquo* to what the other person's judgement refers to *in recto*. Even La Place was well aware of this when he said that probability consists of complex knowledge, first the knowledge that one or the other of several mutually exclusive cases exists, and secondly that I have no more reason to hold the one to be real than the other.[1] We should not allow ourselves to be deluded by the fact that we speak of degrees of conviction as we do of degrees of the intensity of a sensation. We also speak of different degrees in connection with the speed of a movement, yet what we might therefore call the intensity of movement has no more profound relation to

* Cp. Anton Marty, *Untersuchungen zur Grundlegung einer allgemeinen Grammatik und Sprachphilosophie* (Halle, 1908), pp. 244 ff.
[1] According to Brentano the probability judgement is a judgement about judgements. See Brentano, *Versuch über die Erkenntnis*, edited by Alfred Kastil. [A second edition of this work, edited by F. Mayer-Hillebrand, was published by Felix Meiner in 1970; the second edition contains much material that was not in the first edition.]

intensity as it pertains to a sensation. The natural scientist knows that the state of rest is in reality in no way inferior to the state of motion. If the world's center of gravity were to move off in any direction with whatever velocity you please instead of being at rest, this would be totally irrelevant to the internal order of physical, chemical, and physiological processes.[2] It is quite a different matter with respect to the intensity which is peculiar to sensations. Someone who hears something loudly is superior to a person who hears it faintly, as far as the reality of hearing is concerned, just as someone who not only hears but also has sensations of touch and smell and taste is, other things being equal, superior, as far as the reality of sensation is concerned, to someone who only hears. And so if a loud sound existed in actuality as it does phenomenally, it would be a greater reality than a soft one.

This, then, is by way of brief correction to a mistake made earlier. I need hardly add that I do not believe that the collapse of this argument weakens my proof of the distinction between presentation and judgement as basic classes.

VII   *On the Impossibility of Combining Judgement and Emotion in a Single Basic Class*

In my *Psychology* I remarked that if we assign judgement and desire to two different basic classes, we may feel that much less hesitant about acknowledging that presentation and judgement are two fundamentally different classes of reference, because there are similarities between judgement and emotional attitude which do not exist between judgement and presentation. Among emotional attitudes there is a contrast between love and hate just as there is a contrast between affirmation and denial among judgements. But there is no such contrast among presentations. There are further analogies between judgements and emotions, which have no parallel in the realm of presentation. Just as judgements are sometimes correct, sometimes incorrect, there is also such a thing as correctness and incorrectness in the domain of love and hate. On this point see my treatise *The Origin of Our Knowledge of Right and Wrong*, in

[2] Brentano's idea, of course, is this: from the fact that a uniform linear movement of the whole world-system, whatever its velocity, does not bring about a change in any natural event, we see that the state of rest is just as real as the state of movement. (This is the so-called classical principle of relativity. See Kraus, *Annalen der Philosophie*, 1921, *Sonderheft zur Relativitätstheorie*, and in *Kantstudien*, V, XXVI (1922), as well as my open letter to Einstein.) An increase in the speed of a movement is not an increase in its reality.

287

APPENDIX

which I have also shown that many emotional attitudes are immediately experienced as being correct (*als richtig characteriziert*), just as judgements are. In a more penetrating discussion I would have been able to go on to show here, as well, how the emotions which we see with immediate insight to be correct resemble judgements which are, as they say, self-evident *ex terminis*. If we are aware in such cases that our correct judgement arises necessarily out of a presentation, i.e. that by having such a presentation we effectively cause ourselves to judge in that way, something similar holds true of emotions which are immediately experienced as being correct. And just as we see the judgement to be generally and necessarily true because of this, the same thing holds true of such an emotional attitude. For example, we recognize not just in particular cases or just for human beings, but universally and necessarily that, other things being equal, pleasure is to be preferred to pain and knowledge to error. In a note of Marty's to the English translation of my ethical treatise, one may find the idea discussed still further.*[1]

Under such circumstances it may not be so very strange that many of those who were convinced by the arguments in my *Psychology* that judgement is to be separated from presentation as a basic class, should now have hit upon the idea of combining it and the emotions into a single class and interpreting affirmation as a species of love and denial as a species of hate. Quite a few ordinary linguistic expressions might seem to confirm this, as the word "Anerkennung" ("affirmation") is used in the sense of "Hochschätzung." ("approval") and we use the expression "Verwerfung," ("rejection") for denial or contradiction and also apply it to the bad and unpleasant.

It does not seem to be superfluous, then, to say a few words about the fact that despite those considerations, judgements should not be counted as members of the same basic class as emotions, any more than in the same basic class as presentations.

Believing something is quite different from loving it, and denying an object is just as different from hating it, otherwise there could be no such thing as sad news. And in this case it is no adequate defense to point out that because the same thing can be found to be good or bad from different points of view, something could also be hated

* [Editor's note: Brentano refers here to the first English translation of *The Origin of the Knowledge of Right and Wrong*, by Cecil Hague (Westminster, 1902), p. 122 ff. The note he mentions – essentially a biographical sketch of Brentano – also appears in German in Anton Marty's *Gesammelte Schriften* (Halle, 1916), Vol. I, Part 1, 100 ff.]
[1] See also Kraus's essays on value theory, listed in *Jahrbücher der Philosophie* (Berlin, 1914).

and at the same time loved by being believed. For if someone hates an object in other respects, its existence certainly does not make it any dearer to him, since he would rather that it did not exist. And we may not overlook the fact that even if there are analogies between the domain of judgement and that of emotion, they are not to be found throughout. I emphasize here as especially significant a point I also had to stress for a particular reason in my *Origin of Our Knowledge of Right and Wrong*. In the domain of judgement there is a true and a false. But there is nothing intermediate between them, any more than there is something between existence and non-existence, according to the well-known law of the excluded middle. On the other hand, in the domain of love there is not only a "good" and "bad" but also a "better" and a "less good," "worse" and "less bad." This has to do with the distinctive nature of preference, a special class of emotional attitudes which, as I show in my *Origin of our Knowledge of Right and Wrong*, has no counterpart in the domain of judgement. Also, by adding one good thing to another, something better is achieved; indeed even when good is added to something bad, the good together with the bad creates a whole which we might be right in preferring to something else which is purely good taken in and for itself. For example, in theodicy it is usually said that God has permitted evil in the world because, as a result of this inclusion, the world is all in all a more perfect one than a world which is free from evil. So we often implicitly will and choose bad along with good, while in judging according to correct procedure we never permit a falsehood to enter in order to make the whole more true.

Still another point! When we love something correctly, we distinguish between what is good in itself and what is good only for the sake of something else, and we call the latter "useful." When we affirm something correctly there is no analogous distinction. Everything which exists, even if it has its efficient cause in something else, exists as such (and not merely with respect to that cause).

VIII *On the Impossibility of Assuming that Feeling and Will have Different Basic Classes on an Analogy with Presentation and Judgement*

We have just seen how many recent investigators have wanted to reduce the number of basic classes we set up to two by subsuming judgement under emotional attitudes. In addition to them we find others who do not yet admit that everything we call desiring, preferring, wishing, willing and choosing can be united into a single basic class with the feelings of joy and sadness. And when I called attention to the gradual character of the transitions between what is called feeling and what is called willing, I heard *one* point in particular cited as marking a sharply defined boundary. It is said that among those mental references which I put in opposition to one another as love to hate, there are some which are not incompatible with one another even though they are directed upon incompatible things; but the opposite is true of certain other references which I have also assigned to this class. For example, a person could very well simultaneously find pleasure in staying in each of two pleasant places, but he could not simultaneously will to stay in one place and in the other. This is said to be similar to the way in which we can think of contrary things at the same time and compare them in various respects, while in judgement affirming one of the contraries excludes the affirmation of the other. And so willing is supposed to be differentiated from liking, just as judging is from having presentations. It may be that willing presupposes liking, just as judging presupposes presentation, but only in order to be based upon it as one mental reference can be based on another basic class.

Nevertheless the comparison with the relation between presentation and judgement, if employed more precisely, allows us to see that the situation is essentially different in this case. If affirmation supervenes upon presentation, this involves no addition which adds presentation to presentation.[1] Here, on the other hand, it appears that when I choose one of two incompatible things both of which are pleasing to me, a new act of love for the same object is added to the love which was present in my liking that object.

Besides, those mental references to an object which we call willing and choosing are not the only ones which exhibit this exclusiveness. Willing and choosing always have to do with the practical. No one who does not believe that he, like Aeolus, can command the wind and weather can will that in three days we will have this or that weather. But there can still be cases in which on the same day he finds good weather pleasant for certain reasons and bad weather pleasant for other reasons, since here as elsewhere one pleasant feeling is compatible with another, yet he might quite decidedly wish that the one rather than the other should occur.

Should we now say that it is *preference (Bevorzugen)* more than any other emotional attitude which possesses this character of exclusivity? – If this is so, it would be undeniable that we are concerned with a real attitude of love, for ordinary language, too, speaks of *"Vorliebe."* Yet when more than two incompatible objects are

[1] It also emerges from this passage that the existence of "non-additive" complexes or "totalities" has been a well-known fact for a long time and that Gestalt psychology has made no new discoveries in this connection.

involved one of them is often preferable to one and at the same time less preferable than the other, and only this last one is, as they say, "wished for," so perhaps we should regard only absolute preference and not merely relative preference as an example of that new basic class. – We see that this too is unpromising.

But someone might say that it is not a question of distinguishing preference over something, from preference over things one likes, or preference over everything. There are cases in which we prefer the behaviour known to be right, and yet, overwhelmed by passion, we will and act contrary to it. But if this happens, it would have to be thought of as Aristotle interprets it: namely, that passion does not let one's higher love and esteem get a word in; that it hinders them from bringing about their consequences because it predominates both inwardly and outwardly. Although the desire for physical pleasure is not in accord with what reason calls preferable, rational considerations working in the interest of passion find the means to attain pleasure. Love and preference are transferred to the means and lead to action, and the opposing noble preference has no influence. If we interpret the matter in this way, we are dealing with a complex set of relationships. Presentations and judgements attach to the affect, and then, because of them, more feelings of love – those in which we desire something as a means – and finally the outward behaviour. But here too we search in vain for something which would justify the assumption of a new basic class.

IX *On Genuine and Fictitious Objects*

All mental references refer to things.

In many cases, the things to which we refer do not exist. But we are accustomed to saying that they then have being as objects. This is a loose (*uneigentlicher*) use of the verb "to be," which we permit with impunity for the sake of convenience, just as we allow ourselves to speak of the sun "rising" and "setting." All it means is that a mentally active subject is referring to those things. It is only consistent to go on and permit such statements as "A centaur is half man, half horse," although in the strict sense centaurs do not exist and so, in a strict sense, there is no centaur which has a body that is half of human form and half in the form of a horse.

Because reference to things is a distinctive characteristic of someone who is mentally active, we have been led to talk about objects having being or subsisting in the mentally active subject. Similarly, the fact that the subject refers to the same thing in different ways has led people to talk about something which is in some way more than the object, for it includes the latter within itself, and is likewise within the subject. It has been called the "content" of the mental reference. Especially in connection with the mental act of making judgements, there has been talk of a content of judgement as well as an object. If I judge, "A centaur does not exist," it is said that the object is a centaur, but that the content of the judgement is that a centaur does not exist, or the non-existence of a centaur. If it said that this content has its being in the active subject, then once again "to be" is being used in a loose and improper sense and means exactly the same thing as is expressed by the use of "to be," in its proper sense, in the words, "A mentally active subject is denying a centaur in the *modus praesens*."

Some have gone even further than this, however, and taking the difference between correct and incorrect judgement into consideration, speak of contents which exist in actuality and those that do not exist in actuality. Hence, for example, since anyone who denies a centaur judges correctly, it is said that the non-existence of the centaur is actual, while the existence of the centaur is not actual. And contrariwise, because it is true that there are trees, it is said not merely that trees exist, but also that the existence of trees has being and that their non-existence does not. Thus, contents are treated as analogues to objects, among which we distinguish some which have their being only in a loose and improper sense in the mentally active subject, and some which have being in the strict sense outside of the subject, where they belong to the realm of real things. Since there has been some hesitation, however, about declaring the non-existence of a centaur a real thing, it was believed that this difference, on the one hand, and the similarity, on the other, could be taken account of at the same time by calling contents "objectives."[1]

But surely we are dealing here with mere fictions. Anyone who says that the non-existence of a centaur has being, or who answers the question as to whether a centaur does not exist by saying, "That is so," only wants to say that he denies centaurs in the *modus praesens*, and, consequently, also believes that anyone who denies a centaur judges correctly. Aristotle is quite correct, therefore, in saying that the "That is so," by which we indicate our agreement with a judgement means nothing but that the judgement is true, and that truth has no being outside of the person judging; in other words, it exists *only* in that loose and improper sense, but not strictly and in reality. It would lead to the most disastrous complications if we let ourselves go astray regarding this Aristotelian doctrine and took those fictions

[1] Meinong introduced the term, "objective." Others speak of contents, and also of states of affairs, structures. Meinong also invents dignitatives and desideratives in addition to objectives.

to be things which have being in the proper sense of the word. There would then be, besides an apple, also the existence of an apple, the non-existence of the non-existence of an apple, and so on *ad infinitum*, and infinite complications would be multiplied infinitely.

Suppose that, in trying to defend the claim that the non-existence of a centaur subsists genuinely and in reality, someone appealed to the principle, "The truth of a judgement is its agreement with reality," and said that in the case of a negative judgement there would be no such correspondence if there were nothing in reality to correspond to it. The answer is that in this case the meaning of those old and traditional words is being misinterpreted. They mean only that an affirmative judgement is called true when that which the judgement says exists or did or will exist, *does* or did, or will exist. A negative judgement is called true when that which the judgement says does not, or did not, or will not exist, does not, or did not, or will not exist. It is a question of a positive agreement with a thing only in the case of the affirmative judgement in the present tense, while for the negative judgement in the *modus praesens* it is sufficient that there be no disharmony, as there would be, for example, for the denial of centaurs if there really were centaurs.

An analogy is sometimes drawn between contents and objects, which is supposed to lie in the fact that certain contents, like certain objects, have being not only in a loose and improper sense, but in a proper sense as well, and that other contents, like other objects, do not. There is no justification for this analogy.

Just as contents cannot have being in the proper sense, they cannot have being in exactly the same loose and improper sense in which objects have being, either; which is to say that they cannot become objects, just as, on the other hand, no object can constitute the whole of a content. It is easy to see how this statement ties up with what has been said before; for if a content, e.g. the being or the non-being of Napoleon, could become an object, then it would also have to hold true of it that it either is or is not, and we would have to be able to say in the strict sense not only of Napoleon but of the being of Napoleon as well, that it has being at one time and at another time it does not, and that it has a beginning and an end. A content is never presented in the sense of being object of the presentation, nor is it ever affirmed, in the sense in which an object is affirmed, not even by those who believe that it is to be affirmed. In so saying, of course, I do not want to deny that, according to another even more common usage, instead of saying that a person affirms something, we can say he affirms that a thing exists. But absolutely the only thing which is presented is a person who is making the judgement concerned, and we judge that insofar as we are thinking of such a person, we are

293

thinking of someone who judges correctly.[2] Strictly speaking, therefore, we are not even expressing ourselves quite accurately if we say we deny that the content of a judgement exists. We ought rather to say we deny that anything exists for which the word "content" is a name, just as words like "of" and "but," have no meaning by themselves and do not name anything. "An of does not exist," "A but, does not exist," make no more sense than "A Poturi-Nulongon does not exist." But it does, indeed, make sense to say, "There is no thing which is named by the preposition, 'of,' or the conjunction, 'but.'"

Hence we are certain that one cannot make the being or nonbeing of a centaur an object as one can a centaur; one can only make the person affirming or denying the centaur an object, in which case the centaur, to be sure, becomes an object in a special *modus obliquus* at the same time. And so it holds true generally that only that which falls under the concept of a thing (*Reales*), can provide an object for mental reference. Nothing else can ever be, like a thing, that to which we mentally refer as an object—neither the present, past, nor future, neither present things, past things, nor future things, nor existence and non-existence, nor necessity nor non-necessity, neither possibility nor impossibility, nor the necessary nor the non-necessary, neither the possible nor the impossible, neither truth nor falsity, neither the true nor the false, nor good nor bad. Nor can the so-called actuality (ἐνέργεια, ἐντελέχεια) of Form (ἔιδος, λόγος, μορφή), of which Aristotle speaks, and which we express in our language by means of such abstractions as redness, shape, human nature, and the like, ever be the objects of a mental reference, and this is true further of objects as objects (*Objekte als Objekte*) as for example, the affirmed, the denied, the loved, the hated, the presented.

It would be going too far to demonstrate this for each particular case here. And so let us just remark in general that anyone who studies carefully a case in which one might be inclined to assume the contrary, will discover that we always have things as objects in those cases too – sometimes *in recto*, sometimes *in obliquo*. And he will discover further that for every sentence which seems to have one of the items just mentioned as its subject or predicate, he can form an equivalent sentence in which subject and predicate are replaced by things. Leibniz knew this, particularly as concerns the so-called *nomina abstracta*, and in his *Nouveaux Essais*, Book II, Chap. xxiii,

[2] "I affirm that a certain thing exists" could mean the same as "I believe that someone affirming a certain thing cannot be in contradiction with someone making an evident judgement; anyone who affirms it, is making a true judgement."

Sect. I, he gave a translation such as we have given, which can be seen to relieve us of a profusion of subtle and abstruse debates which have perplexed metaphysics and logic.[3]

This is not to deny that in many cases the fiction that we can have something other than a real thing as an object – that non-beings, for example, may be objects just as well as beings – proves to be innocuous in logical operations; and in fact these operations can even be facilitated by this fiction because it simplifies our form of expression and even our thought processes themselves. It is similar to the way in which mathematicians benefit from the use of the fiction of numbers less than zero, and many others. By using such a method a presentation and judgement which are complicated in various ways can be treated as though they were simple, and one is spared the trouble of going through a more detailed, and in certain cases useless, explication of a confusedly understood mental event.

From time immemorial ordinary logic has had a lot to say about judgements being elementary and simple, which they really are not. It was believed, for example, that in the four classes of categorical propositions which are designated by the letters A, E, I, and O, classes of simple, elementary, judgements were being distinguished, while in fact many of them, indeed all of them to a certain extent, are complex, and include judgements of inner consciousness in particular.

I will not refrain from going into their psychological analysis to a certain extent. If we compare the complexity which emerges from it with the simplicity attained by applying certain obvious fictions, we shall have a fuller appreciation of the services rendered by the latter.

Of the four categorical forms named, the I form is the easiest one to analyze. "Some S is P," is equivalent to an existential proposition which affirms in the *modus praesens* the whole arrived at when I think of S identified with P. And if the proposition did express, in accord with the logical fiction, a simple judgement, it would be identical with the judgement expressed by this existential judgement. Looked at more closely, however, it signifies a double judgement (*Doppelurteil*), one part of which affirms the subject, and, after the predicate has been identified in presentation with the subject, the other part affirms the subject which had been affirmed all by itself by the first part, but with this addition – which is to say it ascribes to it the predicate P.

We find something similar with the O form. Logicians call it the particular negative, which is extremely inaccurate, and if it were taken to be a precise expression would say something which is downright

[3] See Anton Marty, *Die "Logische," "Lokalistische" und andere Kasus-theorien* (Halle, 1920), p. 96.

impossible. For a purely negative judgement cannot be anything but a universal denial, just as when we are concerned with universal concepts, it is impossible for an affirmative judgement to be anything but a particular affirmative. The proposition, "There are no trees," is a universal denial, while the proposition, "There is a tree," is a particular affirmative, and the same holds without exception for "There are no A's," and "There is an A." It is only when an S which is identified with P has been restricted previously by a supplementary proposition that someone who denies the combination of an S with a P can deny it without denying it in terms of the whole denotation of S. But there is just such a restriction in the O form in virtue of the fact that, seen precisely, it, like the I form, expresses a double judgement. The one, as in the case of the I form, consists of the affirmation of S, and this is the basic constituent of the double judgement. The second part relates to it and presupposes it in such a way as to be inseparable from it. And this second part is negative; it does not, as in the I form, ascribe an attribute to the S which was affirmed by the first part of the double judgement, but rather denies one of it. It does not deny the combination of S and P *simpliciter*, then, but denies instead the combination of P with an S which I affirm and which, since every affirmation is particular, I make particular by virtue of this very affirmation. Thus, as we said, it is not an S as such whose combination with P is denied, but an S restricted in its range of denotation. It is as a consequence of the particular character of the basic affirmative part of the double judgement O, then, that the negative part constructed upon it also seems to be particular, but really is not. Still, if one prefers, one might also say that the second judgement is truly particular, but only because it is not purely negative but implicitly involves an affirmation.

We found that in the case of the I form the double judgement, "S is P," was equivalent to the simple existential judgement, "There is an SP," i.e. "an S which is a P." In view of what has been said, the same cannot hold true of the O form in relation to the existential form, "There is no SP." For in the latter, in which affirmation is entirely absent, there is no restrictive factor to explain the apparently particular character of the negative judgement.

I must, however, call attention to a linguistic peculiarity of the I and O forms as they are usually expressed. We do not ordinarily say simply, "An S is P," "An S is not P," but "Some S is P," "Some S is not P." This "some" is actually employed only when we are talking of one among several. Thus, for example, we cannot say, "There is some God," as we can say, "There is a God."

The ordinary expression of the A and E forms gives rise to a similar comment. We say, "All S is P," or "Every S is P," sometimes using the plural and other times the singular, which refers, however, to a plurality to which the individual belongs. It is somewhat less obvious that there is a reference to the plural when we express the E form as "No S is P." But here too it is easy to understand "no" as meaning "none among all." In practice the forms are used in a much more general way. People give as examples propositions such as, "Caius is a man," "No absolutely perfect being is unjust," even though in both cases the subject refers to something which cannot be in the plural. And I can also say, "Every round square must be round and square at the same time," even though there is not and cannot be even one round square, let alone a large number of them.

So we see, then, that only the modes of expression and not the sense of the forms as we now use them has to do with the plural. And thus in the analyses which I have just given of the I and the O forms, I have not taken it into account. Nor will I take it into account in the A and E forms which we still have to investigate. But if I did so, I would have to extend the concept of number in a fictitious way, so that it would include both "one" and "zero." For it is obvious that there is a total number for each subject. For that very reason, however, we would have gained nothing by asserting this expressly and, for example, instead of "An S is P," saying "In the totality of things S, there is one which is P," and instead of saying, "An S is not P," saying "In the totality of things S, an S is not P." And in the two other forms there is virtually no reference to a collective, either. It makes not the slightest difference whether we say that a certain thing is not present or that it is not present in the class of all things. And someone who says a class is something or other, for example, that it is green, but includes "one" and "null" among classes, would obviously not be predicating anything of a collective either collectively or, as the logicians say, distributively, since in the case when the class is null, there are no individuals in it of which the predicate "green" could be asserted one by one from beginning to end. Away then with the ballast which shows itself as something which would require much more extensive psychological analyses in order for its content to become completely clear. In particular, this would lead us in various ways to presentations of someone making a negative judgement, but would then also protect us once and for all from the error which has just loomed before us, namely, that the terms "number" and "class" and the like are concepts not derived from any intuition, either of outer or of inner consciousness. I have gone into this briefly in order to head off an objection which could otherwise easily be raised both against that part of our analysis which has already been set forth and especially against the part which is yet to come.

Having studied the I and O forms, we now turn to the E form. Just as the I form proved to be like an equivalent to the existential proposition, "There is an SP," i.e. "an S which is a P," the proposition, "No S is P," is clearly like an equivalent to the existential form, "There is no SP."

I say "like an equivalent," and by this I indicate that, considered psychologically, it is not quite the same. We want to make this clear by a more thoroughgoing analysis. Anyone who says, "No S is P" is thinking of someone judging that "An S is P," and declaring that in thinking of him in this way he is thinking of someone who judges incorrectly, someone who maintains something contradictory to his own judgement. Now we saw that someone who judges that "An S is P," is making a double judgement, of which the first component judgement affirms S and the second attributes the predicate P to the S affirmed in the first. It is implicit in what has been said, then, that he holds at least one of the two judgements to be false, the second one at any rate, for it implies the first and consequently if the first is false, it cannot be correct either. And for this reason the equivalence with the existential judgement, which denies the combination of both attributes, is quite obvious.

The A form is related to the O form as the E form is to the I. If the O form means the double judgement, "There is an S and it is not P," then the proposition, "Every S is P," says that anyone who makes both of those judgements is judging falsely. I think of someone affirming an S and denying P of it, and say that in thinking of someone judging in this way, I am thinking of someone judging incorrectly, someone maintaining something which contradicts my own judgement. This makes it plain that, as a result of the standpoint I have adopted, I believe that there could not be anyone at all who correctly denies P of S.

These are the somewhat complicated results of a psychological analysis of the four logical forms of categorical statements, A, E, I, and O, when they are reduced to their most essential elements. Now let us see how the logician can simplify these operations when such complications threaten to make them difficult!

All he has to do is to create the fiction that there are negative objects, too. This fiction, like many others, is a commonplace to the layman; he speaks of an unintelligent man as well as an intelligent one, and of a lifeless thing as well as of a living thing. He looks on "attractive thing" and "unattractive thing," "red thing," and "non-red things," equally, as words which name objects.[4] And in *De*

[4] Instead of "to name objects," it would be better to say "to name something," for the word "object" is synsemantical here. See Supplementary Essay XVI, Note 46, on negatives and privatives.

Interpretatione even Aristotle, who knows very well that a negative cannot become an object, includes, along with ὄνομα, the word which names something, ὄνομα ἀόριστον which is supposed to comprise just those negative expressions such as "non-white," "non-human," and the like. The expression, "infinite judgement," which Kant uses for a third class of judgement he distinguishes in addition to affirmative and negative in his *Critique of Pure Reason*, seems to have a historical connection with this Aristotelian term.

Logic has long made use of this fiction in various ways, and could have made even more skilful use of it, as I showed in my *Psychology* and as Hillebrand, following in my footsteps, showed in his book on categorical syllogisms. One then comes to see how, just as the categorical proposition, "An S is P," is reducible to the existential proposition "There is an SP," or "There is an S which is P," the categorical proposition "Some S is not P" is reducible to the existential proposition "There is an S non-P," i.e. "There is an S which is not P." Further, we can see how the categorical proposition "No S is P," is reducible to the existential "There is no SP" and the categorical proposition "All S are P" to the existential "There is not an S non-P." In my *Psychology* I stated the three simple rules which, if this artifice is available, make superfluous all of the complications which the theory of categorical syllogism has arrived at since Aristotle by distinguishing figures and modes, all of which complications were not enough to guard against errors in all cases. At the same time such a treatment reveals in an unmistakable way the important truth that the whole of syllogistic consists in nothing but a continuous application of the law of contradiction. Alexander Bain went so far astray on this point that he said we have no other assurance of the correctness of the rules of the syllogism than the fact that they have heretofore been confirmed in practice without exception.

A similar artifice simplifies the theory of hypothetical and disjunctive inferences and makes their propositions reducible to the existential proposition. Here I need only hold to the fiction that contents of judgements, too, can become objects to which we can refer affirmatively or negatively, both taken by themselves or insofar as they are identified with others or are related in some other way. For example, the proposition, "If all A is B, then some C is not D," can be converted into the existential proposition, "There is no non-being of A non-B without the being of C non-D." If one adds to this the proposition, "The non-being of A non-B is," then "the being of C non-D," follows by *modus ponens*, or if one adds the proposition, "The being of C non-D is not," by *modus tollens* it follows that "The non-being of A non-B is not." Substituting the letter α for the term "non-being of A non-B," and β for the term "being of C non-D," the arguments take this simple form:

> "There is no α without β.
> α exists.
> Therefore, β exists."

> "There is no α without β.
> β does not exist.
> Therefore α does not exist."

To be sure, the application of the artificial device is of lesser importance here, since the theory of conditional and disjunctive syllogisms is less complex than that of the so-called categorical syllogism. That may be the reason why Aristotle, who knew it as well as we do, did not consider it at all in his *Prior Analytics*.

But in order to guard against misinterpretations, I remark explicitly that I have not touched upon all the issues that arise with regard to the categorical syllogism here, any more than I did in my *Psychology*. For example, for the sake of brevity, I have not even glanced at the complications which consideration of the temporal mode or of the apodictic character of judgements introduces,[5] nor have I shown how the special difficulties and dangers which arise because of them are very easily confronted.

The fact that such fictions are useful in logic has led many to believe that logic has non-things as well as things as its object and, accordingly, that the concept of its object is more general than the concept of a thing. This is, however, thoroughly incorrect; indeed, in view of what has been said, it is downright impossible, because there cannot be anything at all other than substantive objects, and the same unitary concept of a thing, as the most general concept of all, comprehends everything which is truly an object.[6] Also, the

---

[5] See above, Book Two, Chap. 7, note 12.

[6] To be more precise, the passage should read: ". . . has led many to believe that logic has non-things (unreal entities) as well as things as its object, and accordingly, that the concept of its object is more general than the concept of a thing. This is incorrect; indeed, in view of what has been said, impossible, because we can never have anything but things as objects, i.e. we can think only of things, and the same univocal concept of thing, as simply the most general concept of all, comprehends everything which can truly be made our object." Since the concept of the thinking thing is one univocal concept, namely that of "the subject as having something as object," that something would also have to be one univocal concept.

According to Brentano, then, there can be no irreal entities, indeed, we cannot think of *anything* except real entities, i.e. *things*. One may object: "But it makes sense to raise the question of the existence of non-things,

terms of ordinary language are in most cases not psychologically, but
only grammatically names. They do not name things, but it is nonetheless true that the discourse in which they are involved is concerned
only with things. The object of logic is really much narrower than
the concept of thing; logic is a technical discipline, and is intended
to put us in a position to acquire knowledge by means of inquiry and
proof. It is an art of judgement.[7] Only insofar as, in judging, we have
things of all kinds as objects, do these come within our view, so to
speak, indirectly, while directly, it is knowledge (strictly speaking,
the knowing subject) which should be called the object of logic.

X On Attempts at the Mathematicization of Logic

Others, like myself, have felt a need for a reform in elementary
logic. In particular, many people have attempted to give logic a
thoroughly mathematical character, in the hope of imparting the
perspicuity of mathematical proofs to all demonstrations. The
universality which, on our account, is characteristic of all negative
judgements as such has been interpreted in the case of categorical
statements as a quantification of the subject concept. As a consequence, people were struck by the idea that it would be better if
both the predicate and the subject were quantified. This idea was not
wholly unfamiliar in antiquity and Aristotle himself pays some
attention to it, of course only polemically, when he says pointedly
that anyone who repeats the words "all" or "every" before the
predicate rather than applying them solely to the subject will consistently arrive at false conclusions. For no such propositions as "All
men are all men," and "Every man is every man," could ever be
admitted to be correct. Instead of it being true that all men are all
men, it is true, on the contrary, that no men are all men. And no
man is every man; for if this were true of even one man, Caius, for
example, that would imply that Caius is not just Caius but also
Sempronious and Tully, etc. We have here a complete misunderstanding of linguistic form.

[7] Brentano means a theory of the art of judgement, as ethics is such a
theory applied to emotional acts. He rejects all of the modern revisions
of the traditional meaning of those practical disciplines, ethics, logic,
esthetics.

---

and this would not be possible if we could not even think of the concept
of non-things." Brentano would reply: "That question has to do with
whether it is possible to affirm something and then deny of it that it is a
real thing." The term "non-thing" thus signifies an identification (synthesis) *in obliquo*, of presentations which are thoughts which things think.

Recently Gomperz remarked in an account of Theophrastus's philosophy that Theophrastus had anticipated the modern doctrine of the quantification of the predicate. But when you take a closer look at the passage cited, you find just the opposite; he mentions the idea, as Aristotle did before him, only to condemn it.

A similar misunderstanding guided those who said that every categorical judgement expresses a relation of identity between subject and predicate. Lotze seems to have been led by this notion to the peculiar theory that when we say, "A tree is green," by "tree" we implicitly understand a green tree, and by "green" we understand not just green alone, but a green thing identical with a tree, and so a green tree again. We would then have the equation, "A green tree = a green tree." But what would be the value of categorical statements all consisting in equations where the same thing is identified with itself? If all of the mathematicians' equations said only 2 is 2, and 10 is 10, and the like, they would be of little service to the advancement of science. If the proposition, "A tree is green," is really transformed without essential change of content into the proposition, "A green tree is a green tree," it is easy to see that the predicate, "a green tree," can be left out entirely without any loss. We arrive at the simple existential proposition, "A green tree is," as the equivalent of the proposition, "A tree is green," and this is entirely in accord with our view. One would fare even worse if one thereupon chose to explicate propositions such as, "All men are good," as synonymous with, "All good men are good men." For the latter is as self-evident as the former is contrary to experience.

So, no matter how much I sympathize in general with the efforts to make the rules of elementary logic more self-evident and to facilitate its operations, I am nevertheless unable to approve of these attempts to make logic mathematical. And I take steps to prevent my attempt to reduce categorical statements to existential propositions from being confused with them. We spoke previously of those who wished to give the object of logic an exaggerated universality. Now we must say of those who believe that the judgements with which logic is concerned deal only with equations and other quantitative relations that they have fallen into the opposite error. They limit the task of logic too much and want to make it a part of mathematics, while it seems to me to be the other way around; all of mathematics is a part of logic, that part which tells us how certain questions of knowledge (namely those of quantitative measurement) can best be dealt with in a methodical way.

Among the recent attempts to reform logic there are some which do not quantify the predicate but which nevertheless still suffer from the mistake of a restrictive mathematicization of logical operations.

302

They quantify at least the subject, which, as I believe I have shown, is not at all necessary in order to be able to speak of universal and particular judgements. I find this something of which I cannot approve, even though I do not at all disapprove of the use of letters as general signs for concepts and complexes of concepts as well as for judgements and complexes of judgements, in the manner of algebra, or the use of other signs analogous to + and −, =, >, <, and the like for indicating logical operations and relationships. I do, however, consider it questionable to use signs and expressions which are already in use among mathematicians in an altered sense. Examples of this would be representing a green tree as a multiplication of "green" and "tree" or defining a line raised to the third power not as a cube but as something identical with the line itself on the grounds that "a line which is a line which is a line," is identical with "a line," and yet according to the way of speaking just proposed, it would be the line multiplied by itself repeatedly. Where one of our most essential interests is protecting ourselves against equivocation, we should be very careful not to create new equivocations such as the ones which have just been mentioned. And it appears that this has come about as a result of the entirely accidental circumstance that algebra permits the adjective and the relevant noun simply to follow one another for purposes of expression in speech.

This could be especially detrimental if people wanted to deal with mathematical problems, too, by the new method, as the universality of logic would compel them to do. And this in fact is happening. But if you consider the fact that the entire attempt was brought about by the desire to confer upon other kinds of argumentation the perspicuity which mathematical operations possess, it seems very strange to try to reform the mathematical operations themselves. I do not expect any real success here – just the opposite. And when I hear the friends of this new logic prophesy in their enthusiasm that they will also bring about incomparably more rapid progress in science, I am reminded of the high expectations which Raymundus Lullius had for his "Ars magna." It turned out to be completely unfruitful. Nor do we find now that one of the significant discoveries of recent times has been made thanks to the application of the new algorithm which is in many ways so strange.

The following is another sign of the fact that this mathematical logic has not paid sufficient attention to making logical operations certain, something which is of still greater interest than abbreviating and simplifying them. It criticizes the old logic, and objects, as I do, to its incompleteness. But nowhere, so far as I could discover, does it call attention to the many errors and contradictions in the rules of the traditional logic, which I brought out in my attempted reform.

For example, it does not point out that it is false to say that the statement, "All S is P," implies the statement, "Some S is P." We saw that an entire class could have only one member or it could be null. In the latter case, although it is still true that all S is P, it is not true that a single S is P, for in fact no S is P. And consequently, the rule which says that the truth of "All S is P" is incompatible with the truth of, "No S is P," is also false, as is the rule which says that of the two propositions, "Some S is P" and "Some S is not P," one or the other must be true in every case.

There is no way of defending the old logic. If one wished to do so by saying that all categorical statements presuppose the existence of the subject and should be viewed merely as hypothetical judgements, this, even if accepted, would still leave standing the charge of self-contradiction. For of two assertions which are both supposed to hold true only under a certain presupposition, we can no longer say that they could not both be true at the same time. On the contrary, we can, as in a dilemma, infer the falsity of the presupposition from the truth of the two of them. So, for example, from the truth of the two propositions, "All S is P," and "No S is P," if both of them require the hypothesis that S exists, it follows that this very presupposition is false, that is to say, that there is no S. To reply that categorical judgements should not be thought of as implicitly restricted by hypothesis to the case in which the subject exists, but instead that they include in them the claim that the subject exists, would be no salvation either. For if the A form and the O form both include the claim that S exists, they can and must both be false the moment S does not exist. They are, then, no longer contradictory.

Only when I tried to reform logic did these and other aberrations in the most elementary logical rules (including four of the usual modes of inference), emerge immediately and clearly. And this is thanks to the energetic insistence on the proposition that anyone denying a universal denies the entire range of the concept and that everyone who affirms it affirms each particular, and conversely, anyone who affirms something in which several attributes can be distinguished, affirms all of its attributes, and hence its entire content, but no one who denies it also denies every part of it, every single attribute included in it. We can say, therefore, that when the concept is not entirely simple the negative judgement never makes a judgement about the entire content, just as when the concept is not an entirely individual one, the affirmative judgement never makes a judgement about the entire denotation.

The new mathematical logic has invented a new language. It seems to me, however, that it is less of a service to speak to us in a new language than it would be to teach us how to move about correctly in the mode of speech common to everybody. People will not stop making connections between these sorts of linguistic signs and the course of their thoughts. And so the most important thing is to eliminate the dangers which can arise from this. We do this by making the function of every part of speech intelligible. Then the equivocations which so often exist and which are repeated by analogy in all languages, and which, therefore, serve certain purposes, will not be set aside but will be rendered harmless. That the proposition, "A is A," used to express a self-evident *a priori* judgement, is not affirmative was noticed neither by Descartes, Spinoza, Leibniz, nor Kant.[1] If it had been, the first three would have been spared from falling into the fallacy of the ontological argument for the existence of God. And Kant would not have let himself be misled into a false definition of analytical judgement, according to which an affirmative judgement is supposed to be analytic if its predicate is included in the concept of its subject. This error is connected with many further errors in the *Critique of Pure Reason*, among others the disastrous illusion that mere analytic judgements do not add to our knowledge. This view lives on even today, although it had previously been objected to by Aristotle, and Kant himself inadvertently offers striking evidence against it on one occasion. According to him, logic is supposed to be purely analytic and yet truly a science, and hence an enrichment of our knowledge. Albert Lange, Kant's great admirer, noticed the contradiction and, in order to remove it, it occurred to him to make logic dependent upon synthetic *a priori* knowledge as well. But since that is supposed to have only phenomenal validity, Lange declared that the intuition of space was an essential foundation of all logical operations. The geometric diagrams, showing circles inside of, or outside of, or overlapping one another, which often accompany the exposition of the categorical syllogism in logic books were not supposed to be something incidental, but to contain the very heart of the demonstration.

But are we really supposed to be able to believe, contrary to what Cicero once said, that there exist in a literal sense round or square concepts of virtue, justice, and other universals? – Certainly not. Calling them spatially extended would be only a metaphor. But just as certainly as this transferral would lead us out of the domain

---

[1] A genuinely predicative or categorical judgement is a double judgement and includes the affirmation of the existence of its subject. "A horse is a horse" can be a true affirmative judgement, then, only if there is a horse. But that there is, is not certain *a priori*. If we understand the judgement negatively, it is only a disguised form of the law of contradiction, according to which an A which is not an A is impossible.

of spatial intuition, it would no longer permit the application of synthetic *a priori* truths, since their applicability depends on it.

XI   *On Psychologism*

The charge of psychologism has been made against my theory of knowledge. This is a word which has lately come into use and when it is spoken many a pious philosopher – like many an orthodox Catholic when he hears the term Modernism – crosses himself as though the devil himself were in it.

In order to defend myself against such a weighty accusation, I must first of all ask what is really meant by it, for the dreadful name comes up again and again, even when very different things are meant. When, during a friendly encounter, I sought an explanation from Husserl, and then, as the opportunity arose, from others who use the newly introduced term, I was told that it means a theory which contests the general validity of knowledge, a theory according to which beings other than men could have insights which are precisely the opposite of our own.

Understood in this sense, I am not only not now an advocate of psychologism, but I have always very firmly rejected and opposed such absurd subjectivism.

But then I hear it replied that I am nevertheless an advocate of psychologism and that I do away with the unity of truth for all, since this, it is said, exists only because there is something outside of the mind corresponding to the true judgement, something which is one and the same for everyone who judges. In the case of negative judgements and those which indicate that something is possible or impossible, past or future, this something could not be a thing, however. Consequently, since I do not admit that there are certain non-things, such as non-being, possibility, impossibility, pastness, futureness, and the like, in addition to things, this is where I do away with the unity of truth for all.

I reply that even if the elimination of the general validity of knowledge were a consequence of such a denial, it still would not do to call me down for being an advocate of psychologism, because I myself do not draw this conclusion.

But even this is incorrect; for why could it not be self-evident without presupposing such non-things, that two judgements, one of which affirms in a certain way what the other denies in the same way, are no more both correct if two different persons make the two judgements than if one and the same person makes them? And surely no one would maintain, even if there were such non-things, that in order for us to know if our judgements were true or false we would first have to perceive these non-things and compare them with our own judgements to see whether they agree or disagree.[1] On the contrary, it will always be the case that immediately evident perceptions of things, and immediately evident denials of the combinations into which things enter in our presentations, provide the final support for our critical evaluation of other people's thoughts as well as of our own.

This by way of defense against defamatory talk which I can scarcely believe has really come from the lips of one of my own students. In order not to put an even worse interpretation on it, I must assume that this is an indication of an extraordinarily poor memory.*

But no! There is still a third possibility. You know how human beings are, and how their concepts shift without their being aware of it, and so, because of the equivocations which have arisen, they do not really know what they are saying. This sort of human failing may be what has happened to those who call me an advocate of psychologism. And in fact, psychologism is supposed to be imputed not only to the subjectivist, but also to the man who believes that psychology has anything at all to contribute to epistemology and logic. But no matter how much I condemn subjectivism, I will not be misled into denying that truth. Rather, I am so convinced of it, that it would have to be paradoxical, even absurd, to me, if someone denied that knowledge is judgement and that judgement belongs to the domain of psychology. It also holds true that if beings other than ourselves share knowledge with us, what they share must fall within the domain of human psychology and is directly accessible to scientific inquiry only in this domain.

* Today we may still see many who, failing to recognize the distinctive nature of *Evidenz*, confuse logical validity with the genetic necessity of a thought, whether for the individual or for the whole human species. *I*, at least, both in my lectures and my writings, have always very firmly distinguished between lawfulness in the sense of natural necessity and in the sense of the correctness of an activity. Indeed, no one before me and not one after me (Husserl included) has been able to express himself with greater clarity and emphasis on this matter than I have.
[1] See above, p. 139, and the Introduction.

ADDITIONAL ESSAYS FROM BRENTANO'S *NACHLASS* CONCERNING INTUITIONS, CONCEPTS, AND OBJECTS OF REASON*

(Appendix to the 1924 Edition)

* [Editor's note: Despite blindness and advanced age, Brentano continued to function as an active and creative philosopher between 1911, the date of publication of the *Classification of Mental Phenomena* with its supplementary essays intended to "explain, defend, expand and correct" his theory (Appendix I), and his death in 1917. From the large mass of unpublished material available from Brentano's later years, Oskar Kraus selected the essays constituting Appendix II for inclusion in the edition he prepared for the *Philosophische Bibliothek* in 1924.]

XII *Thinking is Universal, Entities are Individual*
[*Dictated November 21, 1917.*]

There are philosophers who deny that we ever think of anything universal. Others, perhaps the majority, believe that we sometimes think in universal and sometimes in individual terms. And again, there are those who say that even if we think in an intuitive (*anschaulich*) way, we can still only think in universal terms. This is in direct opposition to the second opinion, because those who advance that view usually maintain that it is precisely our *intuitions* which are all individual and that only through abstraction from them do we succeed in thinking in a universal way. Berkeley was a famous proponent of the first view, Kant a famous proponent of the second, but the third point of view is undoubtedly the correct one. Neither so-called outer perception, nor what Locke called reflection and we might call inner perception, provide us with examples of *individual* intuitions. In the case of inner perception, no one can cite any attribute which individuates the intuition. If someone perceives himself making a judgement, there is nothing to prevent someone else doing so as well,[1] and he may indeed perceive himself as someone making a judgement about the same thing in entirely the same way. And two people could likewise have emotions which correspond with one another completely. In fact, it may be that there always are differences when we look at the sum total of inner experiences, but there would be no absurdity if the differences were all to disappear. And the number of individuals who would share them is sufficient proof that intuition is not individuated on that basis. Those who say that substantial determinations in inner perception are never entirely absent may be right. Nevertheless they cannot be cited as something which individuates intuition. They are restricted to generalities to such an extent that it is a matter of dispute whether that within us which thinks is corporeal or spiritual. It is easier to believe that outer perception reveals something individuated to us, e.g. a red point individuated by specification of color and place. But an advanced psychology teaches us that the sensory intuitions of vision (*Gesichtsanschauung*) present us with the colored thing with respect to its localizations, not *in modo recto* but *in modo obliquo*. What we

[1] That is to say, someone else could also perceive him as judging in exactly the same way.

311

think of, in the context of location, *in modo recto*, is only an un-qualified *place*,[2] from which the colored thing is intuitively perceived as in a certain direction and at a certain distance. *The same relationships of direction and distance, however, could be repeated with any spatial point, and along with the general character of the spatial point which is perceived* in modo recto[3] *the general character of outer intuition as a whole is demonstrated.* If the psychologists who study sensation have not become clearly and distinctly aware of the character of visual sensation just explained, Johannes Müller nevertheless touched on it when he speaks of an outward "projection", of the objects seen, as did Petroniewicz just recently when he maintained that the person seeing something perceives a certain point as the location of his Self and appears to be at a distance from that which he sees as colored.

[2] Brentano's theory is that we intuitively perceive an *unqualified* position completely generally, in order to refer to it as a center of the so-called "field of sensation." It is not the colored patch, or one filled with any other quality, then, which we intuitively perceive *modo recto*, but that unqualified spatial datum.

[3] I.e. with the generality of the spatial (local) intuitively perceived *in recto*. The question is: does Brentano mean that we intuitively perceive in *modo recto* an unqualified point, as center point in the proper sense of this word? According to him it is completely impossible for *a point in and of itself* to be presented; so we can only think of a point as the boundary of something bounded. See Carl Stumpf, *Über den psychologischen Ursprung unserer Raumvorstellung* (Leipzig, 1873), pp. 180 ff. and Essay XV of the present book. We should hold fast to one thing in any case: We do not intuitively perceive that spatial center as in any way *absolutely* determined, i.e. we are not given any ultimate specific spatial determination in intuitive perception. In this connection Brentano would no longer be in agreement with what Stumpf has stated on p. 181. Instead, it is his conviction that we have only "relative" spatial intuitive perceptions, and the knowledge that *actually* all spatial things must have individually ultimate (i.e. absolute) determinacy of position is knowledge which arises *a priori* from the concepts. (See the following Essay.) The opinion that we do *intuitively perceive* absolute, i.e. ultimate, differences of position has its explanation in the fact that we commonly import our *a priori* knowledge into observation, mingling the two, as Brentano explains in the concluding section of Book II, Chap. 6. Kant would even have intuitive perception of the possibility of infinite extension of the spatially real and therefore held the doctrine of an infinite intuition of space. It is a related mistake when Brentano and Stumpf and others following him supposed there are ultimate spatial differences intuitively perceived. Just as we cannot think of a surface without thinking of it as the boundary of a bounded three-dimensional thing, neither can we think of a point except in connection with something contiguous.

We can go further, however, and say that the characterization of visual sensation which has just been given holds true for all sensations. It is true of auditory sensations, for example, of which a great many people would deny localization entirely, even though the fact that we can tell the difference between a buzzing in the left ear or the right already clearly proves that they are localized. But if one studies it more closely, one finds that in this case, too, it is possible to speak of projection. The buzzing seems to be something from which an unqualified point stands at a certain distance in a certain direction, exactly like the colored object in the case of visual sensation. In this way not only is one buzzing in the ears located in relation to the other, but each of them is located in relation to colored objects which we see. This has often been so completely misunderstood that even people who wanted to admit a sensory space for different senses have had doubts as to whether we are dealing here with genuine space or a heterogeneous analogue.* Surely sound and color

---

* Stumpf is one of these people. Still, in his own writings we find a remark which testifies to the generality and merely relative differentiation of spatial position which we have insisted upon. He says that determinations of both temporal and spatial position are given without exception from a certain standpoint. In the case of time, that standpoint is the present, while past and future signify only a distance from the present; in spatial terms, here corresponds to now. When we see Stumpf thinking that the sensory spaces for different senses are not homogeneous but only analogous to one another, it follows that we would only be able to speak of "here" for different people in an analogous sense. But it must be true of each "here" that it is thought of in *modo recto* and everything else is thought in *modo obliquo* and relative to it. Perhaps Stumpf believed that the "here" thought of in *modo recto* was individuated, and then relative determination of other spatial points could be thought of as individuated through their relation to it.[4] But in truth there is nothing to be said for the view that in the case of space the "here" is thought of any less universally than "now" is in the case of time. And it is obvious that the latter appears without any specific or individual differences, for the present always arises completely undifferentiated from other present moments. Aristotle was convinced of the necessity of emphasizing this point.[5] But the "now" actually changes, so if it manifested itself with some special character, it would manifest itself falsely – a conclusion which Marty drew[6] but which led him to further very mistaken doctrines. To avoid them, one simply affirms the opposite view, namely, that the present, which alone is affirmed in *modo recto*, appears only in quite universal terms. We shall have to make a corresponding judgement about the spatial present – the "here" – as well.
[4] See Stumpf, *Über den psyshologschen Ursprung unserer Raumvorstellung*, p. 181. For this reason Stumpf believed in absolute location in perception.
[5] See my introduction, p. 376.
[6] In his posthumous work, *Raum und Zeit* (Halle, 1916).

313

phenomena are projected in the same space, and we can go even further and say that such projection from the same unqualified point takes place with all other sensory phenomena, such as sensations of taste and smell and touch and temperature, whether they are or are not accompanied by affects. We are, then, dealing here with a law which encompasses the entire realm of outer perception and we find, therefore, that our claim that neither inner nor outer perception ever reveals anything individual is fully confirmed.

But how does it happen that despite the fact that intuitive thought is so thoroughly universal, we can still very firmly maintain that everything which is must be individual, indeed that anyone who held the opposite view and said there could be two things with all attributes the same and not differentiated from one another in any way is involved in a self-contradiction? The answer is that the concept of there being two things implies that we do not mean by the one what we mean by the other. Only in this way would there be one thing and another. To be sure, they must both have in common the property of being a "thing" and they may have many other properties in common as well, but when one is thought of in terms of an exhaustive definition, it must be presented in some way that the other is not. We can go even further and say that the individuating attribute must be a positive determination, one which was merely negative would itself be universal and hence could not possibly be an individuating factor.

If we are not in a position to have an intuitive presentation of the individuating property of a thing in accordance with this, we can still say that it is in reality never absent, and it would be discovered in an exhaustive definition of the thing. The young Leibniz had already clearly recognized this when, upon taking his doctorate, he discussed the principle of individuation: *Omne individuum sua tota entitate individuatur.*

In view of the above, it is not difficult to see how we can think of an individual thing in an unintuitive way, however, even though we are incapable of thinking intuitively of one. We need only consider that, just as something which is conceived in specific terms is more fully conceived than something conceived in general terms, and just as every new specific differentiation supplements the concepts and hence restricts its range, a person who conceives of the thing in terms of its full definition would be conceiving of it as determined in such a way that it would be impossible for more than one thing to correspond to the concept. We then arrive at what Aristotle called τὸ καθ᾽ ἕκαστον or τὸ τί. We call it a certain thing, a *quoddam, une certaine chose.*

XIII   *Intuition and Abstract Presentation (Presentation with Intuitive and with Attributive Unity)*
[*Franz Brentano's last dictation, March 9, 1917, eight days before his death.*]

1. How is an intuition (*Anschauung*) distinguished from other presentations? – People have frequently said that in an intuition the object of presentation is something individual, but in a concept it is something general. Of course, some deny that we can ever have anything but an individual thing as an object of presentation. If someone thinks that the geometer does this when he sets up a theorem and gives a demonstrative proof of it, he is said to be deluding himself. You can convince yourself of this immediately, it is said, when you see how he looks at a particular triangle drawn in black and white on the blackboard in the course of his demonstration. The existence of general ideas is denied not only by the Medieval Nominalists, but by famous modern philosophers as well, Berkeley in particular. But their doctrine is certainly untenable; without general ideas it would not be possible to have general judgements or demonstrative proofs. The universal is not to be thought of as a collective which cannot be exhausted by induction. Kant did not let Berkeley win him over; he firmly maintained that there are general ideas and he called them concepts. He contrasted them with intuitions as particular presentations. We are supposed to have examples of the latter before us when we see or hear something, as well as when we have an inner perception of something. The ideas of space and time are also supposed to be presentations of particulars and therefore not concepts, but intuitions.

But here Kant has fallen into several errors. We do not have *a priori* ideas of an infinite three dimensional space and an infinite one dimensional time, and when we see or hear something or have an inner perception of a thinking subject, careful psychological study reveals that the presentations do not show us individual differences. No one who is having an inner perception of himself perceives anything different from what another person could at the same time have an inner perception of.[1] It is proof enough of this that he is aware of no individuating factor. With respect to outer perception, however, there emerges the relativity of localization and the lack of absolute determinations, the latter being the only things which could individuate. It is apparent, then, that although Berkeley wrongly denied the generality of certain ideas, Kant wrongly asserted the individuation of those we usually call intuitions.

[1] See Brentano's treatise on "Zeit und Raum," in *Kantstudien*, XXV, I (1921), and Essay XII.

2. Now since these intuitions do constitute a definite and distinct class of presentations, the question arises as to how we should characterize them in contrast to the others.

This can easily be explained by means of examples. Any sensation or any fantasy image (which differ from sensations only in their origin, not in their content) can be cited as an example. And presentations of *inner* perception can be included along with those of outer perception.[2] They are the starting point of our conscious life (*Vorstellungsleben*). But they lead to other presentations, which, even if they are not our *first* general ideas, can nevertheless be described as more general and more generalized than the first one. Thus the concept of red in general is abstracted from any particular localization in this or that direction and at this or that distance from a certain standpoint, and *the concept of the colored* is abstracted from the specific difference of red and preserves only that element which is common to red, blue, yellow, and so on. That which in contrast to sensation is simplified in content[3] we might refer to as an abstraction. But like sensations they still have a kind of simplicity which prompts us to group them with sensations as *presentations* of intuitive unity. In contrast to these presentations of intuitive unity, there are others which are unified only through a peculiar kind of association, composition, or identification[4] as, for example, when one forms the complex concept of a thing which is red, warm and pleasant-sounding.

No matter how familiar we all are with this identification, it probably requires an explanation. The first thing to be said is that it does not consist in a predicative judgement. It is not a judgement at all; it belongs rather in the realm of presentational consciousness. When I say "a warm red thing," I am not saying the same thing as "A red thing is warm," nor does "a red-colored thing," express the same thought as "A red thing is colored," or "A colored thing is red."[5]

---

[2] See the Introduction, pp. 392 ff., and Brentano's *Untersuchungen zur Sinnespsychologie*. What is involved is not pure presentation, but a presentation which takes something to be true, i.e., an instinctive belief. But this is of no importance to what follows.

[3] Content = object.

[4] Identification = attribution. See Supplementary Essay IV.

[5] "A red warm thing" is a synthesis of ideas (presentations), "A red thing is warm" is a judgemental synthesis; so is "A warm thing is red." The latter two judgemental syntheses (double judgements) are psychologically different, but logically equivalent. Furthermore, they are both logically equivalent to the simple thetic judgement: "A warm red thing exists," and "A red warm thing exists."

Furthermore the identification of which we are speaking is connected with the fact that because of their lack of individual specificity, two presentations with intuitive unity can become presentations of one and the same thing despite their difference in content.[6] That very thing which is red is also colored, and in coming to be or ceasing to be this red thing, it also comes to be or ceases to be this colored thing. *One and the same thing thus becomes the object of two presentations,* and someone who makes one and the same thing the object of two intuitive presentations[7] is doing precisely what we call identification. He arrives at what we call an idea not with intuitive, but rather with mere attributive unity.

In this connection there are still different cases to be distinguished. When we say, "a red warm thing," the two things presented in intuitive unity[8] are not totally identified but *identified only in terms of the subject.* It is possible for something red to remain the same red thing without being warm any more, but not without the continued existence of the substance (*Substanz*) which is the substance of this warm thing. The substance of the one and of the other are what are conceived as being totally identical in this case. The red thing and the warm are conceived as identical with each other only in terms of substance, but not totally identical with one another, nor is the red thing conceived as totally identical with the substance of the red thing.

We must also take notice of another difference. There are various kinds of intuitive presentation, since sometimes things are objects of presentation *in recto* and sometimes *in obliquo.* The same presentation does not have both a thing and someone denying the thing as its object, even if the latter is thought of as denying the thing who is an object of presentation *in modo recto*; the thing denied is an object of presentation *in modo obliquo* and furthermore the *modo obliquo* are diverse.[9] Now it can happen that two things both of which are thought of *in modo obliquo* are identified with one another, but it can also happen that something thought of *in modo recto* is identified with something thought of *in modo obliquo,* or that two things both of which are thought of *in modo obliquo* are identified. But then we always get ideas which lack *intuitive* unity and can only be said to have *attributive* unity.

[6] Content = object; more precisely: despite the difference in what they have as object. On this point see especially my Introduction, pp. 392 and 402 ff.

[7] What is meant is: of two presentations having "intuitive unity."

[8] Read: presented things.

[9] See O. Kraus, *Franz Brentano,* Sect. 12, et seq.; the Introduction; and Supplementary Essay III and the following.

317

We have affirmative and negative judgements. There is no such contrast in the realm of presentations. But we can think of someone making a negative judgement and of someone correctly denying something, so we can have a presentation *in obliquo* of something as denied and rightly denied. And in its case too there can be an identification,[10] as when I say, "An A which someone rightly denies." Here one is easily tempted to ascribe the contrast between affirming and denying to presentation itself rather as it is ascribed to judgements.[11] Hence I will give an explicit warning against this mistake. The contrast between affirming and denying no more pertains to presentation than the contrast of love and hate does. But this lack of contrast is entirely compatible with having as objects of thought a person who loves something and a person who hates something, a person who rightly loves something and a person who rightly hates something, and thus to have as object of thought in the *modo obliquo* what that person loves and what he hates, as "loved" and "hated" or "lovable" and "hateful" (*"liebenswert"* and *"hassenswert"*).[12] Here, too, we can then combine things by way of identification.

On the basis of what has just been discussed, what should we say about the question of whether, in the realm of presentation as we have just elucidated it, there might not be, along with identification, the opposite process which we could call detachment, isolation, separation, diversification, and the like? In discussing judgement, Aristotle spoke of synthesis and *diairesis* of subject and predicate. At the same time he remarked in this connection that the term *diairesis* as well as the term synthesis could well be extended to both classes. We are dealing here, however, with something which has to do with the contrast between the affirmative and negative attitude in judgement. We just stressed the fact that such a thing does not exist in presentation, and this seems to prove that we cannot speak of such a process in contrast to identification in the realm of presentational consciousness. We only have to say that just as the *modi obliqui* of presentation manifest various differences in general, the *modi obliqui* are also different when we are thinking of someone affirming or denying something. This will naturally have significance in the case in which what is thought of one way or another *in modo obliquo* becomes involved in an identification. If Aristotle said of the two classes of judgement which he first distinguished as synthesis and *diairesis* that they could also both be called synthesis, we will main-

[10] See the last paragraph of Essay IV and my note to it.
[11] Brentano undertook this attempt but gave it up as mistaken. See his letter in the Introduction, p. 386.
[12] See *The Origin of our Knowledge of Right and Wrong.*

tain with the utmost conviction that in those cases in which one might speak of diversification instead of identification in the realm of presentation, it is the expression *identification* which rightly characterizes the nature of the process.

3. We have thus been led to differentiate the following classes of presentation: there are those which have intuitive unity and those which have attributive unity, the latter being obtained by the identification of those which have intuitive unity, whether *in modo recto* or *in modo obliquo*. Those which have intuitive unity are then divided further into intuitions and abstractions, the latter of which are obtained by *simplifying* and generalizing intuitions, but may not be distinguished from them by saying that they alone are general while what we intuit manifests itself to us as individuated.

4. With this we have rejected as mistaken all of those theories, whether they are called psychological or epistemological, which wish to ascribe *a priori* as opposed to empirical ideas to us, whether they be intuitions or unintuitive concepts not arising from the abstracting and joining of intuitions. If they have managed to gain entry, it has to do with the imperfect state of psychological analysis, which was so extreme that no one even noticed that there are certain words which were supposed to be names of particular objects (whether things or non-things), when in fact there were no such objects at all, as, for example, redness (*Röte*) as distinct from a red thing (*Rotes*), extension as distinct from the extended, possibility, reality, necessity, being, non-being, and indeed also the possible, the impossible and the thought-of thing. A person who says he is thinking of a contemplated mountain is really thinking *in recto* of someone who is contemplating a mountain, and he is thinking of the mountain itself in a certain *modus obliquus*.[13]

5. But there is one more pressing question. If, as we said, not merely our abstractions but also our intuitions are general ideas, how do we come to speak of particular presentations at all? Are there any such things? Obviously they could only be found among those which are the products of identification. But how could identification lead from universal ideas to individuation? Are we perhaps speaking of individual presentations without having any, even among those obtained by identification? And are we even certain that there could be anything of the sort? And how is it supposed to be made intelligible that, as the most competent philosophers suppose, we quite legitimately go still further and say that in reality there can be nothing universal at all, nothing at all which does not have individuating determinations? Leibniz in particular

---

[13] There is a more nearly exact discussion of this in the following essays.

expressed this point of view in his *principium individuationis* and in doing so, presumably without knowing it, he was merely repeating a thesis of Aristotle's, who made such extensive use of it in his *Metaphysics* that he wanted to use it even to prove the unity of the divine principle. Shouldn't we be inclined to suspect, rather, that there is nothing at all corresponding to the *principium individuationis* – that everything there is has a universal character so that it could occur, just as it is, in as many instantiations as you like? Newton, Clarke, and, in express opposition to Leibniz, Euler, maintained this of at least certain classes.[14] But if it is possible in one class, it would be equally possible, one would think, in any other class. Schopenhauer said that space and time were principles of individuation, but according to Euler it is precisely here that there is no individuation. Given that, would it not be easy to conclude that there is no individuation at all? That is what it would come to, going beyond those contemporary philosophers who say that universals as such have being along with individuals, and saying instead that true being should only be ascribed to the universal.

6. In proceeding to answer this question, we begin by granting that it is correct to infer that none of our presentations with intuitive unity can be particular. On the other hand, it is obvious that, if they are all general, they are not all general to the same degree. For example, both the concept of something colored and the concept of something red are general, but not *equally* so, for the concept of the colored comprehends the blue as well as the red, and so on. But the red and the blue are mutually exclusive and so we arrive at the concept of another, the concept of a different thing, and at the concept of two. For the latter arises from the combination of one with another. If we now ask whether it is possible for a red thing and a red thing to be two, just as a red thing and a blue thing are two, the answer is that this is only possible if the one red thing is *another* red thing, or the one is different from the other. Just as the red is distinguished from the colored thing, then, the one red thing must somehow be distinguished from the other red thing. This would be so if I saw a third thing separated in one direction from the one red thing and in another direction from the other. Another case would be that in which I think of something separated from the one red thing and the other in the same direction but different *distances* away. But at this point I can very well arrive at the idea of a concept *for which further differentiation is not possible at all*, and then I would have the idea of the concept of something individual.

Once this has been attained, it is easy to understand how we also

14 See Brentano in *Kantstudien*, XXV, 1.

come to know that there cannot be anything other than individuals. For supposing the opposite to be true would only mean that we would think of something completely in terms of all its determinate properties (*Bestimmungen*) and think of something like it in all of these properties, and hence not at all different from it, and yet the one would not be the other, which is contradictory, since the totality of partial determinations (*Teilbestimmungen*) makes up the complete determination (*Gesamtbestimmung*). If all of the partial determinations are the same, then what is defined by them as a whole must be the same whole. To be without any difference means to be one and the same. In the Medieval period, the following definition was given of the *one: unum est quod est indivisum in se et divisum ab omni alio.*
[The dictation breaks off at this point.]

XIV *On Objects of Thought*
[*Dictated on February 22, 1915.*]

1. Anyone who thinks thinks of something. And because this is part of the concept of thinking, this concept cannot be a unitary one unless the little word "something," too, has a single meaning.

2. But what *is* the meaning of this word? Should we say, something means the same as a thought-object (*ein Gedachtes*)? – This interpretation does not seem to be acceptable. What is a thought-object supposed to be if not something which is thought of or something which someone is thinking of, and here it will certainly not do to substitute the recurring "something" in order to elucidate a thought-object.

One might also try the following. We can say not only that whoever is thinking is thinking of something, but also that he is thinking of *something as something, as for example one thinks of a man as a man or in a less definite way as a living creature.* But that second something we added, and always have to add, must obviously be univocal, too, if the term for thinking is univocal. But nothing is more apparent than that this second something is not to be taken in the sense of "a thought-object." Someone who is thinking of a stone is not thinking of it as a thought-of stone, but as a stone. Otherwise, when he affirms it he would also be affirming it only as a thought-object, and a person who is denying the stone will do that, once he is conscious of denying it, just as much as the person who is affirming it will.

3. Now if the "something" is a univocal concept, it can only be a generic concept under which everything which is supposed to be an object of thought must fall. And consequently it must be maintained that anyone who is thinking must have a thing (*Reales*) as his object

and have this as his object in one and the same sense of the word. This is in opposition to Aristotle, who denied that there was any generic concept common to the ten categories he distinguished and to many moderns who say that we do not always have a thing, but often have a non-thing (*Nicht-Reales*), as our object.

4. Yet there seems to be this objection: many terms in our vocabulary do not seem to designate a thing. This is so of the entire class of abstractions which are associated with concrete terms, as "thinking" is associated with "thinker," and "shape" with "a thing which has shape." Obviously the thinking of the thinker is not the thinker, it is distinct from him (a thing), and yet it is not another thing.[1] If someone wanted to claim the thinking is a thing he would have to say that it constitutes a part of another thing, the thinker. If the thinker ceased, there would still be another part of the thinker left and the thinker would be interpreted as a collective made up of two things. It would also be assumed, conversely, without absurdity, that the other part could cease to exist and only the thinking – the very same individual thinking unchanged in any way – would remain. But this is impossible.

It is still simpler to see that terms such as "nothing," an "impossibility." a "truth," as for example, that no man is a lion, and that all even numbers are divisible by two, are not properly called things (*Dinge, Realia*). But is it not true, nevertheless, that we make such terms the subjects of sentences, and we even say that there are "truths," the "impossibility" of a square circle exists and the like? How can this be reconciled with the fact that only things can be objects of our thinking?

5. I answer that *this is explained by the fact that not every word in our language taken by itself means something. Many of them signify something only in combination with others.*[2] Prepositions and conjunctions are proof of this. And besides this, one must take account of the fact that language makes use of many fictions for the sake of brevity; in mathematics, for example, we speak of negative quantities less than zero, of fractions of one, of irrational and imaginary numbers, and the like, which are treated exactly like numbers in the strict and proper sense.[3] And so language has abstract as well as

---

[1] We have before us the peculiar relationship of substance and accident (mode). See the notes to Book Two, Chap. 4, and then Book One, Chap. 1, note 10 and my Introduction, pp. 407–8.

[2] Mill spoke of syncategorematic expressions; Marty called them "synsemantica." See O. Funke, *Innere Sprahformc: Eine Einführung in A. Marty's Sprachphilosophie* (Reichenberg i. B., 1924), pp. 21 f., 23, 84.

[3] In my opinion, "numbers in the strict and proper sense," 2, 3, 4, etc., is synsemantic since it must be supplemented by "things."

concrete terms and uses them in many ways as if they referred to things which are parts of the relevant concrete entity. It also says of the abstraction that it is and is in the concrete thing. If one does not wish to be seduced into a great tangle of speculations here, one must become clear about the fact that this is all said in a very loose sense. What is here said to be does not exist in the strict and proper sense. Instead, everything must first be translated into concrete language. This, as Leibniz noted, can be done without any change of meaning, in order to make clear to oneself what it really is that is affirmed or denied in this case.[4]

Even when we say that there is something in our mind or heart, because we think about it and love it, we are using being in an entirely improper sense, and so an object of thought as an object of thought and an object of love as an object of love are certainly not things. The only thing which should be called the object of thought here is the person thinking and the person loving, who are things as such,[5] just as it is equally true, then, that what they are thinking of and loving are things (as, for example, when someone thinks of a house or feels love for his friend).

If someone says the impossibility of a round square exists someone who carelessly heeds only the grammatical form may think that he is affirming something, while in fact he is negating something, since he is apodictically denying the round square. In so doing he is thinking about the round and the square and in both cases the reference has a thing as its object.

6. Still another objection could be raised. It could be said that we think of universals in various ways, but nothing can exist unless it is individuated as a thing, hence we also think of non-things. But if the objector pays attention to the way in which we stated the requirement, he will see immediately that his objection is entirely futile.

The concept of a thing is itself a universal and the most general of them all. *Less general* concepts fall under it just as much as do the particular things to which these concepts truly apply. The fact that they are entirely determined and individuated in no way contradicts this; on the contrary, something which was not individuated in any way would no longer correspond to the concept. Thus a triangle

---

[4] See Leibniz, *Nouveaux Essais*, Book II, Chap. XXIII, Sect. 1, and *Dissertatio de stilo, philosophico Nizolii*, 1670, XVII. – See also Anton Marty, *Die "Logische," "lokalistische" und andere Kasustheorien* (Halle, 1910), p. 96, which diverges from Brentano's path at decisive points, however.
[5] That is to say the person thinking and the person loving are "objects" in the sense of things, just as what they are concerned with in thinking and loving are things. See the Introduction.

which was not right-angled nor obtuse-angled nor acute-angled would not be affirmed to be a triangle without contradiction.

7. All of our thinking has a thing as its object. The thinker himself belongs among his objects of thought[6] and he is also a thing. But there are various ways in which we refer to things in thought. We have already seen that a person sometimes thinks in more specific terms and sometimes in less specific terms, as we think of the same person at one time as a man and at another as a living creature. Our way of referring to a person in thought also differs depending upon whether we merely have a presentation of him, or at another time make him the object of an affirmative or negative judgement, or at still another time, refer to him in terms of an emotional attitude, i.e. love or hate.[7]

8. Just as judgement is divided into affirmation and denial and emotional attitude into love or hate, presentations also refer in various ways. *In particular, it is unmistakable that there is a great difference between something being an object of presentation* in recto *or* in obliquo. So when I think of someone denying God, I am thinking of the person himself *in recto*, but of God *in obliquo* and this always occurs when one thinks of a so-called *relative* (*Relativ*). If I think of the larger *in recto*, then I think of the smaller *in obliquo*. If I think of the cause *in recto*, then I think of the effect *in obliquo*. Also, when I think of a boundary *in recto*, I must think *in obliquo* of something bounded by it, and if I am thinking of something which differs from something else in color or size, place or time, here too, in addition to the thing I am thinking of *in recto*, I am thinking *in obliquo* of something else from which it is differentiated.

9. We see that there is one *modus rectus* as opposed to a great number of *modi obliqui*. People have already long since divided them into three classes of relations, into *mental, causal*, and *comparative* references to an object. We should not overlook the fact, however, that in each of them the *modus obliquus* varies; for example, even when something is more or less different from another, the *modus obliquus* in which we think of the latter is already no longer quite the same.

10. Another classification of the *modi obliqui* appears to be especi-

---

[6] That is to say the person thinking refers to himself in secondary consciousness as thinking. See Supplementary Essay II.

[7] According to Brentano, generalization (abstraction, universal presentation) is no new way (no new mode) of presentation, and so it is not analogous to the direct and indirect modes. It belongs to the "differences in the object." Brentano's theory becomes clear from Essay XII and XIII. If on one occasion I think of a man as a man, and on another as a living creature, at each time I have him as my object *as something different*.

ally important, however. It divides them into two groups; first those in which, if the first term or fundament of the relation exists, the terminus of the relation also exists, as for example, if Caius is taller than Titus, not only Caius, but Titus, too, exists. Secondly, in contrast with this class, there are other cases in which a person thinks about something, has a presentation of it, denies it, wishes for it, etc. That the thinker exists, however, in no way implies that what he is thinking of exists.[8]

11. With comparative relations, such as "Caius is taller than Titus," we find that the existence of the fundament requires the existence of the terminus as well. But there are certain cases of a more complicated kind, in which the comparative relation is mixed with the mental reference to an object, as for example, when I say that Caius is taller than Titus thinks Sempronius is. In this case the existence of the terminus is not required. Titus must exist as well as Caius, but it is not *his* height which is involved, but the height of Sempronius. But since it is not a matter of the height Sempronius has, but of the height imputed to him, then what has being in thought would have to belong to being in the proper sense, if Sempronius were also required to exist as someone shorter than Caius. We have seen that this is not the case.

12. But there is still another kind of comparative relation where we must deny that the thing thought of *in obliquo* must also exist along with the thing thought of *in recto*. This deserves our special attention. It is the case in which one thing is earlier or later than another. If something is later than something else, it is by no means required that the latter thing also exist, but only that it has been. Similarly, if something is earlier than another, it is not required that the latter

[8] *This* classification does not seem to be one which concerns the modes of presentation themselves. Further, note should be taken of the fact that in the case of so-called comparative relations we cannot take so-called *denominationes extrinsecae*, i.e. assertions about things lying entirely outside the subject, to be relative predicates. In a large treatise on metaphysics dated February 6, 1916, Brentano says: "In view of what has been discussed, we must say of comparative determinations that, apart from what appears in them as *denominatio extrinseca*, there is only a more or less *indefinite idea* of a substantial or accidental determination which would fall under one of the classes already otherwise differentiated." See also Kraus, *Franz Brentano*, pp. 44 ff. If I say, "The number of inhabitants of Germany is greater than that of Holland," I am making two assertions since in this case I am affirming the existence of the inhabitants of both countries. The linguistic expression in this case mixes up a relative attribute with the affirmation of the existence of something which lies entirely outside the subject – with a *denominatio extrinseca*. See Introduction, pp. 373 ff.

exists, but that it will be. In the one case, that which is thought of *in modo obliquo* can no longer be, in the other it does not yet need to be. We immediately notice the difference between this case and spatial distances, for if something is at some spatial distance from another thing, the thing from which it is distant exists just as much as it does itself.

Still other comparative relations can be formed, however, in which the existence of the fundament does not require the existence of the terminus. These occur in combination with other relative determinations similar to those we have seen earlier to occur in the combination of comparative relations with mental references to an object. We find this, for example, when we say, "Caius is taller than Titus was and he is richer than his son is going to be."

13. The similarity of this case to that of mental reference to an object is unmistakable, and yet the difference between the one case and the other is very noticeable. Thinking of a thing does not imply being at any distance from it, and consequently with thinking one cannot speak of something which corresponds to the contrast between things which are earlier or later. And consider the case in which someone thinks of someone thinking of someone who is again thinking of someone, and so on; here we get a series of things thought of *in obliquo*, a series in which every member is in a certain way further and further removed from being thought of *in recto*. One could certainly find a certain similarity between this case and the case in which something is earlier than something else will be, which is earlier than still another thing will be, and so on, where with the addition of intermediate members, the distance from the first thing affirmed *in recto* as earlier is increased. But there we have a series of discrete members and here a continuous series. And perhaps it also makes an essential difference that there all of the intermediate members must be thought of. But in the case of the interval between the earlier and the later, a more remote relationship, with the apparent omission of any closer relationships, can be thought of.

14. It will be necessary for us to make the distinctive character of this class of relations somewhat clearer. What we are concerned with are *temporal relations*, and the question arises first of all how we come to understand them. It seems certain that we can never think of anything without thinking of something as present,[9] that is to say, however, *as on a boundary line* which exists as the connecting point of an otherwise non-existent continuum or as providing its beginning or its end. So along with the idea of the present, we also get those of the past and future *in modo obliquo* as that the boundary of which is formed by the present.

[9] I.e. as "now"; see Essay XII, note 3.

15. A thing can be present in three different ways:

1. By bringing something in the past to an end.
2. By beginning something in the future, and
3. By doing both and so serving as the connecting link between past and future, in which case we say that something continues to be. In the continua of which the present is the boundary, there are further boundaries to be distinguished, *ad infinitum*. Some are to be seen as those which *have* formed the connecting link between earlier and later, others as those which *will* form it. We can even say of the present boundary that, as it now is, it was once in the future and as future it was located successively at a continuous series of intervals away from being present. And we can just as well say of it that, quite as it is now, it will have been and will be successively located at a continuous series of intervals away from being the present.

We have said that the present as the present constitutes the end of the past and the beginning of the future. But we can also say that in becoming present a thing ceases to be future, and begins to be past. It is true that we ordinarily say that one and the same thing can continue to exist and, therefore, that it holds true of it at the same time that it has been, is, and will be. But this continued existence cannot be understood except as a continuity of ending and beginning, and so as a continual renewal of the same thing. And the continuous aggregate of these renewals produces, then, the length of its duration, which is only in terms of a boundary line; in terms of everything else it does not now exist, but was or will be.

16. Since the very same thing at one time is, at another time was, and at another time will be, it is obvious that when we specify something as present, past, or future, it is not a matter of citing diverse real attributes. We do this no more here than when we say that something exists. Indeed, when we say that something exists and that something presently exists, it comes to the same thing, and when something is said to be past or future, this must therefore also refer to a mode of thinking. The thing which is said to be is affirmed in the strict sense. The thing which is said to be past or future, however, is obviously not being affirmed in the strict sense, but only in a loose and improper sense, just as a thing is only affirmed in a loose and improper sense when we say it exists in thought. And just as it is not the thing thought which is being affirmed in the strict sense, but the thinker as thinking of the thing thought, so too, every time something is affirmed as past or present, we will be affirming something present as later than the past thing, or earlier than the future thing. If we could not say of something present, which is a certain

interval from the past or future thing, that it exists, then it could no longer be said of the one that it has been nor of the other that it will be. Also, everything past or future must be past or future by some definite interval from the present. So everything seems to point to the fact that when something is affirmed as past or future, we are dealing with an affirmation, and thus also with a presentation *in modo obliquo*.

17. But just as there is great diversity in general among the *modi obliqui* of presentation this class is easily differentiated from all others and is most especially distinguished by the fact that, without its being in combination with a mental reference to an object,[10] it is a comparative mode in which the terminus of the comparison does not have to exist if its fundament does. But this is connected with the fact that in temporal relations we are concerned with relationships based on a multiple and diverse continuity of modes of presentation, which produce corresponding modifications in judgement and in emotional attitude.

From what has been said, people will understand my position well enough to recognize that, in my view, if something past or future is to be distinguished from what is, in the strict sense of the word, it is not to be distinguished in the sense of being merely something which has being in thought. It exists, rather, in the same sense in which a thing exists when it can be said of it that something is to such and such an extent later or earlier than it, while it, for its part, is not earlier or later than the other to this same extent, but rather was or will be.

18. The few points we have made, which in part only repeat things that are common knowledge, nevertheless include many things that are worth noting and have consequences which are of the greatest significance.

I stress the fact that those who want to trace the origin of our idea of time and our idea of "before" and "after" back to differences in sense-objects, as is done with the origin of our ideas of space, and of next to, above, and behind, are on the wrong track. To be sure, when we have a presentation of a succession of notes in a melody, we are having a presentation of a number of things following one after the other (*ein Nacheinander*), just as when we see flecks of color in our visual field, we are aware of a number of things alongside of one another (*ein Nebeneinander*). But in the latter case all of the colored flecks appear to exist uniformly as do their spatial differences, but in the former case only *one* of the notes appears to exist and it, too, will subsequently appear to us as quite the same thing

---

[10] Object = to something as object.

yet no longer existent, but rather as a note from which the one that does exist appears to be separated. And thus it appears itself to be to a certain extent removed from existing. And it is precisely this which makes the whole difference with regard to before and after. And so a person could in no way think of it in its distinctive temporal characteristic without thinking of something as present (*gegenwärtig*).[11] This indicates that it is an object of presentation only *in obliquo* and not *in recto*.

The objection might be raised against this that there are cases in which a note is followed by a *rest*. Then one hears nothing as present, yet the note still appears to be past and, if the rest continues, even longer past. Here, then, the note is supposed to be given in experience as past in and of itself and consequently *in modo recto*. But this overlooks the fact that when the note appears to be past, one always simultaneously sees himself as perceiving or, so to speak, hearing the note as past, and as appearing in inner perception with like intensity.

Among other things this leads to a new and quite convincing refutation of those who deny that our outer perception is always accompanied by inner perception. If this were so it would then be impossible to experience outer phenomena as past.

19. People have often asked whether we can be certain that the temporal continuum goes in a straight line. The answer to the question is affirmative, as certainly as "before" and "after" are precisely converse relationships, and ending and beginning are contradictory alternatives. We have seen that in the case of simple duration, where time is noticed without the addition of any variation in objects such as motion or change of quality, we are dealing with nothing but a continuous ending and beginning of one and the same thing. The length of the duration corresponds, then, to the interval between the first temporal beginning and the final temporal ending.

A further question has been raised as to whether we can be immediately certain that there is one *single* time and that it somehow has an influence on or underlies every temporal thing in the way that spatial extension underlies the sense-qualities. Taking the above discussion into account, we see that this is not the case.

This is not to say that it cannot be proved that everything which falls within our experience endures only because it is steadily renewed by the creative influence of the first immediately necessary principle; that this first principle manifests a perfectly uniform infinitesimal change which contradicts neither its necessity nor its uniform perfection, but is rather required by it; and further, that as

---

[11] I.e. as "now"; see Essay XII, note 3.

a consequence of the change in the first supporting principle, all creatures, too, manifest a certain uniform variation in their continued existence by virtue of which everything which exists at the same time bears a certain common characteristic, which is, however, transcendent. In order for us to comprehend it, God himself would have had to become an object of our intuitive awareness.[12]

But we can say that not just human beings and other animals, but every conscious being, thinks of things with a certain temporal mode, as surely as it thinks of things at all; among these modes are the present as *modus rectus* and a past and future as *modi obliqui*. We can assert this no less confidently than we can assert that all beings who make judgements affirm and deny.

It is true that the continuum of temporal modes is not unlimited for us. But rather in the way that our thought goes beyond sensory space, it also goes beyond what might be called sensory time and is consequently able to extend times indefinitely into the past and future.

The differentiation of time as a continuum which consists of past, present and future, bears the character of a primary continuum. The endurance and varying course of things in time, on the other hand, has the character of a secondary continuum.[13] Only of the life of the first divine principle and the variation in that distinctive characteristic shared by all things which exist simultaneously does this fail to hold true.

XV *On the Term "Being" in its Loose Sense, Abstract Terms, and*
Entia Rationis
[*Dictated on January 30, 1917.*]

1. That which has being as object has, as such, no genuine being. This is equally true whether one says, in general terms, that an

---

[12] It is only the continuum of modes of presentation or judgement which falls within intuitive perception, then. Temporal "differences in object" are not directly perceived; *the same* note "A" appears to us first as present, then as past. But transcendentally a continuum of substantive differences must also correspond to the temporal state or change. – The more detailed reasoning in support of this idea is given in the essays on the problem of time.

[13] An account of the difference between "primary" and "secondary" continua" is given in Brentano's unpublished studies on the problem of continuity. There are multiple continua; the spatial surface is the primary continuum as compared with the color which modifies it. In the case of rest and motion the temporal continuum is the primary one; the place which persists or changes with time is the secondary, and so on. Brentano's investigations on this matter extend far back and are very numerous.

object of thought exists, or whether one says specifically that an object of Caius' thought exists as thought of by Caius. And it holds true again if one says still more specifically that an object of presentation exists as presented, something presented *in recto* exists as presented *in recto*, or something presented *in obliquo* as presented *in obliquo*, whereupon still further specifications of the way in which it is presented *in obliquo* can be adduced (the temporal mode is one of these). It is equally true if one specifically says that something judged exists as the object of someone judging, and again if one says that something affirmed or denied exists as object of someone affirming or denying it, or that something denied with evidence exists as object of someone denying it with evidence and so on, or that something loved exists as the object of someone loving it.

There is another question which is connected with the question of whether something which has being as object has being in the strict sense, and that is the question whether concepts, presentations, phenomena, contents of judgement, judgements, images, fantasies, affects, inferences, decisions, doubts, suspicions, plans, intentions, hopes, fears and so on, have being in the strict sense. Naturally we always have in mind those cases in which it is true to say that there is a concept, a presentation, an intention, a judgement.

Additional questions connected with this are whether a universal, a category, a species and a differentia have being in the strict sense of the word; this applies, of course, only to those cases in which they are truly said to be. Indeed, in these cases it would seem as though we cannot always say that a genus or a species exists in the same sense of the word, for sometimes we are thinking of the generic concept and sometimes of the collection of all those things which fall under the generic concept. One might perhaps say that a certain genus has died out, even though the generic concept still exists in us and could never appropriately be described as having died out. The same holds true of species, and equally of universals, for both the species and the genus are universals. People have often argued over the question of whether universal entities exist in reality, and the reason it has been so difficult to agree on this probably stems from the fact that the question is ambiguous. It is essentially the same ambiguity which we find in the question of whether a genus exists, where it is usually said that it exists and continues to exist provided there are individual things which fall under the generic concept. But if in asking about the existence of a genus, someone is thinking of the existence of the generic concept, he can say that a genus exists if someone is thinking this generic concept. But this will be an instance of "being" in the loose sense which applies to the object of thought. Even if we say as in the first case that a genus continues to be, we are still speaking in the loose sense of the term. In order to speak of "being" in the strict sense one would have to say that there are in reality individual things which fall under the generic concept (an equivocation on the term "genus"), but that the generic concept does not exist in reality. The question of whether the major and the minor premises of a syllogism as well as the conclusion also have being in a strict sense or only in a loose one is itself connected with the question concerning what has being as an object.

Another part of this whole area is the question of whether we are concerned with "being" in the strict sense when we say the rose is a flower. "The rose," does not seem to have as much being as a rose; we seem to be thinking of the universal which, as such, exists only in thought and in this case only as an object.

Now should we say that by a concept we mean an object of thought, or perhaps something thought of in a certain special way as such, and should we say the same thing of a presentation, a phenomenon, a content of judgement? In the case of concepts, we also speak of their content and extension, and the question of whether the content of a concept is its extension is to be answered in the negative. Now how is all this interrelated? Do any of them have being in any other than a loose and improper sense, and does perhaps even this loose and improper sense vary? All of this needs to be considered. Nevertheless, from the very beginning there seems to be hardly any doubt but that we are dealing with "being" in a loose and improper sense, for reasons which stem from what we have said about being as an object, and at best some new reasons will be added.

If we wish to achieve perfect clarity concerning the questions here discussed, we must, as we just said, take into account the possibility of equivocations such as we encountered in our example of the term "genus." Furthermore, we must also pay attention to the fact that although whenever a word is used it is related to a meaning, there are still differences in the way this comes about, since many words can be used by themselves, but some can only be used in conjunction with other words, and so are designated as merely synsemantic (*mitbedeutende*) words. Prepositions, conjunctions, adverbs, genitive cases and many others are included among these so-called synsemantic words. Substantives and adjectives have been included among those which have meaning by themselves, although they are ordinarily used only as parts of speech. This was done because they are said to evoke ideas in and of themselves and, what is more, to evoke the idea of the thing which, thought of *in modo recto*, is associated with the word. But it is doubtful whether nouns and adjectives are not often synsemantic too. So, particularly in all the cases in which a term is used as the name of an *ens rationis* of the kind we have just been contemplating, we should consider whether it is really possible to say that here the name by itself designates an *ens rationis* in the same way as in other cases names designate real things. If a thing which is thought of can, as thought-of, be an object just as truly as a real thing can, then the question must be answered in the affirmative. It is to be answered negatively if it should turn out that when we believe we are having a presentation *in recto* of something thought-of, we are really only having a presentation *in recto* of someone thinking of a thing, just as it is also true that when we affirm something as thought-of, the truth of the matter is that we are really doing nothing but acknowledging someone thinking of it. The correct interpretation would then be that someone, on hearing the words "something thought-of" ("*ein Gedachtes*") is thereby led to have a presentation *in recto* of something thinking. In doing so, since the thinking subject as such is one term in a relation, still another thing becomes an object of presentation *in obliquo* as terminus of the relation.

With other terms the question again arises whether they have meaning in and of themselves or only synsemantically. This applies in particular to the *abstract terms*[1] which we usually derive from concrete ones, for example, the term "size" ("*Grösse*") from "a thing with a size," ("Grosses") "thinking" ("Denken") from "a thinking thing" ("Denkendes"). One will scarcely claim that "size" or "thinking" exist by themselves and it seems equally false that they could be thought of by themselves. I shall always have to have a presentation of something with size or of someone thinking. Shall I then also be in a position to distinguish its size as one part of it, or will it all come down to my distinguishing the thing as having a certain size, for example as having the size of a cubic foot, from the thing as having a certain shape, for example as being spherical? The spherical thing is not the spherical shape, however, and the thing which is a cubic foot large is not the size of a cube. It is the sphere not the spherical shape which has being in the strict sense and so too it is the thing which has size not the size. And just as they alone have being in the strict sense, they alone seem to be present to the mind in the strict and proper sense.

When we speak above of judgement, denial, and affirmation, the question arises whether we are to understand by these terms judging, denying, and affirming, which are the abstract forms of someone

---

[1] The word "abstract" has quite a different meaning in connection with "abstract terms" than it does where there is talk of abstract ideas. "Largeness" ("Grösse") is an "abstract term," a grammatical abstractum. "A large thing" ("Grosses") signifies an abstract concept, i.e. a concept which is achieved by the so-called process of abstraction.

judging (*Urteilendes*), someone denying (*Leugnendes*), and someone affirming (*Anerkennendes*), or whether we mean by them something which is thought of, denied, affirmed in a certain way, which exists in the thinker as object in a certain qualified way. Or do we perhaps want to say that "affirmation" is an abstract term, though not synonymous with "affirming," but an abstraction which is related to the concrete term "something affirmed" in the same way as the abstraction "affirming" is related to the concrete term "affirming subject"? In the same way, "denial" would be something to be regarded as the abstract form of "something denied." Similarly, as the thing denied is related to the term "denial," the thought-of thing would be related to the "thought," the thing presented to the "presentation," the thing desired to the "desire," what is conceptually present to the "concept," the thing sensed to the "sensation," the thing perceived to the "perception," and the thing appearing to the "appearance." Here the question would also arise as to what we are to understand by "phenomenon"; does it mean the same as "appearance" or as "the thing which appears"?

But people go even further than this in the formation of abstract terms. Having in mind a concept, for example, they speak not merely of its content insofar as there is something objectively before the person who has the concept, but insofar as this thing or that *falls* under this concept, more or less, they also speak *of the extent of the concept* and then, with regard to this extent they also speak of the limits of the extent of the concept. Should it be proved that the abstract term, "concept," has no independent meaning to begin with, the same thing would naturally apply to the other abstractions just mentioned. Anyone ascribing independent meaning to them would be mistaken and would be thinking of something which truly exists neither in reality nor in thought. It would be a question of someone erroneously believing that he was joining a word to an idea, when he does not have such an idea at all.[2]

This is also true of the case in which someone says that he associates with the term "actuality" something presented *in modo recto* which is a part of an actual thing and by virtue of which the actual thing is actual.[3]

A certain group of equivocations needs special attention. When we say a man is thought of, "man" no longer refers to a real entity and no longer refers to anything in and of itself. What is involved is a

[2] The more precise term here would be "concept," but "conceptual thinker," or better, "someone thinking of something conceptually".

[3] "Actuality" here means the Aristotelian *energeia, entelechia*, which, being added on to matter as its form, first makes it an actual thing. See Franz Brentano, *Aristoteles und seine Weltanschauung* (Leipzig, 1911).

thought-of man and if he is affirmed, what is really being affirmed is only someone who is thinking of him. The same thing also holds true if I say, "a man was" or "a man will be tomorrow." If a past man is affirmed, what is actually being affirmed in the strict sense is a thing as being at some distance from him in time, as being later than he is in time. Strictly speaking, a past thing has being no more than a thought-of thing.

2. In the foregoing we have introduced a "thought-of thing" as an *ens rationis*. It became clear that when something is affirmed as being thought-of, it is being affirmed in a loose and improper sense, but that nevertheless there is also something affirmed in the strict and proper sense, namely the person thinking of it. So we see that we are dealing here with a relation in which something appears as fundament and something as terminus. And if what makes its appearance as fundament is affirmed in the strict sense, what appears as terminus is affirmed in the loose sense; the one is affirmed *in recto*, the other *in obliquo*.

We found the same thing when we introduced a past or a future thing as another example of *entia rationis*. It became clear that here, too, we are concerned with a relation in which, when the fundament is affirmed in the proper sense and *in recto*, the terminus is affirmed in the improper sense and *in obliquo*. Indeed, someone who affirms that there was something yesterday is not affirming it, but is affirming something else as being a day later than it, and therefore at a temporal distance from it while it does not exist at all.

There are *Relativa* of very diverse kinds involved in this case and that, yet they all have this in common: the terminus, as distinct from the fundament, is an *ens rationis*. *May the same thing perhaps be said generally of all Relativa? Do they all have a real fundament and a terminus which is an ens rationis?*[4] So it would appear, yet objecttions can be raised. If one says that Caius is smaller than Titus, Titus as terminus seems to be just as real as Caius, who is the fundament of this relational determination. But a closer look reveals that anyone saying Caius is smaller than Titus, in making this comparative determination, is doing something else besides; he is making Titus the object of an affirmation. But this is not always the case in making comparisons. Indeed, one can also say Caius is smaller than Titus will be, or than Titus was a year ago, or than Titus would be if he were still alive, or than I thought he was, or

[4] In a metaphysical treatise dated December 16, 1916, Brentano asserts "The object present to mind in *modo recto* must exist if the relative is supposed to exist, but the one present to mind in *modo obliquo* need not exist, except in special cases, for example, someone affirming something with evidence cannot exist unless his object also exists."

than a man I am imagining. Accordingly *that with which something is compared, so far as it is compared with it,* seems to be an *ens rationis* just as much as something thought-of as being thought-of.

Reference to causal relations could constitute another objection. If something is caused by something, it seems that not only does the thing caused have being in the strict sense, but the cause does too. Nevertheless, here, too, it can be said that when something is caused, the thing by which it is caused seems, as such, to be an *ens rationis*: it undergoes no change by virtue of having an effect, and becomes, therefore, in no way different. For it, the specification is, as it has been expressed, a *denominatio mere extrinseca.* But the question deserves further consideration.

Could someone not say that the fact that something *does* exist a hundred years before something else (which is then the affirmation in the strict sense corresponding to the loose and improper affirmation that the other thing will exist in a hundred years) also conveys *nothing* that makes the thing in question seem to be *modified* in any way? Exactly two classes of relations have been distinguished, then, of which the one relates to a real terminus, the other to an *ens rationis*. A question calling for special consideration is connected with determinations which require that the terminus of the relation, in order for it to be the terminus, should have being in the strict and proper sense. Must we not say that here we are not dealing with an *ens rationis,* particularly in connection with certain comparative and causal determinations, since the cause and the effect must exist at the same time?

3. Grammarians designate certain subordinate clauses as objective clauses. They are those which can function as subjects and predicates as names do. . . . I cannot say, "Although there are roses, is true," but I can say, "That there are roses, is true." The question now arises whether we are concerned here with real entities or with *entia rationis.* In fact, we answer the question, "Are there roses?" by saying it is so. And we also say it is so if someone asks whether there are no ghosts or whether there can be no perfect virtue.

The being with which we are here concerned is what Aristotle called *ens tamquam verum,* i.e., being in the sense of the true. In this connection he states that true and false do not have their being in reality but only in the judging mind. This would be an indication of an *ens rationis.* But we may not simply say that the word "being" is here used in the same sense as when it is said that something has *being* as being thought of; we do not say that the object is true, but rather that the judgement about the object is true. We must be reminded of what was previously said about the meaning of the word "judgement." But people who say that subordinate clauses signify something which, while not being a thing, nevertheless is something which has being in the same strict and proper sense as things have, are entirely wrong. They call it a fact (*Tatsache*).[5] It is true, to be sure, that when we are concerned with the being of a fact (*Tatsache*) we are also concerned with being and non-being in the strict and proper sense. But that is also the case when one speaks of the being of some *ens rationale*. We have said that someone affirming something thought-of as being thought-of is really affirming someone who is thinking of it. Similarly, we should always substitute for the sentence affirming something as a fact an equivalent sentence which affirms or denies something in the strict and proper sense. Perhaps one might say that for the proposition, "That a thing exists, is true," there is the equivalent proposition, "A thing exists," and for the proposition, "That centaurs exist, is false," the equivalent proposition, "There are no centaurs." But if someone prefers to say that "Everyone who affirms a centaur is someone affirming falsely," is the equivalent proposition, "the person affirming a centaur" and "the person judging something falsely"[6] are names of things.

The upshot of our discussion is, therefore, that we are dealing here with "being" in the loose and improper sense, and if one were to call anything which is a "being" in the improper sense an *ens rationis*, then here, too, we would be dealing with an *ens rationis*. But we are not dealing with an *ens rationis* in the way in which an object is said to have being as something thought-of, but in the way in which a judgement we wish to designate as true is said to have being.[7] We can then express the same, unaltered thought by uttering a proposition in which being is used in the sense it has when we say something has being as an object, and once again it can be expressed by a proposition in which it is said of some real entity that it is or is not. I remind the reader of the fact that just as much as when something is affirmed as being thought-of, we are equally concerned with an *ens rationis*, to the extent that an *ens rationis* is involved when something is said to have being in the loose sense, when something is affirmed as being past or future – yet not in the sense of something thought-of. If, in the case of the thing thought-of, the thing really affirmed was the thing thinking of it, in the case of the past thing,

---

[5] The terms "*Sachverhalt*" ("state of affairs") and "*Inhalt*" ("content") are used more frequently than "*Tatsache*" ("fact"). In addition, Meinong uses the term "objective."

[6] The "person judging falsely" is a thing-name insofar as when I am thinking of him, I am thinking of someone making a judgement, someone who could not possibly be judging self-evidently. See p. 282, note 3, and p. 283.

[7] In that we say, "It is so."

the thing really being affirmed was the thing coming at some temporal interval later than it. In the case of the *ens tamquam verum*, one might say that it is someone judging, which cannot be said to be synonymous with the object of the judgement nor with the judgement or its content and the like.

Not merely what is expressed by so-called objective subordinate clauses, but participles as well belong to the *ens tamquam verum*, so instead of saying "Someone is unhappy," we might assert as a fact "Someone's unhappiness exists."* If we say, "The past existence of someone is," we are also confronted with an *ens tamquam verum*, and one would first have to translate it into "someone is in the past," but then, in order to arrive at "being" in the strict sense, we would have to go on to translate it into "A real thing is later than a certain man."

Abstract substantives can also stand in place of participles, as when instead of asserting "The being of a man" as fact, we assert "the existence of a man." All this amounts to the same thing but many have failed to see this and have been led to grotesque conclusions, as in saying that if there is a stone, there is an infinity of things, for there is also the existence of the stone and the existence of the existence of the stone and so on *ad infinitum*, as well as the non-existence of the non-existence of the stone, and the existence of the non-existence of the non-existence of the stone and the non-existence of the non-existence of the non-existence of the non-existence of the stone, and so on and so on. I do not want to dwell on the absurdities which people have been led into by their failure to recognize the truth of the matter, namely that we are always concerned with one and the same thing, while they say that we are dealing with countless objects affirmed *in recto*.

4. "Existence" is an abstract term. We have many other abstract terms as well. Now should we say of them all that they are synonymous with participles and objective clauses – in other words that they are beings in the sense of *ens tamquam verum*? Many people are inclined to believe this. It cannot be denied that there are still more abstract terms of which it must be said, as with "existence" and "non-existence," that they belong to the *ens tamquam verum*. Among them are *impossibility* and *possibility*. The former is equal to the objective clause, "that something is impossible" (which is sometimes true, and we then say, "So it is.") "Impossible" serves, however, like "is," to express a denial, in which its apodictic character

* [Translators' note: Brentano discusses the German infinitive in this connection. His examples are "das Unglücklichsein von jemanden ist," and "das Gewesensein von jemandem ist." Of necessity, the translation is very free.]

also finds expression. The word "possible" is the opposite of "impossible"; it means the same thing as "not impossible." Now a double "not" is equivalent to an affirmation and for this reason many would take "it is possible" as an affirmation, too. If one says something is possible, one is ascribing to it a being which has been weakened somehow. But nothing at all is said about being or non-being. It is only that someone apodictically denying it is contradicted. It is not just in affirming in a loose sense the impossibility of something that one gives expression to a denial; one also does so in affirming, in a similarly loose and improper sense, the possibility of something. In these cases, we are concerned with an *ens tamquam verum*. In an odd way, many impossibilities and possibilities of things have been conceived of as having being from eternity outside of God and alongside of God, as something which participated in the creation – sometimes limiting, sometimes aiding the Cause. But the truth is that there is only *one* Principle of all things.

Even if this or that abstract term still belongs here, it nevertheless seems wrong to want to include them all in this class. Even Aristotle, who first mentioned the *ens tamquam verum* and who also distinguished between a real thing and its reality which he called form, species, nature, held the *ens tamquam verum* and the form to be entirely distinct from one another.

XVI *On* Ens Rationis
[*January 6, 1917.*]

1. There is one concept of the highest generality under which all the objects of our thinking fall.[1] This is as true as it is to say that the concept of thinking is univocal. It is the concept of being (*das Seienden*) in the sense in which a thing has being.[2]

[1] More precisely, this should read: "There is, i.e. we conceive of, a general concept under which all the things we have as objects of our thought fall." As noted previously, Brentano is merely making use of an abbreviated manner of speaking when he speaks of "relation to the object" or has the objects of our thought falling under concepts. Nothing can be present to our mind except "objects" in the sense of things.

[2] Brentano speaks of being in the sense of the substantive thing. The expression "being" is misleading, since it is possible for a thing to be thought of which has being, e.g., a man, and it is possible for one to be thought of which does not, e.g., a Pegasus. But "*Reales*" [Translators' note: It is this word which has been translated as "thing" throughout] is also ambiguous, for sometimes we use it in the sense of thing, entity, and at other times in the sense of real, existent. Consequently it would be best to speak neither of beings nor of *realia*, but of things or entities.

2. It has been known since antiquity that the term "being" is equivocal.

Aristotle, for instance, distinguished first of all between *ens per se* and *ens per accidens*. This gave him a reason to hold that when we say something is something, we frequently mean only that the two things are combined in a certain way but this is in no way to be confused with real identity. In fact, under some circumstances the one can cease to exist while the other continues to be, or the one might not yet exist while the other already does. If I say this man is a man or is a living creature, then there is real identity, but if I say this man is armed or is learned, there is no identity in this case. The man is included as a part of that which is armed or that which is learned, but the part is not actually the whole and the whole is not actually the part. I speak only in a loose and improper sense, then, when I say that this man is this learned person and this armed person is this man. I would have to say: "This learned person contains this man within itself as subject." It is like saying this person who is hearing is this person who is seeing. He isn't really. As a seeing person he can cease to be, while he still continues to be as a hearing person. In the strict sense of the word, I can only say here that this hearing person and this seeing person include one and the same thing as subject.

When you compare the example of the learned man and the armed man, it is easy to see how it is that being *per accidens* never has to do with identity, but that what is asserted of something else is related to it in many different ways. The man who hears is contained in the hearing person as subject; the arms are not a property of the armed man. Not just he, but the arms as well could remain as such if the armed man were no more. The armed man is the result of the fact that the man and the arms are spatially related in a certain way. We are dealing here with what has been called a *denominatio extrinseca*.

Aristotle distinguished still another loose and improper meaning of being. This is the one he called *ens tamquam verum*.[3] For example, it is customary to make what are linguistically complete sentences the subjects of other sentences, as when we say that a certain tree

---

[3] *Ens tamquam verum* is the ὄν ὡς ἀληθές. Compare Brentano's Aristotelian works (*Die Psychologie des Aristoteles, Von der Mannigfachen Bedeutung des Seienden nach Aristoteles*, etc.) with this historical observation. For a long time Brentano's true significance in the interpretation of Aristotle has been underestimated. His acute mind is revealed here, where he takes up a position in relation to a congenial spirit, in an admirable way. Zeller's authority has prevented Brentano's Aristotelian works from being properly appreciated.

is an oak is true. When asked whether it is so, we reply: "It is so." Aristotle of course remarks that what is involved here always has to do with things and could always be expressed by affirming or denying a thing. He says therefore that the metaphysician does not have to pay any further attention to the *ens tamquam verum*; it has being only in the loose and improper sense in which anything at all could be said to be. It "is" only in that the thing is or is not, and it has no coming to be or passing away of its own. Because a certain tree is, in the strict sense, an oak, one can say that the fact that it is an oak exists. Naturally participles* and certain abstract terms which are used in the place of such objective subordinate clauses belong here, too.

Aristotle also spoke of the difference between something's being "possible," and being "actual," and he designated *what has being in possibility* as a being in a loose sense of the word. On careful consideration, according to him, one would also have to say that the actuality of the thing which has possible being exists only in a loose and improper sense, too. For on his view it is supposed to hold true generally that a group of things is not itself a thing and therefore that no part of a whole thing is to be called a thing. The "actuality," however, is contained along with the possible being as a part of the actual thing.[4] This had to lead him still further, to saying that accidents, in and for themselves, cannot be allowed to count as things in a strict and proper sense, even if the substance is to be regarded as a thing and the accident contains it as subject. He came to the point where he set up, in his theory of categories, a variety of ultimate classes of being and he denied the presence of one single concept of the utmost generality under which all objects of our thinking fall.

Still other important conclusions arose for him. He could not let a collective count as a thing.[5] A troop of men, a herd, a galaxy – on his view none of these could be a thing. Nor could a state or a house. Nor could he even have called a man a thing if he had claimed that he consisted of a body made up of atoms or even of various organs as diverse actual physical substances. And how did he have to conceive of a continuously extended body? If the whole was a thing the part was not a thing for him, but if it was divided into parts, the bodies which had existed potentially become actual, while the body which had been a thing up to that time now becomes only a possible thing. Leibniz, who shared with Aristotle the conviction that a group of things is not a thing, was thereby led to deny reality of all physical

* [Translators' note: In German infinitives perform the function to which Brentano is referring, while in English it is performed by participles.]
[4] See Brentano, *Aristoteles und seine Weltanschauung*, p. 41.
[5] *Aristoteles und seine Weltanschauung*, p. 36.

objects. He said they consisted of entirely unextended monads and by virtue of this he fell into the contradiction of saying that something extended arises from an infinite number of entirely unextended things. Here Aristotle has the advantage. But to say that a single continuum, extending perhaps for millions of miles, should, by virtue of having a millimeter separated off one end, undergo a total substantial transformation at this very moment, seems preposterous.[6] It seems rather to be no more affected in its distant parts than would a life-history be a different one in its first hours if something interfered and brought it to an end before it had run its actual course. So the theory that a number of things cannot be a thing does not seem very acceptable. But the claim that several things can be a thing is no more contradictory than the claim that several groups can be a group, which no one denies. There would be a contradiction only if someone said that a number of things is identical with one of the things which comprises it. Similarly, the group which is formed of several groups is identical with none of its component groups.

And if we look more closely, we shall find not only that Aristotle's interpretation of the continuum and the relation of whole and part is unsatisfactory, but that what he says of the relation of substance and accident does not really resolve the difficulty, either. According to him part of a thing is not supposed to be itself a thing, but the substance, which enters into the accident as part, helps constitute it, and individuates it, is, according to him, in the strict sense; therefore he not only refused to let substance and accident together count as a thing, he also denied that any accident was, like a substance, a thing in the strict sense. In fact there was no difference at all between the accident *with* the substance and the accident *without* it, since the latter never existed and its concept presented a *contradictio in adjecto*.[7] But if, on the basis of this, he did not choose to call the accident a thing in the same sense as the subject, would he not then have to say that it could not count as a unitary thing in any other sense, either? Without substance it was nothing, with substance it was something one part of which was an actual thing in and of itself. As a consequence, doesn't the whole seem to be only in potentiality or, if we let the accident count as actual, does it not prevent us from regarding the substance, insofar as it is bound up with it, as something actual? In the beginning of Book 12 of the *Metaphysics*, Aristotle seems uncertain whether he should define the actual unit as the substance together with all its accidents, and the substance and every accident taken by themselves only as parts of this one reality,

[6] *Aristoteles und seine Weltanschauung*, p. 36, note 1.
[7] I.e. a thought without a thinker, an attribute without something whose attribute it is, is absurd.

or each of these parts as an actual unit, even if it should have to be understood in an analogous rather than the same sense, whereupon there would be an ordering of parts, and the one part would be the primary actuality, the other the secondary, and so on. Here he seems close to giving up his thesis that a number of things is not a thing. So we may hesitate that much less to renounce his doctrine. But then all the reasons we had for being tempted not to let an accident count as a thing in the same sense as a substance collapse. We shall not hesitate to apply the term "thing" in the same univocal sense to parts of a continuum and to any composite of a number of actual things.[8] It is not the case that this will make us any less able to retain the full significance of the difference between these classes of real entities.

This result requires us, however, to look back once more at what Aristotle said about being in actuality and potentiality. According to him, the former is supposed to be composed of the latter together with the relevant actuality. He called this a compound of *matter* and *form*. On the basis of his theory that no real thing consists of more than one actual entity, it appeared to him out of the question that the "actuality"[9] should itself be actual. Now that theory has collapsed and so the question reappears: Is the "actuality" of an actual entity perhaps also something actual? In order to become quite clear about the question, we might offer examples of "actualities." Abstract terms offer us a ready and varied supply.[10] "Extended thing" is supposed to be the name of an actual entity, and extension the name of an "actuality." Similarly opposed pairs of actual entities and actualities are "colored thing" and "color," "sphere" and "spherical form," "thinking subject" and "thinking," "man" and "human nature." Most of these *abstracta*[11] belong to the realm of the accidental; in general, however, the actuality was not supposed to be the actual entity *but included as a part in it* naturally along with another part which together added up to the whole. Now is this really the case, can the *so-called actuality* exist in and of itself or at least be thought of in and for itself? We already heard when we were speaking of the accident, that no accident could exist without including substance. And Aristotle explicitly affirmed that it also had to include the concept of substance in its concept. Now is what was said supposed to hold true just of the concrete accident, but not

[8] Those who call Brentano a "Scholastic" can learn from this and many other examples (e.g., the theory of judgement) that Brentano often subjected Aristotle and the scholastics to incisive criticism.
[9] "Actuality" = *energeia, entelecheia.*
[10] "Abstract terms" (= "grammatical *abstracta*") are not to be confused with abstract concepts. See Appendix XV, note 1.
[11] Abstracta = abstract terms, as before.

343

of the specified real accidental reality? – In one passage in the *Metaphysics* Aristotle says we think of the accident *in abstracto* with the exclusion of substance. But if he had been asked whether one is really able to do this or only imagines being capable of thinking in this way, he would have to admit that the latter is the case. A *fiction replete with contradictions* is involved, then, when one treats the whole accident in relation to the subject contained in it, in a manner similar to treating the whole of a substance composed of parts in relation to a particular one of its parts. One imagines that the thinking belongs to the thinking subject's mind as the tail belongs to the dog which has a tail and that both the thinking and the tail can be made objects in and of themselves, exclusive of their substance. This is all a delusion, even though it may happen that the substitution of a fiction here is in many respects free from disadvantageous consequences and indeed even facilitates the progress of our studies.[12]

Let us also consider the following. Aristotle said the actual entity was composed of two parts, one of which was the actuality, the other the potentiality. The actuality would then be something which did not imply its possibility. But no one could believe anything of the sort, and so it is clear that, as we have said, we are dealing here with nothing but a fiction.

We must also linger a bit longer on being in potentiality and ask whether what Aristotle said of his *ens tamquam verum* does not hold true of it, namely that everything said about it can be expressed in assertions which refer to things in the strict and proper sense as objects. Examples of being in potentiality are afforded by something capable of thought [*ein Denkfähiges*], by something movable and the like. How do we get to that to which we refer with this term? Aristotle himself says that we are led to it by certain experiences. We find that something is thinking at one time, not thinking at another, is at one time at rest in one place or another, at another

[12] I have called attention in my Introduction to the fact that this theory of the usefulness of "absurd, contradictory fictions" reveals points of contact with Vaihinger's theory of fictions. Brentano, who only rarely took account of contemporary philosophical production, did not, to my knowledge, know of Vaihinger's book. The *Classification* appeared in 1911, the same year as the *Philosophie des Als Ob*. The main ideas in the Supplementary Essays had already been established for Brentano over a period of years, as emerges from his correspondence with Marty and me. In *Annalen der Philosophie*, II, No. 3, "*Zur Relativitatstheorie*," in the article, "*Fiktion und Hypothese in der Einsteinschen Relativitätstheorie*," pp. 337–338, I have also called attention to the respects in which two philosophers agree and to the fact that in questions of metaphysics Brentano adopts a standpoint which is diametrically opposed to Vaihinger's. See also Book One, Chap. I, note 8.

time moving from one place to the other. So we see that it is not impossible for it to think and also not impossible for it not to be thinking. And we also see that it is not impossible for it to be present at another place and not impossible for it to change places. What sort of ideas are being applied here and where do we get them? It is obvious that we have nothing but ideas of objects,[13] of which some are affirmed and others denied. They are in part external objects,[14] and in part inner objects, since we do perceive ourselves as affirming and denying. On further investigation of the occurrence, one will discover in particular that still other inner experiences seem to be employed, in which we deny something not merely assertorically but apodictically, conscious of complete certainty. In this way we acquire the idea of someone *making an incorrect apodictic denial*,[15] of someone making an *incorrect apodictic affirmation*,[16] and of someone who rightly believes of the one making the apodictic denial as well as of the one making the apodictic affirmation that they are both in error.[17] This also applies, then, to the case in which a substance is united with an accident or one substance is transformed into another.[18]

It is apparent, then, that just as with the *ens tamquam verum*, everything which can be said about that which has potential being, that which is capable of something, that which has the ability to do something, can also be expressed by means of assertions which refer to things in the strict and proper sense. At the same time, however, we see perhaps here even more than we did in the other case, how much *linguistic convenience* pressures us to introduce not only other words which are merely synsemantical, but names as well, which do not serve in and of themselves to designate a real thing. This in turn has led to a distinction between being in the strict sense and being in the improper sense.

Let us summarize the results of our study of the variety of meanings of being which Aristotle taught. We could not concur with him

---

[13] The word "object," is to be understood as equivalent to "thing" here and in many other places.

[14] Here, too "object" = "thing."

[15] The so-called concept of "the possible," "possibility" is connected with the idea of someone "incorrectly making an apodictic negative judgement."

[16] The so-called concept of the "non-necessary" is connected with the idea of someone incorrectly making an apodictic affirmation.

[17] This is the case of something of which we say it is neither "impossible in itself" nor "necessary in itself," i.e., the concept of the so-called "contingent thing."

[18] See *Aristoteles und seine Weltanschauung*, p. 57.

when he would not allow the accident to be called a being in the same sense as the substance. On the other hand we could not very well say he was mistaken when he maintained that the *ens per se* and the *ens per accidens* have being in a different sense nor when he differentiated between the *ens tamquam verum* and what has being in the sense of a thing. We must also acknowledge that what has being in potentiality and its actuality are not real things. *But it does not follow from all this that anything other than a thing is ever the object of our thought.* The equivocations involved were not equivocations in which each of the meanings designated an object in and of itself. It is rather that being – in the sense of "thing in the strict sense" – designates an object in and of itself; the other meanings, however, are related to those which attach to prepositions, conjunctions, articles, etc., and so there seems to be no objection to repeating what was said earlier, namely, that everything which we are capable of thinking of falls under one and the same concept of the utmost generality, as could also have been inferred from the unity of the concept of thinking. The concept of thinking is the concept of someone thinking something and if the concept of a something did not have unity, the concept of the thinking thing could not have unity either.

3. Much more could still be added to what Aristotle took into consideration in his studies of the diverse meanings of being. One could speak of the *class of objects as objects of a thinking subject* in the widest sense of the word, which includes in particular, just as it includes the specification thing thought of, the "thing affirmed, the thing denied, the thing loved, the thing hated," and so on, in which the mental references appear to be much more specialized still. Many have called this class in particular that of *entia rationis*, things which somehow exist in the mind. It is clear, however, that it also holds true with respect to them that when someone says he is thinking of them, strictly speaking, it is not them but an *ens reale* that he is thinking of. For example, the person whom we say is thinking of something thought-of, is actually thinking of a person thinking of a thing.

We find something similar to this when we investigate other cases, as for example *disjunctive or conditional attributes*, as when we say, "A man who is either very ingenious or very well taught." As with Aristotle's being in potentiality, the psychological analysis in this case may be a more complicated one, but it can always be carried out in such a way as to show that we are not dealing with anything but real things in this case.

An objection could be made with respect to *certain absurdities* (*Absurda*), as for example when someone makes a round square an object, as seems to happen, not, to be sure, with intuitive unity but with attributive unity. But here too we find that nothing but real elements are employed in the absurd composite, indeed, if a cubical sphere did exist in reality, it would be a sphere and cubical and consequently for the one reason and the other, it would be a thing. The only reason it is not, is because it does not exist at all, and in such a case, without being subject to a charge of absurdity, a real thing of which *I think* would *not be* a thing. (If one says, "A man is a man," or more generally, "A is A," this is not a linguistic expression of an affirmation but of a negation. It means the same as "There is no man who is not a man," or "A man who is not a man is impossible."[19] One might also be inclined to interpret the sentence in such a way that the term man does refer to a man, but then we would not be dealing with something necessary.) As it is convenient to say that one has an idea of something which does not exist, it is also convenient to say that we often have ideas of impossible things. In my opinion, one should not say "that in such cases it is not some thing, but an *ens rationis* which is our object."[20] A "thought-of black palomino" does not have the same meaning as a "black palomino." If I say there is a black palamino, I claim an absurdity, but if I say there is a thought-of black palomino I do not. What I say, however, only amounts to saying that there is someone thinking of a black palomino. We must be very much on our guard against the common confusion between objects[21] formed by absurd combinations and *entia*

---

[19] This locution is also a linguistic abbreviation. "A man who is not a man" (see note 3 to Appendix IV concerning identification *in obliquo*) is apodictically denied.

[20] Brentano means the following: It is not improper to say that we are thinking of something which does not exist, or which is impossible. But it would not be suitable to say, when we are thinking of "a thought-of black palomino" that we are thinking of something which is not a thing, but an "*ens rationis*" (something irreal). Instead, in thinking of "a thought-of black palomino" we are not thinking of anything but "someone who is thinking of a black palomino," a person thinking then, a substantive thing. And even if we are thinking of "a black palomino" with "black palomino" we are conceiving of something substantive (a thing), but one which does not and cannot exist. One should keep in mind that Brentano's dictated essays were composed when he was almost entirely deprived of sight and that their immediate publication was not intended. In this type of investigation it is necessary to use locutions that are more difficult than those of ordinary language.

[21] "Objects formed by absurd combinations": e.g. I think of something as white and think of something else as black, and now if I think of one and the same thing as both black and white at the same time, I have made something my object in presentation, and synthetically, attributively in presentation, the existence of which is absurd.

rationis, which cannot become objects at all[22] and in which the word "is" is used only in a loose and improper sense.

4. It is definitely worth while, however, to speak in somewhat greater detail of *abstracta.*[23] They sometimes play an important role in our methodical proceedings, they are formed for a purpose, are adhered to throughout long conversations and finally, after having served their purpose well, they again disappear from the end result. In contrast to other *absurda,* with which this is not the case, we might designate them as somehow rationally justified, or if you prefer, as *absurda cum fundamento in re.* What I mean can very well be illustrated by examples borrowed from the procedure of the mathematician.

Mathematicians speak of *negative quantities.* Now what does this mean? It is often said that they are quantities which are smaller than what has no quantity at all: (-3) is said to be a number three less than zero. And indeed this is in accord with the fact that just as we get 3 when we subtract 4 units from 7, to get (-3) when we subtract 7 units from 4. Just as 3 is 4 units less than 7, (-3) seems to be 7 units less than 4, and thus 3 units less than 0. Others, Carnot for example, have believed they had to protest against this, because, they said, 2 is supposed to be related to (-2) as (-2) is related to 2, and yet it is absurd that the greater should be related to the lesser as the lesser to the greater. But the fact that the idea of something less than nothing is an absurdity did not have to be proved by argument. It is not a matter of freedom from absurdity but of a certain technical usefulness and this can very well exist in spite of the absurdity. If it is impossible for there to be intervals from 0 in opposite directions, there are other cases in which we do encounter intervals which are truly in opposite directions. In the case of a straight line, for example, the two ends are at a distance from the middle in opposite directions and so we encounter in the midpoint of the line something analogous to the absurd fiction concerning 0. And there are thousands of other similar cases. I may, then, turn what I have calculated by using *absurda* to good account by substituting analogies which are not absurd. I can also say that asking for the addition of the absurd (-3) to 4, is equivalent to asking for an opposite procedure, i.e. the subtraction of the non-absurd 3 from 4. Since both give the same result, the use of the absurd fiction has proved to be harmless. When I speak of multiplying by (-3), this is something in and of itself undeniably absurd, but here too I can think of it as a harmless substitution for something that is not absurd. Anyone who

[22] "*Entia rationis* cannot become objects" ("*Entia rationis* cannot be presented") only substantival things can be present to the mind.
[23] "Abstracta" is to be understood to mean *nomina abstracta.*

takes a quantity three times, uses it as an addend three times. The opposite procedure would be to use it as a subtrahend three times. And so when I say that (-3) times 3 should be added to 10, as an equivalent I can also say that 3 times 3 should be subtracted from 10, whereupon any absurdity seems to be eliminated. We can say similar things of still other processes, as when I speak of (-3) times (-3). In (-3) and " -3 times" we are dealing with absurdities. But not even this reduplication of absurdity can detract from its usefulness. And once again operations using negative quantities can be carried out perfectly well when I divide $(-)$ into $(+)$, or $(+)$ into $(-)$, or $(-)$ into $(-)$. And I may also raise a number to negative powers and say that as the third power of 3 is related to the second and the second to the first, so the first power is related to the 0 power and the 0 power to the power -1. This makes the latter appear to be equivalent to 1/3, then.

Like negative quantities, *proper fractions* are in and of themselves something quite absurd; 1 cannot be divided into halves, but this is possible with other numbers, as well as with a continuum. And so it happens that by analogy something divisible is substituted for the indivisible one. The denomination (*Benennung*)*[24] of a number can be something divisible in cases where the number itself is represented by a fiction of something divisible. And something of this sort also holds true of other obvious absurda as, for example $\sqrt{2}$ and other irrational numbers and still more so of $\sqrt{-2}$ and other imaginary numbers.[25] Considered in themselves they are out and out absurdi-

---

* [Translators' note: Brentano's usage of *Benennung* here is a relatively unfamiliar one from arithmetic. The *benannte Zahl* is the concrete number, the number conceived in terms of a certain number of *things*, e.g. the apples, pencils, nickels and dimes of schoolboy arithmetic. These, then, constitute its *Benennung*, denomination.]

[24] Since, according to Brentano, nothing can exist, nor be capable of presentation, except things, the concept of thing must be included in that of number. Accordingly, an abstract number (*unbenannte Zahl*) would be nothing but the number denominated by the most general term and every number taken in and for itself, in abstraction from its so-called denomination, a synsemanticon. Anyone who took it to be an "object," would be guilty of an unconscious fiction.

[25] The mathematician, E. Study, writes in his book, *Die realistische Weltansicht und die Lehre vom Raume* (Brauschweig, 1923), "All mathematical assertions are reducible to assertions about natural numbers and consequently they are no more fictitious than are the natural numbers themselves." He adds as a note, "Naturally that does not prevent mathematics from being used for the purpose of presenting fictions." In Brentano's treatise it is shown how certain mathematical assertions about negative, irrational numbers, etc. can be reduced to assertions about natural

numbers. But that does not hinder those "negative, imaginary numbers, etc." from being designated as "fictions," for after all, the word "fiction," too, is only a term to which the words of Whitehead, which Study quotes, apply: "There can be no question of the names being right or wrong: They may be judicious or injudicious." It is necessary, therefore, to become clear about the term "fiction" itself. It has a number of meanings. It would be an unusual usage, and one which would be hardly to the purpose, to call every conceptual presentation formed by abstraction a "fiction"; for although "*fingere*" means the same as "to form (*bilden*)," the *formation of general ideas* by abstraction is a fiction only for the extreme nominalist. It would be more suitable to call a presentational synthesis, the attributive combination of presentations (Essay XIII above) a creature of presentation, a fiction; but by doing this we would create an unnecessary and pointless equivocation. For we are accustomed to *speaking of fictions only when we are thinking of something which does not exist* or the existence of which is absurd, something in reference to which therefore an affirmative judgement would be incorrect and a negative one true. Sometimes, for this reason, the negative judgement itself is called a fiction (p. 292 above). If the affirmative judgement is not only false, but absurd, we speak of an *absurd fiction*. For Mach the idea of an "atom" was a fiction, since he believed that atoms did not exist, while the idea is regarded by many as a safe hypothesis, namely by all of those who hold their existence to be certain. *As I have said, the concept of fiction always has reference to false positive judgements.* Vaihinger prefers the expression, "conscious false fiction." Here we have before us what is ordinarily called an "assumption"; a judgement is thought of, i.e. someone is thought of who is making a judgement about something (Essay V, p. 284 above), while such a judgement is not actually being made. We act only "as if" we are judging in a certain way. In this case the opinion that one is *actually* making that sort of judgement would be false, the judgement is only imagined.

The so-called legal fictions of which Brentano speaks also belong here; we speak and act *as if* we held St. Stephen's to be a property-owner, as if we made such a judgement.

In the case of those fictions which Brentano calls "abstracta," what is involved are *words*, words of which it would be a mistake to believe that taken by themselves, i.e. in abstraction from their linguistic context, they signify a concept. But we use these words as if they had an independent meaning. The independent meaning ordinarily ascribed to those words is that of something other than a substantive entity (of a so-called irreal thing). Anyone who does this, conscious that they do not have independent meaning, is making use of a conscious fiction. Otherwise the fiction is unconscious, i.e. an error.

It might still be remarked that the word "fiction" is a *synsemanticon* itself (what can be conceived is only a "being which is imagining something"). A distinction between the various concepts bound up with the word "fiction" is to be found neither in Brentano nor elsewhere in any systematic fashion. The inspiration which comes from Brentano and Vaihinger in this connection will no doubt continue to be fruitful, no

ties. But once it has been shown that it is harmless to use them, we can go still further and show that it is even useful. And so they show themselves to be just what we were speaking of, absurd fictions which are rationally justified by their practical application. Such absurd fictions are also used in other sciences. In jurisprudence, for example, we speak of St. Stephen's Cathedral in Vienna as the owner of a large fortune because large sums have been bequeathed for its maintenance or we speak of the will of the people and decrees of parliament. Such absurd fictions can also appear in metaphysics and may be harmless, indeed they may be recommended, if only we do not forget to hold fast to the knowledge that they are fictions and absurd fictions. A "thought-of man," a "ruler of 1000 years ago" becomes an absurdity right away if I ascribe to him the characteristics of a thing and say that he is to be affirmed in the strict and proper sense. The truth is that the only thing to be affirmed is something which now exists as 1000 years later than the earlier thing. And similarly we have already remarked that those "actualities" or forms of Aristotle's, which, upon being combined with something which has being in possibility (a potentiality), are supposed to jointly constitute an actual thing, would at once become absurd fictions if we wished to claim for them the character of an *ens reale* in the strict and proper sense and affirm them in that sense.

5. It will be well to take particular account of some *absurda* which are nowadays frequently not regarded by mathematicians and metaphysicians as absurd fictions, but as things which can be made objects, without contradiction, either because they believe that we are dealing here with real things which exist, or because they fail to see that only a thing could become object of a presentation.

One such example is the so-called *actu infinitum* and that which is infinitesimally small. We have said that just as a single man is to be called a thing in the strict sense, so are three men together. The same thing can be said of any number of men no matter how great. And there are also other aggregates of whatever finite number of units you please. Now since we can continue additions infinitely, we may add 10 to 10 and 100 to 100 all at once, as well as 1 to 1. And thereupon people have come to invent aggregates *which are not just larger than any arbitrarily chosen finite number, but larger than any of them.* These are the so-called *actu* infinite numbers of things. Now it

matter how critically, like Brentano himself, one may think of fictionalism as a *Weltanschauung*. Against those theories which attempt, with Aloys Müller, to interpret numbers as "ideal objects," it is sufficient to cite what has already been brought out with respect to *Gegenstandstheorie* and phenomenology in the present and other essays.

is not difficult to show that it is impossible to assume these without absurdity. Those who assume them would have to deny many self-evident truths, as for example, that the whole is greater than the part, that a quantity to which nothing is added and from which nothing is taken away does not change, so that transposition, for example, brings in no increase or decrease.[26] Just as they would have to deny of the principle that there can be no actual infinite number of things, they also deny of all the consequences which are inseparable from that principle that any of them involves an obvious contradiction. They wanted a proof, as if it had not been known for a long time that not everything which is *evident* is capable of being proved. Anyone who does not know that two things one of which is equal to part of the other are related to each other as smaller and larger, has no concept of larger and smaller at all.

Of course people have believed that it is possible to offer as proof that there is an infinite number of things, the fact that two things together can also be called a thing. And so, someone who has two apples is supposed to have still a third thing in addition to these two, namely the pair of apples. If this third thing is granted, then besides the one apple and the other and the pair of apples, we have still a fourth thing, which is made up of the individual apples and the trio of things consisting of the individual apples and the pair of apples. And so it goes on into infinity and they maintain that we have straightaway *actu* infinitely many things. But here what is missing is what is requisite to a genuine addition. Someone who has one apple and another apple does not have a pair of apples in addition, for the pair which he has simply means the one apple and the other taken together. *So what people wanted to do was to add the same thing to itself, which is contrary to the concept of addition.* Nothing is more true than that a thing[27] can be understood just as well to be a duality as a unity. It is entirely false, however, that because this is so, a third thing is added on anew to the two real entities. The pair is completely distinct from either of the two apples which make it up, but it is not at all distinct from both of them added together. And so it is incorrect that a third thing is added on to the two apples.

Others have been just as wrong if not more so, when they say the *actu* infinite was undeniable because it is not only true that a man exists but it is also true that it is true, and true that it is true that it is true, and so on and so on. But, as we have seen, truths are not

[26] These thoughts were carried through more precisely in Brentano's essays on the problem of continuity, in numerous letters to mathematicians and philosophers, and in his lectures on metaphysics.

[27] Obviously this only applies to physical things or dimensional things generally.

things and for that very reason they do not have being in the strict and proper sense.

The same mistake is obviously present if one chooses to cite an infinite number of "possibilities" as proof of the *actu* infinite. A possibility is not a thing and therefore has no being in the strict and proper sense. So every objection can be easily refuted. The mathematicians often hear it said that for them existence means the same as absence of contradiction. But in the first place we must beware of ambiguity. To say that *each one* of an infinity of things involves no contradiction is quite different from saying that *all of them together* involves no contradiction. The former is correct, the latter false, and many seem to have been taken in by this equivocation, and the more readily, for when existence is taken, not in the sense of absence of contradiction, but in the strict and proper sense, it cannot apply to every individual without applying to the aggregate as well.

Leibniz sometimes spoke about the infinite in words that are very difficult to understand, in particular when he says that there are undoubtedly infinitely many things, but they may not be comprehended altogether as an aggregate, since this would lead to the greatest absurdities. How is it, one might ask, that if infinitely many things exist together in actuality without contradiction, when I unite them in my mind they are supposed to be afflicted with contradictions? Indeed this seems to be inconceivable, and so Leibniz' assertion only makes rational sense if we interpret it to mean that infinitely many things could not exist together in reality either, but that each one of the infinitely many could very well exist. In this sense an infinite multiplicity would be no contradiction, but not an infinite multiplicity in the sense of the joint existence of them all. Still, it is easier to decide with certainty the only thing which can be accepted here without absurdity, than it is to figure out what Leibniz thought.

There is one more instance which we may not leave out of consideration. It is the one based on the fact that there are things which have continuity. In this case, as we have already said, every part of the continuum is a real thing. And since parts are to be differentiated *ad infinitum* but do not become things merely in virtue of being differentiated, the continuum seems to consist of an infinity of things. In fact, Leibniz conceived physical objects as consisting of infinitely many monads and precisely this makes it doubtful that he clearly and consistently adhered to the correct limits in his admissions concerning the theory of infinity.

If someone who admits a continuum cannot avoid believing in the existence of an *actu* infinite number of things, he would consequently have to retract his admission, for it would involve a contradiction. In fact, until the most recent times there has been no dearth of philosophers as well as natural scientists who actually deny any continuum on these grounds. For example, Renouvier and Boltzmann have done so just recently.[28] This leads to the most inconvenient consequences and things which we consider most securely established in the natural sciences would be thrown overboard. The truth is, however, that even if we assume the continuum, we can reject the inference to an *actu* infinite as invalid. Someone who assumes a continuum one meter long can, of course, describe it as two entities 1/2 meter long or as a continuum of three entities 1/3 of a meter long instead of describing it as one entity. He can just as well describe it as any number of correspondingly small entities he pleases, but he cannot understand it as an infinite number of infinitely small entities. Just as the concept of the *actu* infinite number of entities is absurd, so is that of a thing which is infinitely small. Archimedes maintained this and asserted it as a principle that if one of two homogeneous quantities is conceived to be as large as you please and the other as small as you please, if you add the latter to itself *ad infinitum* it would eventually reach and exceed the former. In fact if this were not the case we would have to distinguish within the larger quantity one part which it was still possible to reach and another part adjoining it which could no longer be reached. One can say of a continuum, then, only that it can be described as being as large a finite number of actual entities as you please, but not as an infinitely large number of actual entities. One may only maintain that there are potentially infinitely many entities. And in order to call attention to its distinctive character, we may also use the expression "a continuous number of things," but this must be distinguished from the *actu* infinite number.

6. We must ask those who say that the continuum ultimately consists of points what they mean by a point. Many reply that a point is a cut ($\tau o \mu \acute{\eta}$) which divides the continuum into two parts. The answer to this is that such a cut cannot be called a thing and therefore cannot be an object of presentation in the strict and proper sense at all. We have, rather, only presentations of contiguous parts. Someone else might say that he understands a point to be a thing which belongs to the continuum with which it or one of its parts ends. It is the initial, itself unextended, element of the extended thing. And if one should resist affirming such a thing, the doubt can be overcome merely by taking note of its analogy in time, where "now" is an unextended moment and time exists only in terms of this moment.

[28] Brentano was acquainted with Boltzmann's theories in this connection through letters and personal discussions. When Boltzmann visited Brentano in Florence for the purpose of philosophical conversation, these and other methodological questions were discussed.

Now it is true that everything which is in time is present, existing now. But nevertheless it is not something existing in isolation in and of itself. It is rather continuing, or ending or beginning. It cannot exist without a *relation of continuity* (*Kontinualrelation*) to what is earlier or later and it is thereby connected with things which are separated from it, some by a greater and some by a lesser interval. The interval may be conceived to be as small as you please but not infinitely small. Having a finite far-ranging connection of this sort with other things is part of the concept of the present. Without this relational character it could not be conceived nor could it ever be an element of something with temporal duration and development. But it *is* an element of such a thing, however, and so an element of something which has continuity but which exists only in terms of this element and can only be an object of presentation *in recto* in terms of this element, but in terms of every other element *in obliquo*.

The present belongs to a continuum which does not exist except in terms of the element in terms of which it is present. Someone might find it to be simply inadmissible to say that the continuum exists, since only one element of it exists. But this element does not have being in and of itself, but only insofar as it belongs to the continuum. In order to express this peculiar feature of the case, we also make use of the following form of discourse: the continuum does not exist perfectly, but imperfectly, not in terms of its totality, but in terms of a boundary. If you understand "part" to mean an extended part which has parts itself, this means not only less than total, but less than partial as well. In view of this, Aristotle describes motion as an imperfect actuality (ἐνέργεια ἀτελής).

If we ask to what does the present belong as a boundary, the reply is that it belongs to a continuum which exists only in terms of this boundary and not in terms of any of its other bounds. If we ask: "Does it also belong to each of these bounds?" the answer is that it does only insofar as it belongs to a continuum, and if we are reluctant to say that the present belongs to every part of the continuum we would also have to be reluctant to say that it belongs to every boundary of the continuum. A careful way of expressing it might be this: It belongs to every part of the continuum insofar as the part is part of the continuum and so to every boundary, too, insofar as it is a boundary of the continuum. If it is asked whether it pertains directly to one part of the continuum, the answer is yes; if it is asked whether it pertains directly to one of its bounds, the answer is that it pertains to one insofar as it is possible to say of something that it pertains to itself, for it is itself one of the bounds of the continuum, but it pertains directly to no other one. There can be no question of an *actu* infinite number of parts and limits on this basis, however, because no more than *one* of the limits is actual [but of the parts only those to which the present limit pertains directly and they are only those wherein each larger one contains the smaller ones within itself].[29]

7. If that is how things stand with the *temporal continuum*, it will also be possible to give an account of the *spatial continuum* and to show that affirming it does not make one guilty of the contradictions contained in the affirmation of the *actu infinitum*. The spatial point cannot exist or *be conceived of* in isolation. It is just as necessary for it to belong to a spatial continuum as it is for the moment of time to belong to a temporal continuum. A difference, however, lies in the fact that a spatial point can belong to a continuum which exists in terms of more than this point. I say "can belong," not "must belong,"[30] for if one imagines a cone being annihilated bit by bit from the base up, then at the moment the apex itself was annihilated, only one of its points would have being and it would belong to a continuum which did not exist in terms of any other of its points. The same would be the case if at the same moment the cone was annihilated up to its highest point an act of creation restored it again. Then the highest point would be the only one in terms of which it had never been annihilated, since it would constitute both the end point of its decline and the beginning point of its restoration. There is, then, a possibility of belonging to no continuum except one which exists in terms of this one point only. *For the most part*, however, the spatial point also exists in relation to a continuum which is real in terms of its totality, and it is this case in which it does not seem so easy to avoid admitting an actually infinite multiplicity.

One thing is easy to see, namely, that the point which belongs to a spatial continuum existing in terms of its totality is something only in virtue of belonging to the continuum. The relational character of the continuum is essential to it. *Anyone who conceives of it must conceive of it as something in a continual relation of this sort* (*ein solches kontinuales Relativ*), and if he conceives of it as belonging to an existing spatial continuum, his thought encompasses the continuum in question not merely *in obliquo* but also in itself *in recto* in terms of its totality. It is possible for this to occur sometimes determinately and other times indeterminately, for just as the specific numbers are related to the concept of number in general, the presentations of spatial continua with determinate size are related to the presentation of a spatial continuum in general. But the concept of

[29] This actuality is only that "actuality of an imperfect kind" which has just been mentioned. It would do no harm to drop the passage in brackets.
[30] In manuscript the sentence reads: "I say: 'can exist' and not 'must exist,'" but it should read: "'can belong,' not 'must belong.'" That this is merely a linguistic slip is obvious from what follows.

number can only be specified in one way or another and so too the concept of the spatial continuum can be actual only in some specific degree. And so the idea of the point implies belonging to a continuum of some determinate extension. This can be as small as you please, but it must always be assumed to be finite. No matter how small, it cannot be contained an infinite number of times in the continuum to which the point, as existing, appears to belong. Consequently, we never come to understand the continuum as something which permits an actually infinite number of points to be differentiated in virtue of containing a set of points to be differentiated as you please, or as an aggregate of infinitely many points which can be added together. We come to conceive of the point as belonging immediately, just as it does to the whole continuum, to its parts as well and to smaller and smaller parts *ad infinitum*. We cannot conceive of it as belonging to an infinitely small part, however, nor to one to which it belongs exclusively, so that it is quite impossible to avoid an intersection of the domains it belongs to. But an addition would require, as we have already said, the complete novelty of each individual item added.

Various other thorough studies could be made in this area, such as a study of the impossibility of adjacent points and the *possibility of coincident points*, which have, despite their coincidence, distinctness and full relative independence. It has been and is misunderstood in many ways. It is commonly believed that if four different-colored quadrants of a circular area touch each other at its center, the center belongs to one only of the colored surfaces and must be that color only. Galileo's judgement on the matter was more correct; he expressed his interpretation by saying paradoxically that the center of the circle has as many parts as its periphery. Here we will only give some indication of these studies by commenting that everything which arises in this connection *follows from the point's relativity as involves a continuum and the fact that it is essential for it to belong to a continuum*. Just as the possibility of the coincidence of different points is connected with that fact, so is the existence of a point in diverse and more or less perfect *plerosis*.[31] All of this is overlooked

---

[31] The concept of "*plerosis*" is one of the most important in Brentano's synechology. The word "*plerosis*" means fullness; "more or less in *plerosis*" means the degree of fullness or completeness of a boundary. Even single boundaries still have parts in a certain sense and these parts can either all be realized or only some of them. These parts are the different relations of continuity which can belong to one and the same boundary in terms of different directions. See *Aristoteles und seine Weltanschauung*, p. 37, and the work now in preparation, *Raum, Zeit, Kontinuität*. [This work was never published.]

even today by those who understand the continuum to be an actual infinite multiplicity and who believe that we get the concept not by abstraction from spatial and temporal intuitions but from the combination of fractions between numbers, such as between 0 and 1.[32]

Nevertheless, in mentioning space and time just now, we alluded to something which is a particular source of doubt concerning whether we should really deny the *actu infinitum* without exception. People maintain concerning space and time that it is certain, indeed immediately self-evident, that they have no limit and that the one extends to infinity in one dimension, the other in three dimensions. If this is so, it would seem that, as regards space in particular, a real infinite number of parts cannot be denied.

8. *But what should we understand by "space" and "time"?* The layman is embarrassed when the question is put to him; he hesitates to answer. But up to now philosophers have been unable to achieve unanimity in their answers and there is hardly one among them who has not proposed something quite preposterous. Also we cannot just ask what space and time are, but whether there really exist such a space and a time in the strict sense. And, as we have said, when we hear various philosophers give various definitions of the concepts of space and time, it is easy to see that we might have to say that what one of them means by time does not exist, while perhaps admitting that what someone else identifies as time does exist.

We will attempt to classify the views.

The first to be considered are those which deny that there is space and time at all.

The philosophers who seem to belong here are those such as Kant who ascribe only phenomenal truth, as they say, to space and time; the one is supposed to be the form of intuition of outer sense, the other of inner sense. What exists only in intuition exists only in thought, and what exists only in thought does not exist at all in the strict sense; it is only the thinking subject which exists. Now Kant says, to be sure, not merely that space and time exist but that they exist necessarily, it is impossible for us to deny them at all, or, as he puts it, to think them away. But all this is only a misleading way of talking, by which the concepts of truth and being are falsified once phenomenal truth is introduced as equally genuine as truth in itself.

According to Schopenhauer, too, time is only a form of intuition and has only phenomenal truth, and so, as has been shown, no genuine existence. How large a part vagueness plays here is shown by the fact that Kant and Schopenhauer seem to have answered the question of whether time goes by or things go by in time in opposite

[32] These remarks aimed at Dedekind and Poincaré are developed more extensively in other essays.

ways without Schopenhauer even being aware of his deviation. He holds that time flows by, but according to Kant it seems that time stands still; it is the abiding form of inner perception and the only thing that changes is what we inwardly perceive. Neither the one idea nor the other is tenable.

We must also say of those who say that there is no single time and space, but only a multiplicity of enduring and spatially extended things that they ascribe no genuine being to time and space.[33] If this is so, the expression, "Time (*der Zeit*)" and "Space (*der Raum*)" could be put alongside of "the rose," "the horse." It is a case of the fiction of a universal, which would exist as a universal, which is not the case. There are only individual roses and individual horses and so too there are only individual spatially extended things and individual enduring things. Someone could come to declare time and space to be fictions in another way, by saying that nothing within the realm of the spatial is stationary and nothing within the realm of the temporal changes in a completely even and uniform way. And so we would not have anything in relation to which we could fully determine the positions of physical objects and the temporal relations of events, the speed of changes which occur and the duration of the state of rest. Hence we created the idea of such a perfectly evenly and uniformly varying temporal thing, to serve as the measure of all simultaneity and succession. It is not present in reality, but it does exist, so to speak, in our mind.

Descartes understood time as duration. Locke, too, where he speaks of time, deals with duration. He also speaks of the fiction of duration *simpliciter* which we think of as without beginning or end.

There are others who belong with those who deny space and time for a special reason. They know well enough that space and time are bound up with the concept of *continua*, but they believe any continuum is beset by contradictions; Herbart and Renouviere are examples. Many of those to whom any continuum seems absurd have, to be sure, permitted themselves to substitute quite unfamiliar meanings for the ordinary ones (Boltzmann, for example). Boltzmann has gone so far as to transform the concepts of earlier and later into the concepts of belonging to a world which contains less or more heat.

Teichmüller also rejects time as an absurdity, on the grounds that cause and effect must be simultaneous.

Now let us turn to those who affirm time and space. In this group belong people who regard them as real things which provide us with

[33] Brentano has been – for a long time – among these. For the present, see Brentano's posthumously published essay on space and time in *Kantstudien*, XXV, 1.

standards for simultaneity and succession. For example, Aristotle thought that the highest sphere of heaven, which rotates uniformly and which as a whole always remains in the same place, can be designated as time and space. Yet when he speaks of time and space he does not always seem to adhere to these ideas, for if he did he could not regard motion as a transformation which the object moved undergoes and say that when we judge that something has been or will be, we always think the time along with the judgement and add it on.

In the Medieval period Bonaventura declared that a thing's time is its existence. In view of this, he, too, seems to deny the uniqueness of time. The Church fathers often said that time was created along with the creation of the world, and perhaps not all of them meant by that that it was created along with it as a particular thing.

In modern times many people have wanted to understand time and space as attributes of God. This is perhaps true of Newton and is particularly true of his friend Clarke. For him, they became the attributes of eternity and immeasurability.

The opposition to them, Leibniz, supposed that space was nothing but the order of things next to each other (*die Ordnung des Nebeneinander der Dinge*) and time the order of things succeeding one another. And the doctrine that all spatial properties and all temporal properties are merely relative is very widespread among modern natural scientists. Differing from them, Reid and more recently Marty[34] maintain that there is a single absolute space and a single absolute time, which, however, are not things. Bolzano's thinking is similar to Leibniz's, but it has been modified and expanded here and there in a somewhat peculiar fashion. Causal relations are sometimes more and sometimes less direct. This fact, he says, finds expression in spatial relationships. Hence the three-dimensional character of space is supposed to be deducible *a priori* on the basis of the one dimensional character of time. Still more could be added to illustrate what a great diversity of opinion there is.

9. In order to arrive at a sure judgement of one's own, it is necessary first of all to recall that many expressions are ambiguous and that it is easy to see that the word "*time*" is one of them. Sometimes time is called a criterion for earlier and later. This is true of certain passages in Aristotle, and we usually seem to do it when we speak of times of day or year. When we ask, "What time is it?" ("*Wie sind wir an der Zeit?*") we mean "What o'clock is it?" ("*Wieviel Uhr ist es?*"). But that is like wanting to call the thermometer the temperature because it measures the temperature.[35] We are dealing

[34] In the work of Marty's on space and time which was quoted.
[35] This is what the relativity theorists understood by time.

with a derivative meaning here. There are further signs of ambiguity in the fact that we sometimes speak of time and also of space as a unity, and sometimes as a multiplicity. We use the plural, times and spaces. But then again we say, Time, Space (*die Zeit, der Raum*).

Now it is undeniable that all of these expressions are brought about by that which actually exists. It could well be, however, that we are dealing with words that are only synsemantical, but which at the same time designate absurdities, introduced into our thought with a certain rational justification, in the way we have explained previously, where they serve us well.[36]

If we understand space and time as non-things,[37] i.e. as not to be subsumed under a common concept with everything else which can become an object of our thought, then, according to what has been said before, we must surely deny existence to space and time. And so the view of Reid and Marty seems to be one we should reject. Descartes, who identified the substance of bodies with its spatial extension, would have been led to identify a body's place with its substance if he had reflected upon how this extension is related to specifications of place. In accordance with what we said previously, the *concretum* would then replace the *abstractum* and hence we would obtain a thing, which is certainly not describable as merely relative, but yet as something with continuity and inconceivable without a relation involving continuity (*etwas Kontinuierliches und ohne Kontinualbeziehung Undenkbares*).[38] Then, when we spoke of space rather than spaces or extents, we would be signifying the totality of all real physical bodies. Nothing would prevent us from saying that this totality, no matter how large it might be, is still not of unlimited size. And then all of the doubts tied up with an *actu* infinite multiplicity cease to exist.

Descartes, to be sure, had said that it is impossible for the totality of all physical bodies to have a limit and just as no physical object could be the last for that reason, so a gap between bodies is also inconceivable: it would be an empty space and this is a *contradictio in adjecto*. The bodies between which there is supposed to be a gap would be separated by nothing. But to be separated by nothing is not to be separated. But this was all completely false. If red and blue are separate from each other this is a consequence of their specific

---

[36] See note 25 above.

[37] Here Brentano implicitly gives the definition of the concept of "substantive entity, thing, being in the sense of the substantive, the Aristotelian *ov*," of which I spoke in the Introduction.

[38] Accordingly, the spatial and temporal are to be conceived of as something which is not *merely* relative (i.e. as something which is absolute), although necessarily standing in relations of continuity.

characters and not a consequence of something which actually exists in-between them in the sense that it diverges from them in opposing directions. The absence of actual colors which could exist between red and blue does not bring them any closer to each other as colors. The same thing is also true, then, when one spatial thing is separate from another. The absence of some actual spatial thing will not bring what exists here and what exists over there any closer together either. There is nothing to prevent a body[39] which is already at a distance from another one, without anything between them, from becoming even farther away from it. All that is required is that one of them undergo a change of place; this is similar, for example, to the fact that there is an even greater difference in color between a reddish brown thing and a previously red thing which has turned yellow than there was between it and the red thing. If it is said that there must already be space there in order for the physical object to enter it, the reply is that if one is speaking of a real space, which amounts to the same thing as the existence of something *spatial*, this is so far from being necessary that it would on the contrary be a hindrance, since the one body would have to push the other one out because it is impossible for two things to have the same specific spatial location. The requirement seems no less improper, indeed even more improper, than the requirement that for something to take on a color, something else would have to exist which already has that color and then surrenders it. It is only the "possibility" of a bodily thing with this spatial location which is called for, then. But from what we have said before,[40] it follows that it is not a positive requirement that this should exist but rather the negative requirement of the absence of contradiction. And if it is said that this possibility must be unlimited, even this concession arouses no more objections from us because it concerns an *infinitum potentia* but not an *infinitum actu*.

10. Now how does the view we have advanced stand in relation to the dispute in which Newton and Leibniz once engaged with respect to the spatial? We cannot say that either one is correct or incorrect in all respects. Newton was certainly correct in maintaining that every spatial point as such must be specifically located. It would not first acquire specification through the existence of a second point only having a location in relation to it. We cannot say this any more than we can say that something blue would not be blue unless there were something red. But he was mistaken when he said that the assertion of such absolutely specific spatial locations would require

[39] Here "body" is to be understood to mean the same as "something spatial and qualified."
[40] See p. 352.

the assumption of a single something to which all possible spatial locations belong in reality. Leibniz was right in opposing him on this point, but he was completely mistaken when he made spatial location something entirely relative, so that something could go from one place to another, without changing in any way at all.[41]

It is most remarkable how he could fall into such an error. There must be a special temptation which also exists for temporal specifications, but not for others such as colors, sounds, heat, number, etc. No one will say that 3 is not 3 in and of itself, but only relative to 6 or 10 or other specific numbers. How could it happen then, that Leibniz committed such an error and indeed that after him men of science quite generally have committed it again and again? The answer emerges in the light of the *very remarkable characteristics of our sensory intuitions*, which, up to the present day, psychologists have for the most part failed to recognize. They believe that the things our intuitions reveal to us are revealed *as individualized*.[42] In fact Kant simply defined the contrast between intuition and concept in such a way that the latter is universal and the former individual. But just the opposite is the case. *Inner* perception never reveals to us anything which another person could not find exactly the same in himself. The other person could sense what he senses, judge what he judges, desire what he desires, and so on. Something similar also holds true of outer *intuition*, and the reason is that when various sense-organs are stimulated the spatial differences of sensibly qualified things always appear to us in relation to something else which stands apart from them. This can be noted quite clearly in the case of seeing. Johannes Müller spoke of a projection of the objects outward. What does this mean except that the colored objects are localized in reference to a point at a distance from them, a point which is colorless itself, but which alone is presented *in modo recto*, while they are objects of presentation *in modo obliquo*?

Stumpf touches upon this when he says in his *Tonpsychologie* that everything spatial seems to be an object of presentation as from a definite standpoint. Petroniewicz said that the point presented *in recto* is the point of the perceiving mind itself. But of course this is not so. Rather, it is only the presentation of a point, which is unqualified and without precise location, which enters into intuition as standing apart at a certain distance and in a certain direction from colored

[41] This resolution of the conflict between Newton and Leibniz provides a way of escaping from the predicaments of modern natural philosophy, especially a way out of relativity theory.
[42] See the Introduction and Kraus's book, *Franz Brentano*, and then Essays XII and XIII.

places, and so with a certain generality.[43] For precisely *the same relationships* can exist for every point in space. Thus we have nothing but general concepts of the spatial and apart from the generic concept of the spatial, they are *only relatively specific determinations of something spatially at a distance in various directions and degrees.* If our presentations of the colored should be subject to the same limitation, it would undoubtedly be a very common mistake to suppose, here too, that there are, in reality, only relatively colored things, but nothing that is colored absolutely. This can be said with all the more confidence, since it has now come to the point where, following Hobbes, people have claimed, similarly to what we have said concerning specific determinations of space, that *all* our concepts are merely relative, and we could never think of a concept in and of itself alone. In the strictest sense one could say that one is none.

11. Something very similar to what was said of the concept of the spatial should be said of the concept of the temporal. All special determinations turn into something that was present more or less long before the present, or that will be, after the present. If something is affirmed temporally, if it is affirmed as past or as future, it is affirmed only in the *modo obliquo*, which is to say it is not actually affirmed at all. Something now existing is affirmed as more or less separated from it in one of two opposing directions. Past things and future things do not actually exist at all, and (no matter how strange it may sound to some), if there were no longer anything present, there would also no longer be anything past. In antiquity it was said, "For this one thing even God cannot do – make what has happened not happen." But they did not notice that this can only be true if God cannot make it the case that nothing is present, either. This is certainly true, of course, but only because being present pertains to Him as it does to everything else which truly exists. This has often been denied in antiquity and still is right down to the present time.

12. In view of all this, what is to be said of the spatial and temporal as such? *The spatial is the physical (das Körperliche) and the temporal is the real (das Reale) as such.* Neither the one nor the other can exist or be conceived, not even in a general way, without a relation involving continuity whereby both the extent and direction of the relation of continuity can remain entirely unspecified. It is not possible to produce an effective argument against the proved impossibility of an *actu infinitum* either on the basis of an allegedly infinite space or an allegedly infinite time. There is truly no space and time but only the spatial and the temporal and the temporal is only the

[43] Consequently an intuitive general presentation of something spatial without qualities.

present, regardless of how it may be set apart from the earlier as the later, and from the later as the earlier, at every conceivable distance. There is no infinite continuum here – only a point belonging to the non-existent continuum. As regards space we must admit that there are not only spatial points but spatial continua as well, namely physical objects and physical accidents, but like the physical points, the physical continua are never *actu* infinite.

13. Let us look back on what we have said about the *ens rationis*. The term arose in the Middle Ages. We do not find it in Aristotle.* Perhaps it can be said that it has not always referred to the same concept. Sometimes it is used in the sense of an object thought-of in some way or other, the "thought-of thing" (*das Gedacht*) taken in as wide a sense as Descartes took it.⁴⁴ Sometimes it is used in a restricted manner and hence we find Suarez raising the question of whether only objects of conceptual thinking or objects of imagination too, whether only objects of presentation and discernment, or objects of judgement, or of desire as well can be called things as such. He himself decides to include objects of imagination but to exclude those of desire. He then goes into the question of what kinds of *entia rationis* there are. He distinguishes three classes: *negatives*, *privatives* and *comparatives*. Relative determinations of this kind are supposed to count as *entia rationis* and not as things, because they can be acquired or lost without the least change in the thing they belong to; Caius, for example, becomes shorter than Titus when the latter grows. *Absurda* created by combining concepts of things are also counted as *entia rationis* according to Suarez. With respect to the relationship between the *ens rationis* and the *ens reale* he maintains that only when the latter are produced or destroyed are certain *entia rationis* brought about or destroyed concomitantly. We see that it does not occur to him to assume space or time as self-existent *entia rationis*, necessary in and of themselves or created. But we may criticize him for an apparent vagueness in his concept, as for example when he deals with *absurda*. *Absurda* surely do not exist, so in their case we cannot speak of something being concomitantly produced. This is possible only in the case of a thought-of absurdity as thought-of, in that loose and improper sense in which the thought-of exists.

As far as comparative relative determinations are concerned, we

---

* He prepares the way for the introduction of the term when he says that in healing, the health that the physician produces exists and when, in distinguishing the three classes of πρός τι he says that for one of them, namely, the relation of the thinking subject to the object thought of there exists no real correlate.

⁴⁴ In Descartes, *cogitatio* includes *ideae, judicia, voluntates*. See Brentano, *The Origin of our Knowledge of Right and Wrong*.

should not agree that they are simply to count as *entia rationis,* because the person who ascribes such a comparative determination to something is also implicitly ascribing absolute real determinations to it. For example, someone who calls Caius taller than Titus is ascribing a size as well as a substance to Caius. But then we must notice that the person who says that Caius is taller than Titus is saying the same thing as a person who says that Caius is taller than Titus *is,* and hence in this case Titus is affirmed as well as Caius, and a size is ascribed to him too. Indeed, one can also say that a collective is affirmed, a collective composed of Caius and Titus, which has a size in terms of each of its parts and one part of which, Titus, is surpassed by another part of itself, Caius. Unquestionably this collective is also a thing, yet this does not contradict the fact that in the case of the comparative determination we are supposed to be dealing with an *ens rationis.* Indeed we have said of *entia rationis* that in their case we are always dealing with something which is an *ens reale* and it is *only in virtue of the form of linguistic expression* that it appears *as though* we were concerned with something non-real.

With reference to *privatives,* which Suarez cites as one class of *entia rationis,* the same holds true. Anyone who says, for example, that someone is deaf, is ascribing certain real properties to him; he must be an animal, by which it is usually meant that he belongs to a species in which the capacity for hearing is present. Such properties as *immaterial* are also counted among privatives in a wider sense. A spirit is immaterial insofar as it is not extended in terms of length, breadth and depth. But the thing which I call immaterial is nevertheless at the same time affirmed as a thing and something substantial. Presentations of other things are involved here in addition, however, including those of someone making a judgement, someone denying and someone rightly denying, for something immaterial is a thing of which it is right to deny that it has extension in length, breadth and depth. In thinking of something as immaterial, then, I am also forming the idea of someone who rightly denies of it that it is corporeal.

With reference to *negatives,* we should take account of the fact that the same expression is sometimes understood in pure negative terms and sometimes in privative terms. An *immortal* can mean either a being which is not mortal or *a thing of which it is to be denied that it is mortal.* In that case we have to do with a privative.[45] Someone

---

[45] This is to be taken into account in interpreting Essay IX on genuine and fictitious objects. Brentano there says, in connection with the O form in syllogistic theory, that it is sufficient for us to imagine that there are negatives as objects. But the form, "S Non P" concerns not a negative, but a privative. "A man is non-seeing" (O) is logically equivalent to the

could apply the expression "non-human" to something which does not exist at all and of which it is therefore false to say that it is human. From this point of view a round square would be as much a non-human as a horse would be. Aristotle seems to have used the expressions in this way. In the latter case we are indeed dealing with an *ens rationis,* and we cannot substitute for its affirmation the affirmation of a thing but rather the denial of a thing which includes among its real specifications the concept *human.* It is as if one said that a certain thing being human (*ein gewisses Reales Mensch-Seiendes*) does not exist.

14. If one wished to make a *complete* survey of *entia rationis,* one would have to go into the great variety of locutions which make *words* the subject and predicate of propositions *which do not refer to real things in and of themselves.* One would have to show how each of them is related to the linguistic expressions which express the same thought in such a way that names of real things become the subject and predicate. Naturally, this variety of locutions arises from complications in our thinking. They make possible abbreviated discourse which is highly advantageous. The whole of ordinary language is so much under their influence that we could not possibly give them up without giving up the use of that language completely and resolving to invent an entirely new and extremely unwieldy language. Even in discussions such as the present one we cannot avoid continually making use of such locutions, locutions which could tempt the unwary into believing that there are non-things to be affirmed in addition to things. Even in the modern period a number of such non-things have been spawned by people who are always going around accusing others of psychologism. They imagined they were enriching science by their many weighty discoveries. *Gegenstandstheorie* or, as they called it,[46] *Phenomenology,*

---

[46] "As they called it"; it should read, "as others called it." Meinong speaks of *Gegenstandstheorie,* Husserl of phenomenology; the two of them have carried on an argument over priority as far as the term and the matter are concerned. In this connection the theory that there are *a priori* truths in both the mental and the physical areas is common to them both. This is an important truth and it is already implicit in *Psychology from an*

---

form, "A non-seeing man exists." In this case it is not really a negative, but a privative which comes into play. Therefore, the combination, "a non-seeing man exists" is to be regarded as identification *in obliquo*: "a man of whom it is to be denied that he sees." In all four cases, therefore, Brentano's simplifying transposition is such that it replaces a predicative judgement by a predicative (attributively identifying) presentational synthesis.

was proclaimed to be a special science entirely independent of psychology. They revived the error of Plato and the ultra-realists like William of Champeaux with certain modifications, by ascribing a being to universals as universals. This discovery was supposed to open the way to the true metaphysics, and, harking back to Kant, *a priori* intuitions and concepts were distinguished along with the presentations of experiences. All of Aristotle's achievements were abandoned and that was supposed to be an eminent advance. A concept such as that of number, of which it is so easy to give an account in terms of the experience of counting, was supposed to be one of these *a priori* concepts. No wonder they could not succeed in deriving the concepts of substance and cause from empirical data. All of mathematics, arithmetic, and geometry were supposed to revolve around concepts which have no empirical origin. This was supposed to be adequately proved by the fact that no one has ever found a perfectly straight line or a perfect circle and that we never encounter a line without width or a point without extension. In the foregoing we have already given enough indication of what can serve to clarify these questions. Diverse operations of thought, among them negation, abstraction, comparison, repetition as many times as desired, composition of attributes *in recto* as well as *in obliquo*, have a large part to play, to say nothing of the fact that experiences, not only of presentations and judgements but of emotional attitudes, too, make an essential contribution. The alleged discoveries of things which have not originated from experience do nothing but disclose the flaws in their own psychology, which is incapable of analyzing the pertinent concepts and showing their true origin.

Empirical Standpoint (see my Introduction). It was expressed explicitly in Brentano's *The Origin of our Knowledge of Right and Wrong*. The recent emphasis on it is to be valued as a service. The attachment to the theory of irreal things which Brentano abandoned, on the other hand, is a hindrance. Extending it by introducing objectives, dignitatives, ideal objects, *Wertverhalten*, etc., is an unconscious fictionalism which makes it seem as though the charge of sterile verbal scholasticism is not unjustified.

Introduction to the *1924 Edition* by *Oskar Kraus*

I   *Brentano's Distinction between Descriptive and Genetic Psychology, and his Position with Regard to Phenomenology and the Theory of Objects*

In 1895 in his *"Letzte Wünche für Osterreich"* Brentano wrote, "My school distinguishes between Psychognosie and genetic psychology (on the basis of a remote analogy with geognosy and geology). The task of the former is to exhibit all of the basic mental phenomena. All other mental phenomena are derived from the combination of these ultimate psychological elements, just as all words are built up out of letters. Completion of this task could provide the basis for a *characteristica universalis* such as Leibniz, and Descartes before him, envisaged. Genetic psychology, on the other hand, is concerned with the laws according to which these phenomena come into being and pass away. Because the conditions of their occurrence are largely physiological, owing to the undeniable dependence of mental functions upon events in the nervous system, we see how investigations in genetic psychology are necessarily connected with physiological investigations."

As far as I have been able to determine, Brentano first lectured on *descriptive psychology* in the winter semester of 1887/8; and subsequently, under the title "Psychognosy" in the winter semester of 1890/1 at the University of Vienna.

The method of *genetic psychology* is that of the natural sciences; it is, therefore, primarily inductive, and in that sense empirical. The method of descriptive psychology can also be called "empirical" because it is based on inner experience; but descriptive psychology requires the experience and apperception of mental events too, in order to ascend to more general ideas on the strength of the intuitions included in that experience, just as mathematics cannot do without intuitions in order to attain the most elementary concepts

369

for its axioms. On the basis of the general concepts obtained in this way, descriptive psychology arrives at *general truths* directly "at one stroke and without induction"; this point was made by Brentano in his work *The Origin of our Knowledge of Right and Wrong* in 1889.

In his *Psychology* of 1874 Brentano had already acknowledged some such evident apodictic cognitions; he maintained, in fact, that they were all negative. "Nothing can be an object of judgement unless it is present to the mind as an idea." "We can neither love nor hate unless the object of the emotion is present to the mind as an idea." These and many other psychological truths dealt with in *Psychology from an Empirical Standpoint* and *The Origin of our Knowledge of Right and Wrong* are *a priori* in character. In a letter written in 1904, Brentano analyzes in detail the acquisition of *a priori* value judgements (see *Origin*, p. 111). The knowledge of general laws attained in this way should not, then, be classified as "natural science." Unlike the laws or regularities of genetic psychology, they are not psycho-physical. They are not about matters of fact; they are *vérités de raison*, apodictic *a priori* judgements rather than *vérités de fait*. They "have no existential import" because, like all *a priori*, i.e. apodictic judgements which are evident from the very concepts involved, they are negative. This very disclosure of the thoroughly negative character of these judgements, despite their affirmative linguistic form, is one of Brentano's most important discoveries.

Enough has been said to indicate the extent to which Brentano's "descriptive psychology" ("*Psychognosie*") is echoed in Husserl's "Phenomenology" and to a certain extent, too, in Meinong's "Theory of Objects." But it also clearly demonstrates certain differences. Unlike Husserl, Brentano recognizes no "ideal, timeless, general objects" to which true being is to be ascribed; and unlike Meinong, he acknowledges no objects which are "subsistent" yet "non-existential." For him, Husserl's "*Wesenschau*" is a fiction as soon as it claims to be more than the forming of more abstract, simplified and generalized concepts. It becomes a mere fiction as soon as it accepts real entities which can never be individuated or specified – *in specie specialissima*.

It is of the utmost importance that we should be clear about the term "object." When it is used to mean the same as *thing* or *real entity* it functions as a term having a meaning of its own – it is auto-semantic. In this case it refers simply to what we comprehend by the most general concept that we can obtain by abstraction from perceptual data; and Brentano treats it as equivalent to the expressions "entity" and "thing." But when "object" is used in constructions such as "to have something as an object" it has no meaning of its own (although the construction as a whole has a meaning which can always be conveyed by the expression "to have something before the mind"), it is synsemantic. We can illustrate the ambiguity and the occasionally synsemantic function of "object" by pointing out the equivalence of the two sentences, "I have something, i.e. a thing, as object," and, "I have something, i.e. an object, as object." In the latter sentence, the first occurrence of "object" exemplifies the auto-semantic use of the term, the second the synsemantic. Taken as a whole, the sentence is equivalent in meaning to, "I am thinking of a thing," "A thing appears to me," "A thing is a phenomenon of mine," "A thing appears to me objectively, or as given, or phenomenally, or immanently."

Some ambiguity, therefore, is unavoidable unless one quite definite use of the word "object" is adopted. The Theory of Objects has failed to create the necessary terminological and conceptual clarity here; and Phenomenology, too, entirely overlooks the fact that in such constructions the meaning of "object" is dependent upon other words. This failure to take account of the synsemantic nature of the word "object" is characteristic, however, not only of those lines of thought which have evolved from Brentano, but of contemporary philosophy in general – I am thinking of Rickert's "object of knowledge" in particular.

Just as disturbing as the complete failure to note the synsemantic character of "object" in cases where we speak of "intentional or mental object" is the failure to distinguish between this sense of "object" and Brentano's "object *simpliciter*" or "thing." The remainder of this section will dwell in detail on this major point, since its neglect can only plunge philosophy into a "sea of delusions."

In an attempt to show why it has been necessary to develop a special theory of objects distinct from our knowledge of things or real entities, it has been pointed out that there are *a priori* truths about colors. But colors are not physical objects, so it has been claimed that we must be able to talk about "existence-free objects." Certainly we can do this insofar as we are speaking of things which do not exist and therefore have no existence, no Being, and not even any "subsistence." The further claim that "white and black and sounds and sensory qualities" are nothing mental is also correct, but it would be false to say that we are not thinking of anything physical (extended) when we think of colors, sounds, and other sensory qualities. Indeed the objects of our perception are all physical even though they are physical objects of a sort which physicists themselves teach us do not exist! Physicists inquire as to whether there are colors and sounds and they give a negative answer. It is a matter of *a priori* knowledge (based on concepts derived from intuition) that, if there were colors, they would possess certain characteristics and relations. For example, if there were such colors as yellow and blue, they could not but be of a certain degree of brightness, and be more similar to each other than, say, black and white. What these *a priori* truths are concerned with are *truths that have to do with impossibility, negative judgements*. In this sense, but in this sense only, are they "existence-free."

The *a priori* does involve a special *way of knowing*, namely apodictic-negative, but it does not involve a special *domain of knowledge*. Consequently, Theory of Objects cannot stand as a science having its own special subject matter. But if the word "object" is understood synsemantically, as it must be in the case of Meinong's "Every experience has an object" then "to have an object" is simply to be conscious of something, or to have something as object. And on this interpretation the Theory of Objects is no more than the Theory of Having An Object, that is to say, it is descriptive psychology or Phenomenology in the sense described – that of a body of *a priori* psychological laws.

I believe that enough has now been said to demonstrate the ambiguity of the Theory of Objects. Common to both its interpretations is the central concern with the *a priori*, and in particular with *a priori* negative truths derived immediately from concepts which are in their turn derived from intuition; thus it is *a priori* knowledge that is derived from what have been called "intuitive concepts." There may even be some methodological advantage, as Marty has pointed out, in assigning the task of discovering such *a priori* truths to psychologically trained investigators who might be best fitted for it by their special skills and experience. Geometry and mathematics, on the other hand, have a somewhat different methodology: these are also areas of *a priori* knowledge but since they go beyond the derivation of axioms from "intuitive concepts" and employ complicated "conceptual syntheses" or "creations of the human mind," they require a rather different type of approach. In particular, they make extensive use of synsemantic symbols and inventions such as imaginary numbers, negative numbers and points lying in infinity, as heuristic tools. Thus the unifying concern of Meinong's Theory of Objects is not in fact a special class of *object*, but a certain method of deriving *a priori* concepts and laws from perceptual intuition. We can take a similar view of Husserl's Phenomenology.

These, then, are the basic differences between Brentano's view and the theories of Meinong and Husserl. Both Meinong and Husserl fail to recognize the synsemantic function of the word "object" and the negative character of *a priori* axioms; and this led them to postulate different strata or kinds of being, to distinguish between "being," "subsistence," and "external being" and finally to introduce such fictions as "objectives," "dignitatives," and "contents" having a timeless existence. These points are discussed in the Appendix to *The Classification of Mental Phenomena* and in the essays that have been added to the second part of this book, as well as in the following chapters of this introduction.

To recapitulate, Brentano admits no modes of being, no ideal objects, none of the non-things which proliferate in modern philosophy. *All modes of being can be reduced to modes of conceptualization and to modes of self-evident a priori judgements based on such concepts and also to self-evident assertoric judgements.* Far from destroying the objectivity of our knowledge and impugning the validity of self-evident judgements, Brentano, while firmly confining himself to the discussion of consciousness, is concerned to show how we can attain knowledge of an external world. This will become clearer in what follows.

II *The Historical Development of Brentano's Theory of Mental Reference*

Brentano took over the theory of "the mental inexistence of the object" from Aristotelian philosophy and provided it with its most complete expression in his psychology. He made it his own theory of "intentional reference," although this title is not meant to suggest the sense of intention in which we "intend to reach a goal." As he writes in Book II, "Reference to an object" or, as he later puts it more clearly, "Reference to *something* as an object is characteristic of mental phenomena." (Book II, Chap. 1, Sect. 9.)

According to the accepted theory, every so-called relation presupposes the *existence* of the two terms between which it holds. Now Brentano spoke about intentional reference, so it was easy to interpret him as saying that an intentional relation exists between the subject who thinks of something and an object which somehow exists in his mind. Thus people also spoke of the mental inexistence of an object.

Brentano did not remain unaware of the inadequacy of such an interpretation. It was the subject of discussions between him and Anton Marty, and in his *Untersuchungen*, Marty provides a noteworthy history and critique of the theory – although Marty's own attempt to replace it with a theory of "actual or possible correspondence to something" cannot be regarded as a satisfactory solution. (Brentano touches on this expedient of Marty's in a letter to which I shall refer again below.) Some of Brentano's other former students have also tried to improve upon the theory, but they all retained the assumption that consciousness is a "referential relation," i.e. that it requires the existence of *both terms* of the so-called relation. Since it was realized that the "intentional object" could not be viewed as existing *within* consciousness, attempts were made to provide some alternative explanation of its status; but there was no attack on the original theory that consciousness consists in a correlation between two existent terms. It is to Brentano, always his own most rigorous critic, that we must turn to find such a departure.

Besides abandoning the theory of "the mental inexistence of the object," Brentano demonstrated in the Appendix to *The Classification of Mental Phenomena* that consciousness should not be called a relation in the normal sense of that term. For example, "comparative relations," such as those of size ("A is larger than B") are said to presuppose the existence of their two terms, or "bases" (A and B). Generally, it is held that every relation must hold between two such existing bases. If we accept this view – without further examination of this account of relations – it must be clear that Brentano was correct in holding that "mental reference" cannot be called a "relation" in the sense defined. For a special feature of the "referential relationship of consciousness" is that its existence requires the existence of only one term: it never requires the existence of the second term, to which the mental act refers. For example, if I think of the God Jupiter, there only exists the person who has the God Jupiter before his mind; the God Jupiter does not exist (or subsist) at all.

But consciousness does have *some* similarity to a relation such as that of comparison. Brentano explained this similarity in the following way. Anyone who thinks of something which is larger than something else must think of two terms; and he must think of one term directly and of the other indirectly. Similarly with "mental relations"; if anyone thinks of a "mental reference," for example of someone who likes flowers, then he is thinking *directly* of the person who likes flowers, and *indirectly* of flowers. The difference is that, while both terms of the "comparative relation" exist, this need not be true of the "mental relation." It was for this reason that Brentano came to describe consciousness as "quasi-relational" ("relativliches"). . . .

Brentano came to hold that consciousness is not a relation in the usual sense of that term, i.e. it is not a relation between two existing terms (or co-existents). Briefly, we may say that it is not a "co-existential relation"; it is not a "correlation." "Existence" is taken here to have exactly the same meaning as "subsistence" or "being." Brentano also made the special point that consciousness is not a referential relation to something in the mind – whether that "something" does not exist, exists mentally, appears, or is "given." . . .

Many of those who theorize about consciousness do not make it sufficiently clear that consciousness cannot be characterized or distinguished by a factor which does not belong to consciousness itself – and still less by something which sometimes does and sometimes does not exist. Accordingly, the existence (being, subsistence) of the object of consciousness is essentially irrelevant to the concept of consciousness. A further point now arises, for if the existence or non-existence of what is before the mind in a presentation is irrelevant as far as the concept of presentation is concerned, then the concept of presentation does not include anything of the "individuality" of its object. In fact, Brentano went on to show how the concept of an *individual as a thing incapable of further differentiation* arises by means of a conceptual synthesis; and he demonstrated that it is a necessary truth that anything which exists (or subsists) must be an individual.

This generality and indeterminacy which is shown to characterize presentations would also apply to all other basic forms of consciousness; for these, whether they are judgements or emotional attitudes, are based on presentations and must share their characteristics. Even our intuitive perceptions – though they are acts of belief rather than *pure* presentations – are never concerned with *individuals*. Mental life begins with *general ideas*, presentations upon which beliefs (judgements) and occasionally emotional attitudes are superimposed. Such intuitive perceptions – and Brentano distinguishes between "inner" and "outer" perception – do not reveal any individual thing nor do they contain any particular idea of an individual. Whether the object which we intuitively perceive is material or mental, its individuating features remain hidden to us. In an intuitive perception we are always aware of the substance which is part of the thing perceived in an extremely general, and never in a completely individuated way. (Brentano returned to this Aristotelian doctrine at the end of his life.) So the real problem is not how general ideas are attained, but how ideas of the individual come about. One of Brentano's most interesting advances is the idea that the intuitions of inner and outer perception are general forms of consciousness – even though they are of minimal generality. The process of "abstraction" proceeds from lesser to greater generality, not from the individual to the general.

It is our affirmative or negative self-evident judgements which establish whether a thing exists or does not exist. In the case of objects of secondary, self-evident, affirmative, self-awareness, the judgement will give us certainty. In the case of a transcendent object which does not fall within "inner perception," it will yield probability. (Brentano had always held that certainty of the affirmative kind could only be attained within the realm of *inner* perception.) Solipsism is not necessarily false; there is no internal contradiction in the notion that nothing exists besides myself as thinker-of-something. But even in this case, my consciousness could vary in terms of differentiation in the object.

It follows that this "variation in object" is not determined by variation in things that exist or "objects" simpliciter." The question of the existence of what is before the mind is quite separate from the analysis of an instance of presentation. We can be conscious of something which does not exist at all, and even, indeed, of something which could not possibly exist. In conscious activity the mind is concerned with something, and this concern may change in two ways: we may change the nature (or *mode*) of our concern, or we may become concerned with something else. Both of these are differentiations of the *same* mental entity in different ways.

Now we may assume that it has been established beyond reasonable doubt that there are *many* things, and we know *a priori* that, if they exist, they must be individuated. But a single general idea may represent one thing as well as another, for example the idea of a person thinking might be the idea of me as well as of you, although we are two distinct individuals. Conversely, I can think of Socrates as a man, as a living creature, as feeling, as willing, seeing, etc. This makes it even clearer that it is not the *individual* differences between existing things which distinguish between presentation on the "object side"; rather, this distinction consists in our being concerned with something *as something* at one time and *as something else* at another. Generally speaking, in any instance of presentation *there is something to which something is present as something.* This characterization by means of a threefold something may be abstract, but it would still seem to be the most adequate account that we can give in words of the obscure processes of consciousness.

So we think *of* something *as* something. When we change from thinking of X as A to thinking of X as B, our idea undergoes a specific change; here we could speak loosely of a "difference of object" as the differentiating feature. But we must always remember that this is not a difference imposed from outside or a difference in some "object" which exists within the mind; we must remember that "object" is a synsemantic word.

According to Kant's famous Copernican Revolution in philosophy, it is impossible to claim that our intuitive perception is determined by "objects"; on the contrary, "objects" (as "objects of sense") are determined by our intuitive perception and by the concepts we use. But, when expressed as bluntly as this, *both* of these views are wrong, for both presuppose the existence of "objects" in the first place. In fact, what Kant pointedly called an "object as an object of our senses" is a creation of the mind (or rather of the senses) and, as such, does not exist in any way at all; it is the object of presentation as such, a "phenomenon" pure and simple. It is just ourselves who exist, being conscious of something or having something as phenomenon or as object. The expressions "object as object of the senses" and "the intentional, mental object" only have meaning in connection with other terms – they are synsemantic. Thus, to retain Kant's analogy, neither the Aristotelian–Ptolemaic nor the Copernican theory is correct.

When I have some real thing before my mind, when I truly think of something, my thought may be of something which does exist, which does not exist or even which could not exist. At least in the last two cases, there can be no question of my thought resembling or copying some actually existing object. So "copying" is no more essential to our analysis of the concept of consciousness than is the *existence* of the object of my concern. Only if what is before my mind is *known* to exist, i.e. when its affirmation is self-evident, can we ask whether some "image" of it exists in my consciousness. And the answer is emphatically no. For, when I correctly affirm something or correctly make a predication of something, I affirm I know that thing itself and not just something similar to it. The knower's intention has to do with the *Ding an sich* not the "immanent object" or the "image" of a thing; otherwise the intending could never be a transcending of phenomena. The person engaged in an act of mental reference is concerned not with images of things but with the things themselves which he thinks of, affirms, denies, loves or hates. . . .

As we have said before, Brentano holds that consciousness can never be thought of as a reference to something existing as such; it is always a "relative determination" in the sense of something quasi-relational. After all, we should never forget that the primary task of an analysis is to correct the errors which have arisen from the inadequacy of ordinary language and from the "inner linguistic form," and from the inadequacy of philosophy which takes its bearings from language to begin with. Already our understanding has been furthered by seeing how we should *not* interpret consciousness. It is not a co-existence relation of any kind – whether with something existing immanently or with something existing transmentally or transcendentally.

Husserl, for his part, has rightly seen that the so-called referential relation of consciousness cannot hold between the state of consciousness or the conscious subject and an immanent object. But he has retained Brentano's earlier interpretation of consciousness as a co-existence relation and has therefore had to find some correlative that could exist in any instance of consciousness. This was how he came to discover, or, more accurately, to invent his "ideal objects."

Other writers, too, have entirely overlooked Brentano's later works on the topic of "mental reference," though it is obvious that scientific progress will be hindered by this neglect of the most mature achievements of his intellect. . . .

But Brentano did more than just show that mental reference cannot be called a relation in the traditional way, and I shall now try to explain how he fundamentally transformed the theory of relations.

We have already remarked that, according to the traditional and most widely-held interpretation, relations exist between two existing "bases": a relation of similarity might hold between one ball and another, a relation of being-larger-than might exist between Caius on the one hand and Titus on the other. But the paradox which follows from this view is well-known, for example the predicate of similarity to ball B that I assert of ball A can be lost to A without A undergoing any change at all. It is enough for B to lose its round shape. Thus it is clear that ascribing "similarity to B" or "being larger than B" cannot concern predicates of A; if it did, how could they be lost without A changing? We can resolve the difficulty by saying that *two* judgements are expressed in the statement "A is larger than B." B is affirmed as well as A. But it is not strictly necessary for us to affirm B in order to ascribe the predicate "larger than B" to A; it is sufficient for this purpose for me merely to *think* of B as being smaller in size than A.

So if I hear that Titus is an inch shorter than Caius, and I know the height of Caius, I learn exactly how tall Titus is. In this way I arrive at a predicate of Titus indirectly, by way of my idea of the height of Caius. And this predicate will not be affected at all by the fate of Caius; it is a matter of an indirect, derivative way of defining height for which only the idea of the height of Caius is necessary, and not his existence. There is no size-relationship of any kind between the two that would involve some "real connection." If Caius disappears, Titus and his height remain the same; and I can still specify his height on the basis of my idea of Caius, whether by thinking that Titus is taller than Caius was, or by thinking that he is taller than Caius "as I imagine him." So language misleads us in this case; in saying "Titus is smaller than Caius," we affirm Caius as well as Titus, and therefore make a statement about something which lies entirely *outside of Titus*. It is the linguistic form which leads us to understand a *denominatio mere extrinseca* as a relational attribute and to suffer the illusion that a relational attribute of a subject can be lost without the subject undergoing the slightest change.

In expressions such as "The population of the world is less than eighteen milliards" it is quite clear that we do not affirm "eighteen milliards"; we only have in mind what is associated with the term "eighteen milliards" so that we can evoke a general idea of size in order to specify the population which really is affirmed. Thus we have to be careful to disentangle the relative determination from its linguistic camouflage and adulteration. Such examples are typical of the "comparative relations" of identity, similarity, and difference.

It is such comparative relations as these which are held by the prevalent theory to typify genuine relations, i.e. relations of co-existence. Once Brentano had seen that the "mental relation" is fundamentally different, since it does not require the existence of two terms, he described it as merely *relation-like*. But considerations like those just set forth persuaded him that the conventional theory of relations suffered from obscurities, and that precisely what it took to be a paradigm of the concept of relationship least deserved the name. This concept cannot be derived from the "co-existence relations" that have been mentioned, since they contain *denominationes mere extrinseca*. Rather, consciousness itself is a prototype of all relationships and can only be called "relation-like" if we have an inappropriate concept of relation.

According to Brentano's definitive theory, just one thing generally characterizes "relative determination": *if a person thinks of one determination directly, he must also think of another indirectly*, and the indirect thought is capable of a great diversity of modes. It is best to avoid the grammatical abstraction "relation" and to speak rather of the "relative" or of "that which is related to something." Understood in this way, every "relative determination" (every relative thing) is something real and is a real attribute of its subject. What groups or classes of the relative are to be differentiated is a difficult problem.

Certain other varieties of the relative come into question here; the continuous (the "relation of continuity or connection"), the causal (the "relation of causality"), the subsistent (relation of substance and accident). But we are concerned here only with the mental, with "that-which-is-mentally-related-to-something" or, as we can now say without danger of misunderstanding, with that which mentally refers to something. For it is also part of the concept of consciousness that the presentation of some "consciousness of something" always involves the presentation of two terms, one directly and the other indirectly; and we must add, of course, that only one of these terms need exist.

379

If we now reconsider "comparative relations" from the position at which we have arrived, we may truly say that they are similar to the "relative" in only one way: the idea of a consciousness which makes comparisons and joins things in relations plays a part in both of them and in *this* sense "establishes relations."

I cannot go further into this matter since my aim in this Introduction is merely to trace the historical development of Brentano's theory. We must now consider another aspect of Brentano's theory which has become something of a turning-point, namely that whatever we are thinking of or have before our mind, we have as our object something which falls under a most general and supreme concept which Brentano referred to as a *thing, substance*, or *real entity*.

III *Brentano's Theory of Things as the Only Objects of Consciousness*

We have spoken repeatedly of Brentano's view that it is impossible to have the "irreal" – that which is not a real thing – before the mind, and, consequently, it is impossible for anything other than a real thing to be the object of affirmation or denial or of love or hate. This view contains the germ of another point of irreconcilable opposition to almost all the earlier schools of thought which developed from Brentano.

The new theory is based on the unity of the *concept* of consciousness (not to be confused with the so-called unity of consciousness); since the concept of "consciousness of something," i.e. the *cogitare*, or of "having something as an object," is a unitary concept, it follows that this "something" is similarly a unitary concept; and Brentano sometimes calls it "thing," sometimes "substance," sometimes "real thing." But here "real" does not mean "actual," for whatever one has before the mind is a real thing, whether it is one which exists (i.e. is actual) or not. If, for example, I am thinking of Pegasus, I am thinking of a substance or real thing which is not actual. (Since we frequently use "real" and "actual" interchangeably, it would probably be more appropriate to use another term such as "substance," or "substantial," or "thinglike" thing.) Thus Brentano's rejection of Platonic realism – even in its most modern versions – with its admission of the existence of universals, is total. But in his theory of categories he is in accord with Plato rather than Aristotle for he admits a single supreme category under which everything that we think of, judge, or evaluate can be subsumed. Simple as this idea seems, it represents an extremely important innovation which has hitherto been almost completely ignored.

Aristotle believed that a whole and its part could not *actually* exist at the same time; one or the other must exist in potentiality only. Now from this and his correct belief that a subject which thinks something and then ceases to think still continues to be the same thing, he concluded that substance and accident (in this example substance and thinking; that is, the act of thought as such) are both to be called an ὄν or real entity, but in different senses. This *theory of the manifold significance of being* (cp. Brentano's *Von der mannigfachen Bedeutung des Seienden nach Aristotles*) that is, of things, is rejected in Brentano's later philosophy; instead he takes the concept of ὄν, i.e. of a substantial or real thing, to be the most general concept.

Thus, whenever I have something as object, that thing falls under the highest category – that of real things. It is impossible to have an idea of a non-thing. To the objections that one must have an idea of a non-thing in order to deny the possibility of having an idea of a non-thing, the answer is that this denial means simply that it is impossible rightly to affirm that a subject is thinking of something and at the same time rightly to deny that he is a subject thinking of a real thing.

This is only one of innumerable cases where a highly condensed linguistic form has to be reworded in order adequately to express a thought which is much more complex than the language would suggest; other cases are more complex still. This complexity in ideas arises from those modes of presentation which Brentano calls direct and indirect modes; until now these have eluded explicative analysis, although language does give a clear hint of these important differences in presentation with its distinction between the direct and indirect cases in declension. We have already touched on such oblique modes of presentation; an indirect presentation occurs whenever we think of a relative idea such as *a cause of something*, or *consciousness of something* or *limit of something*.

Anton Marty, so far the only person who has studied Brentano's new theory, says in his "*Die logische, lokalistische und andere Kasustheorien*," and in his small discussion "*Funktionen der Kasus*" (both reprinted in his *Gesammelte Schriften*) that "our most appropriate means of expressing correlatives and relational properties is by means of indirect speech, together with the governing words." But he did not adopt Brentano's theory of direct and indirect modes of presentation, since he believed that, if there were different modes of presentation, the contrast between "correct" and "incorrect" would apply here too, just as it does in the case of judgements, where the difference between the correct and incorrect is bound up with modes of affirmation and denial. But Marty's objection fails, because the correct–incorrect dichotomy relates to the self-evidence of the judgement and to nothing else.

The self-evident judgement is justified of itself; the judgement is as it ought to be. It is only in comparison with the evident judgement that we can know something to be true or false, correct or incorrect. In the realm of presentations, however, there is nothing resembling self-evidence or insight, although there are differing modes of presentation, which naturally exert a manifold influence on those judgements and emotional attitudes which are founded on presentations – this is shown in the Appendix to *The Classification of Mental Phenomena*. And consideration of these modes of presentation allows us to give an account of all the forms of consciousness which provided the excuse for the construction of "contents" (Marty), "states of affairs" and "ideal objects" (Husserl), "structures" (Stumpf), and "objectives" and "dignitatives" (Meinong).

Brentano recognizes no plurality in the supreme category of those things which can be present to the mind as its objects; but inasmuch as he reduces the plurality of *what* we can think of to the unity of a single supreme conceptual category, he introduces a corresponding multiplication and complication in *how* we think of them.

Here we may introduce a letter from Brentano to me, dated September 14, 1909, which is particularly useful in the understanding of the historical development of his theory. In my own letter I had attempted to defend the theory that things which are not real, and in particular such *irrealia* as *states of affairs*, *contents*, and *values*, can be and are objects of presentation. Brentano replied in this rather long letter:

Dear Friend: I am glad to learn from your letter more precisely why it is that you cannot agree with certain views of mine which I reached after years of reflection.

.I can only approve of the fact that my authority does not sway you. For you to accede to my authority would be quite contrary to what I have always urged on my students. Neither I nor any other mortal is proof against error, at least not in philosophy. Allusion to successive changes in my thinking would not, then, have been necessary in order to make me understand why the trust with which you honor me does not extend so far as to ascribe infallibility to me.

But I cannot pass over in silence the fact that you have not presented the development of my thought (of which, as is my custom, I allowed my friends to be fully aware) quite accurately, in that you depict me as holding a series of the most diverse and contradictory theories. This I have by no means done; on the contrary, I made no secret of the fact that my investigations were not yet complete. It was not a change of conviction which occurred; I was experimenting with different hypotheses at different times and naturally I was concerned to bring out those factors in favor of the view which I held as a hypothesis at the time and to refute those which seemed incompatible with it.

There is a single exception to what I have just said: it is true that at one time I treated the contents of judgements, as Marty does now, as though they could be the objects of presentations, judgements, and emotions, just as things can be. At that time a man existing in the past and a man existing in the future were both objects of affirmation for me, and, as Marty still does, I believed in an infinite number of impossibilities as well as possibilities existing from eternity. [See Marty's *Untersuchungen zur Grundlegung der allgemeinen Grammatik und Sprachphilosophie*.] So this really was once my conviction, my theory. It appears most clearly in *Psychology from an Empirical Standpoint*, where negative predicates are treated just like positive features, and hypothetical and disjunctive statements are reduced to a categorical form: that is, "If A is B, then C is D" becomes "It is not the case that A is B without C's being D," and "Either A is B or C is D" becomes "Either A's being B or C's being D is the case." Thus I cannot contradict Marty's statement that in his theory of contents he is defending a theory which I had earlier advocated myself; nor can I grant that Meinong has, in setting up his "objectives," been in any way original, unless the substitution of a new and scarcely appropriate term for what I and Marty called "contents" entitles him to recognition as an original mind.

If it is asked how I came to this point of view, part of the answer might be that essentially I came from the Aristotelian school. And Aristotle often speaks as though when you answer the question "Is it true that no triangle has angles whose sum is greater than two right angles?" with an ἔστι, you are using ἔστι in the same sense as when you say of a thing "It is." One need only look at the beginning of the *Posterior Analytics* for an example of this. [Cp. Brentano, *Aristotles und seine Weltanschauung*, p. 25.] And Aristotle did indeed exert a genuine influence on me here, whereas I never drew on Bolzano in the slightest. From this thinker, whom I nevertheless regard as worthy of respect, I received nothing more than the motivation to deal with certain problems; my answers to them were quite different, and necessitated my rejection of his. [What is referred to is Bolzano's *The Paradoxes of the Infinite*.]

At that time, too, I proposed the three fundamental classes of mental reference, and held (as Marty still does) that only the latter two classes differ in respects other than having different objects, namely in their actual way of referring; and as long as I stood by these views, I could not alter my opinion on the question of what can count as an object. But finally I had to recognize what was dubious and even absurd in the theory I held at that time; for even the authority of Aristotle did not uphold it consistently; we find him, for example, asserting repeatedly that the ὄν ὡς ἀληθές does not exist outside the intellect. And no one has been more emphatic than he in condemning the assumption of infinite quantities.

I myself recognized this absurdity; and it was this, among many other considerations, which prevented me from being content with the mistaken view I held at that time – a view which generates more and more contradictions the further its consequences are developed.

To recount all these consequences here would take us too far. But in addition to the question of the absurdity of infinite quantities, I referred in my last letter to this problem, too: if the non-existence of A can come before the mind as a presentation, then so, implicitly, can the non-existence of A and B. It is just like the case of a person seeing twenty balls, who must, implicitly, be seeing every single ball and every pair and dozen of them, even though he does not so differentiate them; it was this consideration which led Aristotle to oppose those who maintain that, when the whole is seen, parts of less than a certain size are not seen. A parallel conclusion follows unavoidably for our own case; the non-existence of A does indeed implicitly entail the non-existence of A and B, provided that the negative judgement is understood to apply separately to both the existence of A and the existence of B, so that an alleged presentation of the non-existence of A leads also to an implicit presentation of the non-existence of A and B. But no one can admit this and still hold fast to the truth that A and B cannot be thought of as negative unless they are present to the mind in a non-negative thought. For then thinking of the non-existence of A would entail not simply the presentation of A, but also that of B, C, etc. You attempted to refute this view in your last letter. Perhaps the way in which I have restated it here will show you that you did not touch the crucial point of the argument.

A similar criticism applies to your attempt to guard against the consequences of the acceptance of infinite quantities. You mistakenly cite my earlier reference to the case in which we could take one and the same thing to be one or two, or indeed as many things as we liked. I still believe today that there is reason for thinking this – provided that the number in question is a finite number – and I was careful to add explicitly, "but not as an infinite number," at that time too. The present case is quite different; it does not concern something which can be understood at will to consist of one or many things up to any finite number we like, but with something which would, throughout eternity, consist of an infinite number of things. The impossibilities, like the possibilities, the non-existents, the future things and events, would all alike be present, not in finite, but in unquestionably infinite number.

So I regard both these arguments as standing untouched, as well as others which I put forward against my earlier theory, with, I believe, no less destructive an effect. It is paradoxical in the extreme to say that a man promises to marry an *ens rationis* and fulfills his promise by marrying a real person; and it is equally paradoxical to say that if everything real were destroyed there would still exist an ongoing process insofar as what existed yesterday would become what existed the day before, and then the day before that, and so on. [Cp. Franz Brentano, "*Zur Lehre von Raum und Zeit,*" *Kantstudien,* XXV, No. 1 (1920).] Nor do I hesitate to maintain that this endlessly continuing change would be a substantial change, provided that nothing else existed as subject undergoing this change; and I hold further that it would deny to God the attribute of unique principle of all being, if something – even an impossibility – should subsist independently of him. But here it is less vital to follow through all the consequences of the argument than to convince oneself – by sober contemplation of the facts – that nothing is ever made an object of thinking but a real thing. Even Marty cannot deny that in the alleged presentation of the "non-existence of A," it is always A itself which is the object of mental activity, and that, should this activity, directed to A, cease, the allegedly different contemplation of the non-existence of A would cease with it. Perhaps he will grant that to assume otherwise is to embrace an absurdity; and that we should accept this not only as an empirical truth applying to men, but, with complete confidence, as an *a priori* truth for any thinking being. And why is this so? The more one studies the subject, the more one grasps the truth that in our thinking we never refer to the non-existence of A, but always to A itself.

But naturally the claim that our thinking has nothing but things as objects leads to the assumption of a much greater diversity of mental reference than we had at one time supposed. When I say, for example, that I am thinking of something larger than A, my idea of something larger than A refers in a certain way to something other than A, but it also refers in a certain way to A, too. When I predicate "larger than A" of something, I do not predicate "A" of it: yet the predication still refers to A.

Having recognized this, I multiplied modes of mental reference; I introduced, for example, temporal modes of judgement, and of presentation and emotional attitude; and also attempted to introduce a negative presentation. This attempt failed to accord perfectly with the truth; yet my thoughts were moving in a progressive direction, and further advances led to attempts to admit an apodictic presentation, and a presentation with modes reminiscent of the modes of emotional attitude.

According to this latest conception, which, as is my habit, I no more concealed from my friends than I did the earlier stages of my development, there would, strictly speaking, be incomparably more modes of mental reference than are capable of being comprised by the three classes which we earlier accepted as fundamental. [That is, just as many modes as there are indirect modes of presentation. O.K.] And these classes now retain their previous importance only because of two considerations; first, there can be no mental reference to an object unless there is also a mental reference to that object in one or more of these three ways. Second, and most important, it is possible by means of fictions to subsume all our mental activities under the three classes of presentation, judgement and emotional attitude. The use of fictions is seen as similar to that of the mathematicians when they speak of adding a negative amount rather than subtracting, and of raising to a fractional power instead of taking a root; and when they treat fractions, irrational, and negative numbers, and even imaginary quantities in the same way as whole numbers. This has a number of methodological advantages. [The division of mental references into presentation, judgements and emotional attitudes stands: the methodological advantage of fictions is that of drastic simplification, as with the mathematical synsemantics. O.K.] It would lead too far if I were to expand on these general intimations; but perhaps they will suffice to show you why –

although I do not really hold "good" and "bad" to be objects –
I could, at our last meeting and in my last letter, appear so
tolerant towards the retention of forms of speech which we
used to express our earlier point of view.

For the rest, I will merely express my surprise that you find
"correct" so unintelligible unless one believes, in the case of
every judgement (and especially negative judgements), in the
existence of an object which corresponds with the judgement.
Certainly only one way of judging is correct for a given object,
and that is that affirmation or denial which corresponds with
it, i.e. is appropriate or right in that particular case; it cannot
be the case that one way of judging is correct for me and
another for someone else. If I remember rightly, it is this
mistake which Urbach makes in his theory of time, when he
permits different things to be true for God and true for us.

But the meaning of "correct" is still not sufficiently clear; we
can only make it clear in the same way we explain to a person
who wants to know the meaning of the word "red"; he must be
put in such a position as to be able to grasp immediately and
intuitively what is involved. We find ourselves in such a position
when, knowing something, we find that many of those who lack
this knowledge make judgements contradicting ours, whereas
others, even without insight, make the same judgement as we
do. We do not then say that they *know*, but that they are
making a *correct judgement* insofar as their judgement agrees
with ours. So we can convey the sense of the word "correct"
so as to make for clarity by saying that a person judges
correctly who judges with respect to the content of his
judgement and to the affirmation or denial of its object, and to
its temporal mode and possibly also its necessity, as he would
judge if he judged with knowledge. And in the sphere of
emotional attitudes, we should explicate "correct" in a similar
way. I have always maintained that in this sphere the meaning
of "correct" can only be clarified by reference to experiences of
love and preference which are experienced as being correct.
[Cp. *The Origin of our Knowledge of Right and Wrong.*] I
cannot understand what you wish to achieve here with your
belief in the existence of goods to which the emotion corresponds. Do you really think that such goods are there to be
perceived in the same way as the emotional activity of the
mind, and that you can compare the perception of the external
good with the internal emotion so as to conclude the correctness
of the emotion from their agreement with one another? I should
imagine that the mere raising of such a question would suffice

to show anyone the impossibility of an affirmative answer; I should do you an injustice if I were to doubt your conviction of the fact that there are not two such perceptions in question, but only the one, which we find within ourselves. But if this is so, then what further proof do we need to show that the entire theory of existence of "goodness" cannot contribute anything to the clarification of the sense of "good"?

As this letter indicates, Brentano himself operated for a long time with those "states of affairs" which are said to be present to the mind and to exist without being real. This is a widely accepted view, and we find it in similar form today in connection with other lines of thought, as, for example, Kant's conceptual categories ("*Stammbegriffe*" such as existence, possibility, impossibility), and the "realm of values" of Windelband's school. It was only later that Brentano saw clearly that consideration of these contents and states of affairs involves the analysis of abbreviated linguistic fictions, and he has published little on the subject. It is because of this reticence that little attention has so far been paid to this new and revolutionary view; and even Marty could not do justice to it. (See Kraus, *Anton Marty, sein Leben und seine Lehre.*)

This is why all Brentano's older students adhere to the theory as he stated it in former years, and have developed it in opposition to Brentano's own later development. It is Meinong and Husserl who have departed furthest from Brentano's intentions, and they charge him with "psychologism" because of his belief that all ideal things, levels of being, and forms of being, all *entia rationis*, are fictions. The editor, who sided with the opponents of the modality theory up until the autumn of 1916, wrote in his introduction to Marty's *Gesammelte Schriften*, "The essence of the disagreement, given a corresponding shift in the point at issue, is like that between Plato and Aristotle; except that here it is the master who charges his former pupil with an untenable hypostatization and reification – with a Platonic realism."

I do not venture to hope that the exposition offered in the present work and by *The Origin of our Knowledge of Right and Wrong* will suffice to convince the reader; it will require the publication of many other dictations and letters to shed the right light on the importance of the matter, although those essays on *entia rationis* published in the Appendix to the second part are extensive enough to make some impression. . . .

Brentano's view that only things can come before the mind in presentation would deserve intensive examination if only because a thinker of Brentano's stature designated it the most important innovation in his inquiry; but it is at least as remarkable, too, for the wealth of far-reaching consequences it engenders. Is it really so improbable that the tendency of ordinary language towards convenience of expression and hypostatization should result in our frequently taking as a meaning what is in fact a mere suggestion? And because of this we take words like "impossibility," "possibility," "existence," "nonexistence," and so on, to be words with a meaning of their own, whereas in fact they belong to that class of words – called "syncategorematical expressions" by Mill and "synsemantica" by Marty – which have meaning only in combination with others.

Kant's table of categories is in part an incomplete table of such *synsemantica*, which could be called "synsemantica derived from judgement." Herein lies the core of the truth in Kant's attempt to derive the alleged "forms of thought" from the "forms of judgement." I cannot think of the impossibility of something unless I have before my mind an apodictic negative judgement; and I cannot think of the existence of God without having before my mind, as an object of presentation, a judgement which correctly asserts the existence of God. Brentano had already written in *The Origin of our Knowledge of Right and Wrong*, "I am saying the same thing when I say that an affirmative judgement is true as when I say that an object exists." This is a move towards his final standpoint, which is presented in the supplement to the *Classification*, and which follows from his consistent adherence to the basic principle of Locke and Hume: for all simple concepts we must demonstrate those intuitive perceptions from which they derive, and for all compound concepts the elements from which they are made up. This view has also been discounted as "psychologism." Brentano's reply is that the application of the epithet does not constitute a proof; and he continues to progress along the lines marked out by the renovators of psychology and theory of knowledge – who were not themselves the first to initiate such progress. The table of the "categories" of pure reason is indeed thereby divested of its *a priori* character; the categories of modality, for example possibility–impossibility, existence–non-existence, necessity–contingency, collapse into rudiments of language.

The same holds of expressions such as "utility," "harm," the "realm of values," "preference," "profit," "good," "badness" and many others including even "genus" and "species"; if we think that we are dealing, in these cases, with words which have meanings of their own, we shall be lost in a realm of endless fictions. There will surely be many who reject Brentano's theory; but no one who views it closely will long be able to resist the realization that its critique of language is, if correct, of immense importance. Not only does it pose entirely new problems for the philosophy of language and grammar in general, but it also implies an essential transformation of logic.

This holds true particularly of the introduction of modes of presentation. This appears in a more favorable light if we remember that, after Brentano had rejected Herbart's simple psychology of ideas, he reduced the entire manifold of consciousness – apart from the distinction between judgement and emotional attitude – to a differentiation between presentations in terms of their differing objects. Thus the class of presentations remained subject to the limitation that they were differentiated only in terms of their "object," but Brentano's latest move is precisely the implementation of his realization that the *activity* of presentation is of far more consequence than he had at first assumed. It is certainly not a return to Herbart, but the attribution to presentative activity of a far greater importance in the realm of mental references. We may cite here not only the importance of the modes of presentation to the consciousness of space and time – particularly the latter – but also the theory of the direct and indirect attributive combination of presentations. (See the Appendix, essays IV and XIII.)

IV *Brentano's Position on Psychologism*

The preceding chapters shed some light on Brentano's standpoint on the issue of psychologism. He has expressed his views most emphatically in the supplement to the *Classification* (Essay XI). Marty, too, has, in his *Untersuchungen*, clearly shown himself to be in accord with Brentano on this issue. Like nearly all the great logicians before him Brentano clearly bases logic, as the theory of how correct judgements are made, on psychology. But in his opinion there is both a descriptive and a genetic psychology; and so there are, correspondingly, two kinds of logical rule. One kind comprises those which utilize the factual truths of genetic psychology and are concerned with empirical regularities. For example, in setting up rules to aid in the attainment of knowledge, we can draw upon experience of bad habits in thinking, and even of the effects of narcotics and alcohol on reasoning. The other kind of rule is based on *descriptive* psychology, and hence also both on the factual truths of inner perception, of secondary consciousness, and on those *a priori* truths which we spoke of earlier. Such truths as these tell us, for example, that two persons making contradictory judgements having the same temporal mode, the same modality, etc., cannot possibly both be judging correctly at one time. We have, then an immediate *a priori* insight into the correctness of judgements, into their validity or justification; and with this we have a criterion for deciding whether or not a given judgement can be a correct judgement, that is a judgement as it should be. Husserl's argument in the *Logical Investigations* (trans. J. N. Findlay, London, 1970), p. 98, originated in the claim that it is "universally agreed" that psychology is a *purely factual science*. But in Brentano's opinion, which he already held at the time of the *Psychology*, this is simply not so; insofar as it inquires into *a priori* laws, descriptive psychology or psychognosy is more than a purely factual science.

At that time Brentano had already formulated certain *a priori* psychological truths; and in 1889 in *The Origin of our Knowledge of Right and Wrong* he emphasized the non-inductive character of certain propositions about emotions. And on page 9 of the same work he says with regard to "logical self-evidence" that "thought processes that conform to . . . rules are naturally superior to those that do not." Husserl agrees: "These laws must have some intrinsic *prerogative* in the regulation of our thought." (*Logical Investig.*, p. 170.) We can, therefore, find in Brentano an anti-psychologistic attitude, insofar as this means simply the acknowledgement of a logical ought, of thinking that is justified in and of itself.

Every self-evident judgement – and not only, as Husserl thinks, every self-evident *universal* judgement – is a judgement as a judgement should be, that is, justified in itself; and it establishes, therefore, a yardstick for what is a "correct judgement." It would be clearly an incorrect judgement for someone at the present time to deny that I am thinking, or to have denied at some point in the past that I should be thinking now, or to deny at some future time that I had been thinking today. There is no point in the argument whether a self-evident or self-justifying judgement should itself be called a *norm*, or whether it merely forms the basis for the establishment of a norm. Insofar as it is a perfectly correct judgement, containing its own justification, it is directive, rule-giving and normative. It could also be called an ideal judgement, since it embodies the logical ideal of being right or correct. Nothing is more mistaken than the common opinion that "is" and "ought," the actual and the ideal, are mutually exclusive. On the contrary, in every insightful judgement the logical ought or ideal is logically actual, just as in every ethically correct emotional attitude the axiological ought or ideal attains axiological actuality – so long as the *synsemantica* "ought" and "actual" are correctly understood as such. There is no reason why a thing should not actually be what it ideally ought to be. We start, then, from the self-evident judgement; this perfectly correct judgement is the criterion against which we measure other judgements to see whether, although not self-evident, they accord with self-evident judgements in other respects.

The self-evident judgement is not normative in the sense of instructing us how to arrive at correct judgements, but in the sense of telling us *this* is the only way in which to judge, to judge correctly. And, bearing it in mind that psychology, despite Husserl, is not an exclusively factual science, it is clear that descriptive or phenomenological psychology can and must be the source of logic. The aim of logic is simply the attainment of logically faultless judgements; and the major exemplars are found in psychology. For we acknowledge that someone is making a correct judgement when his judgement agrees with that of someone who makes a self-evident judgement with respect to the affirmation or denial of the same object, temporal mode, and possibly also apodicticity. "Correct" and "incorrect" cannot be spoken of meaningfully without some reference to the self-evident or self-justifying judgement. Something analogous is true of the origin of our knowledge of right and wrong; this is discussed in Brentano's essay of the same name and in the letter quoted above.

Of course, if by "psychologism" we understand the view that all our simple concepts are derived from experience, i.e. from intuitive perception, and that all complex or attributive concepts are built up out of simple concepts, then Brentano would certainly acknowledge his acceptance of psychologism. But this doctrine should not be confused with another, which states that all judgements are empirical (*Erfahrungsurteile*); Brentano recognizes no *a priori ideas* or *concepts*, but he does recognize *a priori truths*. But Marty has already demonstrated that the *a priori* character of certain judgements does not justify us in distinguishing for them a special science of "pure logic." (See especially his *Untersuchungen zur Grundlegung einer allgemeinen Grammatik und Sprachphilosophie*, p. 63.)

V *The Theory of External Perception*

Brentano reverts to a previous linguistic usage in interpreting "external perception" in its strict sense of a *blind belief* in what is given to the senses in any instance of seeing, hearing, or feeling. Hearing a sound or seeing a color are not only distinguished from the conceptual presentation of a sound or a color by intensity (this may be called "the density of the phenomenon in the sensory field"; cp. Brentano, *Untersuchung zur Sinnespsychologie*), they are distinguished by, among other things, an intense (blind) belief in the sound or color – by a *perception of it as true*. This second factor is not found in conceptual presentation. Hence, the usual view that sense perception is only a *presentation*, and not an *act of belief* (or judgement) as well, is mistaken. Brentano at least takes "external perception" in its restricted sense to mean nothing more than sensation or feeling; and he maintains that sensation is not a simple presentation of something, but an *instinctive belief* in what is sensorily presented.

We have external perception of items that are extended in terms of some quality, extended, in fact, in terms of their color, their feel, etc. According to Brentano, we can equate "perception" with "intuition" and "external intuition" with "external perception," or "sensation." *But since we cannot have sensations of "mountains, forests, houses," external perception in the strict sense is not to be understood as the perception of mountains, houses, forests* – though this claim is sometimes made. Any interpretation of the colorful picture given us in visual sensation goes beyond Brentano's *technical* sense of "external perception." The use of the term in an inexact and broader sense should not confuse us; Brentano repeatedly says that those external perceptions do not deserve to be called "perception" in the strict sense, since physical extended things do not exist as we intuitively perceive them, i.e., as having colors, sounds, etc.

Husserl misunderstands Brentano's theory. He thinks that external perception can only be called deceptive if we take "physical phenomena" to be physical things such as mountains, houses, etc. Husserl says (*Logical Investig.*, II, 864), ". . . Brentano exchanges this authentic and alone permissible sense of the word 'perceive' for an improper sense which relates, not to external objects but to presenting contents, contents, i.e. present as real parts (*reell angehörigen*) in perception, and when he consequently gives the name of 'physical phenomena,' not merely to external objects, but also to these contents, these latter seem infected with the fallibility of outer perception." But there is a rejoinder to this argument. We ordinarily talk both of "perceiving trees" and "perceiving colors," but Brentano expressly remarks that, strictly speaking, we should not talk of "perceiving colors," since colors (colored things as such) cannot be proved to exist; rather, we must assume that qualities of sensation have no kind of being or existence at all. The physicist banishes physical objects with properties of color or sound from the real world. Nor does Brentano hold that external perception is "deceptive" in Husserl's sense of "occasionally deceiving us"; rather, it always deceives, it is always false perception insofar as it blindly believes in things possessing sensory qualities! Had Brentano been thinking of "the perception of trees, mountains and landscapes," etc., in this connection, he would have had to say that external perception only deceives us occasionally – since trees, houses, mountains, and landscapes do really exist. Husserl's mistake was to espouse the opinion that colors, sounds, tactile qualities, etc., do *really belong to perception* – that they are *real constituents* of it. This theory, which has also been held by other distinguished psychologists, is itself based on a confusion.

According to Brentano, external perception is not deceptive or false because it does, or can, delude us as to "the existence of a tree." Rather, it is deceptive because, when we intuit, and thus take to be real, the colored forms in our visual field (Linke speaks, not inappropriately of a "suggestion of reality" which is given along with any sensation), we end by falling into an instinctive (blind) belief which is logically unjustifiable. If I intuitively perceive something that is qualitatively extended – for example, if I have a sensation of so-called "ideo-retinal grey" then I have this grey as an object. But it is a mistake to say that this grey is a part of the whole mental phenomenon, or that it is what Husserl called a "real constituent" of it. (*Logical Investig.*, II, 864, 869.) When I intuitively perceive a thing, in this case an expanse of grey, I have a real, substantive thing as my object (or, before my mind). But what can be said to exist? Just "someone who has a thing (e.g. something grey) before the mind." "To have a thing as object" does not mean "to have a thing as a part." To treat these two expressions as synonymous is to be guilty of an epistemological error which has the direst consequences. "Object of consciousness" does not mean the same as "part of consciousness" since the former is an expression which has no meaning of its own at all. "To have something as an object of consciousness" means nothing but "to have something before the mind."

Husserl maintains that only perception that is directed toward the external world, i.e. toward transcendent things, should be called "external perception," since the physical qualities (such as ideo-retinal grey) *really belong to perception itself*; the physical qualities are not external to it, but a *part*, or real component, of it. But this is to revive unwittingly the theory of the mental inexistence of the object, which he otherwise opposes. Of course, this is bound up with his denial of the intentional character of sensation. For Brentano, sensation (someone sensing as such) is synonymous with the restricted sense of "external perception"; if I see the so-called ideo-retinal grey or see any instance of color whatever, I am sensing something colored. We could equally well say that I refer to it or that I am mentally concerned with it.

A being which had something red or blue or some other such "content" "within itself" without having it objectively, would have to contain it like a spatial object . . . and thus be a corporeal receptacle. (What has been said here of seeing a colored object applies

INTRODUCTION TO THE I924 EDITION

equally to hearing a sound, feeling warmth, etc.) Many psychologists and epistemologists seem only able to understand clearly the essence of the intentional for *conceptual* presentation and thought. Yet it is of decisive importance to our understanding of both Brentano's psychology and of consciousness generally that we should notice "the intentional" wherever it is present – whether in sensory acts of consciousness, in sensations, or in affects. Husserl writes (*Logical Investig.*, II, 558), of "having an idea of Jupiter" in the following way: to say, in this case, that Jupiter exists within me "mentally" or "intentionally" means the same as "I have Jupiter before my mind" or, generally speaking, "Thinking-of-Jupiter is going on"; but this does not mean that the God Jupiter exists either outside of or within the mind. Exactly the same is true of the intuitive presentation of grey, or of any other sensation of color. I have an extended grey thing intuitively present to my mind, but this "intuitive sense-datum" is *not* one of the "real components" of the experience; putting it as Husserl does, it is neither outside nor inside the mind, it does not exist at all. Nature may compel us to have to do with a grey field, intuitively perceiving it and believing in it, but analysis shows that this belief is unjustifiable. Sensation is an intentional experience, just like any other form of consciousness. When I see, hear, or feel something, I have something *sensuously* as my object, just as, when I think of Jupiter, I have something non-sensuously as my object. Every instance of consciousness is a consciousness of something, and every instance of sensation is an instance of consciousness. To tamper with this most elementary piece of psychological knowledge is to undermine any possibility of arriving at an understanding of the essence of consciousness.

If the sensualists, for their part, have attempted to reduce consciousness to sensation, many modern thinkers make the opposite mistake of denying that sensations have the characteristics of consciousness. (Some have even denied this of the "affective sensations" of pleasure and pain. Brentano deals with this point in his *Untersuchungen zur Sinnespsychologie.*) Brentano's psychology has not yet made its full impact on this point. It can be said that there are cases in which contemporary psychology fails to recognize the "intentionality" (or the character of "referring to something") that was indicated by Brentano. Many students of "sensations" take what we have as an object or "that as which we have something as an object," e.g. the blue we see, the note C we hear, to exist, or have some kind of being, and they pay no attention to our concern with it. On the other hand, other psychologists conceive of certain feelings as objectless states of consciousness, as if there could be some form of consciousness which does not have something as its object.

At this point I want to return to the theory of perception. To understand Brentano correctly, sensation and "outer perception" (in the restricted sense) must be taken as synonymous. Thus we are talking very loosely when we say, "I see a landscape" or "I see a box," since whether it is safe to use such locutions depends entirely on the context. "Seeing," "hearing," etc., are words which refer to sensations, and sensations have as their objects qualitatively extended things of such a nature that we must say with Brentano that they cannot be proved to exist as we intuitively perceive them. So important is this point that we must now examine more closely a point that is mentioned by Husserl. According to Husserl, when I see a thing, a box for example, no matter which way it is turned, I still see the same box. If I call the perceived object a "content of consciousness," then I have the same "content of consciousness" throughout. But if, more appropriately, I take the "content of consciousness" to refer to the content of which we are immediately aware, then I have a new "content of consciousness" each time the box is turned. In this way, we may experience many varied "contents," but it is still true that "the same object is perceived." To put this into Brentano's terminology, we may read "object of consciousness" for "content of consciousness." So I actually have a new "object of consciousness" every time the box is turned – that is, I have new and different sense-qualities as objects; but the box that is turned is a transcendent, existing thing. (The term "thing" is preferable here so that we can, with Brentano, reserve "object" for use in the expression "having something as an object.") We can speak of "perceiving" this transcendent thing only in the wider sense of that word; for perceiving is not mere sensation or feeling, but a whole (partly associative) complex of conscious mental activities and intuitive perceptions and of conceptual presentations and judgements. No matter how it is turned it remains one and the same transcendently existing box, one and the same "*Ding an sich.*" Now when Husserl says of this case that "the same object" (in Brentano's teminology "the same thing") is perceived, it is clear that this statement does not have anything to do with the sensation of seeing a patch of color; thus it has no bearing on Brentano's restricted sense of "outer perception." For when I see a patch of color with some sort of shape and shading, the object of my vision is something in which I blindly believe but which does not exist; it is to this object as ἴδιον αἰσθητόν that my vision is directed. Even if there were no box in reality at all – for example, if I hallucinated – the seeing would still be descriptively ("phenomenologically") the same. From such perceptions, i.e. from such visual sensations, I can abstract the concept of an expanse of color with some sort of shape, but not the concept of "box." *The concept of the "box" is emphatically not abstracted from any intuitive perceptions*, but is a concept composed of abstracted elements, a synthetic concept. For example, it is part of our concept of a box that it should be hollow. *But the hollow inside of a closed box simply is not an object of my vision!* I can no more see a "box" than I can taste, smell or hear it. Nor can I "touch" a box, for the concept of a box also includes some *definition of its purpose*, which cannot be touched. Thus what is supposed to be perception of a box involves conceptual presentations and highly complex synthetic concepts.

We obtain from sense-perception, and particularly from the sense of touch, the conceptual elements which we combine into synthetic concepts of ordinary physical objects and similar things; and in some cases we decide that there actually exists in reality something like the cube or hollow prism that we have thus made into an object. If I observe "those qualitative patches of changing shape and shading," I may believe that they cover the surface of a hollow, prismatic, "useful" object called a box; and my conviction, which is based on conceptual syntheses of presentations and judgements, will stay the same no matter how the transcendently existing thing may be moved or turned. Husserl is certainly correct in distinguishing this transcendently existing thing from the "content of consciousness" insofar as we take the latter to be the content of sensation – as, for example, what is present to our sight, or what is present to us as *seeing*. On the other hand it is quite appropriate to say that the transcendently existing thing may be made the content (or object) of our conceptual, synthetic presentation and of our interpretative judgement, for it is this process of judgement which, when it appears together with the sensuous consciousness, first raises the act to the level of that complicated state of consciousness which Husserl, following inexact common usage, calls "seeing a box." What really happens is that, along with what is intuitively present to us and instinctively affirmed by us *insofar as we see* there is something else present to us *insofar as we have a conceptual, synthetic, non-intuitive idea*. We affirm this latter object and identify the two with one another. It is just this complex act – though it could certainly be analysed more satisfactorily and completely – which constitutes what is called "seeing a box." Husserl certainly makes no attempt to analyse this phenomenon; on the contrary, he regards it as something ultimate. Thus his criticism of Brentano must fail, for he merely characterizes as a new mode of consciousness what is really a very complex state of sensuous and non-sensuous consciousness. Moreover Anton Marty had already established this in his *Untersuchungen*.

We can now see how misleading it is to say, in the case that we have been discussing, that we always perceive the same "object" or the same thing. Brentano may have used similar locutions (such as "I see a landscape") but it is quite clear to anyone who follows the whole argument of the *Psychology* that he could only mean by "outer perception" that which is directed towards the ἴδιον and the κοινόν αἰσθητόν. This sensuous intuition of expanses of quality is deceptive just because what is sensuously qualified does not exist in the way that we intuitively perceive it. Other mistakes of judgement may occur, we may take a stage set to be a landscape, or take a black dot to be a bird when it is a fly, but Brentano does not appeal to such mistakes when demonstrating, in contrast to the evidence of inner perception, the untruthfulness of outer perception.

In one respect some lack of clarity on Brentano's part (Book 1, Chap. 1, Sect. 2) may be attributed to his reading of Locke. Brentano mentions that experiments by John Locke and others have shown that "objects of sensation" (which Brentano explicitly equates with "objects of so-called outer perception") do not exist outside of us, since they are not true and real. But it may be replied that Locke's experiment shows only that it would be contradictory for us to ascribe to the transcendently existing water, at the same time and in the same place the attributes warm and cold. Of course, this does not show that it would be absurd for things to exist transmentally, somehow and somewhere, with both these attributes. We cannot have *a priori* knowledge that the existence of so-called physical qualities is impossible, as Brentano later acknowledges (Book II, Chap. 1). All that is certain *a priori* is that, if physical objects exist, they cannot have different modes of the same kind of qualities in the same place and at the same time. The experiments that have been mentioned, therefore, prove nothing as to *the impossibility of existence* of those "physical qualities" that we intuitively perceive, and Brentano may have overstated their force in this respect. They merely show that sense-qualities do not exist where we locate them when we blindly accept what is offered in the wider sense of outer perception – for example, when we believe that trees are green or that the sky is blue.

These considerations may explain Husserl's misconceptions and his belief that Brentano confused the two meanings of "outer perception." On the other hand, there is no objection to Brentano's subsequent claim that "we have *no right* to believe that the objects of outer perception really exist in the same way that they appear to us." For outer perception or sensation is a blind, not an evident, belief in something possessing sense-qualities; all that is evident here is that we have these qualities, in which we believe, as our objects. But secondary, evident consciousness has the objects of primary consciousness as its own objects only in an indirect way. If I rightly affirm someone who has colors as his object, I do not thereby rightly affirm the colors. Similarly, when I rightly affirm myself as seeing colors, I do not hereby rightly affirm the colors, which are affirmed indirectly.

Speaking quite precisely, the incorrectness of outer perception can only be shown indirectly to be highly *probable*. That colored things do not exist is not so much a self-evident truth as a *hypothesis*, just like the assumption that spatially extended things *do* exist. It is only when we look for the causes of "outer perception" that we arrive at the conclusion that the perception of things which are colored or have factual qualities is to be called mistaken – in fact, a deception – since it is extremely probable that such things do not exist at all, and particularly not where we have most confidence that they are present. That is to say, the belief that "We have no right to believe in the objects of outer perception" is blind and not logically justifiable, not *knowledge*. (Moritz Schlick's *Erkenntnistheorie* uses the word "knowledge" in a deliberately restricted sense as "conceptual knowledge" and not for the knowledge of mere facts; we are "acquainted" with facts. This new linguistic convention, of which Brentano also availed himself occasionally, might have something to recommend it, though the traditional distinction between assertoric and *a priori* knowledge makes the point equally well. On the other hand, Brentano never called external perception "knowledge" – not even Schlick's "false knowledge." Brentano took every perception to be a belief, i.e. a judgement, and even if a perception is a mere acquaintance, as Schlick says, it still has what Brentano and Mill meant by *the character of judgement*. It is reasonable to expect that a "theory of knowledge" should be clear about the essence of judgement before it attempts to teach others about knowledge and acquaintance.)

The person who is born blind and then operated on takes these to be extended colors; he affirms it, i.e. he believes in it and then makes a blind affirmative judgement about this extended color. Traditionally this fact is usually characterized in such a way that it asserts that the extended color is immanent. Husserl, too, continues to use this objectionable terminology; it is objectionable because it takes "immanent existence" for real existence. Husserl says on page 865 of the *Logical Investigations*, "What is immanent and thought to be just as it is, it would be evidently irrational to doubt." So while many want to argue away every judgement of external perception, for Husserl such judgements constitute evident cognitions! Certainly something is evident to us, namely, that colors "are immanent" to us, i.e., that we have them as objects, we have presentations of them and blind beliefs in them. We could certainly just as well say "We have something immanent," as "I have something as object." Then, however, "having-something-immanent" like "having-something-as-object" becomes a term that means no more than "having something before the mind," and the word "immanent" like the word "object" is *synsemantic*. We may now reverse Husserl's proposition as follows, "What is merely immanent does not exist at all, and, if it is thought of *just as it is*, it can only be thought of as something non-existent; it would only be irrational to doubt the existence of the person who has it immanently – that is, of the person who has it before his mind."

It is also misleading to say that contents such as colors and sounds are "immediately experienced." We "immediately experience" states of consciousness, having something as object in some way or other (loving it, hating it, etc.); we "immediately experience" having the god Jupiter before the mind, not the god Jupiter, and we "immediately experience" seeing green, but not the green; we "immediately experience" the intuitive perception of extended things, but not the extended things themselves (Anton Marty has already dealt with this point in his *Untersuchungen*). Any one who denies the evident nature of such genuine "immediately experiencing" will labor in vain to establish a "critical realism."

VI Brentano's Use of the Expressions "Physical" and "Mental" Phenomena

Though it would certainly have been better to avoid these terms which have been the cause of so many misunderstandings, Brentano took them over from other thinkers and was most clearly aware of their ambiguity. His choice of the expression "phenomenon" should be attributed less to any deference to Kant (whose phenomenonalism he rejected as firmly as he did Berkeley's and Mach's) than to his knowledge of English and French psychology, in particular that of Comte.

In an essay entitled "Auguste Comte and Positivism" he writes, "It is of the utmost importance to understand that Kant and Comte do not use the term 'phenomenon' in the same way. It would be a mistake to think of Comte's 'phenomenon' as an appearance behind which a *Ding an sich* is unapproachably concealed. This is indicated by the synonymous use of the terms 'phenomenon' and 'fact'; for example, Comte held that, from the standpoint of positivism, the explanation of facts consists quite simply in the establishment of a connection between several particular phenomena and some general facts." When Brentano speaks of the appearances or phenomena as "something given as such," he normally uses the term "mere phenomenon"; on the other hand, he uses the term "phenomenon" to refer to a state of affairs, or occurrences, or an event.

Throughout his work Brentano takes the expression "mental phenomenon" to mean the same as "consciousness," or "conscious event"; he uses "physical phenomenon" to mean either a "sense-quality" (of color, sound or touch), or, quite simply, a "spatial, corporeal, extended thing." Which of the senses is being used on any occasion must be judged from the context, and I have offered appropriate explanations in my notes on the text. Brentano also uses the term "mental activity" for "mental phenomenon," but this should not be taken to imply *activity*; on the contrary, all mental activity of a created thing is passive in the Aristotelian sense.

Nor is the concept of "someone who is mentally active" equivalent to the concept of someone who is mentally referring to something (see Appendix, essay II). We can talk of "mental phenomena" which have only a phenomenal existence, for example those which we only have before our minds (or have as objects) in fantasy. In such cases all that exists is the person who has these mental phenomena before his mind. We can also speak of mental phenomena which have both phenomenal and actual existence, for example those which are present to inner perception and which are affirmed with evidence. But all the mental phenomena of other people actually do exist.

In *Psychology from an Empirical Standpoint* Brentano claims that physical phenomena are only phenomenal. In fact there appears in the table of contents the concise statement "Physical phenomena *can* only exist phenomenally." This is a careless error; it would not be *absurd* if they also actually existed, but here Brentano is thinking primarily of the so-called physical *qualities* (acoustic, visual, tactile, etc.).

Brentano maintains that when we have sensations of colors, sounds, or smells, etc., we have sensations of qualitative things that do not exist. It is not a conceptual truth that these things do not exist; rather, this is a conclusion derived from experience, observation, and experiment. Brentano writes (p. 92), "Knowledge, joy and desire actually exist. Color, sound and warmth have only a phenomenal and intentional existence." We must always bear this statement in mind if we are to understand Brentano correctly. To put it as Brentano did later, "We have colors, sounds, smells, warmth, etc., as objects" but without these qualities being affirmed with evidence. In other words, it is only ourselves that we know with certainty – ourselves who have these qualities as phenomena or as objects! We have already remarked that "having something as an object" means the same as "having something phenomenally or intentionally" and

401

"having something as appearance or phenomenon." We encounter equivocations here every step of the way.

Just as there are two different uses of the word "object" in "I have an object as my object," there are likewise two different uses of "phenomenon" in "I have a physical phenomenon as my phenomenon," i.e. phenomenally. In the first use of "phenomenon" in the expression it means the same as "state," "event," or "thing": but in the second use it is as synsemantic as the term "object" and means only that I have a physical thing before my mind. The following statements are synonymous:

I have a physical object (thing) as object
I have a physical phenomenon as phenomenon
I have a physical thing as phenomenon
I have a physical phenomenon as object
I have a physical thing as object.

They all mean nothing but, "I have something physical before my mind"; and we could equally well say, "Something physical is given to me intentionally or phenomenally," and the expression "It is a mere phenomenon" also means exactly the same.

All this makes it sufficiently clear that the use of the word "phenomenon" is not to be recommended – even if we are aware of its variety of meanings! In particular, it is sometimes used with an independent meaning of its own and sometimes synsemantically (as an incomplete symbol), exactly like the word "object." Of course, the same is also true of the term "appearance."

Brentano has occasionally been criticized for not making his epistemological standpoint unequivocally clear in his writings; it appears that he supports phenomenalism in one place and opposes it in others. But this is true only if isolated sentences are torn from their context, which is a most irregular method of interpretation. One example of this has already been given: despite the statement that appears in the Table of Contents, the text is explicit that the assumption of a transcendent, three-dimensional, "quasi-spatial" world is indispensable to the causal explanation of the flow of sensations. It is only the qualifying terms "quasi-spatial" and "quasi-temporal" which need surprise us here. The point is that, in his *Psychology*, Brentano was of the opinion that the external causes of our sensations are only spatial and temporal by analogy; for example, he argues against Überweg's *Logik* which allows the world to remain simply spatial and temporal.

This is bound up with another opinion which Brentano entertained at the time, namely that we intuitively perceive absolute species of space and time. Now, according to this theory, intuitive perception must always present us with the *same* absolute forms of space and time (cp. Anton Marty, *Raum und Zeit,* pp. 16, 134), although the real ones are constantly changing. Thus Brentano was obliged to maintain that the real world does not have the same absolute spatial species as the objects of our intuitive perceptions, although it has the same relations, for the senses give us no information about the world's "absolute constitution." It certainly follows from Brentano's argument on p. 98 that he had no intention of disputing either the three-dimensionality of transcendently existing space or what has been called the one-dimensional flow of time.

Brentano later returned to the theory that intuitive perception, too, presents us with nothing but things in temporal and spatial relation, and this was in accord with the opinion he shared with Überweg that the external causes of our sensations are not only quasi-spatial and quasi-temporal but that they are spatial and temporal in the same sense as the objects of external or inner perception; in both cases we perceive only things that are related in space and time (or, spatial and temporal relations). (See Brentano "Raum und Zeit" in *Kantstudien,* 1920.) As the following quotation shows, Brentano is clearer on this point in his essay on Comte than in the *Psychology.*

"Comte has no sympathy with Kant's opinion that there is no way by which we can achieve real knowledge. For him the existence of things – indeed, of a number of things – is indubitable; and even Kant, despite himself, held that something must exist besides mere phenomena. Nor does Comte in any way dispute that these things have size, shape, spatial and temporal position, and motion and that many of them have thought and sensation. To be sure, he denies absolute knowledge of the majority of these properties in detail. But, far from being a sceptical error, this is a truth which can easily be verified. Surely, everybody knows that any moment of time presents itself to us in the same way when it is present and that the same is true, analogously, of any spatial determination. And who would believe that we can ascertain the absolute rest or movement of a physical object when astronomy has shaken even the earth from its foundations? No! Comte cannot be criticized on this point, for here we must all side with the sceptic. What distinguishes our position from that of the sceptics is our claim that it is possible to know the true relations that exist between things. For example, we cannot determine the absolute size of an object, but we can calculate its relative size with precision; we can never know the absolute moment at which an event occurs, but we may be able to specify exactly when it occurs in relation to some other event. It is for this reason that there is a vast gulf fixed between ourselves and the sceptics. We must not belittle our knowledge of these relations between things, for such relations are of paramount importance. On some matters we may be quite indifferent: whether human history is played out at one particular time or millions of years earlier or later; whether the center of the universe is at rest or is moving in a straight line; whether the totality of physical objects, and each object in particular, has twice or half as much extension and lies higher or lower, or further to the right or left in space. Such considerations are of no importance to us. But relative spatial and temporal determination – the differences between being together and apart, being simultaneous, earlier, and later, being at rest or in motion, being *relatively* of one size or another – these are quite different. For on our knowledge of these depends both our theoretical and our practical life, both art and engineering. So Comte makes no substantial concession to scepticism, he does not sacrifice the interests of science; he is no more sceptical than we ourselves, and no more sceptical than any genuine philosopher must be."

Thus we are not *acquainted with* the absolutely specific spatial and temporal properties of things; but Brentano, contrary to the modern "theory of relativity," claims it to be evident *a priori* that things will have these properties if they exist. He writes, "What exists does not, of itself, enter into appearance." In other words, we do not perceive intuitively the transcendently existing absolute properties of position and extension or the transcendent attributes (or modes) of things that are spatially extended, nor the "powers" (Book II, Chap. 1, p. 100) which we might call physical forces today. And "what enters into appearance is not actually true": in other words, the sense-qualities which appear in sensation do not exist, but are merely "phenomenal."

Even if physical science tells us that modifications (qualities, attributes) of some transcendently existing, spatially extended thing (such as ether) are to be considered the causes of our sensations, our belief in things possessing properties of sound and color is still blind, incorrect, and untrue. But although the *absolute* qualities intuition presents us with do not exist, the intuited relation between the spatially extended and the qualitatively characterized does exist transcendently as a relationship of spatial substance and accident (possibly of ether and a modification of ether).

As a consequence of presenting spatial things with qualitative modes, intuitive sense-perception leads us to entertain a belief which is, to that extent, blind though correct. It leads us to have before our minds, and to believe in, a relation between the spatially extended and the sensuously qualified; this relation exists transcendently only between something spatial, which is individuated in some quite unknown way, and completely unknown attributes. The blind belief in sense-qualities can be sanctioned subsequently as a belief in symbols, or signs.

VII *The method of Descriptive or Phenomenological Psychology; Inner Perception and Inner Observation*

By "inner perception" Brentano means a "secondary consciousness" which is directed to the whole of our "primary consciousness"; it is inseparable from primary consciousness and is simultaneously directed towards itself. By its nature, it is independent of the will and it is an incidental accompaniment of every primary consciousness; generally speaking, it is part of the concept of consciousness....

One justifiable criticism is that Brentano's *Psychology* of 1874 does not make a sufficiently clear distinction between confused and implicit perception, on the one hand, and distinct and explicit perception on the other; only later did Brentano teach that we apprehend explicitly what is inwardly perceived. The following letter from Brentano to Carl Stumpf, dated June 16, 1906, shows a change in Brentano's position on this problem:

"I have recently given fresh consideration to the problem of psychological observation. In the first place, it is a question of understanding precisely what observation is to mean; and then what is meant by self-observation, as distinct from any other form. For any observation is concerned with ourselves in a way. Anyone who analyses a musical chord is really *apperceiving* components of himself considered as someone who is hearing. He finds that, as someone who is hearing the chord, he is simultaneously someone who hears the different notes. The chord does not exist at all and what does not exist cannot be observed. But this person may be observed as one involved in the many-sided relation of hearing, and thus according to those particular differences which distinguish a person who is hearing one note from a person who is hearing another. Mental references are not differentiated only by differences in their object. Now the question is whether such relations can be studied so well when they refer to the secondary object as when they refer to the primary object; indeed, it may be advantageous for them to become primary objects in themselves, as is the case with reflection on what has been experienced in the past. If I recall having held a certain belief, I do not thereby hold this belief once again. My earlier belief does not become the secondary object, for the secondary object is my present memory of that belief. In my studies of time, my presumption was that I had discovered that only the primary object – and not the secondary object – makes its appearance in a certain temporal extension; indeed, I believed that to think of the mental object as having an extended appearance would necessitate the monstrous assumption of a continuum with infinitely many dimensions. When I hear a melody, what appears to me is a succession of notes, not a succession of hearings. I do not apperceive myself as someone who has heard something, but as someone who hears one note as present and another note as past and retreating still further into the past. *This confers a very definite advantage on the study of the act with respect to its primary object.* Now I must forgo this advantage if I also study my mental phenomenon from any aspect *other* than that of the quality given it by the distinctive nature of its primary object. But I can acquire it if I turn the secondary object into the primary object, in the way that has been mentioned. This makes it clear that the study in memory was recommended with good reason. It still seems to me much easier to show that the course of mental events cannot be altered by my present observation when this course is reproduced by memory than to show this by an attempt at simultaneous observation. In memory, I can be seen as completely overpowered by emotion; but I cannot be in such a state when I begin a careful and precise psychological analysis of something. For me to remember having been overcome by passion is not for the passion to return. If it did, it would be the secondary object; but at the present time this secondary object is my memory of and my reflection on the emotion. But this is only a suggestion – perhaps we can talk it over at greater length sometime."

This letter – which also contains some interesting observations on the problem of time, meets the objection. The introduction of an explicit and distinct perception makes room for attention, and hence for the possibility of inner observation. Indeed, in contrast to the earlier theory, Brentano denies that there can be any kind of observation other than inner observation in the strict sense; for the sense-quality that we have as our object does not exist.

In a dictation made in 1916 Brentano expressed himself as follows: ". . . a person who is making a comparison pays attention to both of the things which he is comparing. In his thinking he must refer to both of them in particular. What I mean is this: a sensation often includes a great diversity in its object. It refers to a whole in its totality, and naturally to its parts as well; but to the latter only insofar as they are implicitly given with the object, not explicitly through a special reference to each one individually. Indeed, certain parts of a whole, e.g. those which do not attain a certain size, can never become the object to which a sensation makes a particular and, as one says, explicit reference. If this is true, there can be no possibility of comparison or correct differentiation." This process of noticing and apperceiving is our most important means of arriving at general psychognostic laws. According to Brentano, then, Helm-holtz's analysis of musical chords contains nothing essentially different from the analysis of a chord with which the letter to Stumpf is concerned. We do not arrive at general laws by induction in the usual sense of that word; rather, *general laws are immediately evident on the basis of concepts for which those apperceptions provide the preconditions.* But such general truths are not properly des-cribed as being deduced from premises. What happens is that I think of one description included in another and take note of myself as thinking of this inclusion; whereupon I make the *a priori* and self-evident judgement that nothing could satisfy the second descrip-tion without satisfying the first. On the other hand, suppose that someone distinguishes A from B, i.e. thinks of it as something different; in this case A will not be supposed to be actual. But thereupon the self-evident judgement can be made, on the basis of the terms, that nothing can be A without differing from what he thinks of as B.

Brentano does not fail to point out the dangers which creep in with this method and which consist particularly in the temptation to confuse habits of thinking with *a priori* truths. This difficulty will be even greater where the comparison is made by means of memory, which is unavoidable in connection with higher mental processes, as with affects.

We shall not go into more detail here. I would only remark that the short essays published in the supplement to the *Classification* do not give anything like a complete idea of Brentano's contribution to this important methodological question. But what has been said already should suffice to clarify the method of the so-called descriptive psychology ("Psychognosy") and to facilitate comparison of it with the so-called "Phenomenology." With this in mind, there are just two more points that I should like to make.

Brentano says that secondary consciousness includes not only presentation but also an evident affirmation of primary conscious-ness and of itself. In the *Psychology* he also inserted an emotional act into every secondary consciousness, but he later retracted this theory. (See *Untersuchung zur Sinnespsychologie* and the Appendix.) It is high time for writers on psychology and psychological literature generally to take account of this and to stop reproducing the earlier theory as Brentano's true opinion.

That Brentano had no intention of writing a "psychology without a soul" – as is often said – should not need to be pointed out. His discussion of the unity of consciousness is an extremely important preliminary to consideration of the problem of the soul. According to Brentano's later theory, words like "consciousness," "presentation," and "judgement" are mere grammatical abstractions which have no independent meaning. However, "someone with something before this mind" *is* an independently meaningful expression. In other words, it stands to reason that mental states must have a subject whose accidents they are; furthermore, in conceptualizing ourselves as mental agents, we perceive this subject directly, even if only extremely generally. So the problem of the soul is only a question of *what* is the subject of consciousness and not of *whether* such a thing must exist.

Stumpf's lecture on "Body and Soul" (delivered at the Third Psychological Congress in Munich in 1896) approached this problem in a way that was favorable to the interaction theory and thus paved the way for change of opinion in Brentano's direction.

The emphasis of Brentano's *Psychology* is descriptive or phenomenological, but the parts which deal with genetic questions are also of historical and current value. I will just mention the criticisms of Fechner's "Basic Law of Psychophysics" which received its first and decisive exposition in the *Psychology*. Although it has often been overlooked, Stumpf has recently drawn attention to the credit which is due to Brentano for his contribution here (see Stumpf's *Erscheinungen und Funktionen*). We should also remember that "genetic psychology" is not exclusively psychophysical and that Brentano is responsible for one of the greatest advances of modern psychology in his struggle against simple associationist psychology. The cognitive psychology of Külpe and Bühler derives its inspiration from Brentano, as was emphasized at the Fifth Congress of Experimental Psychology in 1912. Many of the tasks that Brentano specified as the future program of psychology have been taken up since his time; and the extraordinary *practical* importance of psychological study, to which he called attention, has become increasingly clear, as has its considerable intrinsic *theoretical* value – but these matters need no further comment.

Index

abstract terms, 322, 330ff., 343n.
absurda cum fundamento in re, 348ff.
addition, concept of, 352
aesthetics, 21
Anaxagoras, 109
Anselm, St., 88n., 140, 229n.
aporiai, 15, 73
aptitudes, 22, 59–60
 differences in people's, 37, 39n., 154
Aquinas, St. Thomas, 88n., 89n., 103, 125, 129, 132n., 211n., 212n., 229–30, 242, 245, 248, 260n., 261, 263n.
Aristotle, 4–5, 11n., 14–16, 18, 26–7, 41, 55, 58, 79n., 87, 88n., 94n., 109, 122n., 124, 127, 130–2, 141, 146–7, 156, 166, 179–80, 188, 192, 195–7, 199n., 201, 211n., 212n., 215, 223n., 228n., 229, 230n., 234, 235, 241, 245, 248, 249, 259–60, 262, 271, 273, 275, 291, 292, 294, 299–302, 305, 313n., 314, 318, 320, 322, 336, 339–46, 351, 355, 360, 367–8, 383, 388
Arnauld, Antoine, 213n.
association of ideas, 12, 16, 41, 56, 78, 110, 114, 163, 203
astronomy, 34, 49, 95–6
Augustine, St., 88n., 248, 261n.

Bacon, Francis, 44, 63, 109

Bain, Alexander, xxviii, 17n., 47, 63, 77n., 86–8, 92–3, 94n., 101, 104, 122, 133, 145, 147, 190–3, 196–7, 202–4, 206, 231n., 234, 249, 258, 299
Beautiful, the, 260–3
being
 in the sense of the true, 336–41, 344–6, 384
 in the strict sense, 339–41
Beneke, F. E., 103, 120, 133
Bergmann, Julius, 130n., 198n.
Berkeley, Bishop, 54, 86, 196, 311, 315, 400
Biunde, 183
Boltzmann, L., 354, 359
Bolzano, Bernard, 360, 383, 384
Bonaventura, St., 360
Boole, George, 231n.
brain, the, 56–7, 60–1
Brown, Thomas, 86, 181
Bühler, Karl, 408

Cardaillac, J. J., 96
Carus, Carl Gustav, 183
categorical propositions
 translatable into existential propositions, 213–14, 218, 221, 301ff.
character, 103
 contrast between feminine and masculine, 37, 39n.
chemistry, 15, 23–4, 46n., 50–1
Christianity, 262
Cicero, 248, 305

409

INDEX